THE INDIAN TRADERS

THE
INDIAN TRADERS

By Frank McNitt

NORMAN

University of Oklahoma Press

BY FRANK McNITT

Richard Wetherill: Anasazi (Albuquerque, 1957)
The Indian Traders (Norman, 1962)

Library of Congress Catalog Card Number: 62–16469
Copyright 1962 by the University of Oklahoma Press,
Publishing Division of the University.
Composed and printed at Norman, Oklahoma, U.S.A.,
by the University of Oklahoma Press.
First printing, August, 1962.
Second printing, August, 1963.

This book moves far from the field
of his professional work as an archaeologist,
but in direction may approach
his unusually deep feeling for the Southwest.
In respect and friendship, therefore,
what follows is dedicated to

R. GORDON VIVIAN

PREFACE

IN THE HISTORY of the Western frontier the Indian traders have received little attention. When mentioned at all they usually have been presented as almost shadowy figures moving in a scene changing but unchanged and scarcely touched by their own actions. We have no concept of Indian traders to match our nearly universal picture of the American cowboy, the cavalryman of Indian-fighting days, or the pioneer settlers who followed in their wake. It is my purpose here to consider the traders first for their group entity, and next as individuals, and so to measure their worth and their contribution to the Indian tribes among whom they lived and to their country.

The Southwest is the region in which the traders most boldly realized their full effectiveness, and so the Southwest provides the background for this book. Indian trade and traders of the Spanish colonial period are treated prefatorily, and I hope not too briefly. My principal concern, instead, has been with the American traders in the one hundred years beginning with the era of Charles and William Bent and Céran St. Vrain and ending in the early 1930's. Bent's Fort, typifying other forts of the mountain-plains trade, was erected approximately at the start of American commerce with the Southwest. As Fort Laramie and Fort Hall were important to the emigrant trains bound for California and the Pacific Northwest, Bent's Fort was invaluable as a supply base and haven for trade caravans traveling from Missouri towns to Taos and Santa Fe.

It would be impossible to pinpoint any time in our past when the old-time Indian traders vanished: the field was abandoned gradually, beginning in the early 1900's. Perhaps arbitrarily, the present work ends when an entirely new generation of traders adopted new approaches soon after 1932, coinciding with sweeping changes in reservation and tribal affairs introduced by the administration of Indian Commissioner John Collier. The government's stock-reduction program, a spreading network of new reservation roads, the changes Indians themselves made from ponies and wagons to pickup trucks and automobiles, and the discovery of natural gas and oil—all of these swiftly revolutionized and obliterated an older way of life.

Sons and grandsons and other relatives of the first American traders supplied a large part of the information gathered for this book. James Damon, for example, eighty years old when I visited him at Fort Defiance in 1960, retained a clear memory of his father and his father's close associates. Sam Day II, nearing eighty, on the many occasions when I called at his home at Karigan's Trading Post told me much of the early days at Cienega Amarilla, of Lorenzo Hubbell, and of other early traders of the region. At Flagstaff, Paul Babbitt, the son of Charles J. Babbitt, supplied details of his family's trading activities in Arizona.

These are only three of more than one hundred traders or descendants of trading families who were equally helpful in personal interviews; names of most of the others appear elsewhere in the text or chapter notes. Over a period of four years I visited nearly all of the trading posts—or ruin sites of abandoned posts—that are referred to in the following chapters. One car was thoroughly burned out in these travels and another, a four-wheel-drive Land-Rover, helped to finish the work over the rougher sections of New Mexico, Colorado, Utah, and Arizona. Often I had as companion a Navaho, from the vicinity of Teec-tso-secad, where I stayed during part of 1960, or encountered along a lonely road.

Old newspaper files were helpful, especially those at Gallup, Albuquerque, and Santa Fe. A few specific points were cleared up by consulting old newspapers at the library of the Missouri Historical Society in Columbia, Missouri, and the Library of Congress in Washington. Court records were examined in Santa Fe, Gallup, and Aztec, New Mexico. Various documents, reports, and old maps were found at the Library of the Museum of New Mexico, the Gallup Public Library, New Mexico University Library, Michigan University Library, the New York Public Library, and the Library of Congress. A very considerable amount of material came from a month's work at the National Archives in Washington.

In such far-separated places as the Archives and the reservation trading posts I found information, new or forgotten, casting new light on the traders' close relationship to Indian crafts. These crafts were basic to Indian trade in the old barter system of Southwest reservations. To the extent that some traders viewed the crafts as commodities with certain dollar valuations while others took deep pleasure in fostering and improving native arts, the subject is explored here rather thoroughly. For readers who might wish a more detailed treatment of Indian crafts divorced from trading, a small number of excellent books are available. Of these two may be called definitive: Charles Avery Amsden's *Navaho Weaving* and John Adair's *The Navajo and Pueblo Silversmiths*. Less ambitious but with some information more recent than Amsden's is H. P. Mera's *Navajo Textile Arts*. Gladys A. Reichard's *Navajo Shepherd and Weaver* also should be read, but George Wharton James' *Indian Blankets and Their Makers* might be approached with care, and then mainly for its entertainment value. A number of recent books on Indian arts of North America contain handsome illustrations of Pueblo pottery, but I know of no book in this field that compares with the work of Amsden and Adair. Alice Marriott's *Maria: The Potter of San Ildefonso* gives an interesting account of the famous pottery of that pueblo. Again, the craft of modern basketry has been neglected. For a limited approach, however, the reader might consult Bert Robinson's *The Basket Weavers of Arizona*. An excellent study of prehistoric basketry—from which all of the modern craft in the Southwest derives—is *Anasazi Basketry*, by Earl H. Morris and Robert F. Burgh.

A useful source of information, referred to frequently in following chapters, is a rarely found work by the late Richard Van Valkenburgh, who died at his home at Window Rock about the same time that work on the present book was started. Although his background was in archaeology, Van Valkenburgh had found his later years otherwise occupied, mainly as a research assistant for the Navaho Service. At the end he was devoting almost all of his energy toward helping to settle a boundary dispute between the Navaho and Hopi tribes.

I did not have an opportunity to meet Van Valkenburgh, but soon after his death I called upon Ruth Van Valkenburgh, his widow. We discussed, quite tentatively, the possibilities of finding a publisher for his work, *Diné Bikéyah*, mimeographed in a limited number of copies in 1941 by the Indian Service at Window Rock. Mrs. Van Valkenburgh said that at the time of his death her husband left a large collection of working notes from which he had hoped to correct, revise, and enlarge his manuscript.

Diné Bikéyah, as it stands, is a fascinating geographical and historical guide to the Navaho country. The text is arranged alphabetically under Navaho place names, the material drawn from Van Valkenburgh's extensive travel through the land of The People, and the information his inquiring mind gleaned from Indian informants, traders, and old-time settlers.

To all of these individuals and sources I wish to express my gratitude and obligation. Most particularly I am indebted to the assistance of John Arrington, who was raised and still lives in New Mexico's San Juan Valley. He is the son of pioneers, his mother, a native of Georgia, having come as a small girl by wagon train to LaVeta, Colorado. Thomas Jefferson Arrington, his father, a native of Tennessee, fought on the Confederate side at Shiloh, arrived at Denver in the spring of 1864, and for a time freighted flour by ox team from Denver to Salt Lake City and then on to Montana.

More Navahos and Utes than whites populated the San Juan Valley in 1887, the year John Arrington was born. In a country where hard money was scarcely known, Arrington worked as a cowboy and later as government stockman for the Indian Service. During the winter of 1908–1909 he clerked for John B. Moore at Crystal, in 1915 built his own trading post at Kinnebito, and still later built a second post on a bend of the San Juan a short distance east of the Navaho reservation line. Either alone or with his chum Will Evans, he traveled all of western New Mexico and eastern Arizona. Throughout the Four Corners region there was scarcely a hogan where the two friends were not known and made welcome.

I cannot testify as to John Arrington's formal education, but it does not matter. In the restless, seeking manner of Thomas Keam, Lorenzo Hubbell, and the Wetherill brothers, he absorbed a working knowledge of the Southwest country and its people. This is a plain but uncommon sort of knowledge, beyond the range of most men of those times and all but lost to later generations.

At John Arrington's home and during trips together across the reservation, we discussed many of the episodes, places, and individuals that were to form a part of this book. Much of his counsel and direct information will not be apparent to the reader, but nevertheless it is here. If there should be inaccuracies, the fault is mine, not his.

Frank McNitt

North Woodstock, Connecticut
January 9, 1962

CONTENTS

ILLUSTRATIONS

Bi-joshii
Traders' Booths at Shiprock Fair

Maps and Charts

PART ONE

". . . They [a family of Utes] took us for traders and they
brought chamois skins and other things for exchange; among
these they brought preserves made of small black apples . . .
which are very similar to small grapes and very tasty. We convinced the Indians, though they did not believe us altogether,
that we were not traders."

—Fr. Silvestre Vélez de Escalante, entry of
August 24, 1776, in his journal of an expedition intended to discover a serviceable route
from Santa Fe, New Mexico, to California.

1

The Spanish Traders, 1540-1846

AFTER HIGH EXPECTATIONS of a golden Cíbola were aroused by
Fray Marcos de Niza and Coronado, the northern provinces proved
nothing but a disappointment to New Spain. From Cíbola to Tusa-
yan and eastward to the Río Grande, the stubborn Pueblos, after
brave resistance, had been subdued. Thereafter, each Indian revolt
resulted only in reconquest and firmer Spanish rule. The Pueblos
could offer nothing in tribute to the viceroys of New Spain and
precious little to their secular and religious masters in New Mexico.
The land itself entered a weary conspiracy. Instead of a flow of gold
and silver, the northern provinces yielded only grudging sustenance
to their few hundred Spanish colonizers.

Long accustomed to their own primitive system of barter, the Indians for a century and a half were forced to accept the conqueror's
new concept of trade.

Tutelage of the Pueblos began with Coronado's vain military expedition to Quivira, when the Zuñi people of Háwikuh, first to receive instruction, were compelled to surrender food and blankets to
the Spanish train. In return for these gifts Coronado permitted the
Zuñis to live. Until then the Pueblos' usual manner of trade was a
process of exchange: their cotton blankets or fruit and corn and
squash for fresh Navaho game, or Apache buffalo hides and deerskins.

Further refinements of Spanish trade were introduced shortly after,
when Coronado, on reaching the Río Grande, encountered more
obstinate resistance. Tewan pueblos that refused to trade on the conqueror's terms were besieged and burned. At one village some eighty

3

to one hundred captives provided an example for all others: tied to stakes, they were burned to death. At Pecos Pueblo, desiring guides who might lead them to Quivira's gold, one of Coronado's captains did not barter or pay for their services but seized and placed in chains four Indians he thought best suited to his needs.

A truer appreciation of Spanish commerce awaited the coming of Don Juan de Oñate, colonizer and first governor of New Mexico. Stopping with his large party at Acoma Pueblo in October, 1598, Oñate was submissively received and—in the manner of Coronado— furnished "liberally with maize, water, and fowls."[1] All might have been well if a following company of soldiers under Juan de Zaldívar had not demanded more supplies from the Acomas a month later. Less willing this time, the villagers resisted and in a fight that ensued Zaldívar, ten soldiers and two servants were killed.[2] Oñate responded, not in angry vengeance, but with determination to discourage further rebellion. Seventy soldiers led by the slain Zaldívar's brother, Vicente, stormed the mesa pueblo and methodically over a period of three days massacred more than half of the inhabitants. The village of stone and adobe was destroyed; the survivors, some seventy or eighty men and five hundred women and children, were taken as prisoners to Oñate's headquarters at Santo Domingo.

That this lesson might never be forgotten, Oñate ordered that male prisoners over twenty-five years of age should have one foot cut off and serve twenty years of personal servitude. Males and females between the ages twelve and twenty-five were sentenced to slavery for twenty years.

Oñate directed that those sentenced to servitude "shall be distributed among my captains and soldiers in the manner which I will prescribe and who may hold and keep them as their slaves for the said term . . . and no more." Girls under twelve years were assigned to Fray Alonso Martínez, boys under twelve to Vicente Zaldívar, to be distributed "in this kingdom or elsewhere . . . that they may attain

1 George P. Hammond and Agapito Rey (eds. and trans.), *Don Juan de Oñate, Colonizer of New Mexico, 1595–1628.*

2 *Ibid.* Spanish and Acoma eyewitness accounts of how the trouble arose are contradictory. Survivors among Zaldívar's company of thirty-one men said that the villagers were offered "highly prized hatchets, iron articles, and other things" in trade for the maize, flour, and blankets the Spaniards desired. This evidently was true. But the Acomas felt the Spaniards "asked for such large amounts" of food and blankets that they would have been cheated. Other Acoma survivors mentioned provocations. Xunusta: ". . . the Spaniards first killed an Indian." Excasi: ". . . they killed the Spaniards because a soldier either asked for or took a turkey." Caucachi: ". . . the Spaniards had wounded an Acoma Indian."

the knowledge of God and the salvation of their souls." Two Hopi
men captured at Acoma were sentenced to have their right hands cut
off and "to be set free in order that they may convey to their land the
news of their punishment."

The pattern was set. Spanish governors who succeeded Oñate were
as firm, if usually less brutal. A slave economy foreshadowing the
worst to be imported later from Africa to the Eastern seaboard was
clamped upon the provinces. Plains and mountain Apaches and the
related Navahos were less accessible and more warlike than the
Pueblos and so until the middle or late 1600's were not as subject to
seizure and servitude. Before the Pueblo Revolt of 1680, however, the
Spaniards dropped any pretense of peaceful relations and in scores
of small raids took many Apaches and Navahos as slaves.[3]

Slaves of all tribes might be taken as household servants, used as
common laborers to dig irrigation ditches, till fields, or build roads,
or—closest to the Spanish dream—be sent off to dig for gold and silver ore in the Spanish mines. These were located in Sonora and at a
few places in the northern provinces, mines in the Sierra Azul, near
the Hopi villages, receiving frequent mention in contemporary accounts. A lust for the precious ore exceeded always its actual production, but the search for new mines was tireless and the availability of
slave labor apparently was inexhaustible.

So it was and promised to remain, but the Spanish dream was a
recurrent vision. Not immune, Governor Tomás Velez Cachupin in
1763 authorized an expedition to skirt the La Plata—or Silver—
Mountains of Colorado and penetrate the largely unknown regions
beyond. Ostensibly the purpose of the expedition was to trade with
the Utes and explore their country. More to the point, Cachupin let
it be known that the discovery of precious metals would please him
more than any quantity of peltries. He was not displeased, therefore,
when Father Alonzo Posados, a member of the party, reported to him
in Santa Fe that the expedition had reached the confluence of the
Gunnison and Uncompahgre rivers and near that place found traces
of silver.

Governor Cachupin ordered a second expedition to undertake the
same mission in 1765, under the leadership of Juan María de Rivera.
This and succeeding ventures into the Rocky Mountains gave Rivera

---

3 Jack D. Forbes, *Apache, Navaho, and Spaniard*, 156. Forbes writes that in the
1660's "slaves became so numerous that an Apache woman could be purchased for
twenty-six pesos. Governor Peñalosa declared that he had so many Apache slaves
that he gave away more than 100 of them."

5

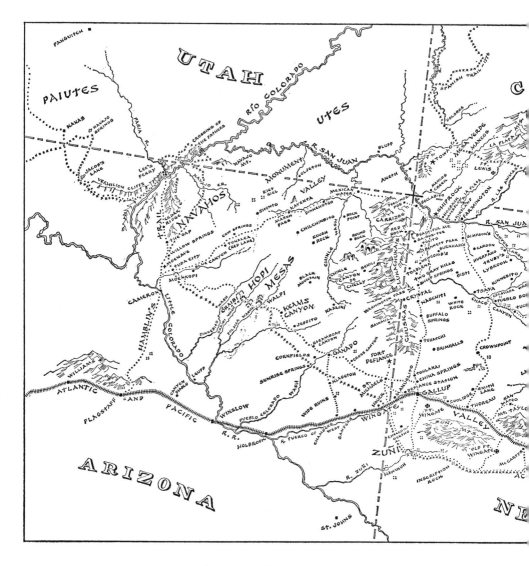

Navaho, Hopi, and Zuñi lands.

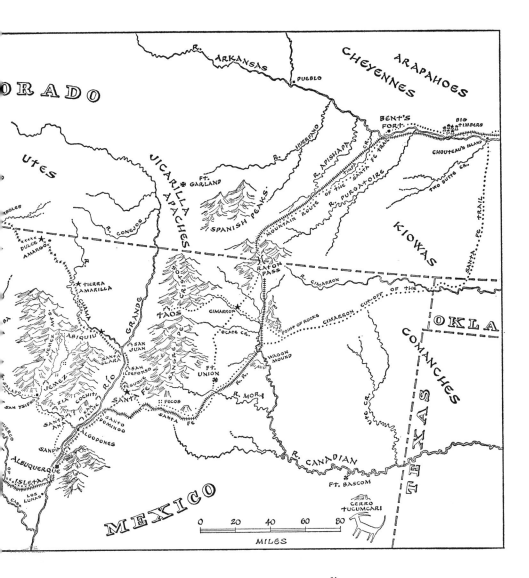

★	agency	●	trading post
✠	fort	xxxxxxx	old Spanish trail
⌐¬	pueblo	••••••	later trail
∷	ruin	⫴⫴⫴⫴⫴⫴	railroad
◼	town	═ ═ ═	state line

a lasting name as trail blazer in all the rough wilderness between the Gunnison and Santa Fe. His success in discovering the minerals so prized by the governor is uncertain, although unquestionably his travels encouraged many of his contemporaries to follow in his steps and begin an increasingly clandestine, if lucrative, trade with the mountain Indians.

Ten years after Rivera's first expedition, three of his companions on that journey—Pedro Mora, Gregorio Sandoval, and Andrés Muñiz—returned to the cottonwood grove where the Uncompahgre meets the Gunnison and looked again on the tree where Rivera had carved a cross, his initials, and the date. If the moment has any relevance in history it is only to underscore the fact that by 1775 the junction of these two rivers, near the present town of Delta, Colorado, was well known to the Spaniards and, so far as the records show, until then was about as far as they cared to go. Of the present trio, however, Andrés Muñiz soon was to travel much farther, for in the following year he served as an interpreter and guide for the expedition of the Franciscan fathers, Domínguez and Escalante.

A resident of Bernalillo and himself a *genizaro*, Muñiz would have been acquainted with the Spanish half-blood trader Manuel Mestes. Documents of the period tell little of these men, but Mestes' name is one of the first mentioned in association with the Utes. He was trading with them at least as early as 1755, and by 1805, when he was in his seventieth year and evidently still active, he was remembered for having journeyed as far as the Timpanogos Valley, near the Great Salt Lake. Governor Joaquín Alencaster referred to him as one "who for approximately fifty years has served as Yuta [Ute] interpreter, [and] was the one who reduced them to peace"—a partially accurate, if overoptimistic statement.[4]

Another veteran of the mountain trade in this period was Juan Pedro Cisneros, whose facility with the Navaho language suggests that before 1775 he may have spent a number of years among the Navahos between the pueblo of Zuñi and the San Juan River. Cisneros accompanied Fr. Escalante on his first visit to the Hopi village of Oraibi in 1775, and—with Andrés Muñiz—numbered one of the Domínguez and Escalante party of twelve a year later. In his diary of that expedition Escalante refers to Cisneros as *alcalde mayor* of Zuñi, and under his entry of November 16, 1776, relates how Cisneros hap-

[4] Joseph J. Hill, "Spanish and Mexican Exploration and Trade Northwest from New Mexico into the Great Basin, 1765–1853," *Utah Historical Quarterly*, Vol. III, No. 1 (1930).

pily intervened when the Franciscans were hostilely greeted by the people of Oraibi.

On arriving at the base of Second Mesa, Escalante writes, ". . . we ascended without incident and on entering the pueblo we were surrounded by a great number of Indians, large and small. In a language which they did not understand we asked them for the cacique and the chiefs, and when we wished to go to the house of the cacique, they restrained us, one of them saying in the Navajo tongue that we must not enter the pueblo. Don Juan Pedro Cisneros, in the same tongue spiritedly asked if they were not our friends. Thereupon they quieted down, and an old man led us to his house and made us welcome in it."[5]

During the next quarter-century nothing produced significant change in the attitude of the provinces or in New Spain's relations and trade with the Indians. Spanish settlements strung out along the Río Grande from Taos to El Paso del Norte depended as before on a continuing flow of manufactured goods from Chihuahua. An intermingling with the native population, a reluctance of Spanish families in New Spain to migrate to the northern provinces, encouraged little progress from the simplest of agrarian economies. Beyond food, leather goods, wooden furniture, and woven articles of wearing apparel, the people of New Mexico produced few other necessities of life and none of its luxuries. Annually, a summer fair for Indian trade goods and Indian slaves was held at Taos, and in turn these commodities—live or inert—were taken for exchange at the January fair at Chihuahua. As though separated by an ocean, there was no trade with the distant Americans, and scarcely any with the Spaniards in Texas or the French of Louisiana.

Next to officials of provincial government in Santa Fe, traders were the most affluent of all in these northern regions of New Spain. And in spite of their enormous profits, even the traders, looking to Chihuahua for hard money and supplies, often played into the hands of merchants there. Hubert Howe Bancroft summarizes the situation:

"There was no coin or other money in New Mexico, but the traders for their accounts invented a system of imaginary currency, including four kinds of dollars. . . . The beauty of this system was that the traders always bought for the cheap pesos and sold for the dearer kinds, all being 'dollars' to the Indians . . . a trader by two or three barters

[5] The quotation is from Herbert E. Bolton's translation of the Escalante diary, appearing in Bolton's *Pageant in the Wilderness: The Story of the Escalante Expedition to the Interior Basin, 1776.*

9

in a year often getting $64 for a piece of cloth which cost him six. . . .
Señor Trebol bought a *guacamaya*, or macaw, for eight dollars and
sold the gay feathers for $492. Another system of swindling com-
merce was the habitual selling of goods to be paid for in future
products. Thus, for a little seed grain six fanegas [about nine bush-
els] at harvest were promised; or for a bottle of brandy in holy week
a barrel was exacted. . . . While the settlers and pueblo Indians were
always in debt to the traders, the latter in turn were debtors to or
agents for Chihuahua merchants."[6]

The treaty signed in Paris in May, 1803, lowered the barriers to
America's westward expansion. Confronted by British sea power, Na-
poleon Bonaparte voluntarily offered France's withdrawal from the
New World. From the Executive Mansion in Washington, Thomas
Jefferson studied the problems arising from his nation's sudden, enor-
mous acquisition of the relatively unknown land called Louisiana.

Congress did not ratify the Louisiana Purchase until October. But
for Jefferson's immediate westering plans this was not important.
Before he became President, Jefferson dreamed of a western expedition, and even before the treaty was signed he arranged for such an
expedition to be led by the Virginian who served as his private secretary, Captain Meriwether Lewis. An appropriation by Congress early
in 1803 authorized Lewis to discover a northwest land route to the
Pacific, determine the nature of the unknown western Indian tribes,
and report on the topography and natural resources of the country
he explored. In July, Lewis left the capital to meet William Clark
on the Ohio, from whence they would proceed to winter quarters
near the mouth of the Missouri.

Meanwhile, for the payment of about fifteen million dollars,
France ceded to the United States all of Louisiana—hazy designation
for unsurveyed territory extending our western frontier from the
Mississippi River fifteen hundred miles to the Rocky Mountains.[7]
The Río Grande, France thought, limited Louisiana on the west.
Spain thought differently. Not until 1819—and then too embroiled

---

[6] Bancroft, *History of Arizona and New Mexico*. A parallel may be drawn between these Spanish traders and the so-called free traders and trappers, American
and French, who in 1830–40 mortgaged themselves to the merchants of St. Louis,
who outfitted them for the Rocky Mountain trade.

[7] From the Louisiana Purchase the United States in time carved all or parts of
thirteen states: Louisiana, Missouri, Arkansas, Iowa, Minnesota, Kansas, Nebraska,
Colorado, North and South Dakota, Montana, Wyoming, and Oklahoma.

in the Mexican War of Independence to care very much—Spain won the United States' agreement to the following boundary: the Sabine River from the Gulf of Mexico to the thirty-second parallel; thence due north to the Red River, and up the Red to the one-hundredth meridian; north along that line to the Arkansas River, and along this to its source; from there north to the forty-second parallel and west on that line to the Pacific.

Two months before Lewis and Clark arrived at St. Louis to complete their journey, a second military expedition, under command of Lieutenant Zebulon M. Pike, set out from that frontier staging point. At the head of about twenty men Pike left St. Louis July 15, 1806, presumably under instructions to determine the source of the Red River, treat with the Indian tribes, and find a suitable southern route into Spanish territory. It is possible that Pike may also have been under secret orders to test Spain's military strength in the northern provinces, though this has never been clearly established.

By mid-November from a vantage point on the Arkansas River, Pike first viewed a snowy eminence in the "Mexican mountains" which later was to be named Pikes Peak. Enduring brutal hardships and after encounters with hostile Pawnees, the party continued to the headwaters of the Arkansas. Here Pike doubled back and cut south into Spanish territory, reaching the Río Grande at a point near present Alamosa, Colorado. While in winter camp on the Conejos, Pike was taken in custody by Spanish soldiers and with his men was escorted down the Río Grande to Santa Fe. Reaching there on March 3, 1807, the Americans were held as prisoners, though treated courteously. Taken first to Chihuahua and then back to Texas and the border, Pike's command eventually was released. Almost a year from the date of their departure they were back at St. Louis.

These events of 1803 to 1807 were all that was needed in a young nation filled with energy and a common desire to broaden its frontiers. From outposts along the Mississippi to the Eastern seaboard the journeys of Lewis and Clark and of Zebulon Pike received wide attention. The explorers were acclaimed from official levels in Washington to the humblest farmhouse and tavern. Trade opportunities in the Spanish Southwest—though illegal and frowned upon by the Spaniards—and a vast wealth to be gained from the Rocky Mountain fur trade, appealed mightily to frontier Americans who until then knew only the scratching hardships of a moneyless economy on wilderness farms.

Pike's brief period of detention by the Spaniards gave him an opportunity to observe the imbalance of commerce between the merchants of Chihuahua and the poor settlements of the Río Grande Valley. Pike observed, and in his journals recorded, the possibilities of a competitive overland trade from the Missouri to Santa Fe. Indeed, while still in Santa Fe, Pike encountered two men who had come there with trade goods and remained. The first of these was the French Creole, Jean Baptiste Lalande, who crossed the plains in 1804 with a pack train supplied by his employer, William Morrison. A merchant of Kaskaskia, Illinois, Morrison perhaps knew something of the sporadic efforts by a few Frenchmen, between 1739 and 1751, to engage in trade between the Mississippi settlements and New Mexico. In several cases the Spaniards dealt summarily with the intruders, confiscating their goods and placing the traders under arrest.[8] If Morrison thought his agent would fare better, he was disappointed. Lalande was arrested and sent to Chihuahua, but in 1805 was permitted to return to Santa Fe, where he lived thereafter.

Before he himself was escorted to Chihuahua, Pike also met James Purcell or Pursley, a Kentuckian, the first American trader of record to reach Santa Fe. After a boyhood on the Mississippi frontier, Pursley outfitted in St. Louis in 1802 and spent the next three years wandering and trading among the tribes of the Great Plains. Pike understood Pursley to say that he went to Santa Fe in 1805 on behalf of one of the Plains tribes, to negotiate trade arrangements between the Indians and the Spaniards. His mission completed, Pursley remained in Santa Fe until 1824, supporting himself as a carpenter at the time of his meeting with Pike.[9]

8 Max L. Moorhead says that trade goods from the French settlements were first brought to the annual trade fairs at Taos by the Comanches, who obtained them from the Pawnees—who initially received them from the French. Moorhead notes four French trade parties reaching Santa Fe, 1739–51. The first was "officially unwelcome . . . [but] . . . was allowed to remain for nine months and return home" (New Mexico's Royal Road: Trade and Travel on the Chihuahua Trail). Located on the Mississippi at the mouth of the Kaskaskia River, the town of Kaskaskia was once the most important French trading settlement in the Illinois country. From 1809 to 1818 the capital of Illinois Territory, Kaskaskia was reduced from leading trading center for the upper Mississippi only with the rise and growth of St. Louis. Kaskaskia was the birthplace, in 1812, of John Doyle Lee, Mormon trader who appears in later chapters.

9 Zebulon Montgomery Pike, An Account of Expeditions to the Sources of the Mississippi and Through the Western Parts of Louisiana. Pike refers to the Kentuckian as Jacob Pursley. Moorhead notes that "an item in the Missouri Intelligencer of April 10, 1824, announcing his return from New Mexico, refers to him as James Purcell." Bancroft, in History of Arizona and New Mexico, speaks of the trader as James Pursley.

Pursley enjoyed a freedom of movement that indicates the Spaniards may have made an exception in his case and not arrested him. Others who followed the Kentuckian were less fortunate, and the policy of the Spanish governors remained nearly consistent: higher profits for their merchants of Chihuahua could be protected only by enforcing the law making it illegal for Missouri traders to enter New Mexico. Thus in 1810 a party of seven traders, including Captain Reuben Smith, Joseph McLanahan, and James Patterson, were arrested on arrival in Santa Fe. Their goods were confiscated, and they were held for two years at the Presidio of San Elizeario. Two years later a party of nine or ten men led by Robert McKnight met the same fate, being held at Chihuahua and Durango until 1821.

Again in 1815–16, the Spanish trade barrier was tested. A large trading-trapping party led by Auguste P. Chouteau and Jules de Mun worked the upper Arkansas through the winter of 1815 and early the following year, laden with pelts and trade goods, visited Taos and Santa Fe. Surprisingly, Governor Alberto Mainez welcomed them and said they might continue their operations without hindrance if they stayed north of the Red River and on the eastern slopes of the Rockies. Mainez also offered to procure a license for them to trap beaver on the upper branches of the Río Grande.

Chouteau and De Mun spent the next months in the mountains north of Taos, unmolested, until early in 1817 the successor to Mainez, Governor Pedro María de Allande, returned to the older policy of exclusion. In June the trappers were arrested and taken to Santa Fe; their caches of furs on the upper Arkansas, valued at $30,380, were confiscated. After forty-eight hours in jail they were released and permitted to return to St. Louis.[10]

Spanish rule in New Mexico was on the wane, however, and for the Americans this was one of its last manifestations. Late in 1821 General Iturbide brought Mexico's eleven-year War of Independence to an end, and all of those still loyal to the king of Spain were removed from positions of authority. Under Governor Facundo Melgares the province of New Mexico openly invited trade with its American neighbors. Captain Hugh Glenn, a native of Ohio, and Captain William Becknell, of Franklin, Missouri, arriving independently in Santa Fe before the end of 1821, were the first to remark the warming change of climate.

Glenn was a veteran in the Indian trade, owning a trading-house

10 Bancroft says that Chouteau and De Mun filed a claim for $50,000 damages, but there is no evidence that any settlement was made.

at the mouth of the Verdigris River. With Jacob Fowler and a few other companions, he followed the Arkansas to the vicinity of present Pueblo, Colorado. Proceeding with three of the party to Santa Fe, Glenn was well received at the capital. His request for a trapping license was granted, and in the months following he and Fowler trapped the headwaters of the Río Grande.[11]

Becknell had no thought of going to Santa Fe when he left the Missouri the same fall. Accompanied by a party of skilled frontiersmen, including the Tennessee trader and trapper Ewing Young, Becknell planned only to hunt and trap the eastern Rockies and trade with the Comanches on the lower plains. After ten weeks out, however, his party met with a group of New Mexican militia whose overtures were so friendly that Becknell changed his plans and accompanied the Mexicans to Santa Fe. Here, like Glenn, Becknell was warmly greeted by Governor Melgares, who urged him to dispose of his small supply of trade goods in New Mexico. This Becknell and his companions did, with "a very handsome profit."

On his return to Franklin, Becknell gave so favorable a report that a number of others outfitted caravans for Santa Fe the following spring.[12] Becknell himself returned several times to New Mexico, his second crossing of the plains, in 1822, adding significantly to the contribution he already had made toward the opening of commerce on the Santa Fe Trail.

Pack trains composed exclusively of mules, occasionally horses, were used by overland traders until this year, when Becknell decided to test the feasibility of wagons. Together with the usual string of pack mules he set out with three wagons. These proved so successful that other traders quickly adopted them, finding that with prairie schooners fewer animals could transport enormously increased loads with greater ease and less chance of damage to the goods carried.

Becknell's other innovation of importance came with his discovery of the Cimarron Cutoff, shortening by many miles the distance to Santa Fe. The alternative, or mountain route, followed the Arkansas to the future vicinity of Bent's Fort and then dropped south over the Colorado plains and Raton Mountains to Taos. Cimarron Cutoff after 1822 was preferred by many caravans, though always the men who followed it paid dearly for time gained by facing perilous days without water.

Seventy men, traveling in perhaps five caravans, made the journey

11 Josiah Gregg, *Commerce of the Prairies* (ed. by Max L. Moorhead).
12 *Ibid.* Further details are given by Moorhead in *New Mexico's Royal Road.*

in 1822 and may be called the true founders of the Santa Fe Trail. Among them, Colonel Benjamin Cooper, with his nephews Braxton and Stephen Cooper and some twelve others, drove a pack train from Howard County, Missouri, to the mountain route of the Arkansas and then proceeded to Taos. Their trade goods were valued at four to five thousand dollars. Another caravan that year was led by Samuel Chambers and James Baird, two members of the Robert McKnight party that reached Santa Fe and internment in 1812.[13]

Others who came out with caravans in the next decade included those free adventurers who disposed of their trade goods in Taos or Santa Fe and remained for varying periods and a hazardous existence as Indian traders and trappers. James O. Pattie, a Kentuckian, was one of these; so, too, were Kit Carson, Ewing Young, Isaac Slover, William Wolfskill, and Tom Smith. Pattie and Young wandered as far as California, between trips up the mountain streams of Colorado, while Tom Smith laid trap lines through the Rockies and on into Utah.

Josiah Gregg, who entered the Santa Fe trade in 1831, estimated that the seventy men who crossed the plains in 1822 brought trade goods amounting in value to fifteen thousand dollars. Max L. Moorhead, annotator of Gregg's *Commerce of the Prairies*, observed that in the next quarter-century—or by 1846, the year of American invasion and annexation of New Mexico—caravans traveling the Santa Fe Trail had increased to 750 men and approximately one million dollars' worth of goods.[14] The greatest quantity of this merchandise was carried on to Chihuahua, usually one-third to one-half being sold in Santa Fe or Taos.

A point generally overlooked is the fact that an important proportion of the trade goods remaining in New Mexico was channeled immediately or soon after into the rapidly expanding trade with the Indians. Without this continuing supply of goods coming over the trail from Missouri, the mountain fur trade originating from Taos could not have existed.

Why, since they always placed a certain value on buffalo hides, were the Spanish-speaking people of the provinces eager as traders

13 Annotating Gregg's *Commerce of the Prairies,* Moorhead observes that Robert and John McKnight, accompanied by eight others, left the Missouri in the fall of 1822 to trade with the Comanches. John was reportedly killed by the Indians. Two years later Robert returned to New Mexico, became a Mexican citizen, and in 1828 started on his way to a fortune when he acquired the Santa Rita copper mine.
14 Moorhead, *New Mexico's Royal Road.*

but so indifferent as fur trappers? Spanish buffalo hunters were encountered frequently anywhere on the plains below the Arkansas on into the Llano Estacado east of the Pecos. By temperament, one suspects, they were not adapted, nor were they by nature patient or aggressive enough, to endure the hardships of a trapper's life.

It is true, many instances are related of Spanish and Mexican parties venturing into the mountains for furs. More often than not, however, the peltries they brought back to Taos and Santa Fe were obtained from the mountain Ietans, or Utes, by barter.

Auguste Chouteau was trapping in the lower Rockies in 1817, as we have seen, and it is likely that others from the distant Missouri were there before him. In the four or five years following, it is certain that many other parties of French and American trappers explored farther into these mountains, but it was not until 1822, when the roving brigades of General William H. Ashley appeared on the scene, that the American fur trade crossed the threshold of its golden decade. That Ashley's men reached the mountains in the same year that overland caravans opened the Santa Fe Trail is mere coincidence. Nevertheless, from that time forward there was a strong interdependence between mountain trade and prairie commerce.

For Indian traders and free trappers, Taos, and Santa Fe to a lesser extent, became headquarters, supply point, and marketing place for the furs and hides and buckskins brought out of the mountains. The names of these men are legion, but would begin with the Robidoux brothers—Antoine, Joseph, and Louis—who maintained a trading-house at Taos to supply their mountain enterprises. The Robidoux', originally merchants in St. Louis, reached Taos before 1825, as did Étienne Provost and his partner, François Leclerc. Working out of Taos, Provost met William Ashley in northern Utah, probably about 1825, and became an Ashley man. A few years later, after Ashley's company was reorganized in 1826 by the Rocky Mountain Fur Company, Provost signed on as one of the principals of John Jacob Astor's American Fur Company.[15] Then, rivaling Jim Bridger as one of the most experienced and knowing of mountain men, Provost in 1839 joined John Charles Frémont at St. Louis as guide for Frémont's exploration up the Missouri and through the Dakota Territory.

American and French traders were not long in Taos before they learned there were two trade items that ranked first with their Spanish colleagues: horses and Indian slaves. At almost any point between

15 Bernard De Voto, *Across the Wide Missouri.*

the Río Chama and Sevier Valley the Americans might run into bands of Spaniards negotiating with Indians for either one or the other commodity.

For the more usual trade goods, as whisky, guns, tobacco, cloth, knives, and beads, the Spaniards traded first with the Navahos or Utes for horses—dearly prized by the various Paiute tribes of Utah who were so poor they ate roots and grasshoppers and owned little more than a few shreds of bark or animal pelts to cover their nakedness. Herds of Indian ponies, usually only the poorer specimens that Utes and Navahos were willing to part with, were then driven on into the Sevier Valley where they were traded for Paiute slaves. Such commerce was frowned upon officially, but was a natural extension of a Spanish colonial attitude, and it appears to have been practiced on a large scale between 1800 and about 1850.

A trading expedition led by Mauricio Arze and Lagos García in 1813, in some respects may be typical. The company of seven men left Abiquiu, on the Chama, March 16 and returned July 12, in the interval having traveled to the Timpanogos Valley and land of the "Bearded Yutas." When it was brought to his attention that the traders were accompanied home by twelve slaves, Governor José Manrique summoned the company before an official inquiry. Affidavits were sworn to by five members of the company, each relating substantially the same story of bland innocence.

At Timpanogos Lake, they related, they bartered with a band of Paiutes for three days, the Indians refusing to offer the Spaniards anything in trade but slaves, "as they had done on other occasions." The Spaniards insisted that they had declined these offers, whereupon the Indians attacked the traders' caravan, killing eight horses and one mule. Escaping from this violent situation, the affidavits continued, the traders were making their way toward the Río Colorado when they met another band of Indians equally determined to barter slaves for Spanish horses. "In order not to receive another injury like the first one," the affidavits agreed, the Spaniards under duress bought twelve slaves and continued their journey. On their return they managed also to barter for 109 pelts, a small number, the affidavits admitted—"but a few."[16]

Dick Wootton, who spent a lifetime in the mountains and in later years built a wagon toll road over Raton Pass, had frequent occasion to observe the slave trade. In reminiscences of his own days as a

[16] Hill, "Spanish and Mexican Exploration," *Utah Historical Quarterly*, Vol. III, No. 1 (1930).

mountain man and Indian scout, Daniel W. Jones quotes Uncle Dick as saying, "It was no uncommon thing in those days [the 1830's] to see a party of Mexicans in that [Great Basin] country buying Indians, and while we were trapping there I sent a lot of peltries to Taos by a party of those same slave traders."[17]

The slave traders made annual trips to Sevier Valley as late as 1851, Jones adds, paying one hundred dollars or the equivalent value in horses for boys, and up to twice that amount for girls.

Trading in slaves was by no means confined to certain elements among the Mexican population. Navahos made frequent raids upon Spanish settlements for livestock and captives, retaining the slaves either for their own use or for trade with other tribes. The situation was so prevalent at the time of the American occupation of New Mexico that it was a cause of positive concern to James S. Calhoun, first Indian agent appointed to the territory.[18]

"It may not be improper to remark in relation to captives," Calhoun observed in 1850, "whether Indians or Mexicans, or in the possession of either, they are bought and sold as *Peons*, and are relieved from servitude only by the payment of such an amount as their masters may demand. Neither a Mexican, or an Indian have the slightest objection to become the purchasers of their own 'kith and kin.' . . . The value of captives depend upon age, sex, beauty, and usefulness. Good females, not having passed the 'seer and yellow leaf,' are valued from fifty to one hundred and fifty dollars each. Males, as they may be useful, one half less, never more."[19]

17 Daniel W. Jones, "Forty Years Among the Indians," quoted by William J. Snow in "Utah Indians and Spanish Slave Trade," *Utah Historical Quarterly,* Vol. II, No. 3 (1929). Snow elsewhere quotes Thomas J. Farnham early traveler to the Salt Lake region, as saying that along the Sevier River "live the 'Piutes' and the 'Land Pitches' (Sanpitch) the most degraded and least intellectual Indians known to the trappers. . . . These poor creatures are hunted in the spring of the year, when weak and helpless, by a certain class of men, and when taken, are fattened, carried to Santa Fe and sold as slaves during their minority." F. W. Hodge *(Handbook of American Indians)* lists thirty-one divisions of the Paiute tribe; the Sanpitch or Sanpet Indians, Hodge says, were of Ute stock and formerly occupied the region of the Sanpete Valley and Sevier River.

18 Calhoun's origins are a bit of a mystery. His granddaughter thought he was born in 1802 or 1803 in South Carolina; Calhoun himself said he was a native of Georgia. From the shipping business he entered the Mexican War with a company of Georgia volunteers. On March 29, 1849, President Zachary Taylor ordered that the Indian agency at Council Bluffs, Iowa, be transferred to Santa Fe. Calhoun was appointed agent for New Mexico Territory, then embracing all of Arizona, on April 7, 1849, at a salary of $1,500 plus $2,300 for expenses and contingencies. He arrived at Santa Fe July 22, 1849, and served with rare ability until early summer, 1852, when he died of illness on the plains while returning East.

If horses were preferred tender in bartering for Paiute slaves, the Mexicans found it otherwise in 1850 when trading with Mescalero Apaches and Comanches, who already were well mounted and quite able to steal any horses they needed. Calhoun, remarking the recovery of four Mexican slaves, three of them boys aged twelve, reported the conditions of their sale: "Refugio Picaros . . . was taken from a Rancho . . . [near] Durango, Mexico, two years ago, by the Comanches, who immediately sold him to the Apaches, and with whom he lived . . . until January last, when he was *bought* by Jose Francisco Lucero, a Mexican, [for] four knives, one plug of tobacco, two fanegas of corn, four blankets, and six yards of red Indian cloth."[20]

Teodora Martel, taken by Apaches, was bought by Powler Sandoval for one mare, one rifle, one shirt, one pair of drawers, thirty small packages of powder, some bullets, and one buffalo robe. Caudalans Galope "was seized by the Apaches . . . at the Rancho Fernandez, near Santa Cruz, Mexico." He was bought by Vicente Romero for "some corn and tobacco," one knife, one shirt, one mule, one small package of powder, and a few rifle balls.

Rosalie Taveris, about twenty-five years of age, was captured by Apaches and Comanches, who at the same time killed her husband and four-year-old daughter. Rosalie was bought also by Powler Sandoval, who paid the Apaches two striped blankets, ten yards of blue cotton drilling, ten yards of calico, as much cotton shirting, two handkerchiefs, four plugs of tobacco, a bag of corn, and a knife.

"The trading in captives has been so long tolerated in this territory," Calhoun observed, "that it has ceased to be regarded as a wrong; and purchasers are not prepared willingly to release captives without an adequate ransom. In legislation upon this subject, it should be distinctly set forth under what circumstances captives shall be released. . . . I may mention that there are a number of Indian captives held as slaves in this territory, and some congressional action may be necessary in relation to them."[21]

Mormon authorities in Utah took notice of the slave traffic in November, 1851, after Pedro León and twenty-seven companions journeyed from Santa Fe to trade horses for Paiute children in the Sanpete Valley. The traders were arrested, brought to Manti before

19 Letter from Calhoun to C. I. A. Orlando Brown, March 15, 1850. *The Official Correspondence of James S. Calhoun While Indian Agent at Santa Fe and Superintendent of Indian Affairs in New Mexico* (ed. by Annie Heloise Abel).

20 Letter from Calhoun to Brown, March 31, 1850. *Ibid.*

21 *Ibid.*

a justice of the peace, and held for trial. León appealed personally to Brigham Young, offering in defense a trading license issued to him by Calhoun the previous August. Young showed little sympathy, telling León that Calhoun's jurisdiction did not extend to Mormon Utah, and, in any case, Calhoun did not intend the license for the purchase of slaves. Twenty of the New Mexicans were allowed to return home, however, on the promise they would not trade again with Utah Indians. The others were tried and later released.[22]

Mormon sentiment against León and his companions was still running high when the Utah Legislature, on January 31, 1852, passed a law prohibiting Indian slave trade in that territory. That the abuse continued for some years, however, is indicated by an order issued by Brigham Young on April 23, 1853, calling for the arrest of "all such strolling Mexicans" caught bartering for slaves.[23]

Of equal concern to authorities in New Mexico were the activities of the Comancheros, Spanish-speaking traders whose name derived from their busy trade with the Comanches and Kiowas. While scouting the course of the Canadian River, Lieutenant J. W. Abert flushed a party of Comancheros in September, 1845.

The traders had come out on the buffalo plains, said Abert, "under the guidance of one of the Pueblo Indians, and told us they had been twenty days in reaching this place from Taos. . . . They were dressed in conical-crowned sombreros, jackets with stripes running transversely; large bag[gy] breeches extending to the knee; long stockings and moccasins. They were badly armed, and presented a shabby and poor appearance though we learned that they were a good specimen of the class to which they belong. They are called 'Comancheeros,' and make frequent trading excursions into the country of the Indians, with whom they exchange their stock for horses and mules."[24]

Livestock traded by the Indians to the Comancheros almost always had been stolen in raids upon New Mexican settlements, this in effect making the Comancheros the instigators of an organized, fre-

[22] Hill, "Spanish and Mexican Exploration." *Utah Historical Quarterly*, Vol. III, No. 1, (1930). Hill notes that twenty-one men of the León party were traders, and the other seven servants.

[23] Snow, "Utah Indians and Spanish Slave Trade," *Utah Historical Quarterly*, Vol. II, No. 3 (1929).

[24] "Communicating a Report of an Expedition Led by Lieutenant Abert, on the Upper Arkansas and Through the Country of the Comanche Indians, in the Fall of the Year 1845." 29 Cong., 1 sess., *Sen. Exec. Doc. 438*. The point where Abert encountered the Comancheros was east of present Tucumcari, New Mexico, in or near the Texas Panhandle.

quently violent traffic in stolen property. As late as 1870 the Comancheros, who always could plead ignorance of Indian theft, were the despair of the New Mexican settlers. Their trade, said the *Daily New Mexican* of Santa Fe, was illicit, and in conducting it they were committing a crime against the people:

"The traffic is immensely profitable to the successful trader, who conveys his articles of merchandise, powder and lead being most in demand, to the Indian country on burros, and gets in exchange for it cattle and horses, and sometimes buffalo robes and other articles. The goods of the trader are disposed of to the Indians, usually at extravagant rates, and the . . . stock is driven up into the settlements in New Mexico, and commands ready sale and at fair prices. . . . The trader returns to his home . . . while the Indians set about procuring [more] stock . . . in the usual Indian way: they *steal* it."[25]

For nearly a century the Old Spanish Trail pioneered by Domínguez and Escalante served as principal trade route from Taos and Santa Fe into the mountains. From pueblo villages on the Río Grande the trail in its lower reaches passed through the northeast corner of Navaho country. Roving bands of Navahos or Utes might be seen at any time crossing the trail in the vicinity of Abiquiu, Tierra Amarilla, and Dulce. The trail forded the Río Navaho, or San Juan River, just north of the present New Mexico–Colorado line, at Arboles, a short distance below the mouth of the Piedra, and then entered mountain ranges and valleys indisputably controlled by Utes. On a winding course the trail proceeded up the Río de los Dolores, to the Uncompahgre and Gunnison rivers, and thereafter northward across the Río Colorado, into Utah, and across the Green.

The Robidoux brothers, following the route of the Franciscans, about 1825 built a mountain trading fort close to the trail and on the Uncompahgre, three or four miles south of its junction with the Gunnison. Their post was in the same valley of cottonwoods visited by Rivera in 1765—and ever since a rendezvous point for traders and trappers. Known variously as Fort Uncompahgre, Fort Compahgre, and Fort Robidoux, the post served a utilitarian purpose. Provisioned with goods packed in from Taos or Santa Fe, the fort was a mountain supply base for Robidoux trappers fanning out from there on the streams and rivers. Returning after trips of several months or more, their pack mules laden with furs, the trappers deposited their catch in the fort's storage room—a log structure of dirt roof, dirt

25 The *Daily New Mexican*, Santa Fe, July 18, 1870.

floor, and no windows. Periodically, freighters employed by the Robidoux' carried the baled furs out by pack train to company headquarters in Taos, the final stage before transfer to the Santa Fe Trail and St. Louis.

Fort Uncompahgre also figured importantly as a trading post for Utes of that region. Besides provisioning the trappers with flour, sugar, coffee, salt pork and dried meat or jerky, gunpowder and rifle balls, the fort stocked trade goods to barter for Indian furs. Herbert S. Auerbach, discussing this and later mountain trading forts, observes that "to the forts the Indians brought their beaver and other pelts, their buffalo robes, their fine buckskin, and their bead-work in moccasins, belts and coats. For these items the white men gave trinkets that the Indians prized—bright beads and gaudy jewelry, pocket mirrors, bright calicos, belts, buckles, axes, brass kettles, tin pans, knives, powder horns, beaver and bear traps, pins, thread, needles, combs— and also, of course, the demoralizing 'fire-water,' which the traders claimed they were forced to give in competition with the Hudson's Bay Company . . . and other traders. Horses and blankets were very valuable to the Indians, so these were used by the white traders as important items of exchange."[26]

Antoine Robidoux, now a Mexican citizen, as technically required by New Mexico authorities before issuing trading licenses—though unheeded by many—continued to expand his firm's mountain operations. In 1831 or 1832, to outfit his trappers in the Wasatch and Uinta mountains, he built a second trading fort in the Uinta foothills in the vicinity of present Tridell, Utah. The log cabins and enclosing stockade became known as Fort Wintey, or Robidoux's Rendezvous.[27]

The fort's company, including trappers, hunters, mule and horse drovers, hangers-on, and their usual complement of Indian squaws, was in all ways typical of the hard-bitten personnel one would encounter at any gathering of mountain men. The Reverend Joseph Williams, a Methodist minister, was therefore naturally horrified by

26 Herbert S. Auerbach, "Old Trails, Old Forts, Old Trappers and Traders," *Utah Historical Quarterly*, Vol. IX, No. 1 (1941).

27 More exactly, Fort Wintey occupied the east bank of the north fork of the Uinta River, called the Whiterocks River. Herbert E. Bolton's map of the Escalante Trail indicates that the Franciscans' route lay south of Robidoux's future post by some fifteen miles. According to Auerbach, a third mountain fort with which Robidoux was associated was Fort Kit Carson. This fort, comprising several cabins enclosed by an adobe wall, was built as winter quarters by Carson late in 1833. Also called Fort Robidoux, the post was located near the junction of the Uinta, Green, and White rivers, in the vicinity of present Ouray, Utah.

what he saw when he spent eighteen days at Fort Wintey in July, 1842. Returning to his home in Indiana from a trip to Oregon Territory, the clergyman was forced to endure this "very disagreeable" delay while awaiting the arrival of Robidoux, who was to accompany him East. His entire stay was repugnant to him, the minister admitted, " . . . on account of the wickedness of the people and the drunkenness and swearing and the debauchery of the men among the Indian women. They would buy and sell them to one another. . . . I tried several times to preach to them, but with little if any effect. . . . No one who has not, like me, witnessed it, can have any idea of their wickedness. Some of these people at the Fort are fat and dirty, and idle and greasy."[28]

The Reverend Mr. Williams was observant, if more mildly, of the fact that Antoine Robidoux, as a sideline, was engaged in slave trading. He commented only that "Mr. Rubedeau had collected several of the Indian squaws and young Indians to take to New Mexico, and kept some of them for his own use. The Spaniards would buy them for wives."

John Charles Frémont was rather less horrified, when he visited Wintey in June, 1844. The fort, he noted, "has a motley garrison of Canadian and Spanish engagés and hunters, with the usual number of Indian women. We obtained a small supply of sugar and coffee, with some dried meat and a cow. . . . I strengthened my party at this place by the addition of Auguste Archambeau, an excellent voyageur and hunter."[29]

Frémont remarked that following his departure Fort Wintey "was attacked and taken by a band of the Utah Indians . . . and the men of the garrison killed, the women carried off. Mr. Robideau, a trader of St. Louis, was absent, and so escaped the fate of the rest." Since Frémont compiled his narratives in 1845, it would appear that Fort Wintey was destroyed in 1844 or early 1845. Not long after, perhaps in 1846 or 1847, the Utes attacked and burned Fort Uncompahgre, killing all of the fort's white personnel. Encroachment of the mountain men evidently had worn out the Utes' patience. At about this time they destroyed a third mountain post, Fort Davy Crockett, located on the Green River and, because of its dirt and squalor, known to some traders as Fort Misery.

28 Joseph Williams, *Narrative of a Tour from the State of Indiana to the Oregon Territory in the Years 1841–2.*
29 John Charles Frémont, *Report of the Exploring Expedition to the Rocky Mountains in the Years 1842–43–44.*

Time, in any event, was running out for the fur trade. Not only were the mountain streams sorely depleted, but as early as 1833 the European market for beaver began to dry up as hats of silk replaced beaver felting. Taos continued to send out and supply parties of trappers well after 1846, but each year their number was fewer. Indian trade in the Southwest was ready to flow in new directions, find new outlets.

2

Bent's Old Fort

ON THE MORNING of November 15, 1806, a few miles east of the mouth of the Purgatoire, Zebulon Pike's small party struck their tents and broke camp early. Large herds of buffalo were seen in the distance, blackening hilly plains on both sides of the Arkansas. At two o'clock in the afternoon Pike first glimpsed his peak, "like a small blue cloud" over the horizon. Half an hour later, from the crest of a hill, the explorer's men saw the Rockies spread almost endlessly before them. "With one accord [they] gave three cheers to the Mexican mountains . . . their sides . . . white as if covered with snow or white stone."[1]

Two days later, and that much closer, Pike "pushed on with the idea of arriving at the mountains, but found at night no visible difference in their appearance from what we had observed yesterday." On November 21 the Americans encountered a war party of Pawnees, homeward bound and surly from failure to count coup on the enemy Utes.

"We found them to be sixty warriors," Pike noted, "half with fire arms, and half with bows, arrows and lances." Outnumbered three to one, Pike counciled with the Pawnees, hoping for the best. For safe passage, he "ordered half a carrot of tobacco, one dozen knives, sixty fire steels, and sixty flints to be presented to them. They demanded corn, ammunition, blankets, kettles, &c., all of which they

1 "The Discovery of Pike's Peak—from the Diary of an Expedition Made Under Orders of the War Department, by Capt. Z. M. Pike, in the Years 1806 and 1807, to Explore the Internal Parts of Louisiana," *Old South Leaflets*, Vol. XII (1908).

were refused." A rough melee ensued in which the Pawnees grabbed haphazardly at the Americans' arms and stores, and then rode off. Pike "felt sincerely mortified that the smallness of my number obliged me thus to submit to the insults of lawless bandits."[2]

Without realizing it then, Zebulon Pike had pioneered the northern route of the Santa Fe Trail. During these nine last days the distance he traveled limited one of the two northern gateways to the Spanish Southwest. Probably on November 16 he camped within hailing distance of the place where the Bent brothers and St. Vrain were to build Bent's Fort.

Charles Bent and his younger brother William came as traders to this region after their father's death in St. Louis in 1827. Some uncertainty surrounds the year of their arrival on the plains, but by 1829 they had established a small log cabin and stockade post on the Arkansas near the mouth of Fountain Creek, future site of Pueblo, Colorado. Charles left William in charge of the post to establish himself as merchant and trader in Taos. Here he met Céran St. Vrain, a former employee of the Indian trading firm of Pratte, Cabanné and Company, who with François Guerin as partner arrived in Taos with a few wagons of trade goods in March, 1825. A friendship between the two men resulted in the founding of Bent, St. Vrain and Company late in 1830 or early 1831.[3]

A toughness of fiber and an innate shrewdness were basic to anything more than survival in the Santa Fe trade. These traits the senior partners, Charles Bent and Céran St. Vrain possessed; William Bent, ten years younger than Charles, had neither the head nor the temperament for complex mercantile organization or hardnosed dealing with Spanish officials. William, though, was a natural frontiersman, an excellent Indian trader. The blending of their talents made this trio formidable. The Bents were of New England stock,

2 *Ibid.*

3 David Lavender, *Bent's Fort.* Lavender questions the statement of George Bird Grinnell, in "Bent's Old Fort and Its Builders," that Charles and William reached the Arkansas as early as 1824. Lavender notes William Bent's testimony before a joint committee of Congress investigating Indian affairs in 1865 *(Condition of the Indian Tribes,* p. 83): "Having been living near the mouth of the Purgatoire on the Arkansas River . . . for the last thirty-six years . . ." and concludes that this would place the Bents' arrival on the plains in 1829 rather than 1824. Elsewhere, Lavender offers evidence that Charles was elected train captain of a caravan of thirty-eight wagons and seventy-nine men that traveled from St. Louis to Santa Fe in 1829. William Bent also was a member of this party. The fact he was chosen as caravan captain might suggest previous experience on the Santa Fe Trail—or the possibility that Charles won this position by virtue of his familiarity with the more rugged aspects of life on the Missouri frontier.

St. Vrain of course was French—on both sides they were sons of large families.[4]

William could have initiated the plan—he certainly had the full co-operation of Charles and St. Vrain—when the partners decided to build a trading fort on the north bank of the Arkansas about midway between Timpa Creek and the mouth of the Purgatoire. The location, seven miles east of present La Junta, Colorado, was strategic. A fort at this point would be a convenient supply base and stopping point for caravans using the mountain route of the Santa Fe Trail. The fort also would provide a southern bastion to a well-traveled trade route skirting the eastern slope of the Rockies from the Arkansas to the North Platte. Most important, placed near the southern edge of the buffalo plains, the fort, if properly handled, could count on a heavy trade by drawing to it the Southern Cheyennes and Arapahoes and their Sioux allies, the mountain Utes and Jicarilla Apaches, and—perhaps—the Kiowas and Comanches ranging up from the Canadian.

The foundations of Bent's Fort may have been laid in 1832, but the fort probably was not completed until 1834.[5] The impressive

4 Charles and William were grandsons of Capt. Silas Bent, a Massachusetts man who was a leader in the Boston Tea Party, December 16, 1773. Their father, Silas Bent II, was born in Rutland, Massachusetts, April 4, 1768. When he was about twenty years old, the young Silas moved to Marietta, Ohio, and then to Wheeling, Virginia (now West Virginia), where he studied for the bar. Here he married Martha Kerr, soon after moved to Charleston, Virginia, and opened a store; Charles, eldest of their children, was born here November 11, 1799. While still living in Virginia, Silas became a judge of the Court of Common Pleas. In 1805 he was appointed deputy surveyor for Washington County, Ohio, and then principal deputy surveyor for the new Louisiana Territory. To fill this post he moved his family to St. Louis, arriving there September 17, 1806. In 1809 he was appointed presiding judge of St. Louis Court of Common Pleas. He served on the Supreme Court of the Territory of Missouri from 1817 to 1821, and died in St. Louis November 20, 1827. The Bent family Bible, now in Denver, Colorado, shows that after Charles came Juliannah (July 18, 1801), John (May 31, 1803), Lucy (March 8, 1805), Dorcas (March 12, 1807), William (May 23, 1809), Mary (June 25, 1811), George (April 13, 1814), Robert (February 23, 1816), Edward (September 12, 1818), and Silas III (October 10, 1820). Of the sons, only Charles, William, George, and Robert moved to the Southwest. (Ina Wilcox Cason, "The Bent Brothers on the Frontier," master's thesis, University of New Mexico, 1939.)

Céran St. Vrain was the son of James de St. Vrain, native of French Flanders, who came to America in 1794. Céran was born about 1802 at Spanish Lake, Missouri, the fourth of ten children. After his father's death, when he was sixteen, Céran worked as a clerk for Bernard Pratte of Pratte, Cabanné and Company until Pratte financed his overland trip to Taos in 1825.

5 Named Fort William by its builders, for William Bent, the post soon became known to traders and trappers simply as Bent's Fort. George Bird Grinnell, in "Bent's Old Fort," says the fort was completed in 1831; De Voto, in Across the Wide

size of the fort, at that time the largest west of the Missouri, and its remoteness from sources of labor and building materials, such as hardware, lumber, and window lights, suggest that construction required more than a year. The tens of thousands of adobes that formed the walls came from the native clay and were molded and sun-baked at the site.

With its rear wall to the river, the fort and its main gate faced north by northeast—not east, as writers on the subject generally have assumed.[6] Occupying a gently sloping plain within a few hundred

Missouri, gives the date 1832; Moorhead, annotating Gregg's _Commerce of the Prairies_, says construction was begun in 1829 and completed in 1832; in _New Mexico's Royal Road_, (footnote, p. 131), Moorhead quotes LeRoy R. Hafen as saying the fort was built in 1842—probably a typographical error; Hafen, in "When was Bent's Fort Built?" (in _Colorado Magazine_, Vol. XXXI, No. 2 [1954]), says the fort was built in 1833. Lavender, in _Bent's Fort_, says: "Supposedly the construction of the fort spread out over four years, 1828–32, but no contemporary record mentions the fort during this period. Surely a significant silence. Farnham, who visited the fort in 1839, says it was built in 1832. Matthew Field, who also visited in 1839, says 1833. William Waldo says 1833. Charles's first trading license was taken out in December [18], 1833. St. Vrain, writing Lt.-Col. Eneas Mackey on July 21, 1847 (Abandoned Military Reservation Series, Box 52, National Archives, Washington), says he and Charles built the fort in 1834. To me it seems likely that planning was begun in the fall of 1832 . . . that construction was started as soon as William and Ceran could assemble workers and materials for operations to start in the fall of 1833; and that the complete job was finished in the spring of 1834." Lavender's conjecture probably is as close as anyone ever will get. Mrs. Cresswell Taylor, in "Charles Bent Has Built a Fort," _Bulletin of the Missouri Historical Society_, Vol. XI, No. 1 (1954), quotes a letter written by a William Laidlaw to Pierre Chouteau, January 10, 1834, saying in part: "I understand from the Sioux that Charles Bent has built a Fort upon the Arkansas for the purpose of trade with the different bands of Indians."

[6] Excavation of the ruins of Bent's Fort by Herbert W. Dick in 1954 revealed for the first time since its abandonment the actual floor plan and wall measurements of the fort. A summary of Dick's findings, including aerial photographs of the excavation, and diagram, appear in "The Excavation of Bent's Fort, Otero County, Colorado," _Colorado Magazine_, Vol. XXXIII, No. 3 (1956). In a personal communication with the author, October 9, 1961, Dick wrote that his original survey lines for the fort were slightly incorrect: "I took the 13° magnetic direction off for true north on the wrong side. True north would be about 13° _west_ of my magnetic north. The east wall is about on magnetic north. . . . Thus a person looking out of the gate would be looking in a NNE direction." After its abandonment by William Bent, Dick notes, his excavation showed that the fort was used as a stagecoach station. During this period the east tier of rooms was torn down and a stage gate twenty-two feet wide was cut through the outer east wall. At a still later period the original north gate was closed off, a second gate was cut in the south wall, and the fort, now almost a ruin, was used as a cattle corral. Responsibility for disorientating the fort—and so misleading Lavender and previous writers—rests with Lt. J. W. Abert. Usually reliable, Abert in August, 1845, visited Bent's Fort, and in his journal carelessly noted that it was "composed of a series of rooms resembling casemates, and forming a hollow square, the entrance on the east side." (29 Cong., 1

yards of a bend in the river, the fort commanded an unbroken view in all directions across a valley saucer-shaped and nearly treeless. Caravans approaching from the east rode the valley rim of sandhills, dropping down in the vicinity of a notch or deeply eroded gap that years later marked a stage road to the town of Kit Carson.

Foundations were marked off in a rectangle, thirteen degrees off true north. The north and south walls measured somewhat over 122 feet, the east and west walls 150 feet. Round rifle towers pierced at the top with loopholes were built at the northeast and southwest corners. Outer enclosing walls were extended from the towers to meet and form the fort's outer southeast corner, the outer eastern wall running diagonally for a length of 168.8 feet, the outer southern wall measuring 170 feet. The effect of the south and east outer wall extensions was to create enclosed compounds. These were protective corrals for the fort's livestock, to be used whenever the threat of Indian raids made it unsafe to leave the animals in the stake and post corrals that were built outside but adjacent to the fort.

Such an occasion arose about 1840 when a war party of Mountain Shoshonis, wandering far from home, reached the Arkansas at this point. A quarrel broke out when their demands to enter the fort were refused, and a sharp fight followed in which one of the Shoshonis was killed.[7]

Lieutenant J. W. Abert, visiting the fort in 1846, estimated that the outer walls were three feet thick at the base and fourteen feet high—the towers rising to eighteen feet. Interior walls of the rooms forming the fort's inner quadrangle were not as ponderous, averaging about one and one-half feet in thickness.[8]

Passing through the main gate and tunnel formed by roof and abutting rooms, one entered an open courtyard ninety-eight feet long and eighty-two feet wide. When originally built, the fort had a quadrangle of twenty-two rooms fronting on the courtyard, thirteen

sess., *Sen. Exec. Doc. 438.*) Returning the following year, Abert reported taking measurements of the fort (30 Cong., 1 sess., *Sen. Exec. Doc. 41*). Again, obviously unaware that an archaeologist one hundred years later would check his findings, Abert was careless. He noted, for example, that the entrance gate "was 7 feet high and 6½ wide." Dick's excavation showed the gate to be 8.1 feet wide, its height undetermined because of the ruinous conditions of the walls.

7 George Bird Grinnell, *The Fighting Cheyennes.*

8 Dick found that at the base the outer walls "had a thickness of three adobe brick widths" and "were originally close to 3.0 feet thick." Traces of the southwest tower had been obliterated by an access road at the time the fort was excavated, but the northeast tower foundations, still intact, showed an inside diameter of 16 feet. The tower walls measured 2.2 feet in width.

of the rooms heated with fireplaces. Running the length of the east side of the quadrangle, to the left, were the main trading room, seventy-three feet long and twenty feet wide, and adjoining that on the south end a smaller room with fireplace.

At some later period, partitions were built to divide the trading area into three smaller rooms. George Frederick Ruxton, visiting the fort in the spring of 1847, found that of these rooms one, twenty by twenty feet, was used for the trading store and powder magazine; the middle room, twenty by twenty-two feet, was "a council-room, where the Indians assemble for their 'talks' "; and the third room, twenty by twenty-eight feet, was "the common dining-hall, where the traders, trappers, and hunters, and all employés, feast upon the best provender the game-covered country affords. Over the culinary department presided of late years a fair lady of colour, Charlotte by name, who was, as she loved to say, 'de onlee lady in de dam Injun country.' "[9]

Nine rooms formed the south side of the quadrangle, the kitchen, with a large fireplace and adjoining pantry, occupying the southeast corner. On the west side of the courtyard were four storage rooms, two on each side flanking a cleared area where there was a deep rectangular cold-storage pit. Extending across the north side of the courtyard, but separated through the center by the tunnel to the main gate, were seven rooms. Floors of the rooms were packed adobe and the walls of all rooms in the quadrangle but the storage rooms were smoothly coated with white or yellow or red plaster.[10]

Over the quadrangle a common roof was laid, poles on beams, covered with a foot-thick layer of adobe, pueblo style, and sloping slightly to allow water to run off. The roof projected on all four sides into the courtyard, supported by heavy posts and thus offering a shaded walkway around the quadrangle. Access to the roof was gained by a broad flight of open steps rising at the south side of the courtyard. Near the head of the stairs were quarters occupied by the fort's resi-

[9] George Frederick Ruxton, *Life in the Far West* (ed. by LeRoy R. Hafen). Dick found evidence that partitions dividing the once huge trading room into three smaller rooms were added after the original construction. The room measurements given here are close but approximate—taken from his scale diagram of the fort. The trading room was so identified by the presence of a gun flint and many trade beads found embedded in the adobe floor.

[10] Description of these rooms is based on Dick's excavation. Fragments of broken porcelain dishes found in the floor around the large fireplace established the southeast corner room as the kitchen. Three of the four storage rooms contained no doorways, leading Dick to believe that access was gained through the ceilings by ladders or stairs.

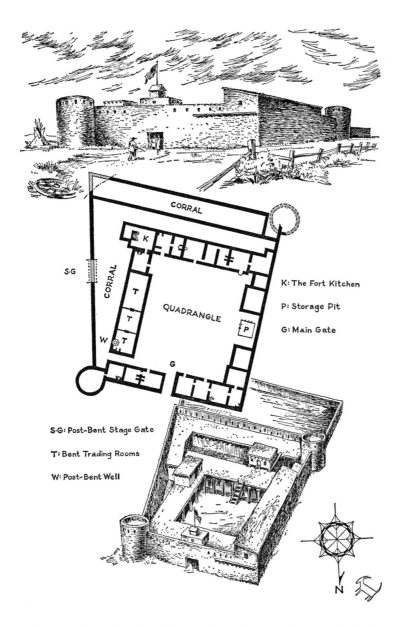

CORRAL

S·G

CORRAL

QUADRANGLE

K

T

T

T

W

P

G

K: The Fort Kitchen

P: Storage Pit

G: Main Gate

S·G: Post-Bent Stage Gate

T: Bent Trading Rooms

W: Post-Bent Well

N

Bent's Old Fort. Sketches of the adobe fort are from original draw-ings by Lt. J. W. Abert. The center diagram is from Herbert W. Dick's plan accompanying the report of his 1954 excavation.

dent manager, William Bent. Directly opposite and situated above the north gate was a guard or lookout room surmounted by a belfry and flagpole. At the southeast corner of the roof a third small building was occupied by the fort's clerk, while extending from the northwest corner, for three-quarters of the length of the west wall, were a series of rooms probably reserved for visitors or members of the personnel of the fort.

During his visit in 1847, Ruxton observed that plains cactus, common to the region, was planted in the coping of the fort walls—a psychological deterrent, at least, to any enemy minded to scale the fourteen-foot wall. Riflemen stationed on all four sides of the roof behind the parapet could fire through loopholes in case of attack.

Lewis H. Garrard, after visiting the fort in 1846, mentioned seeing in the center of the courtyard a robe press, used in baling and tying buffalo robes, and nearby a small brass cannon. In Bent's quarters on the roof he found a billiard table for the entertainment of guests, "and, in the clerk's office, contiguous, a first-rate spy-glass with which I viewed the *caballada*"—or herd of animals attached to the fort—"coming from the grazing ground seven miles up the river. In the belfry, two eagles, of the American bald species, looked from their prison." Looked, no doubt, as Garrard did, upon "a good view of the Spanish Peaks . . . apparently fifteen miles distant—in reality *one hundred and twenty*."[11] An echo of Pike, forty years later.

Indian trade so desired by the Bents and St. Vrain did not come automatically once their fort was completed. Traditional enmity and warfare dividing the allied tribes into several factions prevented their coming freely to the fort to trade, and had to be overcome. William Bent certainly was reminded of this in the winter of 1837 when a war party of Cheyennes stopped at the fort on their way south against the Kiowas, to avenge the killing of forty-two of their Bow String Soldiers. Bent supplied the Cheyennes with Hudson's Bay rifles, flints, powder, and balls, knowing no doubt as he did so that he was acting against his own interests.

Desiring peace between these tribes and the trade that peace would bring, Bent therefore sent a number of his best men south of the Raton Mountains to set up a trading post for the Kiowas, Comanches, and Apaches on the south fork of the Canadian River. The post probably was established between 1837 and 1840, and it accom-

11 Lewis H. Garrard, *Wah-to-yah and the Taos Trail*, 42. First published in 1850, for its freshness and accuracy of observation, it is a classic of western writing.

plished Bent's purpose: in the summer of 1840 these tribes met with the Cheyennes and Arapahoes on the Arkansas some three miles below Bent's Fort. From their camps on either side of the river they met in council, exchanged presents, and made peace. Thereafter it was a common sight to see lodges of any of these former enemies staked out on the river bottom near the fort.

Normally, the number of lodges gathered here would be few, but at least once a year entire villages would trail into the valley to trade, their buffalo-hide tipis forming immense camp circles. Thus, in 1841, Charles Bent advised his friend, Manuel Alvarez, merchant-trader and United States consul at Santa Fe, that "thare will be on the Arkansas early next spring near 1500 lodges of Indians including Aripihoes, Chyeans, & Sioux, and if the Cumanches meete them thare as they have agreed thare will be nearly double that number of lodges."[12]

Not as closely associated with the Indians as his brother William was, Charles nevertheless was familiar with all of the tribes in the region. In 1846 he was able to advise Indian Commissioner William Medill in some detail regarding the nature of his Indian charges.

"First," he wrote, "I will mention the Apaches or Jicarillas a band of about 100 lodges or about 500 souls. The Jicarillas have no permanent residence, but roam through the northern settlements of New Mexico. . . . Their only attempt at manufacture is a species of potter ware, capable of tolerable resistance to fire, and much used by them and the Mexicans for culinary purposes. This, they barter with the Mexicans for the necessaries of life, but in such small quantities as scarcely to deserve the name of traffic. . . .[13]

"The Navajoes are an industrious, intelligent and warlike tribe of Indians who cultivate the soil and raise sufficient grain for their own consumption and a variety of fruits. They are the owners of large flocks and herds of cattle, sheep, horses and mules and asses. It is estimated that the tribe possess 30,000 head of horned cattle 500,000 sheep and 10,000 head of horses, mules and asses. . . . Most of their stock has been acquired by marauding expeditions against the settlements of this Territory. They manufacture excellent coarse blankets

12 Letter from Charles Bent to Manuel Alvarez, January 16, 1841. From microfilm copies, *Bent Letters*, University of New Mexico Library, from Benjamin Reed Collection, N. M. State Historical Society, Santa Fe.

13 Letter from Charles Bent to William Medill, November 10, 1846. Calhoun, *Official Correspondence*. It is clear that Annie Heloise Abel, in editing this work devoted considerable attention to Bent's frontier notions of spelling and punctuation.

and coarse woolen goods for wearing apparel. They have no permanent villages or places of residence, but roam over the country between the river San Juan . . . and . . . the Jila on the south. . . . They have in their possession many prisoners, men, women and children taken from the settlements of this Territory whom they hold and treat as slaves.

"The Moquis . . . were formerly a very numerous tribe in the possession of large stocks and herds but have been reduced in numbers and possessions by their more warlike neighbours and enemies the Navajoes. The Moquis are an intelligent and industrious people, their manufactures are the same as those of the Navajoes. They number about 350 families or about 2450 souls.

"The Yutas inhabit the country north of the Navajoes and west of the northern settlements of this Department. They number 800 lodges and about 4000 to 5000 souls. Their range . . . of country is very mountainous and broken, abounding in wild game, deer, elk and bear, which serve them for food and raiment. They are a hardy, warlike people . . . and several bands of them have been carrying on a predatory war with the New Mexicans for the last two years. . . .

"The Cheyennes and Arrapahoes range through the country of the Arkansas and its tributaries on the north of this Department. They live almost entirely on the Buffalo and carry on a considerable trade, both with the Mexicans and Americans, in Buffalo robes, for which they obtain all the necessaries not derived from the Buffalo. They are a roving people and have for many years been on friendly terms with the New Mexicans. The Arrapahoes number about 400 lodges 2000 souls. The [Southern] Cheyennes 300 lodges 1500 souls.

"East of the mountains of New Mexico, range the Comanches, a numerous and warlike people subsisting entirely by the chase. Their different bands number in all, about 2500 lodges or 12,000 souls. They have been at peace for many years with the New Mexicans but have carried on an incessant and destructive war with the Department of Chihuahua, Durango, and Coahuila from which they have carried off and still hold as slaves a large number of women and children, and immense herds of horses, mules and asses.

"The Kayugas [Kiowas] range through a part of the same country and are similar in their habits and customs and are considered a more brave people than the Comanches. They number about 400 lodges or 2000 souls."

The Navahos, as Charles Bent observed, had no permanent vil-

lages, but individual families did have one or several places of residence and were not quite as nomadic as Bent suggested. At this time,
as for more than a century before, their most common habitation was
the forked-stick hogan, a dwelling roughly conical in shape, the top
flattened, and usually with a low, rectangular passageway providing
entrance from the east. Three cedar logs, forked at the upper end
and set together triangularly in the ground, formed the hogan's basic
structure. Other logs were set against these, a smoke hole was left
open at the top, and the whole affair was then thickly plastered on
the outside with adobe mud. The inside diameter of the dwelling
was usually twelve or fifteen feet. Sheep herders primarily, the people
sometimes might abandon old hogans and move to new ones elsewhere; most of the Navahos, in any case, wintered in the valleys,
summered in the mountains or high elevations.

At the time Bent wrote, Navaho war and hunting parties might be
found anywhere between the Coconino Plateau in Arizona and the
buffalo plains of West Texas. They rarely ventured as far north as
the Arkansas and so were little seen at Bent's Fort. They did, however, go often to Taos to trade, many of their woven blankets finding
their way into the Bent, St. Vrain and Company store and ending up
finally at the fort as trade goods valued by the Plains tribes.

William Boggs, who worked as a fort trader for William Bent in
the fall and winter of 1844–45, found that Navaho blankets were
particularly coveted by the younger Cheyenne women. Although
they were not as large as the American blue trade blanket, the close
weave and natural oil content of the wool made them nearly water-
proof. Boggs described the blankets as "all alike"—which probably is
a simplification—"with a [pattern of] white and black stripe[s]
about two inches wide." On one occasion Boggs recalled watching
"several hundred of these young Indian maidens, dressed in their
Navajo blankets, form a circle at a war dance outside of the circle of
braves, who were dancing around a large bonfire . . . with their tro-
phies of Pawnee scalps."[14]

14 LeRoy R. Hafen (ed.), "The W. M. Boggs Manuscript About Bent's Fort,
Kit Carson, the Far West and Life Among the Indians," *Colorado Magazine*
(March, 1930). William Montgomery Boggs, born October 21, 1826, at or near old
Fort Osage on the Missouri River, was the son of Gov. Lilburn W. Boggs of Mis-
souri, whose first wife, Juliannah Bent, was sister to Charles and William Bent.
Three years after her marriage Juliannah died, and Lilburn Boggs then married
Panthea G. Boone, granddaughter of Daniel Boone. William Boggs and Thomas
Oliver Boggs, who was born August 21, 1824, were sons of this second marriage.
William and Thomas were reared in Independence, Missouri, the latter working as

Lieutenant J. W. Abert described a similar—if not the same—occasion, in August, 1845: "In the afternoon I was kindly invited by the gentlemen of the fort to see a scalp dance. On going up I found about forty [Cheyenne] women, with faces painted red and black, nearly all cloaked with 'Navahoe' blankets and ornamented with necklaces and ear rings, dancing to the sound of their own voices and the four tambourines, which were beat upon by the men."[15]

The number of people employed by William Bent and the number to be found at the fort, idle or active, depended considerably upon the season, conditions of trade, and whether the fort was outfitting a caravan for St. Louis or receiving one just arrived from Franklin or Independence. Among the regular fort personnel were Indian women and at least one Negro woman, a cook, a blacksmith and wheelwright, stock drovers, a few clerks and bookkeepers, and hunters who were expected to keep the fort supplied with fresh meat. Four or more traders might be engaged by the company at one time but would be seen at the fort only between long trips to the Indian villages, camped on the Arkansas or anywhere from Medicine Bow Creek and the Laramie Plains to the middle tributaries of the Republican and Smoky Hill rivers.

Baptiste Charbonneau was the fort's hunter in the 1840's, regarded by his fort colleagues as "the best man on foot on the plains or in the Rocky Mountains."[16] In his worn buckskins and beaded moccasins, his black hair worn to his shoulders, Baptiste might be taken for an Indian, and rightly so, as most of his time was spent with the Chey-

---

a youth in the trading post of his uncle, Col. Albert G. Boone, and there becoming acquainted with the Indians of that region: Pawnees, Delawares, Sac and Foxes, and Wyandottes. In the summer of 1844 the brothers left Independence with the Santa Fe–bound caravan of trader James Wiley Magoffin, and by fall both were working out of Bent's Fort as traders to the Cheyennes and Arapahoes. William Boggs left after the first winter, mined for gold in California, and eventually settled at Napa, California. Thomas Boggs continued working for William Bent, spending months at a time in Cheyenne and Arapaho villages. Early in 1846 he married Roumalda Luna, niece of Kit Carson's wife and step-daughter of Charles Bent by his marriage to the widowed María Ignacio Jaramillo. For a short time Boggs and his bride lived at Bent's Fort but were in Taos in August of that year when Col. Stephen Watts Kearny led his army into Santa Fe. Boggs and Kit Carson were drafted into the army, Carson guiding Kearny's command to California while Boggs served as army dispatch bearer between Santa Fe and Fort Leavenworth, Kansas. After the Mexican War he spent his remaining active years as an Indian scout, mainly with Colonel Beale's First Dragoons in campaigns against the Apaches, Navahos, and Utes.

15 29 Cong., 1 sess., Sen. Exec. Doc. 438.

16 Hafen (ed.), "The W. M. Boggs Manuscript," Colorado Magazine (March, 1930).

ennes and Sioux, and he also was the son of Toussaint Charbonneau and Sacagawea, a Shoshoni, who served the Lewis and Clark expedition as interpreter and guide.

Another *engagé* at the fort at this time, and probably Baptiste's half-brother, was "Tessou" or Toussaint. A somber and indrawn individual, Tessou suffered from fiddlestring nerves, especially after he had been drinking too much "awerdenty" or Taos mountain dew. Shivareed at a party one night, Tessou held his anger against his main tormentor until morning, then aimed his rifle across the courtyard and planted the ball a quarter inch from the skull of the fort's Negro blacksmith. Céran St. Vrain, who was present at the time, gave Tessou a trail outfit and told him to be on his way.

Before starting out for an Indian village, the Bent traders usually were equipped with a pack train of horses or mules laden with trade goods, which would be bartered for mountain peltries and buffalo robes. Trade items would include scarlet and blue flannel cloth, powder and rifle balls, Green River knives, coils of copper and brass wire, hoop iron for arrow points, such staples as tobacco, coffee, flour, and sugar, and such smaller trinkets and gewgaws as packets of vermilion, abalone shells, beads, awls, brass tacks, ribbons, combs, and mirrors.[17] White and blue beads, in that order, were preferred by Cheyenne women. Red beads were least desired.

On shorter trips a wagon or two might be used, as was the case in November, 1846, when Lewis Garrard accompanied one of the fort's veteran traders, John Smith, with a driver and four-mule wagon to the Cheyenne village two days distant at Big Timbers, on the Arkansas.[18] Garrard says that on this occasion they remained in the

17 Green River knives found wide acceptance among frontiersmen and Indians soon after the Green River Works were founded in 1834 by John Russell, a New Englander, who built his plant on the Green River, near Greenfield, Massachusetts. A variety of knives was made, but of all the types, that known as the "Dadley" was most favored by white hunters and trappers. This blade is supposed to have been designed by a frontiersman whose name it bore and was in great demand among both Indians and white men of the upper Missouri country from 1835 to about 1860. Plains Indians often removed the blades from their haftings and reset them in war clubs. Business with western traders such as the Bents was conducted generally on terms of six months. Knives thus sold usually brought $1.50 to $3.50 a dozen wholesale, and retailed in the Indian country at 50 cents to $1.50 each. Among traders and trappers anything done "up to Green River" expressed highest approval of a job well done. On the other hand, when a fight broke out and the cry was heard, "Give it to him, up to Green River!" the words called for a man-sized thrust—up to the Green River stamping on the knife blade. ("Indian Notes," Vol. IV, No. 4 [1927].

18 Garrard, *Wah-to-yah*, 50. In this village were the people of William Bent's

village only two days, trading "tobacco, blue blankets, black (deep blue) blankets, white blankets, knives, and beads" in exchange for "four fine mules."

Garrard returned to the village soon after, with William Bent and Smith, this time "with full complements of goods for robe trading." John Smith, more than Bent, excited Garrard's curiosity, which was alert and intelligent. As a youth in St. Louis, Smith had tired of his apprenticeship to a tailor, joined a party of traders heading up the Missouri, and wintered with the Blackfeet. Not quite at ease with these people, who he thought might lift his hair at any minute, Smith moved on in the spring. For a while he lived and hunted with the Sioux. Then he moved on again, took a wife from a Cheyenne village, and hunted and trapped through the Bayou Salade, or South Park, high mountain meadows of the Rockies headwatering the Arkansas. Returning with his squaw to her village, John Smith lived as a Cheyenne, keeping his own lodge, running buffalo, and dressing the robes for trade. He spoke Cheyenne so easily and was so well regarded by that tribe that his services proved invaluable when William Bent engaged him as a company trader.

New Mexican traders coming to the Arkansas with mules packed with beans, dried pumpkins, and corn to trade for Cheyenne buffalo robes and pemmican often had to treat first with a rather hard-eyed John Smith. He was protecting his employer's interests, no more, Smith felt, when he forced the New Mexicans to pay a certain tribute or duty before settling down to trade. Garrard, who observed this, failed to mention what the tribute amounted to, but evidently it was enough to be discouraging. One party of New Mexicans refused to pay the tithe. Smith and the Cheyennes seized their trade goods, and the New Mexicans were sent flying on their way, "uttering thanks to heaven for the retention of their scalps."

An aging French Canadian, remembered only as Long Lade, another of Bent's traders, projected an image of the vigorous John Smith, perhaps twenty or thirty years older. Garrard's description of the old man is a portrait of almost any plains trader nearing the point of calling his next trip out his last: "His fine face, strongly

---

first wife, Owl Woman, who was a daughter of Gray (Painted) Thunder, a keeper of the Medicine Arrows. Although they usually lived at the fort, Bent frequently visited this band of Cheyennes and with Owl Woman maintained a lodge in their village. On the trip Garrard refers to, he and Smith met Owl Woman and her mother in a lodge near the main village, preparing to go to the fort. After Owl Woman's death in 1847, Bent married her sister, Yellow Woman.

marked with the characteristic high cheek bones and broad under-jaw, proclaimed him to be of a northern tribe. He has been a trader for many years, and like many of the Far Westerns, he is still poor. Now, in his old age, he has nothing on which to depend for a liveli-hood but his salary. . . . From the first time I met the old man, the more tender chords of my heart were touched with sympathy and respect for him. He seemed so lonely, fast growing old, with a few gray hairs struggling through the straight, jetty locks—alone and poor. I have often wondered what has befallen him—he was so sad a picture of taciturn solitude."[19]

Fall's first hint of frost usually found Bent's traders moving to the Indian camps for the winter buffalo hunt. After summer grazing, the cow buffalo were often fat and sleek, their robes long and silky—enough so that "silk robes" became a trade term for the finest ones. A silk robe, William Boggs observed, was "very fine haired and shined like satin, of a slightly lighter color, and would sell for double what a common robe would."[20] It was the cow buffalo the hunters sought, for trade robes as well as meat. Bull buffalo brought nothing: they might do well as a warrior's garment to wear over the shoulders, for moccasin soles, tipi covers, or parfleche makings—but for barter, the traders were not interested.

In the fall of 1844 William Bent sent an invitation to the Arapa-hoes, camped near the South Platte, to winter with the Southern Cheyennes and join them in a buffalo hunt. Boggs and William Guerrier, a company trader married to a Sioux, went out to the vil-lage from the fort, Boggs noting that "the old chief, 'Cinemo,' had the largest lodge . . . in the village and tendered the use of one-half of it to [us], to keep the goods in that we had brought down from the fort . . . we received the buffalo robes as fast as they were dressed . . . the squaws did all the manual labor of stretching and drying the skins and brought them when dressed into the trader and exchanged them for such goods as their men choose."[21]

Mexican pesos and American silver dollars had no value as money to the Cheyennes and Sioux and were not used in trade—except when desired by the Indians for conversion into ornaments. Much as the Navahos, some twenty years later, started hammering out the silver coins for concho belts, men of the Plains tribes occasionally

19 *Ibid.*, 82.
20 Hafen (ed.) "The W. M. Boggs Manuscript," *Colorado Magazine* (March, 1930).
21 *Ibid.*

hammered the coins flat and smooth, to a diameter of about three inches. Fastened to a braided strand of buffalo hair and then tied to the crownlock, the silver disks were worn outside of a brave's robe, dangling down his back. Of greater appeal than silver to these Indians, however, were the iridescent colors of an abalone shell. A shell of especially fiery color, which could be cut into ear pendants or, uncut, could be strung with a few beads, perhaps, on a leather thong and worn as a necklace, might have cost the warrior as much as four buffalo robes.

Bent, St. Vrain and Company controlled the Indian trade of the Arkansas Valley for fifteen years, though in this period there was scarcely a time when the partners lacked for small competitors. A trader named John Gantt and his partner, Jefferson Blackwell, built a small log post near the site of William Bent's original stockade at the mouth of Fountain Creek. Relying more freely on trade whisky than the Bents and St. Vrain cared to do, Gantt and Blackwell operated here for some time after 1833, but without noticeable benefit either to the Indians or themselves.

Nine or ten years later a small trading fort was established at the same place by a trio of partners, George Simpson, J. B. Doyle, and Alexander Barclay. Their post, named Pueblo—as the town of that name would be when founded there—was visited in 1846 by Francis Parkman, who thought it "a wretched species of fort, of most primitive construction, having nothing more than a large square inclosure surrounded by a wall of mud, miserably cracked and dilapidated. The slender pickets that surmounted it were half broken down, and the gate dangled on its wooden hinges so loosely, that to open or shut it seemed likely to bring it down altogether."[22]

William Boggs spoke disparagingly of a man "by the name of Tharp" who in 1844–45 had a small log hut on the Arkansas, "traded the Indians whiskey and sometimes . . . got a robe or two from some straggling Indian from the Cheyenne village, but his trade did not amount to much."

This was the same William Tharpe that Garrard found in one of Tharpe's trading lodges at the Big Timbers in January, 1847. Needing new buckskins to replace his worn-out breeches, Garrard called on the trader, intruding upon a quiet domestic scene: Tharpe, re-

[22] Francis Parkman, *The Oregon Trail.* Parkman noted that nearby but across the river, was a small colony of Mormon families. Their arrival and his nearly coincided, most of the Mormons having recently traveled by wagon from Monroe County, Mississippi.

clining on buffalo robes and smoking a pipe, his Mexican wife and two children seated nearby.[23]

North of Bent's Fort and closer to the mountain foothills, now falling into ruin, was a second large trading fort the Bents and St. Vrain probably built early in the 1830's, to extend their hold on the eastern Rockies trade. Situated a few miles above the Cache la Poudre, on the south fork of the Platte River, this post, named Fort St. Vrain, was approximately midway between Fort Laramie, on the Oregon Trail, and Bent's Fort, which on a smaller scale it generally resembled.[24]

The Bents and St. Vrain were indeed well established. Their company no doubt would have continued to flourish, had it not been for the unrest and turmoil arising from the American annexation of New Mexico and the death of Charles Bent.

The small army of Colonel Stephen Watts Kearny was "the dirtiest, rowdiest crew" that the visiting Englishman, George F. Ruxton, had ever seen.[25] Also, he admitted, they happened to be good fighting men. From Fort Leavenworth they had marched across the plains and, at the beginning of August, camped in the river bottom at Bent's Fort, resting for the assault on New Mexico's capital. Charles Bent previously had communicated with American authorities in respect to the military weakness and apathy prevailing in New Mexico under the corrupt regime of Governor Manuel Armijo. Kearny's forces were not entirely surprised, then, when they entered Santa Fe the evening of August 18, 1846, without the slightest attempt by the New Mexicans to resist. Acting Governor Juan Vigil welcomed the invaders politely and the American flag was raised at sunset over the Palace of the Governors.

[23] Ruxton heard stories of Tharpe while at Bent's Fort in the spring of 1847, later noting in *Life in the Far West* that the trader was killed by Pawnees. Hafen adds that Tharpe was killed on the Walnut Creek branch of the Missouri, May 28, 1847.

[24] Even in its best years, Fort St. Vrain does not appear to have prospered and is rarely mentioned in memoirs of the fur trade. Arthur J. Flynn, in "Furs and Forts of the Rocky Mountain West, Part II," *Colorado Magazine*, March, 1932, says that the fort "was built of adobe bricks and measured about 125 feet in length by 75 feet in width, with walls 14 feet in height." Parkman, traveling from Fort Laramie to Bent's Fort, found Fort St. Vrain in ruins in August, 1846: "At noon we rested under the walls of a large fort, built in these solitudes some years since by Mr. St. Vrain. It was now abandoned and fast falling into ruin. The walls of unbaked [sun-dried adobe] brick were cracked from top to bottom . . . the heavy gates were torn from their hinges and flung down." (*The Oregon Trail.*)

[25] Ruxton, *Adventures in Mexico and the Rockies.*

Before leading his Army of the West on to California, Kearny, by proclamation, on September 22 appointed Charles Bent territorial governor of New Mexico. The senior partner of Bent, St. Vrain and Company thereafter divided his attention between his business and home at Taos and his official duties in Santa Fe.

Lewis Garrard and John Smith were in the company's log post at Big Timbers one day in late January, 1847, when a Bent hunter brought word that Charles Bent had been murdered and scalped by Indians of Taos Pueblo. As the news spread through the Cheyenne camp, causing disbelief and anger, the chiefs suggested that the younger men form a war party to avenge their friend. William Bent thanked them but said that a company of Missouri volunteers stationed at the fort would go if necessary.

"At the following dawn," Garrard wrote later, "Mr. Bent and I left for the fort, some forty miles distant, taking no baggage but the ropes strapped to the saddles. . . . By sundown we reached the fort, having traveled the entire day without ten minutes halt, almost without a word of conversation."[26]

William Bent was present the following April when the Indians responsible for the death of his brother and four others were tried and executed at Taos. He returned soon after to the fort on the Arkansas. There is no evidence that there was a quarrel with Céran St. Vrain, but the driving forces that in the past had made the company so successful now appeared absent or on the wane. Bent had no falling out, either, with the Indians who for so long had been his friends, but profits from the fur and robe trade were smaller each year. Soldiers quartered near the fort or passing through were always thirsty and often unruly, but rarely had more than a few coppers to pay for their fun. Besides a few Indians camped nearby, the soldiers now were almost the only visitors seen, and their presence posed a constant danger of conflict with the Indians. Commercial caravans,

---

26 Garrard, *Wah-to-yah.* Charles Bent was killed at his Taos home January 19, 1847. In the months since his appointment as governor, a reaction against the American occupation, not eased by the disorderly conduct of volunteer troops stationed at Santa Fe, stirred the New Mexicans to rebellion. Leaders of the revolt included such leading citizens as Tomás Ortiz and Diego Archuleta, and the priests, Juan Felipe Ortiz and José Manuel Gallegos, as well as some of the head men of Taos Pueblo. On the morning of January 19 a group of Taos Indians demanded of Sheriff Stephen Lee the release of two Indian prisoners. When Lee refused, the Indians killed him and the prefect, Cornelio Vigil, and proceeded to Bent's house, where they broke in the door and killed him. Before they were through, the Indians also murdered Narcisse Beaubien, son of Judge Carlos Beaubien, and Pablo Jaramillo, Bent's brother-in-law.

which had brought some prosperity to the fort in the past, were seen less frequently; the shorter routes by way of Point of Rocks and Chouteau's Island, or the Cimarron Cutoff, were more heavily traveled.

No document or letter of William Bent's has been found explaining his action, but on August 21, 1849, he moved all of his furnishings and people out of the fort. As they watched from the top of the nearby hills, Bent went either to the northeast tower or to the trading room and set the fort on fire. Flames and smoke were still rising as he and his people turned their backs on the fort and rode down-river to the Big Timbers.[27]

There is no significant connection, perhaps, but only ten days before he abandoned the fort Bent was issued the first trading license in his own name, for trade with the Cheyennes, Arapahoes, Sioux, Kiowas, Comanches, and Apaches.[28] The Bent, St. Vrain and Company holdings were dissolved that winter of 1849, St. Vrain remaining in Taos, William Bent trading from log cabins at the Big Timbers and later from a new fort on the Arkansas.

27 While excavating Bent's Fort, Herbert W. Dick was aware of a persistent legend that Bent attempted to destroy the fort by lighting a fuse to the powder magazine. Charred beams and scorched walls were found in the northeast tower and the trading room showed evidence of a severe fire, Dick noted. In the latter room "possibly explosive charges were used, although there is no direct evidence for this." The fire appears to have confined itself to this area, leaving the main part of the fort undamaged.

28 Dated August 11, 1849, the license named as his employees, "John Smith, P. Carbonir [Charbonneau], Chas. McCue, J. Denison, C. Vasher, R. Fisher, B. Ritier, I. Sanders," and a ninth man whose name is illegible. (National Archives, *Ledgers of Licensed Indian Traders.* This source hereafter is cited as *N. A., Ledgers of Traders.*)

3

Trade Regulations

THE BENTS AND ST. VRAIN, like others of their time in the Southwest, officially—but only officially—were subject to federal controls.
Trading operations from Bent's Fort in fact were conducted very
much as the partners chose. In this they were not alone, but on common ground with other traders along the Western frontier. If the
Bents did not abuse this freedom, it is to their credit; some others
did abuse it. The difference between fair practice and rapaciousness
rested not with the government, but with the individual trader. Congress had power to legislate, but at this period had no means of enforcing its authority on the distant frontier.

Laws controlling Indian trade are nearly as old as our country's
original thirteen colonies. President George Washington, aware of
the abuses of many private traders, several times asked Congress to
establish federal trading-houses for protection of the Indians. Congress did pass a bill, on April 18, 1796, authorizing the President "to
establish trading houses at such points and places on the western and
southern frontiers, or in the Indian country, as he shall judge most
convenient for the purpose of carrying on a liberal trade with the
several Indian nations."[1]

This legislation carried with it an appropriation of $150,000, a
revolving fund, to purchase supplies for the trading houses, and beyond that, an annual appropriation of $8,000 for the salaries of agents
and clerks. The law was a temporary one, coming up for reconsidera-

1 Lawrence F. Schmeckbier, *The Office of Indian Affairs: Its History, Activities,
and Organization.*

44

tion every two years. Trading houses were operated until 1806 by the Department of Public Supplies. They were first located in the South, at several frontier forts in the Middle West, and at the sites of future cities such as Detroit, Chicago, and St. Joseph, Missouri. In 1806 supervision of the trading houses was placed under a superintendent of Indian trade, who maintained headquarters and a warehouse at Georgetown, in the suburbs of Washington, D. C.

The office of superintendent first fell to T. L. McKenney, whose unhappy task it was to maintain the federal trading houses on an ever widening frontier against the private, very determined enterprise of Manuel Lisa. With John Colter and one other veteran of the Lewis and Clark Expedition as guides, Lisa in 1807 followed the Missouri River into Crow country and there, at the mouth of the Big Horn, built the first post for the mountain fur trade. This grasp on the Northwest, far outreaching the operations of the federal houses, Lisa tightened in 1809 when he formed the Missouri Fur Company. For several years more McKenney struggled to meet this resolute opposition, and in 1822, when the federal trading houses finally were discontinued, he placed the blame for their failure on Manuel Lisa and his partners.[2]

Once the government was removed from Indian trade the field lay open to the rapacious pickings of John Jacob Astor's American Fur Company, the Rocky Mountain Fur Company, and lesser competitors who gouged and clawed each other—and in concert battled that "chartered British monopoly," the Hudson's Bay Company. So outrageous were some of the practices of these companies that Congress felt it imperative to intervene once more on the side of the Indians. Thus was passed, on June 30, 1834, the "Act of Congress to Regulate Trade and Intercourse with Indian Tribes." This act, with deletions and amendments, later was extended to control the Indian trade of the Southwest.

Calhoun spoke of traders in 1852 "travelling alone and in parties of two and three" throughout the Navaho country.[3] He implied that these traders went with his approval. If true, this would mean that

2 T. L. McKenney, *Memoirs, Official and Personal.*
3 Letter from Calhoun to C. I. A. Luke Lea, February 29, 1852. *Official Correspondence.* Auguste Lacome, one of the first French traders of note to appear in the Southwest, was granted a license to trade with the Navahos in January, 1853—thus being the first of record authorized to trade with that tribe. (Indian Affairs in New Mexico Under the Administration of William Carr Lane," from the Journal of John Ward [ed. by Annie Heloise Abel], *New Mexico Historical Review,* Vol. XVI, No. 3, [1941].)

they were licensed, but any record of their names appears to have been lost. After them, the first engaged in the Navaho trade from a fixed location were the men who operated trading posts at Bosque Redondo when the Navahos were held there as prisoners from 1864 to 1868. And first among these was George H. Richardson, who received his license to trade at Fort Sumner from Agent Theodore H. Dodd, October 26, 1865.[4]

Richardson came to the Indian country from St. Louis. He posted $5,000 bond for his license and listed as his employees, J. S. Gibson, Benjamin F. Stamp, and H. W. Dodd. The latter may have been the agent's brother, Billy Dodd, who is said to have preceded Thomas V. Keam to Keams Canyon in the late 1860's and from that place been one of the first traders to the Hopis and Navahos. Richardson renewed his license at Fort Sumner for a second year but thereafter allowed it to lapse and, for purposes here, dropped from sight.

Other traders at Fort Sumner were Joseph Alexander LaRue and Oscar M. Brown, both licensed in 1866–67, and William White Martin, licensed in 1867.

Between 1868, when the Navahos were moved to their new reservation, and 1876, traders to the Southwest tribes were appointed by the Indian agents and after that time by the commissioner of Indian affairs.[5]

Major Theodore Dodd, who accompanied the Navahos from Bosque Redondo to be their first agent at Fort Defiance, issued the first trading license at the agency to Lehman Spiegelberg of Santa Fe, on August 28, 1868. Spiegelberg named one of his four brothers, Willi, and Henry O'Neill as his clerks, the license permitting him to trade either at the agency or at any place of his choice on the reservation— a latitude of movement that would be denied Spiegelberg's successors. He does not appear to have been active on the reservation for long, although he does turn up later as a potent force in Spiegelberg Brothers of Santa Fe and New York, wholesale contractors in the Indian trade.

Cole F. Ludlove of Valencia County, New Mexico, was the second man licensed to trade at Fort Defiance. His license was granted in October, 1868, and after the first year it was not renewed. The agen-

4 N. A., Ledgers of Traders.
5 The 1834 Indian Trade Act, Section 5, as amended by Congress August 15, 1876, reads: "And hereafter the Commissioner of Indian Affairs shall have the sole power and authority to appoint traders to the Indian tribes and to make such rules and regulations as he may deem just and proper specifying the kind and quantity of goods and the prices at which such goods shall be sold to the Indians."

cy's third trader was John Ayres, who arrived at Fort Defiance in the spring of 1870 after serving as agent for the Wiminuche and Capote Utes at Abiquiu. Lionel Ayres, who may have been John Ayres' brother, was next in this beginning line of succession, receiving his license in June, 1872.

Penalties for trading on a reservation without a license were severe enough to discourage the attempt in all but rare cases. The Indian trade act provided that in such instances the trader's goods should be confiscated and the trader be subject to a fine of $500.[6]

A substantial part of an agency trader's source of income was removed in the early years of the Fort Defiance regime when the Commissioner of Indian Affairs observed: "It has been the practice at some of the Indian agencies to purchase large quantities of supplies as well as articles of various kinds from the traders. . . . This practice is not considered to be advantageous to the Government and will therefore be discontinued.

"Hereafter, no purchases will be made from any licensed Indian trader by any Agent of the Department, except in cases of actual emergency—when the articles are necessary for immediate use—and then only to a limited extent."[7] A blow to the traders, the ruling was a decided boon to the wholesale contractors of Santa Fe.

The agent–agency–trader relationship was subject to further control when Commissioner E. A. Hayt in 1878 ruled that "no Indian agent or other person employed in the Indian Service is permitted to have any interest, directly or indirectly, in the trade carried on by any licensed trader at his agency."

The sale of arms and ammunition to Indians had plagued the government since colonial days. In the Southwest this remained a problem well into the 1890's. Each new Congress passed laws pro-

6 Superintendent William T. Shelton of Shiprock Agency invoked this section of the trade act against the Reverend Howard R. Antes in 1911. Antes for fifteen years had been conducting a small Methodist mission on the Navaho reservation, near Aneth, Utah. A nearby trader, planning a trip of some months, asked Antes to operate the store in his absence. Antes took the post over as an accommodation, without troubling to apply for a license. Shelton ordered Antes and his wife off the reservation and sent Navaho police to bring in 116 sheep which belonged to the missionary and which Shelton said Antes had secured in unlawful trade. Shelton obtained an indictment against the missionary, and Antes and his wife subsequently moved to California. (National Archives, Indian Office Memorandum addressed to C. I. A. Cato Sells, January 27, 1917. File No. 91845–1911–308.2, Part II.)

7 Letter from Commissioner F. A. Walker to Nathaniel Pope, superintendent of Indian affairs, December 19, 1871. (National Archives, Records of the New Mexico Superintendency of Indian Affairs, 1849–80. Letters Received.)

hibiting traffic in guns, but as always, where need or desire for the contraband runs deep enough, legislation usually was ineffectual. Exceptions to the law might even be sought by authorities of the government, when need was pressingly clear.

Such need and exception were demonstrated when the Zuñis begged Agent Calhoun to arm them against constant raids by the Navahos and Apaches. A census taken at Zuñi in 1849 showed that among the 597 men of that pueblo there were only forty-two muskets and rifles. In the following year, after the pueblo again was attacked by the Navahos, Colonel John Munroe, military governor of New Mexico, ordered that fifty old muskets be sent to the Zuñis.

Even so, before their removal to Bosque Redondo only a relatively few Navahos were armed with rifles, and these were the muzzle-loading type secured from the vagabond traders. In a skirmish in 1858 at Bear Springs, future site of Fort Wingate, Navahos "fired a volley of arrows" at attacking troops from Fort Defiance, and it appears that only a few of the Navahos had guns.[8]

Capote and Wiminuche Utes, traditional enemies of the Navahos, roaming without a reservation but drawing supplies from the agency at Abiquiu, were well armed in 1871. It was not uncommon for them to "trade off an inferior pony for a rifle."[9]

During a visit to Fort Defiance in 1881, Lieutenant John G. Bourke noticed that "The Navajoes who were present at the Agency were poorly provided with warlike weapons, the most dangerous being the old-time Yager rifle. Bows and arrows and lances are still retained in use, but shields have been discarded."[10]

But a year later the situation was changed, at least on the northern borders of the reservation. Colonel George P. Buell, commanding Fort Lewis, Colorado, found that the Navahos of the San Juan Valley were being armed by the settlers in that region. "I have passed through the Navajo Reservation several times," he said, "and have had much to do with them. Where one would see one Indian with an old cap lock muzzle-loading rifle three years ago, he will see today a half-dozen armed with the Winchester and plenty of ammunition."[11] In 1883, Agent Denis Riordan reported that the Navahos "are all armed and well armed."

8 Report of the Secretary of War, U. S. War Dept. 35 Cong., 2 sess., *House Exec. Doc. No. 2.*

9 *Annual Report, C. I. A., 1871.*

10 Bloom (ed.), "Bourke on the Southwest, VIII," *New Mexico Historical Review,* Vol. XI (1936).

11 Letter from Colonel Buell to the Assistant Adjutant General, Department of

The Indian trade act was revised in 1873 to permit the secretary of the interior to adopt any rule he found necessary to prohibit the sale of arms and ammunition "within any district or country occupied by uncivilized or hostile Indians"—but the provision went unheeded in off-reservation settlements.[12] Controls clamped on reservation traders generally were observed, but it was possible for any Indian, without trouble, to buy a rifle and as much ammunition as he could afford in the towns, or from trading posts surrounding the reservation.

Navaho Agent Alex Irvine in 1876 wished that the controls regulating the sale of firearms might be more stringent, "for if I understand it rightly, it applies to Indian traders, and not to any citizen who may see proper to trade with the Indians." He lamented that the southern boundary of the Navaho reservation lay within a few hundred yards of the agency.

"Anyone can establish a trading post within a quarter of a mile and be outside of the control of the agent," he said. "And one party who has such a trading post informed me that he preferred to have his store outside of the reservation, for the reason that no one could prevent his trading with the Indians and getting such prices as he pleased."

In control areas where the laws were enforced there might still be problems. The sole trader for the Uinta Utes refused to renew his license when it expired in 1876 because he was not permitted to sell guns and ammunition on the Uinta reservation. Agent J. J. Critchlow sympathized with the trader, explaining, "He wished to continue trading without license, and indeed I felt inclined to permit him to do so, till I could see if some modification of the regulations could not be procured . . . believing that it was for the interests of our Indians, and that no evil could result therefrom; but as he refused to comply with the regulations . . . I ordered him to remove his goods. . . . He transferred his store to Ashley's Ford, about 30 miles distant,

the Missouri, March 13, 1882. (National Archives, Office of Indian Affairs, Letters Received, 1882.)

12 Section 2136 of the Indian Trade Act, revised February 14, 1873, reads: "If any trader, his agent, or any person acting for or under him, shall sell any arms or ammunition at his trading post or other place within any district or country occupied by uncivilized or hostile Indians, contrary to the rules and regulations of the Secretary of the Interior, such trader shall forfeit his right to trade with the Indians, and the Secretary shall exclude such trader, and the agent, or other person so offending, from the district."

but outside the reservation. Since that time I have been unable to find anyone who was willing to take the post."[13]

Commissioner Hiram Price noted again in 1884 that there was no law prohibiting the sale of firearms off the reservations, and in consequence there had been "much trouble, and, in some instances, loss of life." Price's successor, J. D. C. Atkins, commented on the same problem in 1885: "The licensed traders on the various reservations are strictly prohibited from dealing in these articles without special permit, but the ready access that Indians have to military and other trading posts, located off but near the reservations, makes it an easy matter for them to secure an abundant supply, and the consequence is that the worst and most troublesome Indians are armed with the best breech loaders that can be found in the market."

Atkins called for tighter controls. He could have done better had he whistled "Dixie."

Although the neighboring Utes and Apaches changed little numerically, the Navahos increased in population year by year. Calhoun estimated that the tribe numbered not more than 5,000 in 1849. In 1891 a Census Bureau count showed there were 16,102 Navahos and of these, more than half were living off the reservation.

From the beginning, when the first boundaries were established in 1868, a large proportion of the tribe lived outside of the reservation and stubbornly resisted the repeated demands of the Indian Office that they move within the boundaries. And even though their reservation in later years was more than tripled in size, the extended boundaries never stretched out far enough to embrace them all. Powerless to exert its authority beyond the reservation lines, the Indian Office was constantly bedeviled because its off-reservation Navaho wards were in unending dispute with white settlers. These disputes might be over water and grazing rights, running off of stock, or the plain orneriness of two antithetical peoples knocking heads together.

Agent S. S. Patterson in 1887 placed much of the blame for this situation on traders who, he said, "plant themselves along the border, and . . . invite the Indians to trade with them, at the same time telling them that they have as much right to locate upon the lands of the public domain as the white man."

Patterson's ire was roused by a number of incidents which occurred that year off the reservation. Three white men and a Navaho were

13 *Annual Report, C. I. A., 1876.*

killed in a shooting near Houck's Tank, Arizona, in February; in March, near Navajo Springs, white men ran off 157 head of Navaho horses, and troops had to be summoned to prevent an uprising; in May, a clerk in the Defiance Station trading post murdered a Navaho in an argument over money. Nor was that all.

"About the first of June," Patterson said, "at a trader's store kept by a man named Barton, north of the San Juan River, an Indian who had gone there to trade got into an altercation with Barton . . . in which both lost their lives. The circumstances of this case, as near as I can learn from the Indians, show that the trouble began . . . from the trading of revolvers between the Indian and Barton."[14]

In 1889 there were said to be about thirty trading posts surrounding the reservation, and in the following year Agent C. E. Vandever reported nine traders on the reservation. "The reservation stores carry on about one-half the trade with the Indians," he said, "the balance being transacted by stores beyond the boundary lines and by those on the railroad."[15]

Vandever found the Navahos in an interesting stage of transition and believed that the traders in large part were responsible.

"The proximity of trading posts has radically changed their native costumes and modified many of the earlier barbaric traits, and also affords them good markets for their wool, peltry, woven fabrics, and other products. . . . Firearms have almost entirely superseded the primitive weapons, and silver ornaments of their own manufacture are worn instead of copper and brass . . . .

". . . Within the last two years the price for nearly all their products has greatly increased, and competition among the traders has reduced the cost to them of the articles they purchase, thus materially adding to their resources."

Competition rather than the posting of price lists made the unscrupulous traders behave. Normal fluctuations in wool prices and the prices paid in Kansas City for hides did more than the Indian Office to control the avaricious. Market prices for wool and hides and sheep and horses—the Indians' basic trade commodities—were common knowledge. The traders adjusted their prices accordingly, and where there was any sort of competition, the prices varied by no more than a few cents. It had to be that way. If a trader's prices moved too far out of line the Indians were soon aware of it and took their trade across the mesa.

14 *Ibid.,* 1887.
15 *Ibid.* 1890.

The Indian's difficulty in managing liquor has been no less persistent than the white man's zeal for selling it to him. In the first half of the last century the mountain fur trade would have been poorer by hundreds of thousands of dollars without the inspiration of whisky. No one has presented the situation more clearly than Bernard DeVoto, in *Across the Wide Missouri*:

"Everybody who traded in the Indian Country did so by government permission and on government license, both revocable. It had always been illegal to give, sell, or trade liquor to the Indians. Since July, 1832, it has also been illegal to take liquor into the Indian Country. But from the earliest days on it had always been altogether impossible to conduct the Indian trade without liquor. The Jesuits who first tried to prevent French traders from using it found that their own agents in the trade could not get furs without it. The Hudson's Bay Company had always had an idealistic desire to keep liquor from its Indians—when they got drunk they killed expensively trained traders—and had always supplied it whenever rival traders came into its territory, which was every year. No Dutch or American traders had ever tried to do without it: the Indian trade was based on getting the customers drunk, preferably before they began to bargain. The national government repeatedly prohibited liquor, but that was in Washington: government officials in the field used the prohibition to extract bribes from traders."

As with everything else sold in the mountain Indian trade, profits in liquor were enormous. DeVoto elsewhere observes that straight alcohol, bought in St. Louis for ten or fifteen cents a gallon "sold at a dollar or two or four dollars a pint, after being diluted fifty or seventy-five percent."[16]

To the extent that the mountain fur trade reached as far south as Taos, a similar situation developed along the northern fringes of the Southwest, affecting the Utes of Colorado and the Moache Utes and

---

16 In 1850, Agent Calhoun *(Official Correspondence)* said that a gallon of whisky costing fifty-two cents wholesale at Fort Leavenworth, Kansas, cost $1.52 at Santa Fe. The retail price for whisky at Santa Fe in 1851 was $3.50 a gallon. On April 29, 1851, Calhoun wrote to C. I. A. Luke Lea that the Pueblo Indians "are moody when they come to the Agency, if you do not give them Sugar, Coffee and Whiskey. ... It was with the greatest reluctance that I gave them Whiskey. There are several Distilleries in the Territory which supplies them with ardent Spirits in exchange for their grain ... unless I gave it to them at the Agency, they would roam through Santa Fe, until they could find a small Grocery that would indulge them." Contrary to the impression Calhoun may give here, however, the Pueblo tribes as a general rule avoided liquor, and drunkenness among them was rare until very recent years.

Jicarilla Apaches of northeastern New Mexico. Vagabond traders unquestionably carried Taos Lightning in their pack trains, though in Calhoun's correspondence there is no specific complaint of this. Liquor obtained from these traders evidently was a mere trickle, after the American occupation, to the amount the Indians could buy at trading forts and in the towns and settlements. From the first days of American occupation the Spanish-speaking communities of New Mexico were the worst offenders. And worst among these was the community of Cimarron, New Mexico, headquarters for the Jicarillas and Moaches. Until the Cimarron agency was abandoned in July, 1878, it appears that the town's economy depended mainly upon getting the Indians drunk—an effort in which the Apaches, especially, co-operated with enthusiasm.

"The trading of whisky to the Indians is a constant source of annoyance and of great danger," Charles F. Roedel, the agent at Cimarron, said in 1871. "The Mexicans carry on this trade as a part of their living, and it is done in such a manner that it is almost impossible to detect the guilty parties. Persons are unwilling to give information, for their traveling expenses to attend court are 25 cents per mile, and the Government allows them 5 cents per mile. Thus when a witness has to go to Santa Fe his coach fare is $70, and he is allowed only $15."

Roedel, who was only one in a long succession of Cimarron agents to despair of any cure, pointed out that the cost of being a witness was greater than the penalty of being caught and convicted of selling whisky.

Pueblo Agent W. F. M. Arny in the same year complained that Sol Barth, trading at Zuñi, had been convicted of selling whisky and gunpowder to the Indians and got off lightly with twenty-four hours in jail and a fine of twenty-five dollars. A crusader for virtue, in others, Arny said he was cleaning out a nest of traders who were making Zuñi a headquarters for illicit trade with the southern Apaches.

"This vile and wicked traffic tends to endanger the lives and property of all the people on our borders in Arizona and New Mexico," he declared. "Hence . . . I have expressly prohibited traders [from] locating at this place. A J. H. Whittington, who was licensed last January . . . , declined locating there, and Andrew Napier, who was about the same time licensed in the same manner, I have deemed it necessary to suspend; hence no trader is now authorized at that village."[17]

17 Comments of Agents Roedel and Arny are quoted from the *Annual Report,*

It was sometimes possible to control whisky-selling on the reservation; beyond those boundaries the agents had no power at all. In the
1870's and 1880's, military posts and railroad camps were the easiest
sources of supply; soldiers and railroad gangs, for a few drinks or a
bottle of whisky, could buy an Indian woman. All of the settlements
that mushroomed in the wake of the Atlantic and Pacific Railroad
bootlegged liquor to the Navahos.

The largest and most accessible of these places, the railroad and
coal-mining town of Gallup was a principal offender.[18] The term
"railroad Indian" was coined, a disparagement that might range
in connotation from thievery to fornication but always implied
drunkenness.

One incident of the whisky trade is unusual because the entre-
preneur for once was a Navaho, not a white man. The affair occurred
during Agent Denis Riordan's last days at Fort Defiance.[19]

As the tale came to him, the Navaho was visiting in Gallup when
hailed by a young woman who asked if he would not like to buy
some whisky. He would like nothing better, the man replied, but he
had no money. No matter, the woman said, she would make a trade:
for his pony she would give him eight quart bottles of firewater. The
trade was quickly agreed upon. Weighted down and afoot, the Navaho started back for the reservation, but hardly had he crossed the
line when he was stopped by an agency policeman. Carelessly, he had

---

C. I. A., 1871. Andrew Napier was licensed February 15, 1871, to trade with the
Indians of Zuñi, Acoma, and Laguna. A resident of Santa Fe, he had previously
acted as agent for Willburn and Stockton, contractors, one of the firms supplying
rations to the Fort Defiance Agency.

18 This brief paragraph from the October 5, 1901, *McKinley County Republican* typically indicates the situation in Gallup in the early years: "N. L. Kasano-
vitch was arrested last Sunday . . . for selling liquor to Indians. He was discharged
the next day by Commissioner Hart, who deemed the evidence insufficient. Mrs.
Roat was arrested on the same charge and gave bonds in the sum of $500 for her
appearance before the U.S. Grand Jury next March. J. H. Benson and Dan Miller
were taken to the Albuquerque jail on Monday night . . . charged with selling
liquor to Indians. Francisco Sedillo [on a similar charge] was sentenced last week
at Albuquerque to four months in jail and to pay the costs." C. N. Cotton served
as foreman of a Grand Jury that in October, 1913, examined thirty cases of persons
accused of selling whisky to Indians. The Gallup *Independent* of October 16 quoted
the jury's ultimate findings: "In view of the conditions in the neighborhood of
Gallup, with reference to selling liquor to Navajo Indians and bootlegging, as
shown by the evidence before this jury . . . this jury earnestly recommends that
some steps be taken by which a special deputy United States Marshal be located
at Gallup."

19 Letter from Riordan to C. I. A., June 21, 1884, and Bowman to C. I. A., July
10, 1884. (National Archives, Letters Received, 1884, #12052 and #13398.)

been caught with a little earthen cup. With the cup, which would hold scarcely a gill, he had been selling his bottled cargo at fifty cents a drink. Had he been unhindered, his profit would have bought him fifty ponies.

Intent only upon ending his term as agent, Riordan had the Navaho locked up, and sent off a perfunctory report to the commissioner saying he was turning over this most recent embarrassment to his successor, John Bowman. He recommended that the prisoner, with escort, be returned to Gallup to identify his horse. By claiming the pony as hers, the woman would disclose her guilt.

A few weeks later, with Riordan thankfully relieved of duty and in Flagstaff, Agent Bowman could report the outcome.

"The Indian," Bowman said, "made his escape in the night from the scout who had him in charge, as they were returning from Gallup to the Agency, leaving for parts unknown." The woman who had sold him the whisky, it was learned, was not a Gallup citizen at all but "belonged to a strange freighting outfit which was passing through." After trading the whisky for the pony, Bowman discovered, she too "departed for parts unknown, so it was impossible to effect the arrest."

Off-reservation traders found that whisky-selling was bad for their business and avoided it. Occasionally there were exceptions, and when the abuse was serious, the Indian Office usually stepped in. Thus, in 1889, Navaho Agent C. E. Vandever learned that Thomas Hye, a trader on the east side of the reservation, was developing a largely drunken clientele. Vandever arranged to have Hye caught while selling liquor, and the trader was indicted and brought to trial. When the Navaho reservation was extended in 1901 as far west as Canyon Diablo, Arizona, a trading post at Tolani Lakes was closed down and another trader in the vicinity was threatened with closing because he was selling whisky and gambling with his Indians. These cases were unusual, however, and do not represent the majority of traders who operated in the Southwest after 1868.

A means of trade unique to the Navaho tribe, and which the Indian Office sought to control, originated both from the shortage of money and from the Navahos' skill in working silver and turquoise. At any time of need, but especially in winter and summer, when they usually had no money, the Navahos could pawn their concho belts, silver bridles and bracelets, and turquoise necklaces—even their guns. In the spring and fall, when they sheared their sheep, the In-

55

dians brought in the wool clip and were able to redeem their pawn. The custom became an honored one, as agreeable to the trader as it was to the Indian, when Agent S. S. Patterson in 1887 tried to put a stop to it.

"This practice," he said, "I found to be frequently the cause of a vast amount of trouble and angry disputes . . . which I saw might lead to serious results. . . . I persuaded the traders to agree to receive no more goods on pawn after the first of July last, which agreement has been carried out. As a result of this act both traders and Indians are well satisfied."

And so he may have thought—though a few months more would prove that the system of pawn was too necessary to the Navaho economy to permit abandoning it. Patterson was reminded also of other reforms he felt should be introduced.

". . . my experience," he added, "has led me to the belief that all traders . . . should be persons who are in accord and harmony with the administration in power and in sympathy with the agent. Referring particularly to this reservation, out of the six traders there is but one who supports the administration [Grover Cleveland, a Democrat, was then President]. Most of the others are persons who hold license under former administrations. While it may be held that a person has the right to express his political opinions, yet it should be deemed entirely out of place and improper, in the presence of Indians, especially when such expressions are uncomplimentary toward the Government, as is the case here."[20]

Again, a forlorn hope. Only casually political, traders were not of the breed who would be told what they might say, or how to vote. They did agree, and readily, to the government's rule that pawn must be kept at least six months before it could be sold. Some traders would allow their Indians a year of grace, some even more. A silver bridle taken in pawn would be tagged with the owner's name, the date, and the amount of money loaned for it. A similar tag would be given to the Indian. Many of the old trading posts had "pawn rooms"—a frontier version of a jewelry store—a room flashing with silver and glowing with red and pink coral and turquoise ropes of beads, all tagged, the room smelling of leather and metal, the pawn dangling from hooks on the walls, all waiting to be redeemed.

At the end of six months some traders might move the unredeemed pawn out of the pawn room and hang it up in the store or place it in a glass counter and "advertise" it for sale, for thirty days or more.

20 *Annual Report, C. I. A., 1887.*

If still unclaimed by the owner at the end of this time, it could be sold. A Navaho who found his pawn being advertised for sale, and who still was unable to redeem it, might promise the trader to bring him lambs or sheep on a certain date if the trader would put the jewelry back in the pawn room. In such cases the decision rested with the Indian's record of dependability. A trader was not obliged to accept everything offered to him for pawn, and this, and a difference of opinion over the value placed on an article of pawn, occasionally ended in arguments. On the other hand, many Navahos would pawn their best jewelry for only a fraction of its true value so they would be sure they could redeem it. And it was not uncommon for an Indian to borrow his pawn for some special occasion, such as a big sing, and return it to the trader when the ceremony was over.

Because trade in the Indian country existed on a system of barter and credit, the most successful traders were those who extended enough credit to keep their Indians through the lean months, but not so much that they bankrupted themselves. Most traders carried some families on their books indefinitely and when a trading post changed hands or went out of business, it was often found that the owner was owed large sums of money in uncollected debts. After Richard Wetherill's death in 1910, the ledgers of his Chaco Canyon trading post showed some eight thousand dollars owed to him by Navahos—a situation that was not in the least rare.

Hazards or evils of this credit system might be felt equally by the Indians. After a few traders in the 1890's made unrelenting demands upon their Indians for payment, the Indian Office intervened. Commissioner W. A. Jones ruled that the government would recognize no bills against Indians submitted by a trader, except those for absolute necessities. The ruling has been modified since, but essentially it is unchanged: it is legally impossible for an Indian trader to demand payment of old debts.

Recalling the past, when he traveled about the Navaho reservation as a buyer for the Fred Harvey Company, Bob Evans once said: "Indian traders found a Navajo was a better risk than a white man —once they had judged the Indian's ability to pay. It is doubtful if a Navajo ever took advantage of the government's new ruling." But Evans was speaking of the early 1900's, before the Indians became more familiar with the white man's ways.

4

Fort Defiance

ABANDONED by the military garrison seven years before, the adobe and log buildings of Fort Defiance were in a state of crumbling decay when taken over as Navaho Agency headquarters in 1868. Despite the complaints of agents, the Indian Office for the next fifteen years did virtually nothing to improve the buildings, and such repairs as were made were paid for out of pocket by agency employees or by the traders. Some idea of the squalor and ruinous condition of the agency was given by Agent Denis Riordan in 1883 when he reported that during the preceding winter "there was not a house that would keep out the snow or the rain. . . . I have had to tie my children in chairs to keep them out of the water. . . . I have seen, as soon as the weather began to moderate, the snakes come out of the walls of these same palatial quarters. You wonder we *kick* . . . ."[1]

Conditions under which they lived were no better, but the Defiance traders had less cause for complaint since the dilapidated buildings were furnished to them rent free—until January, 1884, when Riordan imposed rents of fifty dollars a month.

Pay rent to share a room with snakes? The protests were immediate and bitter. Walter R. Fales, who in the previous year had been manager of Thomas Keam's Defiance store, was now the owner of it,

---

[1] *Annual Report, C. I. A., 1883.* Riordan elsewhere in his report said, "It would require the descriptive powers of a Scott or a Dickens to portray the wretched condition of affairs at this agency." He resigned a few months later in disgust, and moved to Flagstaff, Arizona, to become superintendent of the Ayer Lumber Co.

having purchased Keam's stock and fixtures in March.[2] When, as Keam's manager, he moved into these quarters, Fales said, "The buildings (so called) were mere shells—adobe walls, partly covered with poles for roofing—without doors, windows, floors, chimneys or roofs; in short they were wholly abandoned."[3]

Keam had spent $245 to make the place habitable, Fales said, and when he bought the store in March he reimbursed Keam for that amount. He begged leave to ask the agent, therefore, "that in as much as a very high rent is imposed, a due allowance be made for repairs and . . . deducted from the rent."

Another Defiance trader, Benjamin F. Hyatt, was similarly moved to protest. When he learned that Fales' rent had been reduced to twenty-five dollars a quarter, he felt he deserved equal consideration. In June, 1881, when he moved into his building to start trading, the place had no floor and he had put one in—a fine floor of planks and flagstones. Also, he had installed shelving and a counter, new windows protected by iron bars, and he had built a new dirt roof.

"Two years ago [when] the whole of one end of the building fell out, I immediately put up a substantial stone wall in its place. . . . I have braced up the roof in three different places by using heavy timbers, and I do not actually believe that the building will stand five years longer. . . . In place of a ceiling, I have tacked up muslin all through the building to keep the dirt from dropping on the goods, and on us."[4]

Elsewhere, reservation traders owned their own buildings and improvements, but not the land. Ownership of buildings was in name only, however, because if a trader moved away, he was not entitled to sell the buildings except to another trader or to wreck them for salvage. Partly for this reason and also because the Indian Office at any time could cancel or refuse to renew a trader's license, most of the reservation trading posts were built at the lowest possible cost. Also, the traders with few exceptions were men of limited means. Some prospered, but there were more who did not, and so even the

2 Keam's license to trade with the Navahos at Fort Defiance was issued April 3, 1883, and expired a year later. He applied for the license while in Washington, writing to the secretary of the interior, March 9, 1883: "Should I receive the appointment, I am satisfied from my knowledge of the Indians, and the confidence they have in me, I can materially assist the Agent." Keam left the management of the Defiance store in Fales' hands and seldom went there himself. (National Archives, Letters Received, Trader Correspondence, 1883, #4892.)

3 Letter from Fales to Acting Agent S. E. Marshall, May 28, 1884. (*Ibid.*, 1884, #10817.)

4 Letter from Hyatt to C. I. A. Price, September 13, 1884. (*Ibid.*, #17713.)

off-reservation posts—owned, land and buildings, by the traders— were usually modest in size and investment.

Requirements for obtaining a trading license varied. If a trader desired a favored location, it was not enough that he be a citizen, supply excellent character references, and furnish bond. The same brand of patronage and politics that frequently determined the choice of Indian agent often decided the awarding of a tradership. Post traders at Fort Defiance, a good location, in the period 1880– 1900 often owed their appointment and tenure to the vagaries of political influence. Ben Hyatt, native of Findlay, Ohio, offers an interesting example.[5]

Hyatt's appointment at Fort Defiance in 1881 coincided with the inept, politics-ridden administration of Galen Eastman. Hyatt identi- fied himself as Agent Eastman's man—a mistake, as Eastman was detested by the Navahos. When Eastman was succeeded by Denis Riordan, Hyatt's position was immediately threatened. Only a few weeks after his arrival at the agency, Riordan attended an all-night council of the tribe's chiefs and head men at Thomas Keam's trading post at Keams Canyon. Ganado Mucho and Manuelito spoke for the others when they concentrated their anger upon the departed East- man and his close associates.

"They . . . [said] that as long as Eastman was here they didn't care much whether they did right or not," Riordan reported.[6] ". . . they felt bad . . . he made their heads ache and gave them pains in their legs, that when they felt that way, they went and drank whiskey. . . . Manuelito said that Eastman gave him the rheumatism but that he was all right now and would drink no more."

The Navahos told Riordan that the greatest favor the Great Father in Washington could do them would be to remove "every one of Eastman's tools. . . . They demanded in particular that Dr. J. R.

[5] Ben Hyatt's principal claim to interest lies in the fact he is credited with in- troducing aniline dyes to the Navaho reservation—an innovation which revolu- tionized the craft of Navaho weaving and to a considerable extent affected the economy of the tribe. Harsh chemicals of the anilines produced a garish product, gaudier by far than the temperate natural dyes and natural-wool colors associated until then—together with good bayeta and reasonably good Germantown yarn— with Navaho loom work. Traders who adopted Hyatt's anilines share his responsi- bility for broadening the market for Navaho weaving, while degenerating the craft. George Wharton James is the writer who credits Hyatt with introducing aniline dyes, his source evidently being Lorenzo Hubbell. (James, *Indian Blankets and Their Makers*.)

[6] Letter from Riordan to C. I. A. Price, January 22, 1883 (National Archives, Letters Received, 1883, #2051.)

Sutherland be taken away, saying he was 'tarantula No. 2' and a great deal worse than Eastman.[7] They asked that Mr. Taylor who has lately come here from the Moqui Agency, be not placed in charge of the [Navaho] school. . . . They finally demanded that as soon as possible the post trader here [Hyatt] be removed. They said he was a tool and friend of Eastman. Ganado Mucho said they would be in dread just as long as any of these three men stay here."

By midsummer 1883, when Commissioner Hiram Price took notice of Riordan's report of the previous January and asked for particular grievances against Hyatt, the agent replied: "I cannot add one word to what I said . . . and I have no desire to do Mr. Hyatt any injustice, although he is one of the most repulsive men (to me personally) that I have ever met." Generally, Riordan found the trader fostered "antagonisms and dissensions" among the Navahos "and there is no telling where they will end. . . . If my personal wishes have any weight, he will not remain here."[8]

Riordan's wishes obviously weighed hardly at all with the commissioner for Hyatt remained on as an absentee owner until snows of winter provoked Riordan to complain again. In his irritation the agent this time included Thomas Keam, who spent most of his time at the Keams Canyon store and perhaps gave little thought to his affairs at Fort Defiance.

The agency trading posts of both Hyatt and Keam were so poorly stocked, Riordan observed, that the Navahos who could afford to buy clothing found little at these stores to purchase, and, for the complete lack of shoes, actually suffered. Shoes and winter clothes could be bought in Gallup or other towns, Riordan knew, but he knew also that it was he who had most urgently told the Indians to adopt civilized apparel but shun the white man's towns.

"Those who obey [me] . . . suffer. Those who are not amenable to restraint go to the railroad towns and get what they want," he said.[9] "If I understand it aright, one of the objects in establishing traders amongst the Indians is to supply them with their absolute needs without the necessity of their wandering off the reservations to procure them. But the traders here do not keep stock enough on hand to supply them. They have pursued a dog-in-manger policy from the beginning. . . . I have had Indians come to me this very morning,

---

[7] Sutherland was agency clerk during the final part of Eastman's regime.

[8] Letter from Riordan to Price, July 7, 1883. (National Archives, Letters Received, 1883, #12900.)

[9] Letter from Riordan to Price, December 24, 1883. (*Ibid.*, #23588.)

walking with bare feet on the frozen ground, begging for shoes *and willing to pay for them*, with two stores within stone's throw."

Riordan said that this state of affairs had existed for some time, and was getting worse. He had hoped to correct it by talking with Hyatt and Keam personally. "But they are both non-residents. Both are away fully two-thirds of the time . . . the business is run by clerks. . . . If I talk to the clerks they tell me they must write to their principals. I have stood it as long as my duty would permit." If the decision were his alone, he would have closed up both trading posts long since.

The agent's concern for his Indians was real enough, no doubt. But in referring to Hyatt and Keam as equally inaccessible, he stretched it a bit. Between any sunrise and sunset, were he moved deeply enough, he could have traveled to Keams Canyon and talked with Keam personally. In December, of course, this would have been a cold ride.

Nothing further came of the matter until June, 1884, when Hyatt learned that his license would be renewed only upon payment of a bribe. Hyatt took notice of this, and of Riordan's criticism of him, in a letter to Commissioner Price.[10]

He had a large spring stock of goods for his store, he said, but rain and snow and the low price of wool were conspiring to destroy him. Two-thirds of his purchases remained unsold, and "My competitor [Walter Fales, who had taken over Keam's Defiance store] makes the same complaint. To give you some idea of the wool business, season of 1883 to June 21, I bought sixty-three thousand pounds. 1884 season, to this date, have not bought six thousand pounds—quite a difference . . . I can truthfully say that in the three years that I have been here I have not made $4,000; the trade is not what it was before the advent of Rail Roads."

A political acquaintance of his in the East, a man named Vance, had promised Hyatt he would secure renewal of Hyatt's license upon payment of a certain consideration. Vance demanded six hundred dollars and a partnership in Hyatt's store. And Hyatt balked. He had paid Vance well for favors in the past, but this was too much.

"I do not mention the Vance matter in a spirit of malice," he added, "but simply to bring to your notice the manner in which my renewal can be had. I do not wish the office of trader if it's a marketable one."

---

10 Letter from Hyatt to Price, June 24, 1884. *(Ibid., 1884, #12275.)*

Agent Riordan was succeeded in July by John H. Bowman, and in August the Navaho chiefs and head men, again meeting at Keams Canyon, again called for Hyatt's removal. Bowman was present and later reported to the commissioner that "these Indians desired me to write to you and ask that the license of B. F. Hyatt . . . be revoked, and that he be obliged to quit the Reservation. Their causes of complaint against Mr. Hyatt are, as they say, that he is personally unpopular—that he lives and spends most of his time in the East—and that his only object in being amongst them is to acquire money."[11]

Vance's name does not appear again, but on September 15, Hyatt's license was renewed. A year later, Hyatt, now spending nearly all of his time in Ohio, took his clerk, Sam Reeder, as partner and obtained a license for B. F. Hyatt and Company. This was the last time a license was issued to Hyatt.

John M. Weidemeyer, a merchant of Clinton, Missouri, came out to the Navaho reservation in early 1886 to investigate the possibilities of the trading business. He was an able man, so far as the record shows; if he had a fault, it was not of not knowing what he wanted. Weidemeyer learned there were five traders on the reservation, and of these, two—Reeder and Michael Donovan—were competitors for the Indian trade at Fort Defiance. To the man from Clinton the prospects at the agency were inviting, but only if Reeder and Donovan could be eliminated.

Reeder, he had been told, was merely an agent or "front" for Benjamin Hyatt. Against Donovan, whose trade was the lesser of the two, no complaint could be found. Weidemeyer approached both traders with forthright offers to buy them out.

"One asked me a big bonus or advance on cost and carriage," Weidemeyer wrote to U. S. Senator George Graham Vest, on returning home to Missouri. "The other would sell at cost and carriage. The trade at that point is small for two stores."[12]

A man of some power, Senator Vest already had endorsed Weidemeyer's application for a license. They had known each other since the days when the Senator practiced law in neighboring Sedalia.

"I thought best not to buy till I could get [the] license of one of the traders revoked," Weidemeyer told the Senator frankly. "Do you think we can have Mr. Reeder's license revoked at once?"

This was reasonable, Weidemeyer explained, because Reeder "and

11 Letter from Bowman to Price, August 26, 1884. *(Ibid.,* #16716.)
12 Letter from Weidemeyer to Senator Vest, February 8, 1886. *(Ibid.,* 1886, #4580.)

Mr. Hyatt are now building a store house about six miles from Fort Defiance and just on the line of the reservation in New Mexico and it will be no hardship to them to move their Fort Defiance stock there and have but one place to trade instead of two."

His trip to the Navaho country had cost about two hundred dollars; he was anxious to make up the expense as soon as possible. He came to the point: "Unless I can have the only store at the little station of Fort Defiance it will not pay me to attempt the trade on the reservation at all."

The letter found Senator Vest confined to his rooms in Washington by illness. Otherwise, the Senator wrote to Indian Commissioner J. D. C. Atkins, he "would call in person about this matter. I take a special interest in it. . . . Will you be kind enough to drop me a line upon the subject at once?"[13] He enclosed Weidemeyer's message.

One week later John Weidemeyer was issued a license to trade at Fort Defiance, and eventually became well established there as the principal trader. Sam Reeder remained on for about a year. Donovan's Defiance license was not renewed, but a license was issued to him March 7, 1887—to trade at Chinle Valley, Arizona.

Political maneuverings of this sort were not frequent. Officially, the regulations determining who might be licensed were explained first in 1878 by Commissioner E. A. Hayt. Trading licenses, he said, would be "granted only to citizens of the United States, of unexceptionable character, and who are fit persons to be in the Indian country. They are not granted to any person who may previously have had a license which was revoked or the forfeiture of whose bond has been decreed in consequence of the violation of any law or regulation, or who is an improper person to be in the Indian country."[14]

Applications must be made in writing, either to the agent or to the commissioner, Hayt continued, and the applicant must designate the location where he proposed to trade.

The applicant also must state "the amount of capital to be employed, the name of the agent, the names of all the clerks or other persons to be employed. . . . The application must also be accompanied by satisfactory testimonials of the unexceptionable character and fitness of the applicant and his proposed employees. . . . All applications for the renewal of a license are required to be made at least thirty days prior to the expiration of the existing license."

13 Letter from Senator Vest to C. I. A. Atkins, February 10, 1886. (Ibid.)
14 Annual Report, C. I. A., 1878.

A trader was required to furnish a $10,000 bond before receiving a license, and afterwards he was held responsible for the conduct of his employees; any infraction of the Indian trade act could mean revocation of a trader's license. Traders also were instructed that they must furnish the agents with price lists of all their principal articles for sale to Indians and post copies of the lists conspicuously in their stores.

Ben Hyatt's price list for October, 1883, probably is representative of the prices charged in reservation and off-reservation posts at that time:[15]

Pride of K Flour	Per 100 lbs.	$5.50
Standard Granulated Sugar	per lb.	.25
Choice Rio Coffee	" "	.25
Arbuckles "	" "	.25
Seal of N. C. or Durham Smoking Tob.	per pkge.	.15
Calico Simpson Blk	per yd.	.10
" Richmond Pink	" "	.10
All best brands	" "	.10
Cheaper "	12 yds. for	1.00
Muslin Dayton D	9 " "	1.00
" Massachusetts B.B.	9 " "	1.00
Blankets, Mackinac 2½ point blue black		4.00
" " " " scarlet		4.50
Germantown yarn Scarlet & Green,	per cut	.20
Beads Glass per bunch 10¢ or three for		.25
" Gilt " " " " " "		.25
Wool Hats from 1.00 & upwards		
Stetson & other fine grades		4.50
Bayetta	per yd.	2.00

Commissioner Atkins in 1885 further tightened the controls. In addition to the posting of price lists, he ordered that "Traders are required to forward monthly, through the Indian agents, invoices of all goods received. The maximum amount of profit which may be realized on each article of merchandise is fixed by this office; the average of profits allowed will not exceed 25 per cent of the original cost of the goods and the freight."[16]

Invoices of the goods they received during the previous month were reported to Agent Bowman in December, 1885, by the three

15 Hyatt to Agent Riordan, October 15, 1883. (National Archives, Trader Correspondence, 1883, #19528.)
16 *Annual Report, C. I. A., 1886.*

licensed traders then operating on the Navaho reservation.[17] Sam Reeder, managing the old Hyatt store at Fort Defiance, reported purchases totaling $415.30:

500 lbs. Flour	$4.09 per cwt.	$20.45
500 " "	4.14 " "	20.70
75 lbs. ½in. Rope	.13 lb.	9.75
100 lbs. Roast Coffee	.17½ lb.	17.50
2 Pails Stick Candy	.16 lb.	8.40
2 Doz. Cal. Pears	3.85 doz.	7.70
2 " Ger. Prunes	3.40 doz.	6.80
1 " Banda[na]s	1.15 each	13.80
1,500 Yds. Manta cloth	.8¾ yd.	131.25
437 " Richmond Pink Print	.7 yd.	30.59
498 " Simpson Blk. "	.7 yd.	34.86
15 Pr. Blk. Blankets	5.60 pr.	84.00
5 " Scarlet "	5.90 pr.	29.50

The November invoice for Michael Donovan's Fort Defiance post, submitted by the clerk, C. P. Tooly, was short:

6 Sacks Sugar	600 lbs. which cost	$53.40
2 " Coffee	405 lbs. " "	49.61
3 Pails Stick Candy	" "	10.80
Freight on all		23.10
		$136.91

Anticipating the months of winter snow when wagons could neither get in nor out, Clark and Aldrich liberally laid in supplies for their Tse-a-lee store:

12 Black Satinett Pants	@ $1.50	$18 —
3 " Worsted Vests	.95	2.85
12 Fancy Vests	.90	10.80
20 lbs. Red Yarn	.90	18 —
3 Doz. 7 qt. Rinsing Pans	4 —	12 —
50 Lbs. Tobacco	.54	27 —
2 Sacks Coffee 270 lbs.	.16	43.20
3 " Sugar 300 lbs.	.13	39 —
20 Pieces Print 1,080 yds.	.07	75.60
5 Boxes Crackers 173 lbs.	.11	19.03
1 Coil Rope ½ in. 85 lbs.	.14	11.90

[17] Letter from Bowman to C. I. A. Atkins, December 3, 1885, with enclosure of Reeder, Clark and Aldrich, and Donovan invoices. (National Archives, Letters Received, 1885, #29328.)

5 Gross Matches	1.60	8 —
7 Sides Harness Leather 80 lbs.	.42	33.60
2 Bales Tobacco 50 lbs.	.52	26 —
		$344.98

In the same year, 1885, Agent Bowman reported that the value of stock in Hyatt's trading post ranged from $1,500 to $4,000, and Hyatt "does a business amounting to about $5,000 per annum, from which I should judge there would be a net profit of 25 per cent, or $1,200."[18] Donovan's annual business, he estimated, would be $3,000 for a net profit of 20 per cent, or $600 a year. Evidence here that large profits were not made easily by reservation traders in the 1880's.

"Both of these stores are located in buildings belonging to the Government for which they pay rent," Bowman continued. "Their trade . . . consists in the exchange of Wool, Sheep and Goat pelts, for which goods [they give] mostly calico and provisions. The two stores have purchased during the present season about 18,000 [pounds of] wool. The wool sold here is of very coarse and inferior quality, and only used for the manufacture of carpets."

18 Letters from Bowman to C. I. A., August 10, 1885. *(Ibid.,* #18952.)

5

The Trading Posts

TRADING POSTS in the Southwest were offspring of the reservation system. These small unfortified stores replaced the old trading forts after warring or nomadic tribes were confined, with more or less success, within reservation boundaries. No one planned it that way; the posts were a logical answer to a felt need.

This natural sequence was challenged by Colonel John M. Washington's treaty with the Navahos in 1849. The treaty put the cart before the horse: it provided no reservation, but promised the Navahos that the government would "authorize such trading houses at such time, and in such places" as the Great Father might eventually determine.[1] Perhaps merely a talking point, the promise was premature. The trading houses were not built and the Navahos continued to raid, from the Río Grande to the Hopi mesas. And Agent Calhoun, trying to restrict Indian trade by license to the peaceful tribes, warned wandering traders that it was "irregular" to go to the Navahos, the Apaches, or the Utes, and any who did so would be subject to penalties.[2]

Trading posts, therefore, did not appear in the Southwest until 1868, when the Navahos were transferred from Bosque Redondo to their own reservation. Men who built and operated the posts were

---

[1] Section 8 of Navaho Treaty of September 9, 1849, in Charles Joseph Kappler, *Laws, Statutes, Etc., II.*

[2] Letter from Calhoun to Orlando Brown, January 25, 1850. *Official Correspondence.* He doubted, said Calhoun, that his order "had any other effect than to make the traders a little more cautious."

apt to be woolly individualists. First among them were second generation Santa Fe and Taos traders, or native Mexicans like Romulo
Martínez, or the almost mythical Berrando, who about 1870 built
"a kind of trading post" at Horse Head Crossing—a desert location
later to be known as Holbrook, Arizona—and put up a sign at his
door reading, "If you have money, you can eat. No got money, eat
anyway."

They might be Mormons, driven westward by religious persecu-
tions and mob attacks, and now spreading out from the Great Salt
Lake to carry the gospel to the lost tribe of Israel and to colonize the
Great American Desert.

Or they might be Civil War veterans, mainly from frontier-minded
Missouri but in the end from any state, North or South, sick of war
and crowding civilization: men like Anson Damon and Sam Day.

Some were Englishmen, or Germans, or Czechs—like Keam and
Simpson, or Neumann and Cronemeyer, or Dick Heller—but men
who had their special reasons for coming to the Southwest. A rare
few were survivors of the old mountain trade, their leathery hides
bullet-scarred and sun-cured: individuals like old Dan DuBois.

Few if any of these men fitted into the molds of writers of western
lore and fiction. Of heroic deeds they were innocent, and so escaped
the attention of historians. As pioneers who bridled and saddled the
frontier without bravado or six-guns, they were unpromising material for writers. Their most promising period of usefulness fell
between the few romantic decades of the mountain men and the
equally but endlessly colorful era of the cowboys. The walrus-mous-
tached Anson Damon, preferring to linsey coat and pants a buckskin
jacket, silver-buttoned leggings, and worn-out moccasins, may have
been the prototype of the southwestern Indian trader. But the veteran Damon was no man to caper with a bright young school teacher
from the East—he being quietly married to a Navaho—and so could
scarcely interest an Owen Wister or Zane Grey. If not relegated to
obscurity, then, which would have been preferable, the trader in fiction became a stereotype as silly and untrue as Uncle Tom: a money-
grabbing, gun- and whisky-selling rascal.

Rascals among them there were, as in any profession, but by the
nature of the occupation they were uncommonly few. In the post–
Civil War period of which we speak, firearms were not usually a
trading post commodity, nor was whisky freely dipped from a hidden
barrel: the trader, wishing to stay alive, placed too high a value on
his life. The dude storekeepers who moved in with an idea of making

fortunes found no hard money in circulation and the Indians too clever to trade long with anyone who cheated them.

Simple integrity, leavened with understanding humor and personal courage, was helpful. Thomas Keam and Lorenzo Hubbell were successful traders because they had these qualities. Other traders of equal virtue but less talent, and these were the majority, knew little more than loneliness and hardship.

Usually unlettered beyond the grades of grammar school, the trader was bilingual, of course, and tended to think increasingly as an Indian; but of necessity he remained apart and uniquely alone in his own close sphere, even if drawn into a tribe by marriage. He had to be a doctor ready at any moment to treat a snake bite or sew up the most ghastly wound. Many times, with the Navahos, he was required to go miles to bury the dead. He was expected to be banker, adviser, and sometimes father-confessor. In disputes between man and wife, as between men quarreling among clans, he had to be a peacemaker. All but lost and forgotten in his frontier post, he was required to keep himself informed of every new shift in government policy as it affected his Indians and to interpret these policies and counsel his Indians accordingly. Demands upon his time, his patience, and his understanding were unrelenting. If he failed too often in any of these functions, he failed also as a trader.

It was the military—volunteer cavalry for the most part—who beat the warring Utes, Navahos, and Apaches into submission; it was the traders who helped them to recover and start out in a new direction. Indian agents appointed from Washington to superintend the reservations were in office too short a time to begin to understand their wards or care about their problems. A few of the agents, former Civil War officers usually, were able men and, in the year or two allowed to them and with the meager means Washington put at their disposal, were good administrators. Most of the agents, however, were incompetent or corrupt political hacks, accepting a salary of $1,500 a year because they were worth no more, and usually not that. Failure of the Indian Office and its agents to establish any sort of understanding with the Indians, and any continuity of policy in handling their affairs, created a widening breach which only the traders were able in part to close.

Indian trade in the Southwest was either a wandering pack train or a village affair until after 1868. Until that time sedentary trade centered in the towns of Santa Fe and Taos, a few Mexican settlements such as Cubero or Cebolleta, and several of the larger pueblos —as Jemez, Acoma, Zuñi, and Isleta. Old trading forts to the north and northeast were long since abandoned; sutler's stores of military posts which followed neither sought nor wanted Indian trade.

Agencies for the Southern Utes and Jicarilla Apaches at Abiquiu and Cimarron, New Mexico, supplied some of the needs of those tribes: occasional issues of food, tobacco, and ammunition, but little else. But now and for some years more these Indians traded in the Mexican settlements, with other Indians, and with the soon-to-vanish wandering trader with his pack train or wagon of goods.

The trading post emerged when the Navahos were released to the guardianship of an agent at old Fort Defiance and regulated by troops at new Fort Wingate. Posts similar in name but only faintly similar in character were known before 1868 to some of the Plains Indians and, before them, to Eastern tribes. But relationship was distant.

Never more than outposts of frontier settlements, in daily contact with the farmer nearest down the road or with the tavern-keeper over the second hill beyond, the Ohio, Illinois, and Missouri trading posts after 1800 were soon surrounded, swallowed up, and left drowsing in the backwash of the westward movement to the Rockies. Trading posts for the Cheyennes and Sioux and other prairie and mountain tribes were wedded, for safety's sake, to the mining or cow towns, to agencies, or to military camps. Known as traders to the government that licensed them, the proprietors were storekeepers who rarely ventured farther from rolltop desk or cash register than to the nearest church meeting, card game, or saloon.

Not until the years immediately after 1868, then, when the Indian traders moved far out into the desert and mesa wilderness of the Southwest, did the trading post become more than a frontier general store.

The first trading posts on the Navaho reservation were established at Fort Defiance soon after the agency was located there. Posts later multiplied slowly across the reservation while others increased more rapidly beyond the reservation boundaries—and beyond reach of direct government control.

Always the main factor determining the location of a post was its accessibility to a large number of Indians, the Navahos not spreading out evenly over their lands but clustering in a number of favored regions. More often than not this took the trader into remote cracks and corners of country he otherwise would have avoided at any cost. The trader's comfort and convenience, contrary to the Indian's, was never a consideration. If a trading post had the advantage of a good setting, it was by accident.

A single wagon-load of goods often was enough to give a trader his start. Leaving Wingate or Defiance Station, the trader drove his four-horse or ox team out across the desert or into the mountains. Purposely he avoided any region where another white man had located. A week or two later, perhaps, in country that might seem desolate to anyone but a prairie dog and yet managed to support a fair number of Indians—one hundred families might be a fair minimum—he would choose his place and open negotiations with the tribe's nearest head men. If they did not want him there, they would say so and drive him off; otherwise, he could lash up his tarpaulin tent, unload his wagon, and start trading. If he was lucky, he would find a spring close by; more often, he had to dig a well to find water.

Almost always a wagon sheet or trading tent served as a man's shelter and his store in the months when he was deciding whether he would stay, and then while he was erecting his permanent building. Thanks to a writer named Welsh, there is a good description of a trading tent operated at or near Washington Pass in 1884 by Stephen E. Aldrich and Elias S. Clark, with Charles Hubbell, a younger brother of Lorenzo, as their clerk. In most respects it was typical of all trading tents that continued in use from the 1870's through the early 1900's.

"Toward 3 o'clock in the afternoon," Welsh wrote, "we came to the trading-tent of Messrs. Clark and Hubbell, two young men, the former from the state of Maine, the latter of Mexican and American parentage, who have just started what promises to be a successful trading-post among the Navajos. These gentlemen received us with cordial Western hospitality and spared no pains to make us comfortable. Their improvised store consisted of a large tent securely fastened by cords and staples, so as to be capable of resisting the violent winds to which this country is subject. The undivided compartment of the great tent served as a place of business, a kitchen, and a sleeping room. Across the front part of the tent a rough counter had been erected, backed by a high line of shelves on which were piled rolls of red flannel, calico, cans of preserved vegetables and fruits, bags of coffee, sugar, and all the heterogeneous collection of goods suited to attract the eye and supply the wants of a semi-savage people.

"In front and behind the tent huge bags stuffed with the wool of Navajo sheep, that had been received in trade from the Indians, lay waiting departure for the East. Trotting in over the plain from various directions came, singly or in small parties, Navajo men and women carrying bags of wool behind them and ready to do business with the traders. Others within the folds of the tent leaned reflectively across the counter, meditating with the slowness characteristic of Indian deliberation upon the nature and extent of their purchases. A scene so animated and varied could not but give pleasure to one in any degree appreciative of the picturesque."[3]

Sometimes with the help of Indian labor, almost always relying upon materials coming most easily to hand, the trader built his post small and, if necessary, enlarged it later. In the mountains or timbered regions, logs were cut for the walls and roof beams, clay or dirt a foot thick often being used for a slanted flat roof. Where there was stone in any quantity, this was preferred to wood, as it offered greater protection against fire or attack. If neither stone nor wood lay nearby, the trader built his walls of adobe bricks—perhaps to a thickness of two feet—and then hauled in piñon logs or planks to support his dirt or corrugated iron roof. Window sash and glass lights had to be freighted in with the post's supplies. From the start the traders learned to protect themselves by sinking iron bars, vertically, into the walls across every window.

Regardless of structural materials and architecture (or lack of it), all trading posts on the interior were much alike. The heavy front door opened upon a smallish area commonly known as the bull-pen. This for the Indians was a milling-about place, a place to stand, lean, squat, or sit while in the process of trade, sociability, or reflection. Indians who sat in the bull-pen sat always upon the rough plank or dirt floor, since no trader encouraged native tendencies to linger by providing benches or chairs. At some place in the bull-pen, at center or corner, there usually was an iron stove and woodbox, either or both—more frequently than the floor—the target, summer or winter, of spit. Who in seriousness or irony named this enclosure, or when, is long forgotten. The term was descriptive, not critical; it seemed to fit, and it was accepted into regional parlance.

Enclosing the bull-pen on three sides were wooden counters eight inches to one foot higher and wider than store counters found elsewhere in any part of the world. Quite simply, the counters were de-

3 Herbert Welsh, *Report of a Visit to the Navajo, Pueblo, and Hualapais Indians.* As mentioned elsewhere, the Aldrich and Clark tent at Washington Pass probably was for summer trade only, this location high in the Chuska Mountains being so exposed to deep snow and harsh weather as to discourage year-round trade until a later date.

signed as barriers as much as they were loading platforms between customer and trader. Most traders kept at least one gun, usually a revolver, hidden behind the counter and always within easy reach. This precaution continues to the present time. Mrs. Roman Hubbell, as gentle a lady as ever lived upon the Navaho reservation, and who continued to operate the Hubbell post at Ganado after her husband's death, said in 1957 that a loaded revolver and a machete—relic of World War II—were still at hand in the Hubbell counters. Formerly, she said, in Lorenzo's time, two revolvers were held in readiness on each side of the bull-pen. To her knowledge, these weapons were never used.[4]

High counters around the bull-pen were not always a deterrent. Bessie McFarland of Farmington, a brawny girl who married trader Albert Blake in 1914 and went with him to the old and lonely post at Tsaya,[5] near Chaco Canyon, New Mexico, learned this in a violent way. She was tending the post alone one day, Albert being off to town for supplies, when tall young Nez-begay, bold as brass, reached for free groceries.

"I caught his hand," Bessie has recalled, "and he grabbed my arm. There was no one else in the place to help me or to stop him. He was strong and he tried to pull me toward him over the counter. He would have done this, but I managed to grab a poker and beat him on the head and shoulders until he turned me loose and ran for the door.

"There is no accounting for Navahos," Bessie mused. "Nez-begay

[4] After Roman Hubbell's death, October 14, 1957, the famous Ganado post was maintained as before, in the Hubbell tradition, by his widow. From my own observation, on several occasions, the Navahos of Ganado regarded Dorothy Hubbell with great friendship and respect. It would have horrified her, I know, even to touch the armament referred to, but if occasion had required it, there is not the slightest doubt she would have used either weapon effectively. By measurement, the Hubbell counters at Ganado were (and are) four feet, ten inches high and three feet, two inches wide.

[5] Tsaya deserves more than a passing note. One of the most remotely situated of all Navaho trading posts, practically never visited by white men, Tsaya is located in a sandstone canyon just north of the Chaco Wash and some twelve miles northwest of Pueblo Bonito. An early, off-reservation post—and so unaccounted for in Indian Office records—its origins are unknown even to the oldest settlers. One clue, however, is found roughly carved in the cliff wall immediately north and east of Pueblo Bonito:

FEB. 20
1887
H. L. HAINEZ
2 TORE
10 MILEZ
DOWN
CANON

came to our post afterward, to trade and to talk to Albert. He pointed his mouth at me, the way they do, and said to Albert, 'That's the best friend I've got—she's a good woman.' "

Space was a problem. Trading posts were small, and Indians wanted to see what the trader had to sell. Shelves behind the high counters, therefore, were loaded to ceiling level: groceries on this side, dry goods on that side. Still there was not enough room to display everything, and so the roof beams dripped merchandise as a cave roof collects stalactites. From hooks and nails dangled Dutch ovens and frying pans of dull black iron, glinting oil lanterns, and hardware—tin pots and kettles and washtubs—coils of yellow rope, bridles, saddles, and tanned deer hides or skins of mountain lions. The smell of the post always was the same, desert or mountain: a concentrated essence of very dry dust, of sweet tanned leather and sour sweat and oil and metal, an abrasive lining of spit, tobacco smoke, and kerosene, and sometimes, for charity's sake, a whiff of sagebrush carried through the chinks and cracks of walls and roof.

Long gone now, but common to the counters of old trading posts were boxes or tin cans of free smoking tobacco—always nailed down —and a small pile of cigarette papers. The Indians might help themselves, within reason. At the old Naschiti store, following honored custom, Charlie Newcomb studded the bottom of the free-tobacco box with nails pointing up, to encourage a pinch with the fingers rather than a scoop with the fist.

Almost certainly, Haines was the Tsaya trader in the 1880's, and probably it was he who built the post. Haines either died or moved away, the roof caved in or burned, and only the two-foot-thick walls of stone remained standing. In 1906 the ruined building was rebuilt by Harvey Shawver, who a year or two later took George Blake as his partner and then, in 1910, sold his interest to George's brother, Albert P. Blake. When he was in his seventy-ninth year and living in Farmington, Albert Blake told me there were only about twenty-five Navaho families who came to the post in the ten years he was there, and even some of these traveled a distance of fifty miles. The place was known to the Indians as *Tsaya-chas-kesi*—or Dark Under the Rock—reference to a shaded spring three hundred yards distant. Originally the trading post had only three rooms; now it has six. The store itself was and is unusually small, the bull-pen not much more than twelve feet square. A modern, dusty oil field road coming in from the north makes Tsaya accessible to passenger cars in dry weather. This is very recent, however. Albert Blake recalled when old Model T Fords—like grasshoppers, able to go almost anywhere— dragged down on the southern approach and stalled in the sand of Chaco Wash. Many times in summer rainy season, Blake said, he saw cars caught in the deep sand and then literally buried when flash floods, rising to a crest of six feet or more, swept down the Chaco. George Blake, not Albert, was tending the Tsaya store an evening of June, 1910, when Chis-chili-begay plunged in, wildly excited and in need of advice, after murdering Richard Wetherill near Pueblo Bonito.

"Navajos roll a very thin cigarette when using their own tobacco," Bob Evans once observed. "When someone else is furnishing the makings their taste grows tremendously." Evans succeeded Herman Schweizer as buyer for the Fred Harvey Company. His comments here and following were set down in the early 1900's but might have been made fifty years before.[6]

"An Indian trader is supposed to furnish the makings for all Navajos who come to his trading post. If the trader does not keep the tobacco where they can help themselves they will ask for it. If away from the post a Navajo will seldom ask a trader for a smoke no matter how badly he may want one. . . . Many traders will give away three times as many matches as they sell."

Sensitive to Indian ways, Bob Evans noticed other Navaho manners quite as old as the oldest trading posts.

"When a Navajo buys a coat or pair of pants he does not remove the price tag or other marking. He lets them stay on until they are worn off.

"A penny is 'a red,' a nickel 'a yellow,' a dime 'one blue.' Sugar is 'sweet salt,' and a Negro is a 'black Mexican.'

"A Navajo will enter a trading post where there are many of his friends and acquaintances but will show them no recognition for several minutes. After a prescribed length of time he will shake hands with all of them. Navajos do not shake hands but clasp them gently for an interval depending on the length of time since last meeting.

"When a Navajo rides up to a hogan or a trading post he will remain seated and look everything over carefully before dismounting. Before a Navajo will enter he will first peek in and make a thorough survey. When a Navajo enters a trading post or hogan where there are other Indians, he must be the one to make advances and offer his hand. If he doesn't, it shows ill manners and the other Indians will feel slighted. When Navajos meet each other in public they are never boisterous or demonstrative; a light touch of their hands and a low murmur is their form of greeting. . . .

[6] A native of Wales and a giant of a man until illness late in his life left him emaciated but still towering tall, Robert G. Evans joined the Harvey Company at Kansas City, gained knowledge of the Indian trade under Schweizer—"a stubby, bald-headed man who the Navajos called Hosteen Tsani, or Bald Head"—respected for his discriminating taste and choleric temper. When Schweizer retired in 1922, Evans took his place, traveling once a month or not less than three times a year to the major posts on or surrounding the Navaho reservation. As buyer for the Harveys, Evans told me that it was not rare for him to spend $68,000 in four days for Navaho blankets. The quotations here are from a thirteen-page unpublished manuscript which Evans wrote and placed at my disposal.

"A Navajo usually helps in an advisory capacity when his wife is buying but his advice is neglected about as often as it is taken—especially if it is her own money she is spending.

"When Navajos are trading out a certain amount for merchandise they ask after each purchase how much is left, never how much has been spent. . . .

"A Navajo does not wear his hat tilted forward, back or sideways. He wears it square on his head and he uses both hands to put it there.

"Many Navajos cut off the part of the stocking that covers their foot. Navajos prefer brown shoes to black. The Utes wear black. Four out of five Navajo women wear either a five or a five and one-half shoe. A size seven would be called an average for most of the men.

"When buying cloth to be used for ceremonials, Navajos want it torn, not cut."

All of the old trading posts had a wareroom for storing supplies and for goods taken in trade—the room ranging in size, depending upon the post's trade, from a dark, musty little cubicle to an entirely separate building such as that maintained by the Hubbells at Ganado for many years or by Richard Wetherill at Pueblo Bonito for the Hyde Exploring Expedition. Many of the prosperous trading posts also reserved special rooms for storing Navaho blankets. The so-called rug room, however, was a late development, introduced about 1900 or soon after, when a growing market for Navaho weaving made it desirable for the trader to offer buyers or wholesalers the convenience of a separate room where they could examine his collection of rugs in privacy.

Of the old traders, only Lorenzo Hubbell built with feeling or flair for structural materials and architecture, his massive buildings of stone, wood, and ironwork at Ganado and Chinle standing—the latter now in ruins—as unique monuments to his imagination. Thomas Keam built a small colony of buildings in his canyon, and he built them solidly and well, but as plain and utilitarian as a Mormon schoolhouse of the 1880's. Otherwise, there is little to be said in criticism or praise of the outward appearance of the trading posts: unpretentious shelters of stone, wood, or adobe, they had the common grace, like beeweed and toadstools, of blending quietly into their surroundings.

Horizontal patterns of corral fence, dark shadow stripes against light mountain grass or desert sand, caught the eye sooner than the outlines of the trader's buildings. All traders maintained large corrals at the back or side of their posts for the sheep and horses brought in by Indians to sell, in twos or threes or in large herds.

Just beyond the corrals were hay barns, always small and un-painted, in later years roofed with tin or corrugated iron that was mirror-bright until stained red by rust.

And somewhere close by, completing the group of buildings if this was Navaho country, was a guest hogan. With no counterpart in Indian or white society, the function of the guest hogan was a prac-tical extension of early western hospitality. Built by Navahos at the trader's expense, the hogan was reserved for the free use of any Indi-ans coming a long distance by horseback or wagon to trade.[7]

Solitude of the desert posts could be so complete, so unrelenting, as to remain achingly alive in the memories of the older traders. Years after he left Two Gray Hills, H. B. Noel spoke of a winter when it seemed that he and a horse were, alone, the only living things in the Chuska Valley. The sky was gray, snow slanting down, as he stared from a window out at the corrals, at the horse penned there, head low and tail to the blowing snow. For perhaps an hour Noel and the horse stood without moving, regarding each other, "and the thought occurred to me that the horse was as lonely and wretched as I was."

Will Evans once wrote that "sleep was one solace" in which a trader might escape loneliness. Recalling his early life on the reserva-tion, Evans said:

"Perhaps the post was anywhere from 'fifty to two hundred miles from nowhere,' as the old saying went. In some cases the trader was alone, in others he had a male assistant or two, depending on the volume of business. He or they 'batched,' doing their own cooking and washing dishes. The usual fare consisted of sour dough, or else baking powder biscuits, camp style fried, or, boiled potatoes, baked or fried mutton, sometimes Irish stew or mulligan, peaches a-la-can and Arbuckles coffee. This was the routine diet, with a pot of beans occasionally for a change.

"Candles or kerosene lamps were the only available lights. Hot water was obtained from the tea kettle, and cold water was carried in from a well or from the creek. . . . Perhaps the trader would remain

[7] When the guest hogan was introduced, and where and by whom, is entirely uncertain. The oldest of Navaho traders spoke of Indians coming to their posts in journeys of a day or two, or even more. But provision for their shelter appears to be fairly recent, perhaps from the late eighties or early nineties. Guest hogans re-main in use at some posts but the need for them has diminished as the Navahos' use of automobiles and pickup trucks has increased in the last twenty years.

at the post for six months or a year before going to the nearest supply point, and mail and newspapers were brought out by occasional freighters. The newspapers thus obtained were days and sometimes weeks old.

"When the trader did go to his nearest town or source of supply he either had a team and wagon, or, if he was young and inclined to be romantic, sported a 'foxy' team and buggy. In some cases a saddle horse was the only means of locomotion. In most cases the trip took two or three days with outdoor camps between. The nearest post to civilization was a long day's journey. A round trip which now takes but a few hours represented a week's journeying with plenty of hardships attached.

"In those days the only conversations carried on were in the Navajo tongue. Little chance of cultural attainments from that source. A keen and inquiring mind, of course, could get much of value in tribal lore and in native viewpoints; but this fitted the individual but little for intelligent associations with his fellows."[8]

Flour, coffee, and sugar—in that order—were the staples most in demand and therefore most in supply at the old trading posts. Tobacco, by the plug or can, was greatly desired but considered more of a luxury than were yards of bright flannel, velveteen, or calico. Canned goods—fruits and vegetables—stocked the shelves from the early eighties, but the variety was limited and not too well regarded by the Indians for twenty or thirty years more. By comparison, an inventory of the post trader's stock at Fort Wingate was exotic.

"My national pride was aroused," Lieutenant Bourke exulted, with perhaps no irony, when he entered Lambert Hopkins' Fort Wingate store, ". . . aroused by the display of goods of the *very best quality*, and put up in excellent style. These included raisins, almonds, figs, olives, honey, preserves, pickles, canned salmon and other fish and varieties of wines and liquors, all of California production."

These delicacies, needless to say, Hopkins purveyed not to Navahos, not to cavalrymen of the ranks, but to the post's officers and their wives.

"This store is peculiar," Bourke continued, "in having a private room for ladies' shopping, a feature to be commended to other mili-

---

[8] Will Evans, no relation to Bob Evans, traded for many years in the Four Corners region and at one time operated the old Shiprock Trading Company. The quotation here is from "Recollection of Early Trading Days," written in 1938 for the *Times-Hustler,* Farmington, New Mexico.

tary traders. The proprietor, Mr. Hopkins, evidently understands his business."[9]

Bourke observed the ways of Indian-trading a few days later when he arrived at Fort Defiance and poked his head in the door of William Leonard's post: "The scene . . . was in the extreme animated and picturesque, altho' the old den was so dark that upon first entering it was difficult to distinguish the mass of parti-colored blankets, men, squaws and pappooses pressed against the counter. The Navajoes are keen at a bargain and as each unpacked his ponies and ripped open the blankets full of wool he had brought to market, he acted as if he knew its value and meant to get it. Mr. Leonard said that last year he purchased 250,000 lbs. [of wool] and this season expects to buy a greater quantity."[10]

If he heard Leonard correctly and if the trader was truthful, Leonard in 1880 did remarkably well. The price of wool per pound, at Albuquerque, then fluctuated between six and one-half and twelve cents. After freighting charges, here based on available 1885–86 rates, Leonard may have cleared between five thousand and ten thousand dollars on the wool—a considerable sum at that time. Furthermore, if Bourke is correct, Leonard must have purchased about one-third of the entire Navaho wool clip for that year. In 1877, Agent Alex Irvine estimated the tribe's total wool clip sold at 200,000 pounds. In 1880, Agent F. T. Bennett reported that "not less than 800,000 pounds of wool have been marketed this season . . . and I should estimate that at least 100,000 pounds [more] were manufactured into blankets and clothing for [the Navahos'] own use."[11]

9 Here and below, Bourke's comments are quoted from his 1881 diary, "Bourke on the Southwest VIII," ed. by Lansing B. Bloom (*New Mexico Historical Review*, Vol. XI [1936].) Appointed post trader at Wingate August 30, 1877, Lambert N. Hopkins, Jr., did not understand his business as well as Bourke supposed. He built a $4,000 stone house close by on the military reservation—and ran out of cash-paying officers. In 1882 he was bankrupt, his house going to W. S. Woodside, his chief creditor, for one dollar. (National Archives, War Records Division, Fort Wingate File #1251.)

10 Mr. Leonard, as Bourke refers to him—or "Old Man" Leonard, or William B. Leonard—is an elusive person. Under these various references the name Leonard appears in or about Fort Defiance between 1875 and 1881. A W. B. Leonard clerked at Fort Defiance 1877–78–79, for Romulo Martínez (*N. A. Ledgers of Traders*). And in October, 1876, a William B. Leonard is listed as teacher, at $250 quarterly salary, at Defiance Agency. (Letters from Agent Alex Irvine to C. I. A. Smith, October 1, 1876, National Archives, Letters Received . . . 1876.) All of these Leonards, I believe, were the same man.

11 *Annual Report, C. I. A., 1877* and *1880*. The older traders have told me that their greatest profit was in wool, and in the purchase of wool—never knowing how

Hauling and freighting nibbled at a trader's profits. By four-horse team and wagon in the eighties, it cost fifty to seventy-five cents per hundredweight to haul the twenty-five or thirty miles between Fort Defiance and Manuelito, on the Atlantic and Pacific Railroad—the same for "back freight." It cost $1.04 per hundredweight to ship from the lading point to Albuquerque in less than carload lots, which were rare.

By 1888, when the Navaho wool clip increased to an estimated 1,200,000 pounds, the Navahos sold some 800,000 pounds of wool to traders at prices from eight to ten cents a pound. This was a good year: the traders bought 300,000 sheep pelts at ten cents each, and 100,000 goat skins at twenty-five to fifty cents each. Navaho and Ute horses were bought by traders at six or seven dollars a head, but an unusually good horse might bring as much as twenty-five dollars.

As a youngster, John Arrington grazed five hundred Indian ponies on the flat, grassy mesa now bare of grass and criss-crossed by Farmington's air strip—and sold the ponies at an average of eight dollars a head. Charlie Newcomb, trading at Naschiti, could glance out on the Chuska Valley and see thousands of Indian ponies drifting over the prairie, where neither grass nor pony herds have been seen for forty years. And years later he remembered the pony-buyers who came to the Reservation.

"I remember one fellow, especially, who came often," he said. "Always he rode up in the late afternoon with two heavy duck bags of gold and silver tied to his saddle horn, and a quart or two of good whisky wrapped in his slicker and tied on behind the cantle. The whisky was not for trade, but for his own enjoyment.

"Ponies bought at Naschiti usually were shipped to Louisiana and there sold to Negro sharecroppers. The ponies were tough, strong, and cheap, selling for ten to twelve dollars a head. Thousands of them left the reservation this way."

Trading posts in the high wooded country did a considerable business in piñon nuts, a natural crop of the piñon trees occurring in cycles of "good" years—some saying every three or four years, others seven—but always harvested in late September or October.

the market price might change—they gambled heavily. John Arrington said he lost his Kinnebito post a year or so after building it because he bought too much wool at the wrong price at the wrong time. In 1885, Navaho traders paid five to six cents a pound for black wool, about a cent more for white wool. In Albuquerque the wool sold for six and a half to nine and a half cents a pound. In 1886, the market price for wool ranged from nine to twelve cents.

The fall of 1889 came within one of the cycles, Navahos that year selling 117,000 pounds of piñons.[12]

After leaving Naschiti and moving to Crystal, Newcomb remembered one fall when the price paid by traders soared so high that "the Navajos dropped everything else they were doing to bring in the harvest. I never paid cash for piñon nuts, but traded goods for them, buying them in 90-pounds sacks." In a few brief weeks that fall, Newcomb said, the price of piñons went up to twenty-five cents a pound. As his wareroom filled with loaded sacks, supplies taken by the Indians in trade left his shelves bare. Cleaned out of trade goods, unable to hire Navaho teamsters to freight in more supplies because they were gathering piñons, Newcomb finally had to issue promissory notes in lieu of trade goods, payable when the harvest was in and he was able to restock his store.

From the trading posts the piñon nuts were taken to Gallup and sold to wholesalers, and then shipped East where they were salted, packaged, and sold wholesale again to retail outlets.[13]

In the good years entire families went off to gather the piñons, making almost a picnic of the occasion. A good harvest came in the fall of 1921, according to the Gallup *Independent* of September 22: "The Navajo Indians predict that this year will produce the greatest crop of piñons the world has ever seen. . . . The prices are holding up wonderfully. . . . The wholesalers are offering five cents a pound for piñons. One Indian trader in town is offering eight and one is offering ten cents per pound. Of course there has been only a few brought to town up to the present time. Following the first heavy frost the gathering of piñons will begin in earnest, as the frost cuts them all

12 *Annual Report, C. I. A., 1890.* Navaho Agent C. E. Vandever said that for the twelve months previous to August, 1890, the Navahos sold, in addition to the piñon nuts, 12,000 sheep, 1,370,000 pounds of wool, 291,000 pounds of pelts or hides and 1,110,000 pounds of corn. Blanket sales amounted to $24,000. Lt. J. W. Abert with Josiah Gregg, is one of the first Americans to comment on piñons as an article of food and trade. In the vicinity of the Raton Mountains in 1845, he noted that ". . . we collected and ate many of the nuts, and found them exceedingly pleasant to the taste. Gregg says that considerable quantities are exported annually to the southern cities [of Mexico], and that they are sometimes used for the manufacture of oil, which may be used as a substitute for lamp oil. They form the [a] chief article of food of the Pueblos and New Mexicans." (29 Cong., 1 sess., *Sen. Exec. Doc. 438*.)

13 Four-fifths of the piñon crop went to the New York market, according to Kluckhohn and Leighton *(The Navaho,* 22) where nuts were "packaged for sale like peanuts. In 1936 a single trader paid $18,000 for the nuts." The *McKinley County Republican* reported on November 24, 1911, that "the piñon crop this year is very large. S. E. Aldrich of Gallup has already contracted for 60,000 pounds."

loose from the cones, and they either fall to the ground or can be easily shaken from the trees.

"Gathering piñons is a very tedious occupation. When conditions are good, that is when the piñons are lying thickly under the trees, the average picker can pick up about 25 pounds of them in a day, for which he can receive from $1.25 to $2.50 for his day's work."

When, and with whom, metal tokens originated is not known, but this currency, which no government would honor nor any bank redeem, was in popular use among Indians and most of the old traders. Tokens or scrip of various kinds were known in colonial days on the Eastern seaboard, reappearing in another form during the early years of the Pacific Northwest fur trade. In 1820 a brass beaver token was issued to trappers in the employ of the Northwest Company, the Hudson's Bay Company introduced a similar token in four denominations, and the practice spread thereafter among the other companies setting out lines for beaver plews.

Tokens good for rations and trade items appeared in post sutlers' stores in the Southwest after 1851, with the establishment of Forts Union, Fillmore, Conrad, Defiance, Sumner, Garland, and Wingate. The traders borrowed the idea of tokens from the post sutlers, perhaps—certainly the system of tokens was an old one when the traders settled in permanent locations.

Most of the early trade was straight barter: a gun for two blankets and a horse; a pound of flour for a bag of wool. When refinements in trade were introduced, a substitute for legal coinage became necessary. Silver and gold coins were scarce or nonexistent.

The Fort Wingate commissary issued a token that was called a "hindquarters check."[14] One side of the token was stamped "Good

14 M. L. Woodard of Gallup, who has a fine collection of traders' tokens, tells me that the Fort Wingate commissary token is the oldest he has seen. If issued prior to 1868, the token would have been from Old Fort Wingate, near San Rafael. Two years before, Congress abolished the appointments of civilian post sutlers and in 1876, to replace them, established the position of civilian post traders. This formality, however, trailed the fact, as Willi Spiegelberg was appointed and listed as civilian post trader at new Fort Wingate, July 8, 1868. (National Archives, Fort Wingate File #1251.) Post traderships at military installations were abolished in 1893, the secretary of war declaring: "They were a privileged class, exempt from taxation because located on government reservations, and had practically a monopoly of the trade in such articles as were not furnished or sold by the quartermasters or commissary. . . . On the 4th of March, 1889, there were 85 of these traders. There are now but 22, and 7 of these have been notified that their licenses will be revoked." (Report of the Secretary of War relative to Bill S–3117, 52 Cong., 2 sess., 1892–93.)

for 5 lbs. of Beef." The reverse side was stamped "Good for 5 lbs. of Beef Hindquarter." When this chit was issued is uncertain because, in common with all tokens, it bore no date.

Tokens were known by different names in different regions: *seco*, a Spanish word meaning "dry," was used by traders along the railroad lines of New Mexico and Arizona; Navahos called *seco* "dry money" or "thin metal" (*pesh-tai*) or "dry chips." Any of these names was appropriate since tokens were made of aluminum or brass alloy, but invariably a metal lying feather-light in the hand. The chips were stamped out in different sizes and shapes: round, usually, or square, oval, or octagonal. A few traders preferred the elaboration of a petal-shaped rim.

Most commonly, tokens on one side bore the trader's name or his store name and location; the other side was stamped with the words "Good for" and then the denomination, either five cents, ten cents, twenty-five cents, fifty cents, or one dollar. None had a value of more than one dollar. Tokens made for Lorenzo Hubbell and C. N. Cotton differed from most in that they also bore small serial numbers of three or four digits.

Traders in some localities used silver and gold coins in addition to tokens, but checks and paper money were never used in trade with Indians, who regarded the paper as of doubtful value or worthless.[15] A necessity or convenience, tokens were used by most traders, with only a few exceptions. Joseph Schmedding, trading at Sanders, Arizona, in 1918 and later at Keams Canyon, did not use tokens. Nor did the Hyde Exploring Expedition, which from 1898 to 1903 operated trading posts at Chaco Canyon, Farmington, Thoreau, Tiz-na-tzin, Ojo Alamo, Largo, Raton Springs, and on the Escavada Wash.

Mrs. Richard Wetherill once recalled that her husband regularly obtained a supply of Mexican silver dollars from a bank in Gallup for use in the Hyde company stores. Navahos preferred the Mexican pesos because they contained less alloy than American silver dollars and therefore were more satisfactory when melted down for use in silverwork.

Agent C. E. Vandever observed that Navahos would rather have silver coin than gold and were excellent judges of silver.

[15] This disdain for paper money appears from the earliest days of Indian trade down to the present. In 1950, after a pack trip to Kiet Siel in Arizona, I offered the Navaho who supplied the horses a twenty-dollar bill in payment. The amount was correct, but he refused to accept it. Nothing would do but drive ten miles with the Navaho to the Shonto Trading Post and have the bill changed to silver dollars.

"They melt from a third to a half of the coin they receive to make into silver ornaments, but for gold they have no appreciation," he reported in 1890. Before the Atlantic and Pacific Railroad crossed Arizona Territory in the early 1880's, the Navahos were poor, Vandever said, and "they were content with copper and brass. But with the coming of the railway and better markets for their products, they grew rich, and these yellow metals became cheap and were discarded, and gold they reckon in the same category."[16]

Another form of trade money appeared on the Navaho reservation with the development of silversmithing. Buttons hammered out of coin silver and used by both women and men to ornament their clothing or equipment were accepted by traders in place of money or tokens. Agent Bowman in 1886 observed that coin-silver buttons "are made in different sizes and styles" and the Navahos "solder on an eye, and wear them as ornaments. . . . When they wish to buy anything, and have no wool or pelts to exchange, they simply cut off the needed number of buttons. These vary in value from 2½ cents to $1 —and are never refused as legal tender anywhere in this vicinity."[17]

The old-style buttons, cone-shaped or flat or slightly rounded, but usually fluted or otherwise stamped with design, still are found ornamenting moccasins; otherwise, they are rarely seen. In their place, Navaho women in recent years have decorated their velveteen blouses with dimes and sometimes quarters. Eyeholes are soldered to the coins which are then sewed to the blouses, usually in rows down the front over each breast and occasionally from the yoke of the blouse across the shoulders and down each sleeve. As before, in times of need the ornaments may be cut off and handed over the counter as legal currency, worth the face value of the coins.

The circulation of tokens usually was restricted to the area of each trader's operations. Navahos trading with Lorenzo Hubbell, for example, received Hubbell *seco* in change which generally was honored only at one of the Hubbell trading posts. But in rare cases a trader might accept *seco* bearing the imprint of another, even com-

[16] *Annual Report, C. I. A., 1890.* Vandever overstates the case. The railroad did benefit the Navahos economically to some extent, but demoralized those in contact with the towns following in its wake. Navahos' preference for silver money no doubt has a close relationship to the beginning and development of their interest in silversmithing. John Adair, in *The Navajo and Pueblo Silversmiths,* writes that Atsidi Sani, the first Navaho to learn the art from the Mexicans, began working in silver after 1850—possibly as late as 1868. But silversmithing was not widely practiced by the Navahos until the late 1870's and early 1880's.

[17] Letter from Bowman to C. I. A. Atkins, February 22, 1886. (National Archives, Letters Received, 1886.)

petitive trader. Jim Counselor recalled that Navahos of his region, near Largo Canyon, New Mexico, occasionally traded at the Pueblo Alto store when it was operated by Lester Setzer, and would return to him with Pueblo Alto tokens. Counselor said he would take the Pueblo Alto tokens in trade and later, when he had enough of them, redeem them at Setzer's store. Because tokens never were redeemed for hard money, this exchange would be for trade goods, not for cash.

Whether intended or not, the widespread use of tokens often had the effect of encouraging Indians—if not compelling them—to continue going back to the same trader. In some instances this placed the Indians at a disadvantage, particularly when a trader who enjoyed such a monopoly may have been dishonest, charged too much, or carried a poor line of trade goods. There were, on the other hand, advantages in the tokens which the Indians readily understood. A trader reaching into his cash box to make change or payment was almost invariably more liberal with *seco* than he would have been with silver.

Charlie Newcomb, who in 1907 began as a trader clerking at Hans Neumann's post at Guam, New Mexico, explained it this way: "If we had used only gold and silver—which was mighty scarce—many things brought in to us would never have been bought at all. For example, I have often seen Hans Neumann toss out another tin dollar to a squaw for a rug when I knew, if it was silver dollars he was paying her, she would have to be satisfied with half the number."

This wasn't logical, really, because Neumann then would turn around and give full value in trade goods for the tin money.

The Indian Office, too far removed to appreciate such illogic, never regarded the use of tokens with a friendly eye. An attempt to abolish *seco* was made as early as 1878 when Commissioner E. A. Hayt ruled that "the trade with the Indians is required to be for cash only—the use of tokens or tickets prohibited."[18] Hayt's order was universally ignored, as most of the laws governing Indian trade were when they butted against reality.

Good or necessary in the early days, not so good or necessary after the 1900's, *seco* finally was abolished officially about 1935 when representatives of the Indian Office and the United Traders Association, meeting in Gallup, agreed to prohibit its use on the reservation. For some years afterward tokens continued as currency in a few off-reservation posts. But as the need for it diminished, it disappeared, until now *seco* is almost a forgotten word.

18 *Annual Report, C. I. A., 1878.*

PART TWO

"I knew Victorio and Geronimo personally; knew them very well. I knew Victorio particularly well when he came through Fort Wingate. We got them both there in the fort, but they had not broken out on the warpath then; they broke out afterwards and killed a great many people. . . . I knew Cochise and Pedro, knew them well. They captured Sol Barth and several others, Chávez, Calderon and others, and took them out and turned them loose, all naked, and the only thing they had to eat was a dog they found. They had to walk seventy-five miles to the nearest settlement, and had no guns or ammunition."

—*Lorenzo Hubbell*, personal recollections, 1918.

6

Hamblin and Lee

MEMORY OF THE Mountain Meadows massacre, scarcely ever referred to in the Mormon settlements of Utah, was especially clear in the mind of Jacob Hamblin in the autumn of 1858. His travels for the church took him frequently to the region where, in the previous year, the emigrant train of Gentiles led by Charles Fancher had been waylaid and brutally wiped out. Hamblin had no part in the affair. But a close acquaintance of his, a man for whom he developed an almost brotherly responsibility—had been involved, most terribly and pitilessly.

Instead of splitting them apart, this episode during the next fourteen years drew Hamblin and John Doyle Lee closer together. Neither man was an Indian trader by design or temperament: with each, trading came as an accidental circumstance of necessity. Hamblin's Indian-trading was a small but essential part of his explorations and missionary work. With Lee, for the present waiting silently in the wings and wishing to attract no attention, trading was to be a means of support in years of hiding and exile. Fate, then, impelled these two to become the first of a long Mormon dynasty of Indian traders.

With Hamblin in the fall of 1858 were eleven other men, under his leadership and all charged by President Brigham Young to visit the yet-unknown Hopi villages lying south of the Colorado River, and "to take advantage of any opening . . . to preach the gospel to them."[1] The river crossing was made at Ute Ford, a name then com-

1 James A. Little (ed.), *Jacob Hamblin, A Narrative of His Personal Experience.* A native of Salem, Ohio, Hamblin came to Utah in 1849, leaving his first wife,

89

monly used for the crossing-place of Domínguez and Escalante in 1776. Since the Franciscans' time no other ford had been found.

The same village of Oraibi that was hostile to Spanish visitors nearly one hundred years before took the Mormon party into its homes and treated them in such friendly spirit that Hamblin was encouraged to return the following autumn. On his second trip he brought with him sixty dollars' worth of trade goods, including wool-cards, spades, and shovels.

An abortive, tragic end came to Hamblin's third attempt to enter the Hopi country in 1860. On a mesa in the region of Red Lake, or Tonalea, Hamblin's party was surrounded and stopped by a band of unfriendly Navahos, later said to have been foraging out from the Fort Defiance area many miles to the east.

Several Paiutes, including two women, were traveling with the Mormons, and the Navahos' first demand was that these women be surrendered to them as captives. Hamblin bluntly refused, but a compromise was agreed to when the Navahos said they would be satisfied to withdraw in exchange for ammunition and trade goods.

Hamblin camped that night on a table-rock mesa, maintaining a guard at the one narrow approach to his party. At dawn it was found that the Navahos had not gone away, but were pressing closer when the Mormons led their horses down to water in a draw.

Noticing that his horse was wandering off by itself in another di-rection, George A. Smith, Jr., started after it on foot. When he came upon it, the horse was being led away by two Indians, who turned the animal over freely enough and then rode closely in Smith's tracks back toward camp. A few minutes later Smith misjudged his com-panions by handing one of the Navahos a revolver he carried in his belt, the Indian expressing curious interest to look at it. The Indian then passed the gun back to the second Navaho, bringing up the rear, who leveled the gun and fired three bullets into Smith's back. The shots did not kill Smith but did knock him to the ground. While he was lying there, before his friends could help him, the two Nava-hos notched shafts to their bows and planted three arrows in his back.

Even then, Smith did not die, but lived in agony a few hours longer as Hamblin withdrew his people in flight, supporting Smith on the back of a mule. Before nightfall and before the pursuing

---

Lucinda, at Winter Quarters when he discovered her laughing in the arms of a drunken officer. Married twice since his arrival in Utah, father of at least ten chil-dren—two or three of them being adopted Paiutes—Hamblin was thirty-nine years old at the time we find him here.

Navahos gave up the chase, Smith died. To save his body from mutilation, the Mormons buried him among rocks, and then continued homeward.[2]

Hamblin set out a fourth time for the Hopi villages in the fall of 1862, on this trip crossing the Colorado at Grand Wash, far to the west of Grand Canyon and near the present site of Pearce's Ferry. After another trip in 1863, further exploration or missionary work south of the Colorado was interrupted for six years by a nagging war of attrition the Paiutes and Navahos waged against the southern Mormon settlements. The raids intensified after Dr. James M. Whitmore and his son-in-law, Robert McIntyre, were killed at Pipe Spring, twenty-two miles south of Kanab, Utah. In time the continuing raids were referred to as the Black Hawk War—so named after a Paiute chief, although the Navahos throughout were the principal aggressors. According to one estimate, the Mormon-Indian war cost over one million dollars, resulted in at least seventy deaths, and enriched the Navahos to the extent of twelve hundred horses and cattle.

Concern over these losses caused Hamblin to be sent, in October, 1869, on still another mission to the Hopis—this time, however, to "learn, if possible, whether there were other Indians besides the Navajos raiding on our borders." Accompanying Hamblin were twenty Mormons and as many Paiute warriors disaffected from their recent Navaho allies—a force considerably stronger than Hamblin until now was accustomed to leading. For once his Hopi friends received him "rather coldly," fearing reprisals, but told him that the Navahos, unassisted, were planning another raid soon.

Perhaps more significant, Hamblin on this journey made the first crossing of the Colorado at the future site of Lee's Ferry—or Lonely Dell, as it was to be known first. Hamblin's reference to the crossing was brief: "Our luggage went over on rafts made of floatwood, fastened together by withes."[3]

Brigham Young knew something of his visitor's past and was inclined to be helpful when Major John Wesley Powell called upon him in Salt Lake City asking his assistance.

In the previous year—1869—Powell had led a party of nine men on a hazardous descent of the Colorado River. From Green River

2 This episode is related in the *Hamblin Narrative,* and in greater detail by Angus W. Woodbury, in "A History of Southern Utah," *Utah Historical Quarterly,* Vol. XII (1944). Van Valkenburgh notes that in 1938 the Mormon church erected a stone monument with a bronze plaque to Smith's memory, placing the monument on a rocky outcropping immediately north of Red Lake.

3 *Hamblin Narrative,* 93.

Station in Wyoming, Powell's boats traveled the Green to its junction with the Colorado near Moab, Utah, and then through deep canyon gorges as far as the mouth of the Río Virgin. The party—what was left of it—disbanded on the first of September. Of Powell's four boats, one was wrecked in the rapids at Disaster Falls and another abandoned late in August when three of the party, all near the point of starvation, refused to continue and wandered off. The three deserters soon after fell in with a band of Shivwit Paiutes and were murdered. In spite of these reverses Major Powell could claim a major achievement: with the instruments he carried he had mapped the uncharted course of the Upper Colorado and made valuable geological notes of a region blank and marked "unknown" on government maps.

Major Powell's request of Brigham Young was simple enough. For further exploration in the summer and fall of 1870, before mounting a second Colorado River survey the following spring, he asked the services of a dependable guide who knew the country and knew the Indians. One of his objects, said the Major, was to discover if possible the reason for the murder of the three men who had deserted the previous August. Brigham Young at once suggested Hamblin as the man who above all others fitted Powell's needs.

With a letter of introduction from the Mormon leader, Powell sought out Hamblin and secured his agreement to act as guide. The contrast between the two men, as they faced each other, was startling.

The top of the river explorer's large, auburn-curled head came only midway to the buckskin shirt of the Mormon, who stood two inches over six feet tall. Hamblin's age, fifty-one, was not revealed in his face or clear eyes or in his unbent, spare frame. Age told only in the gray-shot hair that grew back from a broad-domed forehead and was chopped off unevenly at shoulder level. Hamblin's junior by fifteen years, Major Powell was as slight as a mature boy, but his erect bearing and the empty right sleeve of his coat hinted of his past. The arm he left behind when struck by a Minié ball at Shiloh, in the Civil War; his commission as major came just before his service with Union forces besieging Vicksburg. The military title fitted him all right, even five years after the war's end, and he may have preferred that to his more recent title of professor—professor of natural science—at Illinois Wesleyan University.[4]

4 Prior to the meeting with Hamblin referred to here, Major Powell had induced the Illinois Legislature to provide $2,500 annually for a natural history society and museum at State Normal University. Powell was curator of that museum until his return from the first Colorado River exploration in the fall of 1869,

Through the summer of 1870, Hamblin guided Powell's party through the redrock and barren plateau country of southern Utah, interpreting for the Major during their frequent encounters with Paiute bands of Kaibabs and Uinkarets. In his notes of these meetings the Major remarked upon the primitive level of the Indians' existence, the nakedness of the women, the usual laziness of the men, and the poor diet of roots and plants by which they somehow subsisted.

Leaving Kanab in mid-September after outfitting their pack train with fresh supplies, the party moved southwest toward Mount Trumbull. Here, it was said, the Howland brothers, Oramel and Seneca, and William Dunn—the three who deserted in 1869—had met their death. Near Pipe Spring the Major's party was visited by a group of Shivwits, who, after assurances by Hamblin and Powell that the white men would do them no harm, told how the three had been murdered.

Whether their account was true or not, the Shivwits said that the Howland brothers and Dunn had been taken for prospectors, and if that alone were not enough, these interlopers had molested their women, even shooting one woman. In revenge, the Shivwits ambushed the three near a spring and killed them all with arrows.[5]

In talking with the Shivwits, Hamblin explained that the small man with one arm was a chief or leader of the white men and would return the next year for another trip by small boats on the great river. He would not be coming to find gold or silver, Hamblin said,

when he resigned to tour and lecture in the East and Midwest. Powell's initial exploration, a trip into the Rocky Mountains in 1867, resulted in his bringing back to his museum a large collection of insects, birds, and plants. In 1868–69 he led a party of twenty-one in exploring the White and Green rivers, and while wintering on the White he spent much time with the Utes, making notes on their language and customs and observing that "these Indians as yet had no firearms and killed game only with their primitive bows and arrows. " (William Culp Darrah, *Powell of the Colorado*.) At the conclusion of his Colorado River surveys, Powell in 1874 completed his manuscript for "Exploration of the Colorado River of the West and its Tributaries Explored in 1869, 1870, 1871 and 1872 Under the Direction of the Secretary of the Smithsonian Institution," and two years later published his "Report on the Geology . . . of the Uintah Mountains." As keenly interested in ethnology as in the natural sciences, Powell was instrumental in founding the Bureau of American Ethnology, Washington, D. C., and in 1879 became its first director.

5 Natives of Vermont, the Howland brothers had little experience to qualify them for the privations and hardships of the river survey. Oramel G. Howland, thirty-six years old, was a printer and editor who came west in 1860. Seneca, ten years younger, was a Civil War veteran, wounded at Gettysburg. William H. Dunn, about thirty years old, was a mountain man who had accompanied Powell on his trips in 1867–68. The Shivwits' version of their murder may not be true in all of its details, but evidently was accepted by Powell and later by others who have written on the subject.

but as a friend, and the Paiutes of all bands must promise not to harm him or his people. Impressed by his guide's manner throughout this and previous councils, Major Powell later wrote: "This man, Hamblin, speaks their language well, and has a great influence over all the Indians in the region round about. He is a silent, reserved man, and when he speaks, it is in a slow, quiet way that inspires great awe. His talk is so low that they must listen attentively to hear, and they sit around him in death-like silence."[6]

When the council ended, Powell put Hamblin in charge of the pack train, directing him to explore the country to the east, north, and south. When supplies ran out, Hamblin was to return, presumably to Kanab, and from there take the Major to the Hopi villages. This would have been in early October, when Hamblin, according to his own journal, "packed lumber on mules over the Kibab [Kaibab], or Buckskin Mountains, to the crossing of the Colorado, now known as Lee's Ferry. With this we constructed a small boat, in which we conveyed our luggage across. Our animals crossed over by swimming."

After guiding the party to the village of Oraibi, Hamblin persuaded Major Powell to accompany him more than one hundred miles eastward, to Defiance Agency, where the Navahos were gathering by the hundreds to receive their annuity goods. Navaho raids on Mormon settlements had been continuing; now, with the principal chiefs, the head men, and a major number of the tribe come together at one place, it was Hamblin's desire to council with them and make peace. Powell intervened on Hamblin's behalf with Agent Frank Tracy Bennett and a meeting with the head chief, Barboncito, and others, was arranged on November 2. Both Powell and Hamblin spoke, eloquently and long enough that Barboncito agreed to discuss their proposals with the other chiefs. Three days later a treaty ending the Navaho-Mormon war was signed.[7]

Returning by the route over which they had come, Hamblin left Powell and his party in the Hopi villages, where the Major pursued

6 Powell, "Exploration of the Colorado River."

7 In writing of the council, Darrah credits Powell with being "the leading spokesman" and adds that with the signing of the treaty "Hamblin had completed the lifework he had set out to do." Darrah overstates the case in each instance. Major Powell unquestionably was helpful during the council, but Hamblin, who says that he spoke to the chiefs for a full hour, made the most convincing appeal for an end to hostilities. The treaty was gratifying to Hamblin but it would not put a final end to raiding and killing—and Hamblin was realist enough to surmise as much at the time. In his own estimation, as emphasized in his *Narrative*, his missionary journeys and colonizing efforts for the Mormon church were his lifework.

ethnological studies of these Indians for the remainder of the month before going back East. From Oraibi, Hamblin was accompanied back to Utah by the Hopi chief Tuba and his wife. His object in taking them with him, Hamblin wrote, was that Tuba, "a man of good report among his people," might "get acquainted with the spirit and policy of our people, and become a truthful representative of them among his people."[8]

First at Kanab and then at St. George and Washington, Utah, the Hopi visitors were introduced to the different customs of these rustic Mormon settlements. At Washington, Tuba was taken to a spinning mill and marveled at the sound and sight of three hundred spindles drawing out endless strands of thread with magical speed. At a flouring mill Tuba's wife mentally weighed the output of the ponderous grinding stones turning without human labor against the trickle of corn meal that came from aching arms and backs bent over the Hopi *metates*. She thought it a pity, Hamblin wrote, "that the Hopees (meaning the Oriba women), were obliged to work so hard to get a little meal to make their bread, when it could be made so easily."

On the Santa Clara River, in fields near Hamblin's home, Tuba and his wife picked cotton for one week, working side by side with Mormon men and women, and were paid for their work. The welcome given these two was sincere and warm enough, but wherever they went no effort was made to conceal the rougher or harder aspects of pioneer life. As agreed, Tuba and his wife remained for one year in Utah, and then in September, 1871, were taken back by Hamblin to Oraibi.[9] In the fifteen years or more that remained to him, Tuba was a firm friend to his Mormon neighbors.

During the period of Tuba's visit Hamblin frequently was called away on personal matters. Between Lee's Ferry and the Uinta Valley he "explored many places," helped to establish a small Mormon settlement on the upper Paria River, and for himself and his own

8 *Hamblin Narrative*, 104. There are various spellings of the name, Hamblin giving it as "Tuba." Van Valkenburgh uses the spelling "Tivi," while another variant appears as "Tuve." Soon after their return from Utah, Tuba granted the Mormons rights to establish a settlement in the Hopi country, the place chosen being named Tuba City and located about a mile north and west of Moenkopi. A bronze and stone marker erected by Mormons in Tuba City in 1941 refers to Tuba as a "member of the Water and Corn Clan, who served as scout of Kit Carson's U. S. Expedition in 1865." According to the marker, Tuba was born about 1810 and died about 1887.

9 In his *Narrative*, Hamblin confuses the year for 1872, as previously he confused the date of the council with Navahos at Defiance, making it 1871 instead of 1870.

numerous family, marked out a ranch and started to build a house near House Rock Springs, a few miles south of the Utah border.

Major Powell, meanwhile, in the spring of 1871 was preparing for his second descent of the Colorado. Sponsored this time by the Department of the Interior, Powell was given a grant of $10,000 by Congress—not for a river expedition, but for a geographical and topographical survey of the country for fifteen miles on either side of the river.[10]

As before, Powell's river boats were constructed to his specifications by a firm in Chicago and transported by rail to the Green River Station starting point. Three boats were launched this time: the *Emma Dean* (Powell's craft, named for his wife), the *Nellie Powell*, and the *Cañonita*. Identical in design, the boats were twenty-two feet long, square at the stern, and each was steered by an eighteen-foot oar.

Also as before, the party of ten men was composed mainly of Powell's friends or relatives, short on experience in the techniques required of them, but fired with enthusiasm. The wonder of it was— since enthusiasm presently gave way to boredom or discouragement— that such a crew of young amateurs could endure as much, and accomplish as much.

Powell's long absences from the river party, while in Salt Lake City or elsewhere, attending to often unrelated affairs of personal interest, did not heighten the men's morale. Not long after the boats pushed off, on May 22, the Major departed on the first of many side trips, leaving the direction of the survey to his brother-in-law, Almon H. Thompson, a geographer.

Late in the summer Powell and Hamblin met and with two of Hamblin's sons, Clem and Fred, rejoined the party at Gray Canyon. Hamblin and the boys remained at the river camp for several days, and possibly at that time worked out plans for the winter quarters Powell's group was to establish at Kanab. When cold weather finally interrupted further progress on the river, at least one of the boats, and perhaps all three, were cached in the vicinity of Lee's Ferry.

For nearly fourteen years John Doyle Lee had lived with his conscience, his thoughts about the Mountain Meadows massacre,

10 "His [Powell's] exploration became a quasi-official survey in a field in which there were already three distinct government surveys: two, headed by Clarence King and Lt. George W. Wheeler, were under the jurisdiction of the War Department; the third, directed by Dr. Ferdinand Vandiveer Hayden, was under the authority of the Federal Land Office in the Department of the Interior." Darrah, in *Powell of the Colorado*.

whatever they were, locked in his heart. He was not a well-educated man, nor a man who read books, but he did keep a diary and what he wrote in those pages about the massacre, so far as his words concerned him, has the sad irony of a man compelled to delude himself.

Frequently, in recent years, he heard his name linked with the brutal affair. Each time the rumor was dutifully entered by Lee in his diary, and each time it was characterized by him as an absurd lie.

But time for Lee was running out. Too many persons knew of his part in the massacre of the Fancher train. The federal government, pressed by families of the victims, had started an investigation and was calling for arrest of the ringleaders. Besides Lee's, the names mentioned most often were those of Isaac Haight, Philip Klingen Smith, and John M. Higbee—but Lee's name was heard most persistently.[11]

Lee was dividing his time between his several wives and his homes at Harmony and Washington when he learned, in July, 1871, that Brigham Young, himself erroneously accused of complicity in the massacre, had "treacherously through fear Made Me a scape Goat" and excommunicated Lee from the Mormon church.[12] By doing this, Young was obviously and publicly adding the considerable weight of his own accusation to that of Lee's other accusers, but regardless of how damaging to him it was, Lee had the grace a few days later to

11 The exact dates are uncertain, but the waylaying and murder of the Fancher party, a California-bound wagon train of some 120 to 150 emigrants from Arkansas and Missouri, occurred over a five-day period in September, 1857. After following the Oregon Trail into Wyoming, the Fancher wagons turned south at Fort Bridger to meet the old Spanish Trail in Utah. Mountain Meadows lies on the west fork of the Virgin River, some thirty miles southwest of Cedar City. Mormons who planned the attack first induced a band of Paiutes to strike at the train; when the emigrants more than held their own, it is said that Lee, under a flag of truce, approached the Fancher wagons. He warned that the Paiutes would attack again and in strength, but promised the emigrants a safe withdrawal to Cedar City— providing they placed all their arms and ammunition in one wagon; that all of the women, children, and wounded men rode in the other vehicles; and that the other men formed, unarmed, in a column under Mormon escort. When these terms were agreed to, it is said that John M. Higbee, a major in the Mormon militia, gave the order to open fire. The number of the Fancher party killed is estimated variously from 115 to 120. The only survivors were 16 or 17 children under seven years of age.

12 Robert Glass Cleland and Juanita Brooks, who edited and annotated Lee's diaries, remark without intended humor that in 1861 Lee had ten wives, "eight of whom lived in Harmony"—a Utah settlement—the other two in Washington, another Mormon town. The number of Lee's children, as in Hamblin's case, including several Indians by adoption, may only be conjectured. The quotation here, and all of Lee's comments quoted hereafter, are from the Cleland and Brooks *A Mormon Chronicle: The Diaries of John D. Lee, 1848–1876,* II.

note in his diary: ". . . let this, My Testimy, suffice from troubling Me on the subJect any More: Brigham Young knew nothing of the Mountain Massacre until it was all over; & verry Much regretted it when he heard of it, & I am satisfied that he never would have suffered it."

Before the month was out, Lee was a fugitive. He sold his home at Washington for two thousand dollars—part cash, part goods and hardware—hiding out in one settlement after another. At Kanab, where he stayed a short time, he found the "town full of NavaJoes in to trade." Finally, on November 16, he noted that "I had a Private interview with J. Hamblin. He gave Me the pass word to Make My way to the Lonely Dell."

The canyon gorge where the Paria River meets the Colorado was known to Hamblin at least since October, 1869, when he first forded the great river there. It was this place that Hamblin later referred to in his journal as Lee's Ferry, the name commonly accepted later but never used by Lee in his lifetime. To Lee it was Lonely Dell, and a lonelier, more remote spot on the face of the earth would be impossible to imagine.[13]

If two rivers should meet in crevices of the moon, the murmur of water meeting could not be more lost in silence. Rising almost perpendicularly, the Vermilion Cliffs wall the river gorges to the north and west, the red stone banded horizontally with strata of pink and white. Through these cliffs the Paria cuts, widening at the mouth to form a spit of flat red sand before emptying into the swift, muddy Colorado. This ruddy palm of land, blazing in sunlight, locked in silence, was Lee's Lonely Dell. Standing here, Lee could look across the barrier of the big river to the opposite escarpment, a wedge-shaped palisade of brown sandstone tilting steeply up and away from him down-river.

As a hunted man would, Lee lost track of dates about this time, but his diary entries place his arrival at Lonely Dell in late December, 1871. Hamblin helped and advised him in various ways, and Lee brought with him a small flock of his children and wives. When one of the wives bore him a daughter in this wilderness, on January 17, 1872, Lee "named it Frances Dell, after the Place of our location."

Two days later Lee's isolation was invaded, and he accidentally moved into his new role as Indian trader when "before sun rise we

13 Van Valkenburgh says that the Navaho name for this place was *Ha'naant'eetiin,* or "Crossing Against the Current." Later, when Lee built his ferryboat, the Navahos referred to Lonely Dell as *Tsinaa'ee dahsi'ani,* "Where the Boat Sits."

was Saluted by the whoops & yells of a Band of 15 NavaJoes, pleading with us to set them over the river. . . . We were but 3 Men Strong, 3 women & 13 little children & 100 Ms [miles] from Setlements, & 15 Braves to come over amoungst us."

The identity of his company is not revealed, but it may be assumed, since Lee was then sixty years old, that the two other men could have been his sons or sons-in-law. In any case: "The spirit said help them over, so I with Samuel & James & My wife Rachel Andora commenced to cork [caulk] an old flat Boat & by noon we were ready to cross. . . . My wife Rachel Andora Said that She would go over with Me & Steer"—since James and Samuel were too afraid to go. On reaching the opposite side, Lee and the sturdy Rachel Andora were met with open arms by the Navahos.[14]

"They were heavy loaded with Blankets full of cloth, calico, Domestics, Made up clothing, linseys & handkerchiefs"—no doubt part of the annuity goods received at Defiance the previous fall, and—"After Much difficulty we Succeeded in getting them & their luggage over Safe." The Indians stayed on to help Lee start building a stone corral, and on the third day, before they left

"I traded them 2 Horses & a Mule for the value of about 6 Blankets Each in clothes, calicoes & Blankets. They seemed well pleased & were not Much inclined to begg, although I gave them Beef & Bread."

Navahos and Paiutes—and Utes and Hopis in lesser numbers—came with increasing frequency to Lonely Dell after Lee settled there. The facilities he offered for fording the Colorado made it easier for the Navahos to reach Kanab and other Mormon towns on their trading trips, and few Indians passed through without stopping to trade with him, both going and on their return. In February, 1872, Lee took some goods received in trade with the Indians to a Mormon community north of him on the Paria and "exchanged Some NavaJo Blankets, Larso, Handkerchiefs . . . for 300 grape Roots & a few varieties of other choice shrubs and seeds."

Several hundred yards back from the willow clumps and swamp grass bordering the Colorado, where the sandy ground was level, Lee built a log cabin, and between the cabin and the Paria River he dug irrigation ditches and set out fields of vegetables, melons, grapevines, and fruit trees. Hamblin continued to befriend him, sending a man

14 The flatboat Lee refers to may have been one built and left here by Hamblin, or it may have been the cached *Nellie Powell*—which Lee calls by name and mentions using three months later.

to help with the fields and, in April, 2,000 grapevine cuttings, garden seed, and 120 apple trees.

When a small party of prospectors found their way into his deep canyon—and it was yet a rare thing for Lee to see white men there—he gratefully traded with them for some of their long-handled shovels and picks, and for flour, bacon, coffee, tea, and sugar and rice, "which to us at that time was certainly a Godsend." His own supplies had run out, Lee notes, leaving the impression that he dared not go to any of the Mormon towns to replenish them.

Isolated and almost cut off as he was, Lee did not have to look for trouble, as it sometimes came to him. He was staying at Hamblin's ranch near House Rock Springs in May when he recorded an ugly incident that occurred several weeks before at Lonely Dell.[15] Seven Navahos arrived on their return from Kanab with ten horses that they had taken in trade. The Colorado was deep and swift with the spring run-off, but the Indians nevertheless demanded that Lee take them across. The only boat available, Lee noted, was the *Nellie Powell*, left there by the Major's party the previous autumn.

"I offered them an enfield Rifle & ammunition," Lee wrote, "if they [would] go to the ute crossing & wait for the River to fall & then ford it. But they said it Might be 3 Moons & insisted on launching the Boat & set them over." Lee finally agreed to take them across when the river subsided, providing they would help him with a dam he was building on the Paria. In the week that followed two of his seven visitors turned lazy and thievish, seizing anything in sight that hadn't a lock on it and could be hidden under a blanket. Tiring of this small larceny, which he knew was intended to bait him into a quarrel, Lee decided to chance the river crossing.

"I told them I would not Swim their Horses over with the Boat as it was dangerous, not having the proper oars. After a long cavel I agreed to take one Horse over & no more. When this was done they wanted two More set over. I refused & was compelled to Buckle on our revolver & take My 2 Henry Rifles & told them if th[e]y wanted us to help drive their Horses in, to bring them to the water & if they wanted to be set over, to stop their Noise or I would take the Boat back; That we were not agoing to be run over by them."

15 Hamblin's ranch in House Rock Valley, Arizona, was situated on the Kaibab Plateau within sight of the Vermilion Cliffs and about thirty-seven miles south-west of Lonely Dell. Lee may have been hiding out briefly near Hamblin's place because a diary entry of May 16, 1872, places him at "Lee's Ranch of Jacob's Pools"—the last name, appearing on modern maps as Jacob's Lake, being the site of Hamblin's home.

Something in Lee's voice, or perhaps the show of firearms, quieted the Navahos. Six of the horses were driven into the water and made to swim across, although two nearly drowned before reaching the far side. An old Navaho who was the leader of the trading party offered to give Lee a buckskin if he would cross the remaining three horses in Powell's boat.

"I finally aggreed & set them all over. . . . But when I got across on the other Side from them, one of those thieves Shouted back, Mormon No wino. Merican Mucho Wino, Mormon no wino. This was doubtless a Band of low Maraders from the chief down."

Leaving their winter quarters at Kanab at the end of May, 1872, Major Powell's party went overland with their boats, after much hardship reaching the junction of the Dirty Devil River and the Colorado, where they pitched camp on June 22.[16] Powell, who had spent the winter in Washington, D. C., did not join them until later in the summer; meanwhile, four of the men explored downstream as far as Lonely Dell.

Lee greeted their boat on July 13, noting that "they were out of Meat & groceries, all but coffee & Flour. They offered to furnish us the Flour & coffee if we would cook for them till the remainder of the co. would come up with supplies from Kanab."

A later diary entry makes it appear that Powell and his entire party may have been reunited at Lee's hideout when, confusing the date of a celebrated holiday, Lee wrote: "We got up a splendid Dinner & invited our Generous friends of Maj. Powel's Expedition to spend the glorious 24th [of July] with us & participate in the festivities. . . . In return for the kind reception & affable Manner in which they had been entertained since their arrival . . . they & Maj. Powel adopted My Name for the place, Lonely Dell & so ordered it to be p[r]inted U. S. Map[p]ed."

Presence of Powell's men at Lee's hideout, possibly in some measure influenced by Hamblin, was slightly ambiguous since the men could not have failed to know that Lee was wanted by the federal authorities—and why. Their willingness to overlook this again suggests some previous understanding with Hamblin. In his writings afterward Powell spoke often, and well, of Hamblin, but did not mention Lee by name. If it is likely that Powell was at Lonely Dell in July, it is certain he was there in August, for in this month, after

[16] The Dirty Devil River is upstream from Lee's Ferry, entering the Colorado near the lower end of Cataract Canyon.

leading a small party in topographical surveys in the vicinity of the Kaibab Plateau and House Rock Valley, he finally reached the mouth of the Paria. On August 17 his boats were reported just below Lonely Dell, in Marble Canyon, and several weeks later the expedition was disbanded.

Lee was visited in October by several members of Powell's returning group, accompanied by the Major's former guide. In his diary for October 13, Lee soberly noted that he had made a shrewd trade: "Jacob Hamblin, J. Hillers, Andy [Hattan] & Clem Powel came en route for the Moquis Nation on a trading expedition & Photograph their vilages & Princeple Men & to obtain ancient relics & antiquities. Stayed 4 days & we built a Skift & Set them over on the 4th day. I traded to Powel a Black Mare & colt for a Henry rifle, colts Revolver & $35 cash, also let Hamblin have 50 lls. cotton at 50 cents."[17]

The year 1873 was the period when John Doyle Lee was most active as an Indian trader, and, whether by design or not, he prepared for it by building the first actual ferryboat ever used on the Upper Colorado His difficulty in "setting over" his Indian friends and their horses no doubt accounted for it. Along with the ferryboat he built a swifter, smaller skiff, naming it the *Pahreah*, and celebrated the event with a party for twenty-two friends and relatives. There was a rashness in this act that Lee would regret, but for the moment his Mormon friends were concealing his whereabouts and he felt safe.

"About 12 noon," he wrote on January 11, "we had a Public Dinner on the bottom of the Ferry Boat, Just having finished Pitching her preparatory to launching her. . . . After Dinner we launched the Boat & called her the Colerado. . . . [She] is 26 by 8½ feet, strong, A Staunch craft & well constructed & a light Runer."

Once in the water the boat was boarded and "all crossed on her to christen her & take a Pleasure Ride. We crossed over and back twice."

Spring sun warming the walls of his deep hideaway made Lee even more careless. Indian trade was increasing with the advent of his ferryboat, and in April, against the better judgment of Hamblin, who advocated another location farther down-river, Lee persuaded

17 John K. Hillers joined the Powell expedition as photographer during the winter 1871–72. W. Clement (Clem) Powell, twenty years old, was Major Powell's cousin, serving as a boatman. Andrew Hattan, of Illinois, was a Powell friend and served as cook.

Mormon friends to use his ferry on a route south into Arizona, and to build a road to the approaches on both sides of the river.

Hamblin probably was one of the first to use Lee's ferry in the winter of 1873 when, on Brigham Young's instructions, he "was sent to look out a route for a wagon-road from Lee's Ferry to the San Francisco Forest, or the head waters of the Little Colorado."[18] By horseback, alone, and by pack train, Hamblin had been crossing and re-crossing much of this country since 1858. He was familiar now with the location of the best springs and, in general, the most favorable terrain. His present objective was to make certain of a route that would be practical for wagons. The road he laid out in 1873 is virtually the same as today's United States Highway 89 as it runs south from Kanab to Flagstaff, Arizona. From Lee's Ferry the old Mormon Trail climbs gently for miles through a broad, treeless valley. Hamblin Wash and the ruddy Echo Cliffs (or Mormon Ridge) parallel the trail and enclose the valley to the east. Small trees begin to appear near Cedar Ridge, and then some seven miles beyond the trail reaches its high summit at The Gap. Thereafter the road drops off into a painted desert, skirting Willow Spring and Moenave and Moenkopi, finally making a crossing of the Little Colorado at the site of present Cameron. Hazy blue in the distance, and almost due south, are the peaks of the San Francisco Mountains.

Snow still covered the ground when Hamblin returned, the mission accomplished, and started preparing to lead the first contingent of Mormon settlers from Utah into Arizona.[19] A few weeks later, at the head of nine wagons, Hamblin was at Lee's Ferry, and on April 23, Lee noted in his diary: "I finished crossing the co. & receid from them $46. I charged them 75¢ for each Horse & $3 for each waggon, the Luggage & Men thrown in."

The second and third trains of pioneers followed: on May 9 and 10 Lee ferried twenty-six wagons across the river, and nineteen more (a total of fifty-four) from May 24 to 26. This last crossing was a precarious one, as the Colorado was running in flood, ten feet higher than usual, and a new road had to be blasted out of the cliffs on the south bank. Everyone concerned appears to have lost his temper, not excepting the captain of the train, Henry Day.

Day "was not a Man of Much firmness," Lee sniffed, "either in Mormonism or Manly deal. The first thing that [Day said] when he

18 *Hamblin Narrative*, 110.

19 First—in this sense—to settle in northern Arizona. Actually, the first Mormon settlement in Arizona was at Tubac, in the fall of 1851.

came to the Ferry was that it was a Poor Shitten arrangemt (to use the vulgar) & that this compay never Should have been Sent on a Mission until a good Road & Ferry had been Made first &c. I felt indignant at the impertinence of the Man."

Brigham Young knew what he was doing when he organized the Arizona Mission, Lee lectured the captain, and Young "does not expect you to be carried through to [Arizona] on Flowry Beds of ease, but to help prepare the way."

None of the pioneers found the expedition a flowery bed of ease. Hamblin's lead party, which he took as far as Moenkopi, quickly became discouraged by the arid country, and all but a few of the group started back for Utah.[20] Members of the two following wagon trains, which went as far south as the Little Colorado, became equally disheartened and turned back.

At his ferry, Lee greeted the first returning stragglers on June 4 and quoted one man as saying he had found "the Litle Colerado dried up & the country a Sandy Desert—nothing But Sand & rock & crooked cotton woods."

A few days later Lee received word that federal officials had discovered his hiding place, which he recently had been so careless in concealing, and that soldiers were coming to arrest him. He fled in June to Moenkopi, remaining there or nearby until he came back to Lonely Dell January 1, 1874. He had no more than a chance to rest his horses, however, for another warning came and five days later he was running again—this time to "Moweabba"—his name for Moenave. During the next ten months there would be other quick, harried visits to Lonely Dell, but he was now truly a fugitive and Moenave was his last refuge.

His new hiding place was a wedge-shaped oasis of cottonwoods and tall poplars, a vivid spot of green at the base of a redrock mesa. From any high point here he could look westward down into a sloping, barren valley and wonder occasionally who the travelers were when far in the distance he saw crawling wagons moving on the Mormon Trail. Somewhere among the trees, which were and are now fed by a clear spring at the mouth of a box canyon, Lee built a rude cabin of two rooms, one of logs and the other of stone. Three tall

[20] James H. McClintock, in *Mormon Settlement in Arizona*, says that John L. Blythe of Salt Lake City "and a number of other missionaries" remained for a time to plant trees and grape vines at Moenkopi and also at Moenave, about six miles west. First permanent Mormon settlement in the Moenkopi–Tuba City region waited until Hamblin brought the James S. Brown party there in December, 1875.

poles set in the ground at front helped to support a brush-and-pole shade projecting from the cabin roof. A stone fireplace heated the one room of logs.

If Lee had been content to remain at Moenave, he might never have been captured. But his restlessness made this impossible, and in Panguitch, Utah, where he came at night to visit one of his wives, he was arrested, on November 7, 1874. At the small Beaver City jail he was held prisoner until his trial the following August. The death penalty was asked, and when the jury returned a divided verdict, Lee was taken to the penitentiary at Salt Lake City.

Jacob Hamblin, during a part of this time, was able to do Lee one last favor. After Lee's arrest and through the winter of 1874–75, Hamblin remained at Lonely Dell to operate Lee's trading post. In his own journal of this period Hamblin is not very informative, mentioning only that he "assisted in carrying on a trade with the Navajoes at Lee's Ferry" and that the Indians by now had built up an extensive trade with the Mormons, "principally in exchanging blankets for horses."

Lee was released on fifteen thousand dollars bail from the Salt Lake penitentiary, May 11, 1876, his freedom lasting until he was brought back to Beaver City for a second trial, beginning September 13. Seven days later an all-Mormon jury found him guilty—nineteen years, exactly, after the crime. Once more held behind bars, Lee spent his remaining months waiting hopelessly, and then was taken back to Mountain Meadows. There, on March 23, 1877, on the same ground where the Fancher party had been slain, Lee was executed by a firing squad.[21]

John Doyle Lee's connection with the massacre, and his death in payment for his part in the affair, raised two questions that have never been satisfactorily answered.

At the time of the attack on the wagon train, Lee was a respected member of the Mormon community. He was a captain of Mormon militia, a sincerely loyal member of his church, a steady if abundantly prolific family patriarch, and a probate judge of Iron County. None of these attributes or attainments, even together, place Lee apart from his fellows or in any way make him an unusual man. He

21 After Lee's death his trading post at Lonely Dell was operated by other Mormons and was "devoted exclusively to the Navajo trade. Old Navajos in the 1930's recalled riding to Lee's Ferry to barter blankets and silverwork for horses, flour, and syrup." Robert M. Utley, "The Reservation Trader in Navajo History," *El Palacio*, Vol. LXVIII, No. 1 (1961).

was, in fact, an entirely usual sort of man—except for five short days in his sixty-four years of life.

Why, then, would such an ordinary man take a leading part in an unprovoked mass killing? Lee asked that question of himself, and his answer is not very helpful. During his last days, while awaiting execution, he dictated, in his "Last Confession," that Isaac Haight had summoned him to Cedar City and told him that the approaching Fancher train "were a rough and abusive set of men . . . that they had insulted, outraged, and ravished many of the Mormon women" in the communities they passed through. Haight then told him, Lee continued, "that it was decided by authorities to arm the Indians, give them provisions and ammunition, and send them after the emigrants, and have the Indians give them a brush, and if they killed part or all of them, so much the better."[22]

Haight's accusations against the emigrants were untrue, and if Lee did not know this at the time, he certainly knew it later. But there was another cause for stirring passions against the Fancher party, not mentioned in the confession.

Not far behind the Fancher train—and this all Mormons knew—was an approaching force of 2,500 United States troops, led by Colonel Albert Sidney Johnston and ordered by President Buchanan to put down any Mormon resistance in Utah to federal law. Approach of the troops raised fear, if not panic, in the minds of Mormons not too far removed from persecutions and cold-blooded slayings of their own people in Ohio and Illinois. The fear may have been transmitted to John Doyle Lee as an impulse to strike out and smash before he himself was hurt.

There is the question, also, of why Lee alone was made to pay for a crime involving many others, and there is no answer.

[22] Andrew Love Neff, *History of Utah, 1847 to 1869* (ed. and annotated by Leland Hargrave Creer).

7

The Contractors

THE SANTA FE CONTRACTORS—operators of the big wholesale supply houses without whom Indian traders could scarcely have existed—trace back more than one hundred years to the Spiegelberg brothers.

As though predestined for his vital role in the Indian trade, Solomon Jacob Spiegelberg joined a caravan in Missouri, crossed over the Santa Fe Trail, and arrived in that thriving town of adobe houses sometime between 1841 and 1848.[1] Both time and country were ripe for unusual men; in 1848, only twenty-four years old, this Solomon Jacob was an unusual young man. He was not long in realizing the

---

[1] The idea that Solomon Jacob Spiegelberg reached Santa Fe in time to join the Doniphan expedition to Chihuahua and then returned to Santa Fe with his regiment to serve as post sutler has been discounted by his grandson, George A. Spiegelberg, who has written: "My knowledge of the subject is, of course, solely based on what my father told me of his father. My father was ordinarily a most accurate man and what he told me was that his father had arrived in Baltimore in 1838 apprenticed to a relative whose name I no longer remember and with whom my grandfather got along not at all, since in the very year in which he arrived, he set out by himself peddling his way westward. At this same time, according to my information, my grandfather was fourteen years of age, having been born in Hanover, Germany in 1824. From 1838 to 1841, grandfather peddled his way west and in the latter year, arrived in Santa Fe where he settled down." (William J. Parish, "The German Jew and the Commercial Revolution in Territorial New Mexico, 1850–1900." *New Mexico Historical Review*, Vol. XXXV, No. 2, [1960].) Solomon Spiegelberg's arrival in Santa Fe as early as 1841 is questioned by Parish (*ibid.*), who says he could not find proof that Solomon reached New Mexico before Colonel Doniphan's regiment, but believes that Solomon was trading in Santa Fe by 1848—perhaps "more than a year or two before."

trade possibilities, beyond the overland caravan trade, of a raw and wanting region that indiscriminately brought together, with the native Indians, the peoples of the Old World and the New, and did not begin to supply the needs of any of them.

Spiegelberg wrote to his younger brothers urging them to leave the family home in Germany and join him. Besides Jacob, there were Lehman, Willi, Levi, and Emanuel, and by 1861 all of them were together, including Jacob's son Abraham. Abe was born in New York in 1848, joining his father and uncles in Santa Fe when he was nine or ten years old.

When the firm of Hockady and Hall established a stage route between Independence, Missouri, and Santa Fe in July, 1857, Levi Spiegelberg was chosen as their Santa Fe representative. As the agent in New Mexico it was Levi's duty to collect travel fare in advance from Missouri-bound passengers: $150 from November 1 to May 1, and $125 from May 1 to November 1; also, to see that the travelers on the stage paid extra if their baggage and bedding exceeded the forty-pound free limit. The stagecoaches were drawn by six-mule teams and under normal conditions required twenty to twenty-five days for the journey. Departures were scheduled on the same day at each end of the route, on the first and fifteenth of each month. As agent for Hockady and Hall, Levi was expected to advise stage riders that they "must conform to the rules which may be established" by the stage driver en route—an awareness of contingencies that might arise on an unnaturally hazardous journey. Levi also was to reassure his passengers that, for their safety, "provision, arms and ammunition [would be] furnished by the proprietors."[2]

The Spiegelberg firm already was well established in a building fronting the capital's old plaza when it advertised in the Santa Fe *Daily New Mexican*, on June 9, 1868:

"Spiegelberg Brothers, Importers, and Wholesale and Retail Dealers in Foreign and Domestic Dry Goods—Clothing, Boots, Shoes, Hardware, Queensware, Liquors, Groceries, etc., etc., etc. . . . Merchants will find it to their advantage to call on us before going East, as we keep on hand an assortment of goods especially adapted to this market and of the adjoining Territories. Two of our firm are permanently in the New York Market purchasing goods; those who deal with us can rely upon our stock being of the best quality and lowest prices."

2 *Western Journal of Commerce*, Kansas City, January 2, 1858.

The family was spreading out. Brother Levi, on returning East, was in charge of the New York branch, which had offices at 132 Church Street. Lehman and Willi, upon the release of the Navahos from Bosque Redondo, secured trader appointments and were off gaining firsthand experience on or near the reservation.

Willi was the first trader at new Fort Wingate when the Navahos, on their long march back from Fort Sumner, reached there in July, 1868, and went into camp. Lehman was waiting to trade with them at Defiance when, in November, the crumbling old army post was opened as their agency and they were allowed to leave Wingate and move to the reservation.[3]

Wingate was a fort in name only as long as Willi remained there (he left the following March, the tradership succeeding to John L. Waters)—more a tent camp than anything else, a few dozen acres aswarm with Indians and blue-coated soldiers. Willi traded through the summer from a tent, over a counter made of planks spread between boxes. A steam sawmill was hauled in that fall, but by the first snow the lumber cut and milled made only temporary shelters for the post's officers and men. Not until 1870 were plans for the fort approved and work was started on the permanent buildings.

Conditions at Defiance Agency were at least as primitive, and during the year he was there Lehman Spiegelberg merely had the consolation of knowing that Major Theodore Dodd, the agent, whom the Navahos called Big Gopher, was as uncomfortable as he was.

The Spiegelbergs were making a reputation as Indian agency contractors when a third member of the family took a fling at trading. Again, the venture did not last long, but while it did, it was without parallel.

A circus wagon, left behind in Santa Fe by a traveling company that evidently had met disaster, was discovered by young Abe Spiegelberg and purchased for him by his uncles. Its gilt paint, fancy scrollwork, and flashing side-panel mirrors made the discarded wagon a vehicle of wondrous beauty. It is possible to imagine Abe sitting high and proudly erect at the glittering prow as he rode grandly among the Río Grande Valley pueblos and out on the Navaho reservation. According to one account: "Its interior was remodeled to transport a full stock of dry-goods, clothing, hats, caps, bacon, ham, jewelry, watches, shoes, rifles, pistols, powder, and bullets. This golden chariot was a blaze of light as the sun reflected from its mirrors and gilding.

---

[3] Willi's Fort Wingate license was issued July 8, 1868, and Lehman's Defiance license on August 28, 1868. (*N. A., Ledgers of Traders.*)

It created excitement among Indians and natives everywhere. This glamorous vehicle even made a trip into Chihuahua."[4]

By the early 1870's, when they founded the Second National Bank of New Mexico in Santa Fe, the Spiegelbergs held a dominant position as agency contractors, challenged by only a few. Among those who were or might become competitive, the firm of Z. Staab and Company, active in Santa Fe since 1860, probably was the foremost. The elder Staab and his brother Adolph also maintained a branch office in New York, at 24–26 White Street. Perhaps next in importance were the firms of Adolph and Bernhard Seligman, Willburn and Stockton, and the young, very promising Charles Ilfeld. With Noa and Bernard Ilfeld, Charles formed an association with the Eldodt trading family—Nathan Eldodt and the brothers, Marcus and Samuel. It was not until later, however, toward the turn of the century, that the Ilfeld firm grew into the powerful organization that it remains.

Even against this opposition a dozen lesser contractors might at any time turn up with a successful bid.[5] Andrew Napier was an interesting member of this aspiring group, not least because he brought down the displeasure of W. F. M. Arny, then agent for the Pueblo tribes. Napier served for a time as agent for Willburn and Stockton and then, in February, 1871, secured a license to trade at Zuñi, Acoma, and Laguna. His license was abruptly suspended a few months later when Arny, stopping at Zuñi, discovered a "vile and wicked traffic" there in whisky and gunpowder. Arny never made it clear whether Napier was engaged in this wickedness, but at least he was suspect.[6]

Before he fell afoul of Arny, Napier—with John Pratt and Bernard Koch—in March, 1871, entered a successful bid for delivering 30,000 pounds of wheat at four and one-half cents a pound, to the Navahos at Defiance Agency. The bid was so low that it is doubtful if Napier came out of it with any gain.

Various factors influenced the outcome of such bids. In February, 1870, Lehman Spiegelberg, Adolph Staab, and Adolph Seligman each

4 *New Mexico Historical Review*, Vol. III, No. 1 (1928).

5 Other contractors operating from Santa Fe or Albuquerque in the 1870's included Frank Chapman; Wendel Debus; Alexander Gusdorf; Gutman, Friedman and Company; D. Bernard Koch; Aaron Michaelis; John Pratt; Charles Probst and Jacob Krummeck; Samuel B. Wheelock and Thomas S. Tucker; Benjamin Schuster; and W. F. Strachan.

6 *Annual Report, C. I. A., 1871.*

entered bids to supply the Hopis with a large shipment of spades, hoes, pickaxes, ax helves, and camp kettles. Staab's bid was the highest, Seligman's the lowest, but the contract was awarded to the Spiegelberg firm—because Lehman assured the quickest delivery.

In March of the same year, on a contract to supply Defiance Agency with 25,000 pounds of wheat, seven contractors entered bids: Lehman Spiegelberg (8¢ lb.), Frank Chapman (7.40¢), Aaron Michaelis (7.03¢), Charles Ilfeld (7¢), Adolph Seligman (6.94¢), Louis Clark (6.75¢), and Z. Staab & Co. (5.75¢). The Staab firm won the contract but later refused to fill it—presumably because the price bid was too low. The contract then was awarded to Seligman.[7]

Apart from the light shed on the personalities involved, interest in such matters rests mainly in discovering the prices paid ninety years ago by the Indian Office to provide food, clothing, and tools for its Indian wards. For the same reason, it is worth noting a bid entered by Lehman Spiegelberg to supply certain annuity goods to the Navahos.[8] Only a few of the items are quoted here:

100	Pairs	Women's Shoes, good quality & assorted sizes	$1.30 pr.
50	"	Boys' Shoes, good quality, No. 5	1.25 pr.
50	"	Misses' " " " , assorted sizes	1.25 pr.
50	"	Children's " " " , out sizes	.85 pr.
600	Pounds	Indigo	1.50 lb.
1,000	"	good Coffee	.18½ lb.
5,000	"	Navy Tobacco	.60 lb.
10,000	"	Flour	6.40¢ lb.

Large contracts usually were issued from the Santa Fe office of the superintendent of Indian affairs. On a few occasions a contract was large enough to require a number of firms to pool their resources. This was the case on March 14, 1871, when Superintendent Nathaniel Pope signed two contracts, naming six Santa Fe firms to supply Defiance Agency with 200,000 pounds of "sound, clean, shelled corn" that would be "put up in good strong sacks containing 100 pounds net each."[9]

7 The three cases cited here are from the files of Maj. William Clinton, superintendent of Indian affairs for New Mexico. (National Archives, Record Group 75, Letters Received, 1870–71.)

8 The list was sent to Arny by Lehman Spiegelberg, April 17, 1875. Correspondence in the file fails to show what action, if any, was taken. *(Ibid.,* Micro. Roll #564, 1875.)

9 *Ibid.,* Micro. Roll # 13, 1870–71.

The amount of the order was divided evenly, Benjamin Schuster, Aaron Michaelis, and Alexander Gusdorf agreeing to deliver 100,000 pounds of corn to the agency between April 10 and May 1, the firms of Bernhard Seligman, Lehman Spiegelberg, and Wendel Debus supplying the remainder between April 15 and May 15.

In this instance the contractors undertook the responsibility and cost of freighting the corn to the reservation, the larger firms maintaining wagons and teams for such a purpose. There were occasions, however, when men independently engaged in freighting were employed by Indian agents or the superintendency. Usually in such cases, freight-hauling was on a contract basis.

There was a time, for example, when Indian Superintendent William Clinton had on hand in Santa Fe 35,000 pounds of agricultural tools and equipment for the Navahos. This was in early May, 1870, and if the tools were to be of any use to the Indians in their spring planting, no time should be lost in their delivery. The respective merits of mules and oxen—argued by wagon-train masters since the opening of the Santa Fe Trail—may have weighed in this case.

Antonio José Luna, of Los Lunas, owner and firm advocate of mules, offered to load his wagons immediately and, without hesitation, promised delivery at Defiance Agency within eighteen days. Luna's bond of $3,000 was assured by Lehman Spiegelberg and one Pablo Delgado. The road Luna would follow would not be easy: a fording of the Río Grande near San Felipe Pueblo or below, thence to Cabezon and over the old Indian trail skirting Mount Taylor to the Wingate Valley, and finally to Defiance—roughly 240 miles. Luna's price was three and one-half cents per pound.

A loyal partisan of the slower but sometimes surer oxen, Joseph Hersch, a Santa Fe freighter, agreed to load a week later and said he would deliver the tools thirty-five days afterward, "provided I am not delayed by Storm, High Water, Muddy roads, loss of Cattle, or other unavoidable accidents."

Hersch's price was lower than Luna's: two and sixty-nine hundredths of a cent a pound. Major Clinton rejected it in favor of Luna's spryer mule teams.[10]

Indian traders themselves ordinarily freighted their own supplies and goods taken in trade, oxen and mules both seeing service until gradually retired during the 1890's by horses.

There were exceptions, of course, Walter Lee Kelly, a Missourian

10 *Ibid.*

who came out to Colorado in 1889, freighted supplies from Durango to the Riverview (later Aneth) trading post when it was owned by Pete and Herman Guillet, as well as to other traders located between Mancos and the San Juan. Kelly drove a six-horse team with a "jerk line" to the lead pair, often hauling more than four tons in his two wagons. It was an eight-day trip between Durango and Aneth, often much longer in bad weather. In rain or snow Kelly at night stowed his bedroll among the freight under the wagon sheet and managed to keep fairly warm and dry. On the return trips, however, when he was carrying hides and wool, Kelly allowed that when he bedded down, it sometimes got a bit smelly.

Some drawbacks attended their dealings with Indian agents and traders, and the one most exasperating to the Santa Fe contractors, which reached its most aggravated level about 1875, was the system of vouchers introduced by the Indian Office several years before. Always provided by Congress with less money than needed, agents of the Indian Office more often than they liked were completely without funds when confronted by some emergency, or even the routine meeting of an agency payroll. In this way, the voucher—or I.O.U. slip—came into currency, and usually, in the end, the contractors were the ones left holding them for collection.

Navaho Agent Arny knew as well as any man the embarrassment of finding his coffers empty when there was a most urgent need for money. Entertaining the chiefs and head men when they visited the agency seemed urgent enough, and to this end Arny ran up a bill of $170.70 with Defiance trader Henry Reed between October, 1873, and March, 1874. Such a transaction had been prohibited by the Indian Office a few years earlier, but more important, Arny obviously felt, was supplying his Navaho visitors with coffee, tobacco, shucks (cigarette papers), sugar, flour, and crackers. And when he decided to settle this account, Arny gave Reed a voucher for the amount owed and Reed promptly assigned the voucher to Z. Staab and Company of Santa Fe in return for trade goods. Staab at the same time accepted another voucher from Reed, in the amount of $53, which Reed had received from Arny when he supplied fodder for the agency animals.

Neither of these vouchers was in any way unusual except that Staab, in turn, forwarded them to the commissioner of Indian affairs in May and payment was allowed three weeks later. As Staab himself must have felt, such promptness was remarkable.[11] Scarcely a

11 Letters from Staab to C. I. A., and accompanying vouchers, May 7, 1874. (Ibid., Letters Received, #10710 and #10717, 1874.)

month later Staab experienced the more customary delay when he sent the commissioner six more vouchers totaling $881.25. Payment was not allowed until five years later.

All but one of these vouchers were issued by the farmer-in-charge at Abiquiu Agency, Chandler Robbins, who evidently sensed an urgent need among the Jicarilla Apaches and Capote and Wiminuche Utes for whom he was responsible. The chits were written for food, clothing, guncaps, lead, and gunpowder because, said Robbins, "the heavy fall of snow [of spring, 1874] made the roads impassable" and because the Indians "were in a half starving condition." The sixth voucher was issued by Arny to onetime agency employee and Indian trader Perry H. Williams, for sixty dollars' worth of grain.[12]

Delay in honoring vouchers might occur before the notes ever reached Washington, since they first required the endorsement of the superintendent of Indian affairs in Santa Fe. Thus, in July, 1874, Thomas Keam's brother Will wrote to Superintendent Dudley: "Please turn over to Messrs. Spiegelberg Bros. the vouchers you hold in my favor for services as Temporary Clerk from Feby, to May 12th 1873, and oblige."[13]

During the short regime of Navaho Agent W. F. Hall, and before Hall was replaced by Arny, Will Keam was employed at Defiance Agency for a little more than four months. His salary as clerk for this period was paid by Hall in part in the form of vouchers, and as Keam's letter indicates, more than a year had passed while he waited for the superintendent's endorsement.

Hall and Arny both evidently had some difficulty in finding money to pay their employees. The Spiegelberg firm, acting as a clearing house for Defiance Agency, accepted dozens of payroll vouchers issued by the two agents, one group of notes forwarded to Washington amounting to $2,360 for the period April, 1873, to June, 1874. The situation, which could have pleased no one, is seen in better perspective when one considers that the agent's annual salary (not paid by vouchers) was only $1,500.

12 *Ibid.*, #10731, 1874. Unlike the Navahos, who with their planting and sheep did much to subsist themselves, the Utes refused all inducements that would lead them to farming. Instead of sheep they collected large pony herds and—apart from occasional rations issued at the agency—lived mainly by hunting. Largely for this reason the Indian Office made an exception in the Utes' case and regularly supplied them with firearms and ammunition.

13 Will Keam was paid $176.66 for his services as temporary clerk at Defiance, January 1 to February 22, 1873. The vouchers his letter refers to were in payment of his salary from February 23 to May 12. (*Ibid.*, Micro. Roll #563, 1874.)

Don Fernando de Taos, a view from the south, probably drawn about
1848–49, artist unknown. *(U. S. Signal Corps, National Archives.)*

Santa Fe and vicinity, seen from the east, drawn by R. H. Kern to
accompany Lt. James H. Simpson's 1849 report, "Route from Fort
Smith to Santa Fe."

Lee's Ferry. An undated photograph, probably taken about 1910, shows the overhead cable-and-winch used in crossing the Colorado. *(Utah Historical Society.)*

Facing page: Lonely Dell, John D. Lee's home in Marble Canyon. One of his log cabins is visible, lower right, among the cottonwoods. The Paria River flows at the base of the pink cliffs, joining the Colorado off the picture at the right.

Views of Fort Wingate, New Mexico, above, looking northeast into Wingate Valley, and Fort Defiance, Arizona, below, the Navaho agency at Canyon Bonito. In the Defiance photograph, the crumbling adobes of the old fort and traders' quarters form a rough quadrangle. Ben Wittick made both these photographs, probably in the late 1880's and early 1890's. *(Museum of New Mexico.)*

Keam's Ranch, Arizona. The seated man, possibly Thomas Keam himself, surveys part of the trader's extensive group of buildings— these evidently farm dwellings upstream from Keam's home and trading post. Ben Wittick's undated photograph was probably taken about 1890. (*Museum of New Mexico.*)

Keam's central group of buildings in the canyon, photographed by Ben Wittick about 1890, when they had become a school for Hopi children. No trace remains today of buildings or trees, and the wash runs in an arroyo forty feet deep. *(Museum of New Mexico.)*

Thomas Varker Keam, an oil portrait painted at Keams Canyon
in November, 1890, by Julian Scott, A.N.A. *(Hubbell Collection,
Ganado.)*

View in Keams Canyon, a Wittick photograph of about 1890. The building in the right foreground may be Keam's second post in the canyon, and in the central background is probably his second home there. *(Museum of New Mexico.)*

In Washington, the strain was felt to some degree by the Indian Office, which could only plead with an otherwise preoccupied Congress for more adequate appropriations. Commissioner E. P. Smith was certainly not overjoyed in the spring of 1874 when he received from Lehman Spiegelberg a voucher in the amount of $5,005.55, originally issued to one Estanislas Montoya for supplying the Southern Apache Agency with 100,000 pounds of flour. Commissioner Smith was in the same predicament as his agent: his office simply lacked funds enough to make the payment. A memorandum on a covering paper attached to Lehman's letter in this matter indicates that the Montoya voucher was referred to the Board of Indian Commissioners in April, 1877, and to the government auditor in April, 1880. Final disposition of the claim is not shown.

On other occasions in 1874, both Lehman and Willi Spiegelberg inquired of Commissioner Smith when drafts for overdue payments might be expected. Lehman's interest concerned a voucher for $9,679 for cattle supplied by his firm to the Navaho agency; Willi wondered when the Indian Office would honor vouchers in the amount of $4,400 for 2,200 sheep supplied to the Hopi Indians.

Replying to Willi, the harassed commissioner wrote that because his appropriations were exhausted, "there are no funds now at the disposal of the Department that can be used in settlement of this account and will not be until the necessary provisions therefor shall have been made by Congress."[14]

Viewing these frustrations in the context of the times, it should be remembered that the interest of Congress and of the people centered then on subjugating the Plains tribes. The welfare of a few thousand reservation Indians in the Southwest weighed as a dram, in the country's mind, against the fascinating cavalry operations against the Sioux and Cheyennes, the Arapahoes, Kiowas, and Comanches.

Santa Fe, Defiance Agency, Abiquiu, and Oraibi all seemed dim light years away from the dome of the nation's capitol. Of course, the contractors were serving a useful purpose, but to a part of official Washington their activities may also have seemed an annoyance.

---

[14] A copy of Smith's letter, February 17, 1874, is enclosed with a later inquiry Willi made in the same matter, August 13, 1874. (*Ibid.*)

8

Solomon Bibo

INDIAN TRADING mainly was an island of loneliness reefed by hardships and small profits. The life required resourcefulness and courage of ordinary men but rarely demanded a gifted imagination. Few traders, no matter how well endowed with other traits, were men of vision. There were exceptions, of course, and among these Solomon Bibo was one of the most imaginative men ever to trade in the Southwest.

Following his brother Simon, who eleven years before was licensed to trade at Laguna Pueblo, Solomon Bibo in December, 1882, installed himself at neighboring Acoma. Sixty miles west of Albuquerque, occupying a mesa-top four hundred feet above the surrounding prairie, the Sky City of Acoma was first seen by a white man in 1540—by Captain Hernando de Alvarado, of Coronado's command. The people of Acoma thereafter tasted Spanish iron so cruelly and often that they formed a lasting aversion for most men of the white race.[1]

Such hostility as may have greeted Solomon Bibo upon his arrival he soon overcame, however, after applying first for the favor and sympathy of the pueblo's Indian governor, Martín Balle.

[1] The largest pueblo of the Keresan linguistic group, Acoma has maintained a population of 1,500 or slightly less since Spanish times. Occupied for at least one thousand years, Acoma disputes with the Hopi village of Oraibi the claim to being the longest continuously occupied village in the United States. The name Acoma derives from the native *Akóme*, or "people of the white rock." Their name for the town is *A'ko*. Since Solomon Bibo's time, the majority of the people have abandoned the mesa pueblo and now live in or near the settlements of McCarty's and Acomita.

Meager profits that he might make as a trader evidently interested Bibo but little. In the spring of 1884 he obtained Martín Balle's signature to a lease giving him thirty-year title to the entire 95,792 acres of the Acoma reservation. Specifically, the lease granted to Bibo all grazing and water rights, exclusive rights to mine for coal on the reservation, and the option to assign to others any or all of the rights for the full term of the agreement.

In return for these truly remarkable concessions, Bibo agreed to pay the pueblo of Acoma an annual rental of forty dollars, or about four-tenths of one cent an acre. He agreed also to pay a royalty of ten cents a ton for any coal he should mine and stipulated that the Acoma people might continue to graze their stocks and irrigate and cultivate the fields on land now under lease to himself.[2]

Word of this private transaction between Bibo and Acoma's governor soon reached Pueblo Agent Pedro Sánchez, in Santa Fe, causing that worthy man to explode in anger. To him the lease was a "complete and bold falsification" defrauding the pueblo of Acoma. He wrote at once to the Indian Office, outlining the situation and asking how he should proceed.

The lease was obtained "by undue influence exercised by Bibo, and does not represent the will of the Pueblo in common," Sánchez assured Commissioner Price. At the same time the agent was aware that a pueblo's governor was allowed unusual authority, amounting almost to one-man rule. True, above Martín Balle was the pueblo's cacique, or chief officer of the village's religious affairs, and three head men or *principales* chosen by the cacique. But Governor Balle, appointed by the cacique and *principales*, was the executive officer of the pueblo and a ruler without whose order nothing could be done.

With nice regard for the legal traps that presently would involve him, Commissioner Price replied that Bibo's lease was valid, providing it had been obtained with the advice and consent of the *principales*. And if not?

"If it was not so executed, or if the lease was obtained by undue influence, misrepresentation, collusion, or fraud," Commissioner Price added, "then I think a court . . . would . . . set it aside."[3]

---

[2] Terms of the lease are contained in a letter from C. I. A. Hiram Price to Pueblo Agent Sánchez, June 28, 1884. (National Archives, Record Group 75, Letters Sent, 1884, #8717.) Bibo agreed to a rental of $300 for the first ten years, $400 for the next ten years, and $500 a year for the final ten years—a total of $1,200 or slightly more than four mills an acre.

[3] *Ibid.*

The commissioner instructed Sánchez to inform Bibo that regardless of legal hair-splitting, the Indian Office would not tolerate this land grab. Bibo must surrender his lease immediately or forfeit his trader's license. Sánchez, meanwhile, should find out if the people of Acoma realized that "under such a lease they actually surrender possession of their lands for an entire generation for a mere nominal sum of money, with the prospect of their being overrun with cattle, torn up by prospectors for minerals, and innundated with a foreign population, all of which are not only possible but probable."

Before Bibo could be found and informed of Price's views, a rival of his for the Indian trade took part in a little drama played at McCarty's Station, a hillside stop on the Atlantic and Pacific Railroad where the Acoma Indians were putting up small adobe buildings and establishing a farming community. Robert G. Marmon, trading at Laguna Pueblo since 1873 and after that with his brother Walter at both Laguna and Acoma, appeared as witness when Governor Balle swore that Bibo had obtained his lease by misrepresenting its terms.

Present at the meeting at Agent Sánchez' request, but in his own right eager to have Bibo's scheme blocked, Marmon stood by as agency interpreter L. G. Read penned an affidavit of two paragraphs —a statement by the governor which Balle promptly stepped forward to sign with his mark.

He signed the lease, the Governor said, with "the understanding that it was only for three years and *not* for thirty years; that it was *so* made known to me. That the will of my Pueblo was not consulted in this case in any way. That no meeting was held for this purpose, either public or private, and that I never understood to convey any coal."[4]

Armed with this statement, Agent Sánchez next called a meeting of some sixty Acoma Indians, including Governor Balle and a number of the pueblo's head men. José Paisano, a native of Laguna, interpreted as the agent explained the purpose of his being there and then read to them the terms of Bibo's lease. There were mutterings of surprise and indignation as he proceeded, and at the end the meeting broke into an uproar when Sánchez, after a dramatic pause, asked loudly if any of those present had agreed to leasing their reservation to the trader Bibo.

4 Governor Balle's affidavit, dated July 10, 1884, is enclosed with a letter from Sánchez to Price, July 14, 1884. (National Archives, Record Group 75, Letters Received, 1884, #13722.)

Only Martín Balle remained silent as the others rose and pressed forward, angrily denying any previous knowledge of the agreement. When the clamor subsided Sánchez turned to Balle with the question: "What do you know about that lease? Have you signed that paper which I have just read to you?"

The Governor in reply repeated substantially his remarks taken under oath before Robert Marmon. And asked further by Sánchez if he would have signed the lease had he understood it was for a term of thirty years, Balle answered: "Then I would not have signed it for all the money in the world."[5]

Before returning to Santa Fe Agent Sánchez located Solomon Bibo, who insisted that his lease was legally binding and therefore refused to cancel it. His refusal brought a brusque order from Commissioner Price to Sánchez: "You will therefore immediately notify Mr. Bibo that his licenses [for McCarty's Station and Acoma Pueblo] have been revoked, and that he must cease his trade and remove with his stock of goods . . . from the reservation on or before the 20th proximo."[6]

If Solomon Bibo protested this action, there is no evidence of it in the Indian Office records. Nor is there any indication that he communicated at any time with Commissioner Price in the matter of the disputed lease. An appeal was made in his behalf, however, to General Whittlesey, secretary of the Board of Indian Commissioners. Some months previously the General had met the Bibo brothers while visiting Acoma in the company of Albert K. Smiley, another commissioner. And now Simon Bibo, remembering that Whittlesey had been friendly, wrote asking for his intervention.

The Marmon brothers of Laguna were the cause of this trouble, Simon wrote.[7] It was they who first thought of leasing Acoma land— the choicest part, in return for which they would give the pueblo one cow a year for ten years. Solomon Bibo was consulted by the Indians, Simon continued, and he told them "he thought one cow was very little pay." He offered them instead his own lease. Agent Pedro Sánchez approved, at first, until the Marmons went sneaking behind Solomon's back and turned the agent's head.

All three, the Marmons and Sánchez, then intimidated the poor

5 This meeting also was held at McCarty's Station. The quotations are from Sánchez' report of the affair to Price in the letter referred to above.

6 Letter from Price to Sánchez, July 25, 1884. (*Ibid.*, Letters Sent, 1884, #10028.)

7 Letter from Simon Bibo to E. Whittlesey, July 23, 1884. (*Ibid.*, Letters Received, 1884, #14660.)

old governor, Martín Balle, taking advantage of his fear to secure his mark to a trumped-up statement discrediting the Bibo lease. Further, said Simon Bibo, Sánchez had called a meeting of Acoma Indians at McCarty's Station, and a pure mockery it had turned out to be, for Sánchez had bullied the Indians and threatened them with punishment if they did not tear up the lease.

"The Governor and his entire people repudiate the action of Agt. Sanchez and go so far as to say they can dispense with him entirely since he has so falsely represented the lease that they voluntarily signed and so thoroughly then and now endorse," Simon Bibo wrote.

He was under the impression, Simon added, that "no ordinary authority" could prevent his brother from trading with the Acomas, as long as they wanted him as trader, and as long as Solomon complied with the laws of the Territory. To deprive the pueblo of Solomon's good services would be an injustice to the Acomas "because the men, women and children love him as they would love a father, and he is in the same manner attached to them."

Simon enclosed with the letter a petition addressed to Commissioner Price and purportedly signed by Governor Balle and one hundred Acomas.[8] A curious document, written in ink on a fragile, yard-long sheet of bright yellow tissue paper, it begged that the commissioner "will not revoke the Traders License granted Mr. Solomon Bibo . . . for he has assisted us in a great many important matters and he has always . . . proved himself our friend. And the lease which Mr. Pedro Sanchez . . . claims to have been taken from us by fraud, we hereby sustain and protect in every particular."

Eleven days had passed since Martín Balle put his mark to the statement that the Bibo lease was fraudulent. Various pressures or considerations in the interval may have caused him to change his mind, but in any case the Governor now was committed to the agree-

[8] Dated July 21, 1884, the petition—including signatures—is written entirely in the hand of Justice of the Peace Margarito Baca. The customary mark made by an Indian appears with only two of the names. Perhaps a coincidence, but if so an interesting one, the names José Antonio and Juan Pedro each appear twice, Juan Esteban and Juan Rey three times, and the name San Juan six times. *(ibid.,* enclosure.) Walter Marmon thought the petition was as fraudulent as Bibo's lease: "The Indians were asked their names—they did not know what for; they did make their marks. The justice of the peace *did not know what the petition was, nor was it explained to the Indians in his presence.* One Indian and his wife who opposed the lease were thrown into jail by the governor. . . . The Indians *are all* opposed to the lease with the exception of the governor and his clique and they still tell the people that the lease does not cover the entire Acoma grant, but that portion West of McCarty's." (Letter from Marmon to Sánchez, July 31, 1884. *Ibid.,* #14852, enclosure.)

ment. Whether his people liked it or not, their reservation would be leased to Solomon Bibo for thirty years.

Far removed from the scene, at his summer place in Massachusetts, General Whittlesey sent a brief note to Commissioner Price upon receiving Simon Bibo's letter. "We were kindly welcomed at Acoma," he said, referring to his recent visit there, "and our impressions of him were favorable. He seemed to be dealing fairly with the Indians, and truly interested in their welfare. . . . I know nothing of the lease of which [Simon] Bibo speaks. As at present informed I think a change in the tradership there would be annoying to those Indians."[9]

Solomon's interest in the Acomas' welfare—which in other matters may have been sincere—soon manifested itself. He subleased his Acoma grazing rights to the Saint and Cleland cattle company, an accommodation no doubt planned weeks before, and on July 31, 1884, a train of thirty-four cars of Saint and Cleland cattle stopped and unloaded at McCarty's Station.

"Whatever is done should be done quickly," Walter Marmon advised Agent Sánchez. "As I write the empty cars are passing back to Albuquerque. . . . It is the most infernal, damnable, high-handed outrage that was ever attempted. If you need a force to assist you to put the intruders off the Acoma land you can get it *here*."[10]

Force would not be used, but the Indian Office would try by every legal means to restore the reservation to the Acomas. The acting attorney general of the Justice Department instructed the United States attorney for New Mexico "to take such steps as he may deem advisable." And on August 2, Agent Sánchez informed Commissioner Price that Bibo had been notified that his license had been revoked and he must leave the reservation.

Between the neighboring pueblos of Acoma and Laguna there existed a long tradition of friendly relations, never seriously strained since the time of an angry dispute over possession of a painting of St. Joseph. The picture had been brought to Acoma mission about 1629 and since then had been believed by the Indians to have marvelous powers to inspire good fortune. Borrowed by Laguna in a period of drought and stress, it was not returned for more than twenty-five years, until a war between the pueblos was averted by a court order in 1857 restoring the painting to Acoma.

But now the two villages were again locked in controversy, each

9 Bibo to Whittlesey, July 23, 1884. (*Ibid.*, #14660, enclosure.)
10 Letter from Marmon to Sánchez, July 31, 1884. (*Ibid.*, #14852, enclosure.)

accusing the other of invading its grazing lands. Most at issue was a strip of government land separating the reservations, claimed by the Lagunas and now overrun by sheep, horses, and cattle of both pueblos. Clearly, to all, the dispute arose from Solomon Bibo's assigning his lease to the Saint and Cleland cattle company.

"These frequent quarrels between the Acoma and Laguna Indians are evidently the direct result of the lease," Agent Sánchez reported in November, 1884.[11] "It appears to me that the Acomas are the aggressors for the reason that they are constantly under the influence of Saint & Cleland or their paid agent, Solomon Bibo, either of whom I believe would not hesitate to incite the Indians to mischief if he could be the gainer thereby."

He was well satisfied, Sánchez continued, "that the chief men of the Acomas are the frequent recipients of presents from these men. Not long ago Mr. Cleland, himself, told me that he was intending to give Martin [Balle] . . . six fine bulls to improve his stock."

On November 18, when the validity of Bibo's lease was to be tested in Valencia County Court at Los Lunas, U. S. District Attorney George W. Prichard, counsel for the Indians, "was particularly conspicuous for his absence." A settlement then was further impeded when Bibo's counsel filed a motion to compel Prichard "to disclose by what authority he [represented] the Indians" of Acoma—arguing that because Pueblo Indians were citizens of the United States, action in their behalf could not be brought to court unless initiated by them and paid for by them.

Prichard did show up when the question was presented to the presiding judge at Santa Fe in January, 1885, but was unable to explain his authority in the matter further than to say that he appeared for Acoma, not under retainer by the Indians, but by the direction of the attorney general of the United States. Knowing well that he had been backed into a corner, Prichard requested time and, this granted, communicated with Washington to ask for instructions. But before there was further action, Prichard resigned.

If the people of Acoma realized that they were being defrauded, and a majority of them probably did, their tribal organization and total ignorance of white man's legal procedures combined against their acting independently of or counter to the personal interests of Governor Balle. With Agent Sánchez their relations were formal, not close, and even if Sánchez had remained in office he could not have

---

[11] Letter from Sánchez to Price, November 26, 1884. (*Ibid.*, #23016.)

provided the counsel they needed to resist or deny their governor. But Sánchez was replaced as agent by Dolores Romero at this time, and Romero knew nothing of the case and perhaps cared less.

This was the situation that confronted James Bell when he succeeded Prichard as United States attorney early in 1885. He was powerless to act, Bell informed Attorney General A. H. Garland in June, because "a suit must be brought directly by their [Acoma's] authority, and not . . . simply by the authority of the general Government"—and the citizens of Acoma, leaderless and confused, were not prepared to sue anyone.[12]

And so the case against Bibo's lease lapsed and died.

Saint and Cleland cattle grazed over the Acoma reservation, and no doubt onto Laguna land, unhindered, and Solomon Bibo, without further challenge, remained in the vicinity to see the Indian Office veer in its policy and consent officially to possible piracy on the Indian lands.

Commissioner John H. Oberly was the instrument of this new policy in 1888 when he observed that Attorney General Garland found the leasing of Indian lands for grazing purposes was "illegal unless there was specific treaty or statutory provision for such leasing," but, "So long as grazing grounds are increasingly in demand, and there is no law prohibiting the use of Indian lands for grazing purposes, cattle owners will continue to make arrangements with Indians for obtaining grazing privileges; and so long as there is no law authorizing such arrangements the Department can give no approval thereof."[13]

In short, Commissioner Oberly was under pressure. He wanted a nice little law that would circumvent the government's "as long as the grass shall grow" treaties with Indians.

"I recommend," said Oberly, "legislation that will authorize such leases. Many tribes would be benefitted thereby."

12 Letter from Bell to A. H. Garland, June 17, 1885. (*Ibid.*, 1885.)
13 *Annual Report, C. I. A., 1888.*

9

Thomas Keam: 1846-1872

H E W A S something of a paradox: a squaw man equally at ease, and voluble, in an Arizona hogan as in calling upon a Washington big-wig; disliked and feared by some officials of the Indian Office; generous host or informed friend to stray wayfarers and scientists; an outspokenly honest and intelligent partisan of Indians, a foe of self-serving political humbuggery. An Englishman, he was one of the ablest, best-known traders in the Southwest. His early years, which concern us at the moment, may be considered in terms of an interesting apprenticeship.

Thomas Varker Keam was born in 1846 in the coastal town of Truro, in Cornwall, England. While still a boy he signed on as a midshipman in the English mercantile marine. His ship sailed to Sidney and Newcastle, Australia; sometime later he turned up in San Francisco, finished with the sea. Traveling overland across the California and Arizona deserts, he came, in 1865, to Santa Fe. He was a slender young fellow of just better than average height, sandy hair lying flat and brushed at a right angle to a high-domed fore-head. When he joined the First New Mexico Volunteer Cavalry, he sported a cavalryman's drooping mustache.

He served for a year and a half, the War Department's impersonal records, beginning with his enlistment in Company E at Fort Bascom on February 18, 1865, revealing an engagingly clear insight to his personality.[1]

1 A relatively modest complex of adobe and brick buildings, Fort Bascom was built on the south bank of the Canadian River, some ten miles north of present

His qualities of leadership were acknowledged with his immediate appointment as a second lieutenant and by his subsequent assignment as company commander—this at the age of twenty, when his troop was often in the field against the Comanches and Kiowas.

His fiery belief in a personal concept of justice and his rebellion against superior authority that crossed this belief are demonstrated by his fall from grace for "seditious conduct." For stirring revolt among his fellows, for complaining against the "tyrannical" treatment of his commanding officer, he was tossed into the brig for three months.[2] His sins were forgiven, it appears, because after his release from custody, and when his company was operating from Fort Stanton in Apache country, he was placed again at the head of E Troop. He was post adjutant when he was mustered out in September, 1866, the good wishes of his superior officers going with him.

Within a year after the treaty of 1868 released the Navahos from Bosque Redondo, Keam became Spanish interpreter for Agent Frank Tracy Bennett at Fort Defiance at a salary of $500 a year.[3]

Tucumcari, New Mexico, and began active service August 15, 1863. Authorized by Brig. Gen. James H. Carleton as a deterrent to raids by the Comanches and Kiowas, the fort was named for Union Capt. George N. Bascom, Sixteenth U. S. Infantry, killed at the battle of Valverde. Five miles west of the fort and immediately outside the military reservation, a civilian town was staked out and appropriately dubbed Liberty by the troops, who frequented its saloons and gambling halls. Fort Bascom's commander at the time Keam was stationed there was Maj. E. H. Bergmann, a strict disciplinarian. Infraction of rules under this man brought harsh punishment. Soldiers might be hung by their thumbs for hours at a time or ordered to march from dawn to dusk around the fort's flagpole, carrying a four-foot length of a heavy green log on their shoulders. Fort Bascom was abandoned in December, 1870, when the garrison and stores were transferred to Fort Union. (James Monroe Foster, Jr., "Fort Bascom, New Mexico," *New Mexico Historical Review*, Vol. XXXV, No. 9 [1960].)

2 "Charge 1st. Seditious Conduct. Specification. In this that 2nd Lieut. Thos. V. Keams did try to excite, or being accessory thereto, or caused to be raised discontentedness & dissastisfaction among the officers of Fort Bascom N. Mex. against their comdg. officer Major E. H. Bergmann 1st Cavl. N. M. Vols. & did without cause or provocation complain to the officers of the ill treatment confered upon him by the comdg. officer and did cause and invite the officers to a meeting for the purpose of deliberating upon what should be done about the comdg. officer who he said had treated the officers of the Post unjustly and tyrannically.

"All this at or near Fort Bascom N Mx on or about the 20th day of July 1865

"Charge 2nd. Violation of the 34 Article of War. Specification. In this that 2nd Lieut. Thos. V. Keams did complain to the officers of Fort Bascom N. Mx about the ill treatment confered upon him by the commanding officer Major E. H. Bergmann and did not make his grievance known to, nor did he ask any redress from his comdg. officer. All this at or near Fort Bascom N. Mx. during the month of July 1865." (National Archives, War Records Division, Thomas Varker Keam file.)

3 Records of the Indian Office, National Archives, show that Keam's appointment as Spanish interpreter was dated February 1, 1869.

Captain Bennett was short of help and more accustomed to military affairs than running an Indian agency. He found Keam an obliging interpreter; by June, 1870, all agency letters going out over Bennett's signature were in Keam's handwriting. Bennett returned to military duty early in 1871, to be succeeded as agent by James H. Miller, a quiet, capable veteran of the Civil War. Soon afterward Keam applied for appointment as special agent, a request that was not granted.[4] But as he had for Bennett, he continued as interpreter and ex officio clerk and letter-writer for Miller.

Pueblo Agent W. F. M. Arny provided a break in this monotony when he appeared at Defiance Agency on May 18 breathing imprecations upon stupid Indian officials and villainous Indian traders. Miller's failure to keep his Navahos on the reservation, Arny implied, accounted in measure for Arny's present difficulty: the reopening of a bloody feud between Navahos and the neighboring Pueblos.

Two of Miller's wandering charges were responsible, said Arny, having robbed and killed two Zuñis; in retaliation the Zuñis applied their own version of an Old Testament rule and killed two Navahos. And just a short time since, off to the west, six more raiding Navahos so enraged the Hopis that warriors of one village—Oraibi, it is said—seized the six and hurled them to death on the rocks below their mesa. Barboncito, head chief of the Navahos and first to sign the treaty of 1868, had died on March 16.[5] Perhaps in a small way this contributed to the Navahos' unruliness, Arny wasn't sure. Miller's laxity in the matter, and that is what Arny called it, only aggravated the feud.

Miller suffered Arny's criticism quietly, complying with the tall, irascible man's request that several Navaho head men be sent with him to Zuñi for a peace council. Keam, meeting Arny for the first time,

[4] Bennett was succeeded by Miller, one of the best agents the Navahos ever had, on February 3, 1871. A native of Huntington County, Pa., Miller enlisted and served for three years in the Civil War with the Fifty-fifth Pennsylvania Volunteers, much of that time as a lieutenant. Keam requested appointment as special agent in a letter to Superintendent of Indian Affairs Nathaniel Pope, stationed at Santa Fe, February 15, 1871. (National Archives, Records of the N. M. Superintendency of Indian Affairs, 1849–80. Letters Received. 1870–71.)

[5] Letter from Miller to Superintendent Pope, March 17, 1871. (*Ibid.*) Death came after an illness of eighty-seven days. Juero Cantadone (or Herrero) was elected to succeed Barboncito at a council of principal chiefs and head men in April. The principal chief of the Navaho tribe, acting more or less in concert with lesser chiefs and head men, governed more by influence than actual authority. Two years after this date the two most influential leaders of the tribe were Ganado Mucho and Manuelito.

joined the group as Spanish interpreter, as did the Mexican-Navaho half blood, Jesús Arviso, who was Miller's Navaho interpreter.

At the Spanish-speaking pueblo, Keam had a part in bringing the angry factions almost to an amicable settlement, but not before old wounds were salted. Zuñi outcries against the recent murders were answered by the Navahos in this way: true, there was bad blood between the *Diné* (Navahos) and *Naasht'ezhi* (Zuñis), and so it had been for as long as the grandfathers could remember. But stop a minute. Had not the Zuñis joined with Mexicans in massacring Navaho women and children at Canyon del Muerto in 1805? And before Bosque Redondo, had Zuñis not served as scouts for Kit Carson? Also this: What of the massacre in Zuñi Pueblo of one hundred Navaho captives in 1863?

As the Navaho words were translated into Spanish words the story came out once more, for all to hear:

Tired of holding their prisoners longer, unwilling to feed them longer, the Zuñi captors grimly offered the Navahos a chance at freedom. The hundred captives, stripped all but naked, were led to the center of the walled, terraced pueblo and were told to escape—if they could—and in the open plaza were unbound, free to run. In Arny's words, upon hearing of this: "Alas! but a poor chance. The town is constructed with houses from five to seven stories high, streets and alley-ways narrow, and difficult to find a way out unless well acquainted with them . . . at each corner were placed a couple of Zuñi warriors, armed with clubs and knives."[6]

Memory of it was bitter. The captives fled blindly toward any corner that promised an opening, a way out, only to be cut down. Not one of them escaped.

For their part the Zuñis related cruelties inflicted upon them by the Navahos, exchanging old grievances until the cause of present troubles was confused. Even so, the talk seemed to have done some good. On May 29 the governor and principal men of Zuñi returned with Arny and Keam to Fort Defiance, and the council was continued there to an eventual agreement. Property stolen by the Navahos from the Zuñis would be returned and hereafter both sides would try to keep the peace.

A similar council was arranged for the Hopis with their agent, W. D. Crothers, and Arny departed, but not before reporting on these and other grave matters.[7] Shortly before the council at Zuñi,

6 *Annual Report, C. I. A., 1871.*
7 Crothers was only a part-time, and absentee, agent for the Hopis, 1871–72. He

he had found at Acoma Pueblo a party of southern Apaches and some Navahos trading in the Sky City for arms and ammunition. He ordered the Acomas to cease this trade, Arny told Superintendent Pope, and now would go even further: "My opinion is that all traders should be prohibited from trading in the villages of Acoma, Laguna and Zuñi for the present. . . . All the troubles in these three pueblos arise from the furnishing of whiskey to the Indians. . . . Last court we did succeed in having one man convicted—but alas! he was only sentenced to *one day's* imprisonment and a fine of *twenty-five dollars*!!!"[8]

His investigations of recent months had convinced him, Arny said, "that the whole system of trade as heretofore carried on in these villages by citizens is wrong and that the traders are a great source of evil . . . as they furnish whiskey and ammunition to the Pueblo Indians and in turn they trade the ammunition to the Apaches and Comanches who use it in their wars against the settlements."

Keam may have heard Arny express similar views when chance brought them together again later in the summer. A Navaho had run off a bunch of Navaho horses and traded them at Acoma; from here the horses were traded to Mexicans. And now Arny, with Keam's help, was attempting to recover them. Small in itself, it was an incident that brought these two together again that they might test each other—interesting only because of the deep rancor that split them apart later.

Keam's effectiveness in treating with the Indians caused Agent Miller, in September, to send him out to another trouble area. With the interpreter Arviso and Chief Narbono, he traveled seventy miles southeast of the reservation to Canyon Juantafoya. Here, in a small Spanish settlement buried in the hills above Cebolleta, Mexicans some time before had killed two of Narbono's men. Reprisals followed, and feelings on both sides were growing worse. In a council with the principal men of Juantafoya, Narbono spoke his grievances, and, as always, there was something to be said on the other side.

With more than his usual authority as interpreter and as the personal representative of Agent Miller, Keam mediated the dispute. It was agreed in the end that Navahos hereafter would not steal the

---

was based at Fort Defiance and gave little attention to the Hopi villages. As Pueblo agent, Arny's jurisdiction was over the Río Grande villages and Laguna, Acoma, and Zuñi.

[8] Letter from Arny to Pope, May 31, 1871. (National Archives, Records N. M. S., Letters Received. 1870–71.)

Mexicans' sheep or graze their ponies on the land of Juantafoya; in return, for the two Navaho dead the village would pay to the families so many sheep and so many horses.

Upon their return to Defiance, Agent Miller reported: "They succeeded in making an amicable settlement of the affair and the Indians are much pleased."[9] In recognition of Keam's services, Miller promoted him from interpreter to agency clerk, with an increase in salary to $700 a year.

His task was more routine, late in November, when Keam and his friend, the gruff Anson C. Damon, agency butcher since Fort Sumner days, were called upon to help distribute annuity goods.

Well in advance of the distribution, Indian families poured into the agency compound from every direction, coming by the hundreds until the old parade ground and all approaches to Canyon Bonito were restless moving pools flashing with bright silver and the color of their dress and blankets. By November 23, when the first goods were doled out, the crumbling agency buildings seemed in danger of falling into dust under the milling Navaho ponies and swarming humanity. Annuity tickets were given to each man and woman, to be surrendered on receipt of goods and prevent the more eager from going through the line more than once, and then the slow process of distribution began.

Keam's job now, after checking Miller's purchase orders against the invoices, was to see that each Indian received an equal or fair share, the goods amounting in value to about five dollars a person. Boxes and crates were spilled open to disgorge a fantastic array of loot, as, for example

3,000 yards of Bayetta
650 pounds of Indigo
72 boxes of Plug Tobacco
300 dozen Tin Pans
50 dozen Dippers
200 Kettles
648 dozen Sewing Awls
25 gross Thimbles
325 dozen Awl Handles
300 sides of Bridle Leather
500 dozen Madras Handkerchiefs
200 pounds of Linen Thread
250 dozen Wool Cards

9 Letter from Miller to Pope, October 1, 1871 (*Ibid.*)

4,500 pounds of Scarlet Yarn
75 pairs of Scarlet Blankets
45,000 yards of Calico "fancy"
30,000 yards of Brown Sheeting[10]

And so on and so on. Agent Miller, when the last crate was emptied on the third day, believed that the Navahos had "behaved in the most orderly manner." And he listened to the pleas of the chiefs who asked if next year they might not have sheep instead of annuity goods for two-thirds of the amount due them—to build up the herds decimated when they were held as prisoners at Bosque Redondo. Miller agreed with them; were this done, he thought, the tribe might soon be self-sufficient.[11]

An event combining the shock and the random violence of a lightning bolt was gathering force in the spring of 1872 in Ute country to the northeast. Effects of it were to lash back at Defiance Agency. Keam's career was to be altered by it.

This is the way it came about.

Sobeta's band of Capote Utes, numbering less than one hundred lodges, based on the agency at Abiquiu but ranging across the San Juan and into Colorado, started warring on the Mexican settlements of Tierra Amarilla and vicinity. As yet no one had been killed. But Sobeta's band had run off twenty-seven Mexican horses, several ugly clashes had occurred, and tension was mounting in his wake.

The Capote chief, just returned from a long journey, had shaken off his usually tractable manner and now seemed spoiling for a fight. He had traveled to the Green River, in Utah, and there had seen and talked with an Indian messiah. The message he received promised a coming freedom from the white man's domination, and a return to the old Indian ways of life. Sobeta's people, like all Indians, would receive "everything they might need, such as horses, all kinds of game, and in fact everything in abundance."[12]

[10] This partial list is quoted from Miller's early-year estimate of annuity goods required, and the invoices filled by eastern contractors, most of them New York firms. (*Ibid.*)

[11] In May, 1872, Miller was authorized to contract for 10,000 sheep in lieu of a portion of annuity goods, these giving the Navahos a total of about 130,000 head.

[12] *Annual Report, C. I. A., 1872.* Report of Armstrong to Pope, August 31, 1872. The appearance of an Indian messiah, beginning among the Paiutes of Nevada in 1870, was known to most tribes of the West in the years following. Tavibo, a Paiute sub-chief, is said to have been the first to receive messianic visions. Upon his death his place was taken by his son who had been reared by a white family and had the

From Abiquiu, Ute Agent John S. Armstrong sent out messengers calling for Sobeta (Big Frock) to come to the Tierra Amarilla sub-agency with the stolen horses, and then went there himself on May 3, finding he had been preceded to the little village by a detachment of cavalry. On the morning of May 6, Sobeta came to the meeting place with about thirty warriors, having stationed others a few miles off and left his women and children in camp still farther away, on the west side of the Chama River.

"After the interview had continued for a long time," Armstrong reported later, "and their answers being very evasive, the Command-ing Officer of the troops [Captain J. D. Stevens] and I asked them to deliver the horses to me . . . and also to surrender their arms."[13] Arm-strong and Stevens demanded also that the Utes guilty of stealing the horses should be surrendered to Stevens for punishment.

Sobeta refused to promise anything until late in the afternoon when, with the council obviously deadlocked and hostility increasing on both sides, Captain Stevens ordered his troops to mount and form ranks in the plaza outside. In the face of this threat Sobeta agreed to bring in fifteen of the stolen horses—the number he had with him—the next morning.

The troops accompanied the Utes back to their camping ground, but before they reached there, some incident occurred to make the Indians break and run, and a fight that lasted an hour ensued. At the end, one Ute was killed, another fatally wounded, and one of the soldiers was wounded seriously. In the darkness the Utes withdrew, crossing the Chama and riding west and north toward the mountains, where they joined forces with Chief Ignacio's band of Wiminuche Utes. They paused long enough in their flight to kill a Mexican herd-er and drive off a large number of cattle.

Armstrong's position at Tierra Amarilla was reinforced on May 18 with the arrival of additional troops under command of Major Wil-liam Redwood Price, Eighth Cavalry. The agent feared the possibil-ity of a Ute uprising too large for his force to cope with, however, and so he sent messengers to alert the garrison at Fort Wingate, and to Defiance to ask Agent Miller for Navaho recruits. Miller's reply in-dicated the Navahos' lack of enthusiasm for this sort of undertaking.

white name of Jack Wilson, but was better known as Wovoka. The son's influence was powerful, spreading across the desert, mountains, and plains and culminating in the widespread Ghost Dance religion of 1889 and 1890.

13 Letter from Armstrong to Pope, May 6, 1872. (National Archives, Records N. M. S., Letters Received, 1872.)

At a council with the chiefs, Miller said, "I got a few of the Indians to agree to go to the Ute country and try to induce Sobita and band to go to Tierra Amarilla . . . [but] . . . the Chiefs seem to hesitate to give any assurance that their people would be willing to act with the Military in a war with the Utes." However, he continued, "Jesus Alviso, my Navajo interpreter, assures me that he could raise five hundred warriors if called on to do so."[14]

Before any test could be made between the chiefs' realism and Arviso's optimism, the problem came quickly to a head. On June 1, Armstrong learned that the Capotes again were on the west side of the Chama and preparing to come in peacefully and that the Wiminuches were close by and of a similar mind. On the day following, fifty Capotes under sub-chief Timpiache appeared in the plaza of Tierra Amarilla driving twenty head of cattle, four calves, and eight horses—a part of the livestock the Utes had run off in recent weeks. The remainder, Armstrong was told, now grazed in the camp of Ignacio's Wiminuches. Sobeta stayed away, taking care of a dying "brother," a Capote wounded in the May 6 encounter.

A war had been averted, apparently, but suspicion and fear mounted in the next few days as more of the Utes appeared at the subagency to ask for rations.

"Small bands are coming in almost daily," Armstrong noted. "This day nine families came in, very destitute indeed . . . they are very much afraid of soldiers and natives."[15]

A brief flurry of violence broke out, increasing the tension.

"On Friday a Mexican met an Indian . . . drew his revolver and told him that he would shoot him, but did not," Armstrong reported. "The Indian went to his camp and related the story. They were all very much alarmed."

Unaware of these incidents, Agent Miller at the same time was preparing to turn the Navaho agency over to Keam's control during a period of his absence. Bottom lands of the San Juan, some hundred miles to the north, were said to be unusually fertile. If the Utes could be persuaded not to raid upon their neighbors, Miller thought a Navaho subagency might be located on the San Juan and the Navahos encouraged to cultivate farms. His enthusiasm over the prospect induced him to make a personal investigation.

Thomas Keam assumed charge of the agency on June 4, the morning that Miller departed for the river. Traveling with him by horse-

14 Letter from Miller to Armstrong, May 25, 1872. (*Ibid.*)
15 Letter from Armstrong to Pope, June 8, 1872. (*Ibid.*)

back were the post trader, John Ayres, Ben Thomas, the agency farmer, and Jesús Arviso. On the evening of June 10, with no premonition of danger, they camped on the bank of the San Juan within sight of Shiprock pinnacle. At dawn the next day, before he or the others were awake, a shot rang out and James Miller lay dead in his blankets.

Official reports of Miller's death are scanty in detail, lacking the information given later by J. H. Beadle, a writer looking for western material, who was then visiting at Defiance Agency.

"We were seated at breakfast the morning of the 13th," Beadle relates, "when one of the party which had gone to the San Juan arrived, completely exhausted, and announced that Agent Miller had been murdered, and all of their horses stolen but one; that he had started out immediately with that, that the rest of the party were coming afoot. Next day the others arrived, quite worn out, having walked a hundred miles in three days, carrying their baggage."[16] Beadle was present as they told of the agent's death.

"On the morning of the 11th, just at dawn, Miller's companions were awakened by the report of a gun and whistling of an arrow, both evidently fired within half a dozen rods of them. They sprang to their feet and saw two Utes run into the brush; ten minutes after they saw them emerge from the opposite side of the thicket, and ride up the bluff driving the company's horses before them.

"They did not know, at first sight, that the Utes were hostile, or that they had fired at them. John Ayres spoke to Miller, who did not reply; he then shoved him with his foot, still he did not wake. They pulled off his blanket, and found him dead. The Ute's bullet had entered the top of his head and passed down behind his right eye, without disarranging his clothing in the slightest.

"His feet were crossed, and his hands folded exactly as when he went to sleep; his eyes were closed, and his lips were slightly parted ... all showed beyond doubt that he had passed from sleep to death without a struggle."

Telegraphic communication between the agencies and forts was then lacking; for this reason news of Miller's death traveled slowly, carried from Defiance to Wingate and Tierra Amarilla by a messenger on horseback. As might be expected, there were official expressions of outrage and regret. But it was not until early July that

16 Beadle spent five years traveling through the West, between 1868 and 1873, visiting the territories of Oklahoma, Wyoming, Utah, California, Arizona, and New Mexico. This passage is quoted from his book. *Five Years in the Territories.*

anyone had any accurate information concerning the murderers' identity—and by then the Utes who had killed Miller had so completely vanished that pursuit seemed futile. Before June was out, Ignacio's Wiminuches faded back from the subagency and disappeared, soon to be followed by Sobeta's Capotes, who, in the uninformed view of Agent Armstrong, "became alarmed, without any cause whatever."[17]

Major Price in late June rode to Wingate and Defiance Agency to collect what information on the murder he could, returning to Tierra Amarilla the evening of July 3—an unusual feat since he covered more than four hundred miles by horseback in eight days. Miller, he determined, had been killed by two Wiminuches. From descriptions supplied by John Ayres and Jesús Arviso he felt he could identify and capture them. He proposed hunting down the pair with a troop of cavalry, but was unable to obtain the necessary authorization. Ignacio's band was reported now somewhere in Utah, trading with Mormons. So far as the Indian Office was concerned, a pursuit would be hopeless and expensive; the case was closed.

Or almost closed, for there was a sequel.

At Los Pinos Agency, in Colorado, Special Commissioner Felix R. Brunot on September 6 opened negotiations with Ouray, head chief of all the Utes, for a drastic reduction of tribal lands, then amounting to some fourteen million acres. At some point during the council, which other chiefs and head men attended, a reference by Brunot or one of his aides was made to Agent Miller's death. Ouray in response offered to find the murderers and bring them to punishment. The issue was not then regarded seriously and all but passed from mind until the following year when Brunot, again in Denver, met again with Ouray to discuss a reduction of the Ute reservation. Miller's name bobbed up once more, and when Ouray said the murderers had been found, Brunot replied that he was glad to hear it. Ouray is then quoted by Brunot as saying: "We killed one. The other escaped to the Moquis Pueblo village. They were Weeminuche Utes; the main band were up in Utah; these two had strayed behind; they followed Agent Miller and killed him to get his mules. They were out all summer, and were afraid to come in, and were almost starved. They eat up both the mules before we found them. I was sorry the one was killed; I wanted to bring him in and give him up to the Agent to be

17 Monthly report, Armstrong to Pope, June 30, 1872.

punished. We followed the other one but could not catch him. If he ever comes back we will get him and bring him to the Agent."[18]

Thomas Keam, in the weeks following Miller's death, handled the agency affairs of the Navaho tribe. Much of his work was routine: asking aid from Superintendent Pope after a severe frost on the night of June 18 "visited the farms of all the Indians living in the vicinity of Canon de Chelly . . . and ruined nearly all of their crops"; reporting that war chief Manuelito had recovered twenty-nine horses stolen by Navahos "which he thinks they stole from the vicinity of Abiquiu, and probably are the property of Jicarilla Apache Indians"; and, again, recovery of ten horses stolen by Navahos, supposedly from the region of Tierra Amarilla.[19]

Hunger was the cause of these depredations, Keam reported to Pope on July 6: "The chiefs are doing all they possibly can to recover all stolen stock brought on the reservation, but tell me at the same time it is impossible to keep their people on the reservation, as most of them have nothing to eat; and stealing is resorted to by some to keep them from starving. I would therefore urge the necessity of corn and beef being furnished them at once, or evil results will surely follow notwithstanding I am making every effort to prevent them.

"I have taken the responsibility to purchase at different times from the Trader at this Agency, Flour, Coffee, and Sugar for these Indians . . . which I trust will meet with your approval."

Increasing the number of Navaho sheep, alone, would not solve the tribe's problem of subsistence. Something more must be done. Keam remembered Agent Miller's interest in developing the fertile land of the San Juan, but for the present his efforts were diverted.

On August 6, in recognition of his management of the agency, Keam was appointed special agent for the Navahos by Brigadier General O. O. Howard, now a special Indian commissioner, who four years later would lead the long pursuit and subjugation of Chief Joseph and the Nez Percés. And with the good came the bad. Soon after Keam's promotion came a communication from General Howard, ringing, this time, with brassy displeasure. He had "direct information," said the General, that some of Keam's employees, due to their profanity, gambling, and cohabiting with Indian women, were morally undesirable, and should be discharged.

---

[18] Interview between Brunot and Ouray at Denver, June 25, 1873. *Annual Report, C. I. A., 1873.*

[19] Letters from Keam to Pope, June 25-26, July 4, 1872. (National Archives, Records N. M. S., Letters Received. 1872.)

Phrasing of the complaint leaves no doubt about the identity of General Howard's informant; it could have been none other than Keam's recent traveling companion, W. F. M. Arny. Keam's anger over the accusations was easily apparent, when he made his reply to Superintendent Pope: "I judge this false information has been given by some party who from mercenary and office seeking motives, under the cloak of Christianity, seeks to injure these men.[20] There are two Employes of this Agency living with and married to Navajo women according to the customs of the Navajoes which in no way conflicts with their morals."

Anson Damon, an agency employee, and Keam himself—by Navaho ritual and custom, which were not the ways of Arny's Presbyterian church—were then married to and living contentedly with Navaho women. General Howard's moralistic censure probably was directed at Keam and Damon, although it may have embraced another: Dan DuBois, married not to one but to two Navaho women, but perhaps excepted by the General since at this writing Dan was not exactly a regular agency employee. His comings and goings were as variable and uncertain as the weather.

"These men have families and naturally look to the women as their wives, and treat them as such," Keam continued. "They have been with the Navajoes and in the employ of the Government from five to seven years; are esteemed and respected by all the Indians.

"While I deem it as [an] act of Christianity as far as their families are concerned, I think it is to the best interest of the Government as well as the Indians, that they be retained.

"As far as gambling and profanity are concerned, I know of no employe addicted to those vices. In all my actions I shall use my best endeavors to carry out the wishes of the Government, and look after the welfare of the Indians."

Colonel Pope, from his army days, had some experience with gambling and profanity, and either vice, in usual or milder measure, was not likely to offend or dismay him. Nor was he likely to think ill of a man who, in this frontier country, took a Navaho woman to his bed and, in the custom of the woman's people, respected her, honored her, and in all usual ways regarded her as his wife. The matter was allowed to drop—for the time being.

Keam returned to the affairs of the agency. With the authorization of General Howard and Superintendent Pope, he concerned himself

[20] Letter from Keam to Pope, August 15, 1872. (*Ibid.*)

during August with the organization of the first company of Navaho police. The force was composed of 130 horsemen, including the tribe's thirteen principal chiefs, each of whom was the leader of nine or ten men. At the head of this Navaho Cavalry—as he referred to it —Keam placed the war chief, Manuelito. Objectives of the troop were simple, in outline if not of accomplishment: to "guard the boundaries of the reservation, to arrest thieves and recover stolen stock for the agent."[21] The idea of a tribal police force was practical and was undertaken with enthusiasm by both Keam and the Navahos, but Keam made one miscalculation. In the interest of efficiency and morale he promised the Navahos more than he could provide: uniforms, the same pay and rations as issued to soldiers, and muzzle-loading rifles, pistols, and ammunition. All of this seems reasonable enough, even necessary to the end in view, but the Indian Office balked at providing necessary funds.

On August 21, reporting to Superintendent Pope, Keam alluded to his promise to equip the police, no doubt expecting that Pope would approve, and added: "I am pleased to state that they have already been actively at work and have turned over to me thirty one head of horses, mules and burros."

Ten days later Keam wrote again to Pope, saying that the Indian police, because of their knowledge of the country, were "far superior in training and do better service than a company of U. S. Cavalry . . . they are willing and active [and] should be encouraged." In the first month alone they recovered fifty-six stolen animals, but were making anxious inquiries about the uniforms and arms and other things promised to them. Were the promises not kept, "it would not only dishearten the good Indians, but have a tendency to convey to the thieves the idea that the actions of the Agent and his soldiers were not upheld by the Government."

The responsibility, however, seemed to rest solely upon Keam, and neither Pope nor General Howard troubled to intercede on his behalf with the indifferent officials in Washington. The Navaho police continued to function through the remainder of 1872 and again in 1873, until disbanded by Pope's successor, Colonel L. Edwin Dudley.[22]

21 Report of Pope to C. I. A. Francis A. Walker, October 10, 1872. (*Annual Report, C. I. A., 1872.*) The plan for a Navaho police force originated with Frank Tracy Bennett in 1869, and was given further support in 1871 by his successor, James H. Miller; it was not implemented, however, until Keam's administration of the agency.

22 Superintendent Dudley acknowledged that the Navaho police "accomplished great good" in 1873, but he felt, mistakenly, that the need for them had passed

A dual control of Defiance Agency, destined to last almost one year, began on September 7, 1872, when W. F. Hall, a nonentity so far as his tour of duty with the Navahos was concerned, assumed the nominal duties of agent. Hall faded at once into the background and during his short tenure the affairs of the agency were largely conducted by Keam, who had remained on as special agent.

Two days after Hall's arrival Keam submitted the annual report of the agency, beginning with the death of Agent Miller and proceeding to matters more routine—as, for example, the tendency of the old agency buildings to melt into mud with every rainstorm. In one brief paragraph he dealt with the nearly inoperative agency boarding school, offering a simple recommendation for its improvement that would be ignored for years.

The school was making little progress, he observed. This was not the fault, necessarily, of Mrs. Charity Menaul, who was in charge, but stemmed from the children's "great difficulty in learning our language."[23] He continued: "I would suggest that a farm should be connected with each school, conducted on the industrial and manual-labor plan, and that the children be furnished with food and clothing."

Keam would not claim to have originated this proposal; a similar plan actually was first suggested by James Miller, whose ideas Keam generally supported and later adopted. Keam was equally sympathetic to the project that most interested Miller at the time of his death—a subagency on the San Juan.

Miller's vision, eventually to become reality with the building of Shiprock Agency, was advanced measurably when Keam visited the region in September and found the fertile valley quite as promising as Miller had described it.

---

and ordered the police disbanded. (*Annual Report, C. I. A., 1873*.) In the following year, with depredations increasing, Agent Arny established a new Navaho police force of two hundred men under the principal chiefs. Profiting from Keam's experience, he agreed to pay them out of a surplus of 1873 annuity goods.

23 Miss Charity A. Gaston was the Navahos' first school teacher. She arrived at Defiance Agency in October, 1869, but finding no provision had been made for a school, was unable to start classes until December. Within the year she was married to Rev. John Menaul, Presbyterian missionary and agency physician. The Menauls remained at Defiance untill 1876, when they went to Laguna Pueblo to establish a mission and school. In 1877, Menaul set up a printing press at the pueblo, printing lesson-cards for the Laguna pupils. Under the Menauls' guidance the school thrived during the next ten years. One of Menaul's innovations was a *McGuffey's New First Eclectic Reader*, which he printed in both English and his own version of the Laguna language, and ran off on his printing press.

"I arrived at the San Juan river on the 20th of September, about ninety five miles due north of Fort Defiance," Keam reported to Colonel Pope upon his return.[24] Locating the grave of Agent Miller, near the river bank and five miles to the west, he made camp close by for the night.

"The morning of the 21st I proceeded up the river about twelve miles,"—probably to a point a few miles east of present Shiprock—"taking care to mark the best and most suitable locality for establishing an Agency.

"In this immediate vicinity I found some of the best and most fertile lands in New Mexico, one strip being ten miles long and averaging one and one half miles wide, containing 9,600 Acres, this and other in the vicinity having advantages over every other part of the Navajo Reservation in climate and water facilities.

"Corn enough could be raised here, and in the immediate vicinity to support the whole Navajo Nation. There is also sufficient wood for fuel to last several years, then it could be obtained from a short distance, say five miles.

"This place I selected as the most suitable locality for erecting temporary Agency buildings, store houses, &c.

"An Acequia of ten miles long will have to be dug, and lumber will be required to flume across small arroyas; a road will also have to be constructed, via Navajo [Washington] Pass to the Tunicha [or Chuska] valley; most of this labor can be done by the Indians themselves at no great expense.

"As the season is so far advanced and no supplies could be taken there before the road is completed, I would recommend that work be commenced on the road as soon as practicable, to have it open early in the spring, so that the necessary rations can be taken to the river for those Indians who wish to farm there."

Keam then mentioned a problem that was to delay the project almost indefinitely. Wiminuche Utes controlled most of the San Juan Valley, frequently raiding south of the river into Navaho country. Before the valley was safe for Navaho farms, the Utes must loosen their grasp upon the northern river valley.

"In connexion with this," he continued, "I would state that a number of the Indians are willing and anxious to go there, but say they are always in fear of a raid from the Ute Indians; they also informed

24 Letter from Keam to Pope, October 5, 1872. (National Archives, Records N. M. S., Letters Received. 1872.)

me that the Ute Indians had told them that they would not allow buildings to be erected there, or farming to be done.

"I would here state that the few Utes who visit this part of the Reservation, in small numbers (as there are not over three hundred in all who pretend to claim this country), are a great source of trouble and dread to the Navajoes, and as they have never made an attempt to work, and still persist in this mode of living, they come to the corn fields of the Navajoes in season and make them common property by helping themselves, and the Navajoes to avoid trouble bear with them patiently.

"These few Utes have now more land than the whole Navajo Tribe, and not only refuse to work themselves, but cause trouble [for] the Navajoes, who are exerting themselves to become self sustaining. It is therefore my opinion that the Government should not only protect the Navajoes, but encourage them and spare no expense to help them make this portion of their reservation on the San Juan be to them what the Rio Grande is to the Pueblo Indians."

Keam estimated the cost of the subagency as follows:

Agency building, Corrals, Stables	$25,000
Employes' Buildings, four Corrals &c	14,000
Blacksmith & Carpenter Shops	8,000
Warehouse	7,000
Grain and Issue Room	7,000
Butcher House & Corral	4,000
Acequia, Flumes & Dams	7,000
	$72,000

Superintendent Pope approved Keam's report, writing to Commissioner of Indian Affairs F. A. Walker on October 10: "For some time past I have been satisfied that the valley of the San Juan River, within the boundaries of the Navajo reservation, afforded better facilities for farming than any other portion of the reservation, and I have directed the agent to establish a sub-agency at a favorable point ... where, it is believed, large crops can be raised next year." Raiding war parties of Utes were a recognized hazard. Troops stationed in the vicinity, said Pope, could handle the situation.[25]

25 *Annual Report, C. I. A., 1872.* Various proposals were made subsequently for a fort in the San Juan Valley, but it was never built. Southern Utes roamed the country freely until a new agency for them was built in late summer, 1877, on the Río Los Pinos in southwestern Colorado. Plans advanced by Miller and Keam for a San Juan subagency did not materialize until September 11, 1903, when Ship-

Thus were plans laid for Shiprock Agency. Instead of next spring or summer, however, thirty-one years passed before the plans became reality—and by then Keam was gone from the country.

rock Agency finally was opened. Van Valkenburgh observes that "the settlement was laid originally on land belonging to a Navajo named Tseheya-begay. . . . Indians had been irrigating here for many years, and there were 275 Navajo farms under some 25 ditches. . . . The first [agency] buildings were constructed of logs and adobe. They were largely replaced by brick after the disastrous flood" of 1911.

10

Hubbell and Keam: 1873-1877

WHEN Thomas Keam and Juan Lorenzo Hubbell first met is uncertain. They may have met near Fort Wingate, where young Hubbell once worked, or at Defiance Agency. Their paths crossed in the early 1870's, however, and a friendship began that might have been closer had they not become the two most powerful Indian traders of the Southwest and, for that reason, rivals.

Lorenzo Hubbell recalled many years later that he came to Arizona in 1871, settling at Fort Defiance "where I established a trading store in partnership with a man by the name of Reed." This probably was the trader Henry Reed, but Lorenzo's memory may have been faulty; the records do not show that Henry Reed had a partner, and he was not licensed to trade at Fort Defiance until 1873.[1] There is, however, some evidence that Lorenzo was clerk or manager of Reed's store at Fort Wingate in the latter part of 1876.

In any event, Lorenzo was a self-reliant fellow, younger than Keam by seven years, when he showed up at the Navaho agency. Short and dark-haired, he was barrel-chested, amiable, and ready to wrestle any man for fun or to fight in earnest if forced to.

His early years we know little of except from legend. He himself was not sure whether he was born on November 21 or November 27

---

1 Hubbell's statement is quoted from a short autobiographical sketch he wrote for *History of Arizona*, VI, by Thomas Edwin Farish. Henry Reed was licensed to trade at Fort Wingate from June, 1872, through early August, 1877. He also was licensed to trade at Fort Defiance in 1873–74. (*N. A., Ledgers of Traders,* and War Records Division, Fort Wingate, #1251.)

—but the year was 1853 and the place Pajarito, New Mexico. His father was James Lawrence Hubbell, native of Salisbury, Connecticut, who settled in the West in 1848 after serving in the Mexican War.[2] James Hubbell was a government contractor, buying large herds of cattle in Mexico and selling them in New Mexico; also he was a freighter, once owning a train of forty-eight wagons with four yokes of oxen for each. In Pajarito the Yankee from Connecticut wooed and married Julianita Gutiérrez, whose family originally came from Toledo and, since 1739, by the grace of the King of Spain, held papers to the Pajarito Land Grant.

Juan Lorenzo, their son, spoke Spanish before he spoke English. He was tutored privately until he was twelve years old, when he entered Farley's Presbyterian School in Santa Fe, his mother's concession to his Protestant father.

"At the age of seventeen," he recalled later, "my education was considered sufficiently complete for me to seek my own future in the world, and I went to work as a clerk in the post office in Albuquerque. The job paid $40 per month, and that was a good wage. . . . But I quit after a year. . . . In 1870, therefore, I invested most of my savings in a saddle horse and outfit and set out for Utah Territory which then was virgin land. . . . After some weeks on the trail I came to Lee's Ferry."[3] Here he encountered the fugitive John D. Lee and— this of necessity would have been after December, 1871—stayed with Lee for several weeks at Lonely Dell.

Hubbell took a strong fancy to the wry-humored Mormon, this enduring long after Lee was dead. "He seemed a thoroughly likable sort of fellow, hospitable, kind-hearted, intelligent, and with utterly none of the traits of character later attributed to him. I have never been able to believe that he was actually guilty of the crime for which he was executed some seven years later."

Soon after their first meeting and after Lorenzo entered the Mormon settlements of Utah, he clerked at a Mormon trading post in

2 A relative, James Boyd Hubbell, native of Winsted, Connecticut, moved to Minnesota in 1857 and there was appointed an Indian trader. In 1864 he bought out the interest of Charles Chouteau of St. Louis, in the American Fur Company, and later organized the Northwestern Fur Company and was its manager until the company went out of business in 1870. James Boyd Hubbell thereafter traded with the Northern Cheyennes, Arapahoes, and Sioux, and in 1881 was engaged in a mercantile business under the firm name of Broadwater, Hubbell and Company, with headquarters at Miles City, Montana.

3 Hubbell's remarks here and immediately following are quoted from "Fifty Years an Indian Trader" (as told to J. E. Hogg), *Touring Topics*, Vol. XXII, No. 12 (1930).

Kanab, there getting his first practical knowledge of the Navahos and picking up some of their language. In the spring of 1872, at Panguitch, he was involved in a fight, the details of which he later refused to discuss, and very nearly lost his life.

With a bullet lodged in his left leg and a bad wound in his side, he "found it necessary to flee, and I fled toward the south. . . . I wandered for days scarcely knowing where I was or what actually happened." Eventually he was found by a band of Paiutes. Instead of harming him, they took him to their camp and cared for him until his wounds healed. From the Paiute camp he "drifted on southward" until he reached the swift Colorado, somewhere below Lee's Ferry, where "I rolled my clothing, lashed the bundle to the saddle, and drove my horse into the water. Clinging to the horse's tail, I steered him for the opposite shore." It was a crossing that few men, before or since, have attempted. He then made his way to the Hopi villages and from there to Defiance Agency.[4]

Lorenzo was on the scene, a fascinated observer, when W. F. M. Arny became Navaho agent in September, 1873. Promoted to this office after several unrewarding years as agent for the Pueblos, Arny was a favored member of the Presbyterian church, then playing a dominant role in Indian affairs and territorial politics. In his own circle known still as "Governor" Arny—he was acting governor of New Mexico briefly in 1866—the new agent soon proved himself a hypocritical rascal, a Bible-pounding moralist who plotted larceny.

Within a week of assuming charge, Arny boldly set in motion a scheme to defraud the Navahos of the best part of their reservation. He opposed, when asked to report on its feasibility and cost, the Miller and Keam proposal for a subagency on the San Juan. The over-all cost, he said, would be $57,500—"and I think this is a very low estimate." He recommended, for reasons to be seen presently, that the San Juan project be scrapped. He urged that the Indian Office, instead, should provide $20,000 to repair the crumbling, snake-infested adobes of Defiance Agency.[5]

4 For much of my information about Lorenzo Hubbell I am indebted to his daughter-in-law, Mrs. Dorothy Hubbell, wife of Roman, who supplied documents and materials and was helpful during several interviews at her home at Ganado, Arizona. Other sources are: Dorothy Challis Mott, "Don Lorenzo Hubbell of Ganado," *Arizona Historical Review*, Vol. IV, No. 1 (1931); Mrs. LaCharles Goodman Eckel, "History of Ganado, Arizona," in *Museum Notes*, Museum of Northern Arizona, Vol VI, No. 10 (1934); and an obituary notice, "Great Southwest Pioneer Passes On," in *The Santa Fe Magazine*, January, 1931.

5 Report of Arny to C. I. A. Edward P. Smith, September 4, 1873. (*Annual Report, C. I. A., 1873.*)

Arny then moved swiftly to remove those at the agency whose knowledge of Navaho affairs, and presence, might embarrass him. Thomas Keam he removed first, and Keam's office of special agent was abolished. Out with Keam went Jesús Arviso, the interpreter, because "he is a Mexican, an immoral man, has a wife at Cubero and lives here with *two* Navajo women (sisters) by both of whom he has children, [and] is also addicted to gambling." Out with Keam and Arviso went Anson Damon, because "he has lived with Indian squaws . . . has several children by them, his moral influence is bad." Out with Damon and Arviso and Keam went Perry Williams, the agency's "man on issue," because "he is similar in his habits to Damon." And out with Keam and Arviso and Damon and Williams went the chief herder, W. W. Owens, because "I do not think he is a fit person to be here."[6]

The purge was drastic. Among the few veteran employees untouched were those of less importance: William Burgess, blacksmith, who "lately married a young lady who was educated at the Presbyterian school at Santa Fe" and by this act of innocent wisdom might stay on, because "I believe his appointment would add to the moral influence which should be exerted over the Indians."

The agent's next blow fell a week later. Keam, undoubtedly warned in advance of Arny's intentions, had previously applied for a license to trade on the Navaho reservation, Lehman Spiegelberg and Herman Ilfeld of Santa Fe assuring his bond for five thousand dollars. As clerk for his trading store Keam proposed his younger brother William, who came to the Southwest from England in the early 1870's.[7] Arny quickly snuffed out Keam's plans. On September 15 he wrote to the commissioner: "I have the honor to report that I have refused to grant a license . . . to Thomas V. Keams. . . . The sureties on the bond are ample, but . . . Thomas V. Keams and his brother William are not proper persons to be here, and . . . the Government, the Agent, and the Indians will be benefitted by their absence."

Refused a trader's license, Keam left Fort Defiance, apparently living and perhaps trading just south of the agency and reservation line. Certainly he was not far away, for he remained in close touch with

6 Letter from Arny to Smith, September 6, 1873. (National Archives, Records N. M. S., Letters Received, 1873.)

7 William Keam's name first appears as temporary agency clerk, appointed by Agent W. F. Hall from January 1 to May 12, 1873. William remained at or near the agency for the next three years.

what was happening at the agency. And Arny was continuing to make a show worth watching. Now rid of what he termed "the junto" of "squaw-men and whiskey-sellers," he turned the rod on the Navahos; the Indians must learn who was boss.

Ganado Mucho, with about one-third of the entire tribe with him and under his control, was living off the reservation to the west and, so Arny understood, trading with Apaches and Mormons. This must stop. Arny read chapter and verse of the 1868 treaty to the chief "and told him he must come with his people to the reservation. This he promised me he would do at once, but I am informed that he has made the same promise to late Agent Miller and other agents."[8]

Manuelito was guilty of the same treaty violation and must be disciplined. All of his life Manuelito had lived on the plains of the lower Chuska Valley, and the war chief only shrugged when told he was living off the reservation. This would not do. At a council of chiefs and head men in January, 1874, Manuelito was absent and scheming with the Utes—so Arny reported—to join in a war with them against the Mexicans and white miners prospecting along the San Juan. Manuelito would not get closer than an angry bow-shot to a Ute, but it suited Arny to believe otherwise. In any case, the Navaho chiefs brought Manuelito to the agency early in February, and he was told he must stay on the reservation except while hunting in certain uninhabited areas.

Arny's brusque tactics caused confusion and some grumbling; the provisions of their treaty apparently were not well understood by the Navahos. This treaty, which promised them land and annuity goods and other things, also had sharp teeth in it. Amid the grumbling was heard a growing demand that a delegation of chiefs be allowed to visit the Great Father in Washington. They wanted these matters explained to them.

Lorenzo Hubbell was drifting about in the vicinity of the Navaho agency unattached and looking for means to keep a full stomach, when Arny early in 1874 found an urgent need for his services. Stories reaching the agent told of the killing in Utah of three Navahos and the wounding of a fourth—the murderers, supposedly, being Mormons. Hubbell was engaged as Spanish interpreter to accompany Ganado Mucho to the scene and investigate rumors of threatened border war between the Mormons and the northern Navahos. Upon his return Hubbell was able to report that the situation was indeed

8 Letter from Arny to Dudley, January 31, 1874. (*Ibid.*, 1874.)

serious, that the Navahos talked of reprisals unless heavy payments were made to families of the murdered men.

Some doubt shadows the episode to this day. Jacob Hamblin, who was instructed by Brigham Young "to visit the Navajos, and satisfy them that our people were not concerned in it," gives the most credible version in his *Personal Narrative*.

A party of four young Navahos, Hamblin said, went to the east fork of the Sevier River to trade with the Paiutes. "In Grass Valley they encountered a severe snow storm, which lasted for three days. They found shelter in a vacant house belonging to one McCarty. He did not belong to the [Mormon] Church. . . . The Navajoes, becoming hungry . . . killed a small animal belonging to McCarty. In some way he learned of the presence of the party on his ranch, gathered up some men of like spirit with himself, came suddenly upon the Navajoes, and, without giving them an opportunity of explaining their circumstances, killed three of them and wounded the fourth."

As Brigham Young's mediator, Hamblin traveled from his home at Kanab to the vicinity of Moenkopi, where a few Mormons were just beginning to establish a settlement. The Navahos he found in the region, relatives and friends of the three dead men, were in an ugly mood but willing to meet Hamblin in council.

"They required me to give them a writing," Hamblin recalled in his *Narrative*, "obligating me to pay one hundred head of cattle for each of the three Navajoes killed, and fifty for the wounded one . . . .

"I answered that I had never lied to them, and that I would not pay for the wrong that other people had done. 'Let the Americans pay for their own mischief, I will not sign a writing to pay for one hoof.' "

Throughout the council, which lasted far into the night, Hamblin insisted that the Mormons were not responsible for the killing.

"I came here on a peace mission," Hamblin told them. "If you will send Hastele [a Navaho chief of the region] into our country to learn the truth concerning what I have told you, let as many more come along as you like. . . . It is no use to ask me about pay. In the meantime your people can trade among the Mormons in safety."

From Moenkopi, Hamblin went on to First Mesa and from the Hopi village of Hano wrote to Arny suggesting that the agent send several Navaho chiefs to that place for further council. The murder of the three Navahos was resulting in serious consequences, "but if all parties try, it can all be settled satisfactorily to all reasonable men." Mormons were not guilty of the shooting, Hamblin said again, but guilt rested with "strangers [who] had lately come in and taken up a ranch."

Hamblin's concern for the safety of the Mormon families at Moen-kopi caused him to confide at the conclusion of his letter, that "we have commenced to make a small settlement sixty miles from the crossing of the [Colorado] River—This will be of much importance in forming other settlements."[9]

Arny, who was convinced that the McCarty ranch affair was the work of Mormons, noted carefully Hamblin's final lines.

A Mormon settlement at Moenkopi would demoralize both Hopis and Navahos, Arny advised Colonel L. Edwin Dudley, Indian super-intendent at Santa Fe, "especially as the leading Mormon who con-trols the ferry on the Colorado river is J. D. Lee . . . who from all I can learn is doing much to encourage the Indians to steal from 'the Gentiles.' " The Mormons now realized their mistake in killing the Navahos, Arny said, and their desire to correct it "should be used in a peaceful way to prevent the settlement of the Mormons too near to either the Moquin [Hopi] or the Navajo Reservations."[10]

To Hamblin, Arny wrote on the same day that "the importance of a settlement in regard to the Indians killed by white men (said to be Mormons) I appreciate . . . and I have used every effort to prevent the Indians from retaliation." He would not agree, however, to a council in the Hopi villages as Hamblin proposed.

"If you will come here at as early a moment as possible, prepared to do justice to the Indians for the wrong done them," Arny added, he would then summon the head chiefs of the Navaho tribe. "This Agency is the place to make the settlement and have an understand-ing, and if not done soon, I fear I will not be able to restrain my Indians."

Lorenzo Hubbell and Ganado Mucho were entrusted with carry-ing this message to Hamblin. It would be rewarding if anything could be found in Lorenzo's words to tell of Hamblin's reaction when he read the letter. We know only that Hamblin, always willing to negotiate when there was any chance of agreement, declined Arny's proposals and returned to Kanab.

Threatened with continuing hostility by the Navahos surrounding them, Mormon residents of Moenkopi in April wrote to Arny, offer-ing their aid in investigating the McCarty murders; also they sent

9 Letter from Hamblin to Arny, March 7, 1874. (*Ibid.*)
10 Letter from Arny to Dudley, March 28, 1874. (*Ibid.*) Arny was premature: a reservation for the Hopis was not established until December, 1882.

Andrew S. Gibbons, former member of the Arizona legislature, to consult with Arny at Defiance Agency.

The Navahos demanded that the Mormons pay 192 head of horses and 100 head of cattle for the murdered men, but this the Mormons refused to do because "we are not in any way guilty or responsible."[11] McCarty and his partners in the shooting were "not members of the Mormon Church," they said, "nor subject to any counsel or advice that we as a people can give." Furthermore, the Mormons told Arny, "the Navajoes boast to us that they are furnished arms and ammunition by the Americans, to aid them in waging war on us.

"It is well known by all persons who have had dealings with us, that we are a peaceable, industrious and law-abiding people. We delight not in the shedding of blood, and as American citizens we appeal to you to use your influence as Agent of the Navajo Nation to conciliate their feelings and avert the threatening evil of an Indian war."

Thus the situation remained, when in June, 1874, Arny decided that a show of force against the Navahos might be helpful. To Colonel J. Irwin Gregg, commanding the Military District of New Mexico, he wrote "to ask that you will please furnish an escort of not less than one company of troops with officers of judgment to cooperate with me in an endeavor to make peace. . . . And as I will be required to take subsistence for the Indians who will necessarily accompany me from this Agency, I respectfully ask, if possible, that you cause me to be furnished with a wagon and six mules for that purpose."

Arny's plan for an expedition was vetoed by Colonel Dudley, who wrote on June 19 to Commissioner Smith: "My own opinion is that the nature of this trouble is such as requires a different man from Mr. Arny to bring about peaceable relations. I am convinced that . . . sending troops to the country might increase instead of diminish the difficulty."

Through winter and spring of early 1874, Arny used the Mormon troubles along the Colorado to conceal his real objective: seizure of the fertile and supposedly mineral-rich northern one-quarter of the Navaho reservation. Arny's unfaltering determination to have the Navahos relinquish this land suggests that powerful interests beside his own were involved.

11 This message is an enclosure with a letter from Arny to Dudley, May 12, 1874. (Ibid.) Among the twenty-one men who signed the message were John R. Young, a son of Brigham Young, and two Mormons who accompanied Hamblin on his early trips to the Hopi villages in 1859 or 1860—Ira Hatch and Francis Hamblin.

Lorenzo Hubbell may have suspected nothing of Arny's purpose when, at a council of chiefs on February 11, the agent's plan was blandly sandwiched into an appeal that the chiefs be allowed to visit the Great Father in Washington. Lorenzo was present as Spanish interpreter during the council, and later wrote the petitioning document in his own hand. So thoroughly had Arny scolded and threatened the Navahos for living outside their reservation that the chiefs wanted the matter of their treaty rights explained to them in Washington. As a concession to Arny, they agreed that "we now desire to comply with and have our treaty so modified as to give us lands south of the present Reservation in lieu of lands we are willing to relinquish north of the Reservation, so as to let the Miners have the San Juan River country."[12]

Soon afterward eleven of the principal chiefs signed an agreement, which Arny prepared for them, relinquishing the northern quarter of their reservation, the San Juan section of some 1,152 square miles. Arny in return proposed that an equal amount of land would be added to the reservation on the south.

Armed now with the chiefs' agreement to his scheme, and eager to press his advantage in person with his superiors in Washington, Arny agitated through the remaining months of 1874 for permission to take his delegation to see the President.

Border troubles between Navahos and the Mormons would inevitably continue, he wrote Colonel Dudley on February 16, "until the Chiefs can see the President, Genl. Sherman, the Sect. of the Interior, and the Commissioner of Indian Affairs together with their Agent, and so modify the treaty as to change the lines of the Reservation." In even stronger terms Arny wrote to Commissioner Smith, suggesting that a border war was likely unless he could bring his delegation to Washington—adding that the delegation should include relatives of the three Navahos killed in the McCarty affair.

Responsive to this pressure, but without enthusiasm, Commissioner Smith replied, on August 4, that "the visit of such a delegation is not deemed necessary or advisable by this office" unless for the good effect it would have in preserving peace, and even then only if the chiefs insisted upon it. With these conditions clearly stated, the commissioner added that he would permit Arny to take $2,500 from the

12 Petition addressed to C. I. A. Smith, February 11, 1874. (*Ibid.*) Among the chiefs who made their marks were Huero, Ganado Mucho, Delgadito, Manuelito, Largo, Narbono Primero, Narbono Segundo, Chiquito Primero, Chiquito Segundo, Armijo, Herrero Primero, Tien-su-se, and Herrero Segundo.

Navahos' clothing fund to defray expenses—if the agent still considered the trip "absolutely necessary."

Lorenzo Hubbell, who on June 1 was relieved of duties as Spanish interpreter and made the agency's man on issue, was an observer of these developments, as was William Keam. In spite of Arny's displeasure, young Keam had managed to remain near the agency with his Navaho wife. Both Hubbell and Will Keam, it appears, were in touch with Thomas Keam and kept him informed of Arny's activities. When the agent departed for Washington with his delegation in November, 1874, Thomas Keam was scarcely surprised. He had, in fact, made plans of his own. He would not travel with the delegation, but he would go to Washington at his own expense and be there when Arny made his proposal to trade off the San Juan country.

As his party progressed eastward, Arny welcomed newspaper reporters aboard his train at every important stop. The ten Navahos accompanying him excited curious interest, and this Arny used to publicize, with shrewd candor, the purpose of this journey.

"Their object," the Washington *Evening Star* reported on the day before their arrival, ". . . is three-fold. In the first place they want to trade a slip of land, sixty by thirty miles, on the north edge of their reservation and embracing a part of what is called the San Juan country, for a strip of land equally large on the south of the reservation, in an agricultural and pastoral region. This sort of a dicker, if consummated, would, as intended by Gov. Arny, open up to the whites a section amazingly rich in the precious metals."

Beyond this, the *Star* reported, the delegation wished to adjust "some complications" arising from terms of the 1868 treaty, "and, third, and last, they will demand some redress for the murder . . . of three of their tribe by the Mormons, who tried to found a colony in Arizona."[13]

More than an amateur politician, Arny evidently sensed that a bold, brassy truth sometimes is more expedient than a big or a devious lie. The country at large would applaud taking gold fields

13 The Washington *Evening Star*, December 1, 1874. In the same story it is noted that members of the delegation "are neatly dressed, in goods of their own fabrication. Next to Gov. Arny, of course, Manuelito, head war chief, is the most distinguished member of the party. Next to him is Cayatanito, second war chief. The others are named as follows:—Juanito Pal ti-to, wife of Manuelito; Manuelito Segundo, son of Manuelito; Barbas Hueras, chief councilor; Mariano, second councilor; Cubra Negra, chief; Tene-su-se, chief; Ganado Mucho, chief; Bueno ci-nia, chief; Jesus Alviso, interpreter; Hank Easton, interpreter." Manuelito may have presented the most commanding presence; Ganado Mucho was the most important Navaho of the delegation.

from savages in return for lands agricultural and pastoral; at the same time, the public at large would care nothing about tribal "complications." Were they able to read, which they were not, the Navaho delegation might have been badly jolted, as Commissioner Smith was, presumably, to learn that the professed reasons for this junket—treaty rights and murder "by the Mormons"—now were matters of lesser importance to Arny than his land dicker.

The President would receive them in due course. In the meantime, before their audience at the White House, strange sights awaited them, and in turn the Navahos themselves were subjects of interest—the *Star* reporting on December 4: "The Navajoe Indians today and yesterday strolled around the city sight-seeing. Their costumes of red blankets and leggings, with heads decorated with the modern stove-pipe hat, gave them a rather novel appearance. . . . Each one wears a silver belt about his waist weighing from four to six pounds, also silver ornaments about the neck adorned with fossil heads. The chief [Manuelito] wears black buckskin pants, with the sides of the legs ornamented with silver buttons."

Six days later the Navahos solemnly trooped into the Executive Mansion and stared into the tired eyes and impassive, bearded face of Ulysses Grant. "The Indians," said the *Star* that evening, "laid before the President a series of complaints relative to their lands, their children held in captivity by their enemies in New Mexico, and depredations committed by Mormons and miners prospecting for gold. The President listened very patiently and in reply referred the delegation to the Secretary of the Interior and the Commissioner of Indian Affairs, whom he said would take the necessary steps to right their wrongs."

After journeying more than two thousand miles, their council with the President had lasted not more than sixty minutes. No mention of giving up the San Juan country was made by the Indians, and almost certainly this was due to the intervention of Thomas Keam. A meeting previously arranged with the President had been canceled when Keam suddenly descended upon the delegation, whisked off the principal chiefs, and after a few quiet words with them scuttled Arny's entire scheme.

"On a certain day," Arny bitterly recalled afterward, "when an interview was to be held with the President . . . Keams came to the hotel where I and the Indians were stopping and in my absence took away with him Manuelito and several other of the Indians and thereby prevented a council being held with the President." And when

Keam returned the Navahos to the hotel that evening, staggering in each other's arms but firmly determined not to trade off the San Juan country, they "were in a condition of intoxication and had to be confined to their rooms."[14]

From every point of view but Arny's, theirs was a salubrious condition. A white man, for once, had gotten Indians drunk—and entirely and unquestionably for their own good.

14 Affidavit of W. F. M. Arny, September 13, 1875. Copy "G" of a series of documents enclosed with letter from Arny to Smith, September 14, 1875. (National Archives, Records N. M. S., Letters Received. 1875.)

11

Arny and the Squaw Men

FOR THE TIME BEING there was nothing more that Arny could do. The Navaho delegation started back for Arizona. Beyond handshaking and palaver nothing had been accomplished—or almost nothing. On a side trip to New York, Arny purchased three hand looms and some spinning wheels, ordering them shipped to Defiance. His backward Navahos might profit by adapting these civilized machines to their weaving.[1]

The broth he was brewing began to boil over soon after Arny returned to the agency. His Washington junket had cost far more than the $2,500 allowed by the commissioner, and it was imperative that Arny find more money, and quickly, to settle the bills. Following a council of chiefs and head men at Defiance Agency on February 28, 1875, Arny mysteriously came into possession of a receipt, signed by the chiefs, acknowledging that the agent had given them a cash payment of $7,500—this "being amount of funds forwarded to him by the Hon. Commissioner of Indian Affairs from the funds for fulfilling treaty with the Navajo Indians for 1875."[2]

[1] A worn-out loom, already at the agency, was repaired and a Miss H. W. Cook was engaged by Arny to teach the Navaho women how to use it. On March 31, 1875, awaiting delivery of the new machinery from New York, Miss Cook reported that ten yards of cloth had been woven on the old loom thus far. The project never was a success. Agent Alex G. Irvine, who succeeded Arny, reported in 1876 that "the hand-looms purchased and set up for them . . . . have not proved to be as great a success as was hoped for. . . . The Navajos seem to prefer their own way of weaving blankets, for which they are celebrated." (*Annual Report, C. I. A., 1876.*)

[2] Documents and statements referred to comprise part of a file enclosed with a letter from Major Price to Lt. J. H. Mahnken, Acting Asst. Adjt. Gen., District of

Other signatures appearing on the receipt as witnesses included those of W. B. Truax, agency doctor, and Lorenzo Hubbell and William Keam. Dr. Truax later said he had no recollection of signing such a paper, and Hubbell and Keam told Major William Redwood Price "that they never knowingly signed such a paper—that they were present at the council . . . and that no reference was made to payments of any money or the giving of any receipts for the trip to Washington." Major Price implied that the receipt Arny held for $7,500 was a forgery.

"As I know that there has never been such an amount of currency paid to the Indians," Price said, "I infer it is a voucher to cover the expenses of the Washington visit."

In April came word that Congress had rejected Arny's proposals for acquiring the San Juan region. No objection to his plan was raised by the Indian Office, but Commissioner Smith notified Arny on April 16, 1875, that Congress had found it unacceptable because the southern extension lay within the right of way granted to the Pacific Railroad Company, predecessor of the Atlantic and Pacific Railroad. Arny promptly drafted an entirely new plan, with the same end in view and arranged to return alone to Washington in July to argue his case before the commissioner.

The Navahos in the meantime were becoming restive. At a council of chiefs and head men on May 28 a petition was drawn up, addressed to Commissioner Smith, calling for the removal of Arny because "We can place no reliance or confidence in his word . . . he being a great prevaricator of the truth"—and because "he also resorts to threats and coercion to make us sign numerous papers of which we have no knowledge whatever."[3]

Upon their return from Washington, the chiefs said, Arny "presented to us a paper, for our signature, which contained an abstract of flour, sugar, coffee &c. given to the Chiefs and sick Indians during the time the greater number of us were in Washington, and of course we had no knowledge whatever of the transaction, more especially of the quantities: 1,000 lbs. of flour, 100 lbs. of sugar and a large amount of coffee." Now to their certain knowledge, the chiefs said, none of these goods had been issued. Beyond this, Arny was withholding from them about half of their annuity goods.

New Mexico, September 25, 1875. (National Archives, Records N. M. S., Letters Received, 1875.)

3 Petition addressed by Navaho chiefs and head men, May 28, 1875, to C. I. A. Edward P. Smith. (*Ibid.*)

The chiefs asked, in conclusion, "that Thomas V. Keams be sent to us as our Agent, in the place of W. F. M. Arny, he having been our Agent, understanding our language, and knowing our wants, we placing the utmost confidence in him."

Dan DuBois was the Spanish interpreter when this petition was drafted, and Anson C. Damon was among the witnesses who signed it.

Receiving no response from the commissioner, thirty of the principal chiefs met again—at Fort Wingate, on July 15, after Arny had departed for Washington—to write a second petition, addressed this time to President Grant. Lorenzo Hubbell was their interpreter and chief spokesman.

Expressing Navaho sentiments, but flowing in Hubbell's most eloquent phrases, the document called again for Arny's removal because he "does not fail to create the opportunity to enrich himself at the expense of the people he should protect" and because "he is trifling, vacillating, and unreliable in all matters connected with his agency" and because "of the parade, pomp and circumstance of all his actions . . . his high sounding and meaningless words . . . his waste of public property and misapplication of public funds."

And finally, and again, "We pray our Great Father to send us an Agent who will talk less and do more, give us less show and more justice. We believe Thomas Keams to possess all we ask for."[4]

Agent Arny, meanwhile, arrived in Washington and on July 24 submitted his second proposal for changing the boundaries of the reservation. As before, the Navahos were to relinquish the northern one-quarter of their land. In return, the government should add new sections to the reservation from the public domain, on the east and on the west.

The eastern section, Arny admitted, "is a barren mountain and broken region and has scarcely any water, there is not a white inhabitant on it, and sufficient arable land could not be obtained there as an equivalent for the San Juan region."[5] However, this arid tract "has heretofore been used by the Navajo Indians to pasture their sheep when water could be obtained . . . and would be useful to them for that purpose."

The western strip, of about equal size (some six hundred square miles), Arny reported as a tract "on which there is considerable arable

[4] Petition addressed to President Grant by Navaho chiefs and head men, July 15, 1875. (*Ibid.*)

[5] Arny's boundary proposals and map are enclosed with a letter he wrote in Washington, July 24, 1875, addressed to C. I. A. Smith. (*Ibid.*)

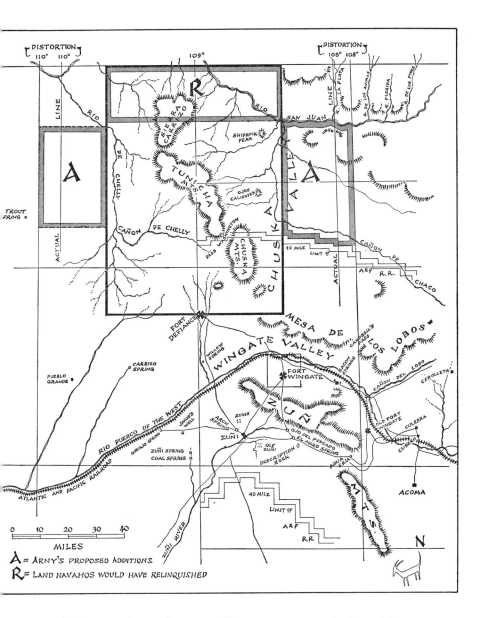

Navaho Reservation and surrounding area, a transcription of Agent Arny's map accompanying his 1875 proposal for changing reservation boundaries.

land and over *two* thousand Navajoes have resided [on it] for many years, and [it] would sustain a much larger number." Furthermore, "There is *not a white* inhabitant on it, except occasionally a couple of white men who live with squaws, and have given much trouble to this Agency. . . .

"I believe that this exchange will be of great advantage to both the Government and the Indians," Arny said, "and at the last council the Indians asked me to do all I could to get it for them. In consequence of the interference and falsehoods of 'the squaw men,' the Navajoes claim portions of the country now occupied by white men and which is not a part of their reservation *and never should be.*"

The squaw men, and most notably Thomas Keam, had advised the Navahos that it was to their interest to hold what land they had— and to obtain more of the San Juan Valley, north and south of the river and east of the eastern boundary line set by the 1868 treaty. This being precisely the land he coveted, Arny naturally was wrathy.

"I would respectfully suggest," Arny continued, "that *the Governor* of *New Mexico, the Surveyor General* of *New Mexico,* and W. H. Manderfield Esq., Editor of the [Santa Fe] New Mexican, be appointed Commissioners with myself to enter into an agreement with the Indians for this change of lands, subject to approval of the Government. . . . This will, I hope, settle the vexed question promptly with economy to the Government and advantage to the Indians."

With this letter Arny enclosed boundary descriptions of the three tracts and a map that had been prepared for him by a private firm in Santa Fe. Arny's proposed east and west additions were distorted in scale to three or four times their actual size. Commissioner Smith, who was not familiar with the country, could scarcely be expected to know this.

Land of the eastern addition was quite as arid as Arny described it—its mesas, dry arroyos, and sand hills picturesque enough, but nearly valueless. The western addition was not as favorable as described, the northern two-thirds being desert wasteland. Ganado Mucho claimed the wooded, arable southern portion for his home and no doubt wanted it made a part of the reservation.

Arny did not describe the San Juan lands. Nearly all of the region was arable, half of it was within the San Juan watershed; the Carrizo Mountains formed its vast heart. To give up this land would mean giving up what Thomas Keam had described three years before as "some of the best and most fertile lands in New Mexico." Also it would mean giving up the subagency advocated by Miller and Keam and, with that, what Pope had agreed were "better facilities for farming than any other portion of the reservation."

The proposals remained for some time on Commissioner Smith's desk, and then were filed. At a later time the reservation boundaries would be changed, to embrace the east and west extensions proposed by Arny—and much more besides. But the San Juan lands, as Keam urged, would be retained and increased.

Arny left Washington to return to his agency, unaware then of his failure, unaware that at Defiance the chicaneries of his regime finally had spawned revolt.

At Santa Fe, where he arrived on August 23, Arny learned that in his absence the Navahos had seized the agency and now threatened to kill him if he returned.

"I was informed," he wrote Commissioner Smith, "that the 'squaw men' and whiskey sellers had so excited the Navajoes by their falsehoods, that it would be unsafe for me and would endanger the lives of my family and the female employes at the Agency if I went there."[6]

Dr. Walter Whitney, who had been left in charge, was brushed aside unharmed when the chiefs rode in on the morning of August 19 and quietly took over. Not a gun was fired. Navaho employees were ordered to put down their work and leave. One, who refused, was tied up and whipped. Guards were placed over all agency buildings, over Arny's wife Cicilia, and over all white employees.

A Navaho employee called attention to a number of wagons that had recently brought in annuity goods and waited now, empty, to move out the agent's possessions. That night the chiefs searched the houses of Arny and his son William and carried out two full wagonloads of goods which they dumped in a pile in a room of the schoolhouse. It did no good for Mrs. Arny to protest that all of this was her husband's personal property, this incredible pack-rat collection of loot: forty-nine bolts of linsey, sixteen of calico and four more of manta, denims, and jeans, seven gross of handkerchiefs, seventy-five pairs of children's shoes, shears and butcher knives, thirteen red blankets, wool cards and knitting needles, packages of linen thread, and enough tin cups to equip a company of soldiers.

Further search turned up more evidence of Arny's propensity for looting the agency's storerooms. In a mail sack in the agent's desk were found a dozen fine shawls of the sort usually given to the wives of the chiefs. Packed away in a rear harness room were 240 tin pails,

6 Letter from Arny to Smith, dated Santa Fe, September 14, 1875. With enclosures marked "A," "B," "C," "D," "E," "F," "G," and "H." (*Ibid.*)

432 tin pans, 54 spades, and 40 pounds of yarn. On retiring as agent, Arny conceivably planned to open a general store.

In one of the storerooms, but labeled by the agent as his personal property, were 3,300 pounds of flour, 54 pounds of coffee, and another 70 pounds of yarn.[7]

Dr. Whitney was allowed some freedom of movement but was virtually a prisoner. He was able, however, to smuggle out two letters before the end of the day, both addressed to Arny and saying about the same thing: The agency was in the hands of the Navahos—and "if you come without soldiers I think your life and that of your family will be in danger."[8]

Whitney managed to get off another message, to Fort Wingate, asking for help. The reply of Captain C. A. Hartwell, commanding, reflects the extent of ill-feeling that had grown between the military and the Navaho agency. He was sorry, said Captain Hartwell, but "without instructions from District Head Quarters it would be impossible" to send troops to Whitney's aid. Nevertheless, he agreed to forward the acting agent's appeal to Colonel Irwin Gregg in Santa Fe and await the district commander's instructions.[9]

This was the situation, then, that confronted Arny upon his return from Washington. He fretted in Santa Fe for two days, hoping, no doubt, for a miracle. Then, quite suddenly, he resigned.

False statements of the squaw men had so incited the Navahos against him that his life was endangered, Arny told Commissioner Smith, and it would be unwise for him to return to the agency. Therefore, "I respectfully ask you to do me the kindness to inform the Chiefs through the commanding officer at Fort Wingate that I have tendered my resignation and that it will be accepted and my successor appointed as soon as possible; that I have taken measures to remove my family and that all I desire is that I be not interfered with till I can close my business at the agency and be relieved.

"Please also have the Indians informed that the statement made that their reservation is to be taken from them is untrue, and that the Government will probably soon send three Commissioners to talk with them and arrange their land matters, I have no doubt to their satisfaction."

[7] Invoice of property found at Defiance Agency, enclosure with letter from Maj. Price to Lt. Mahnken, September 25, 1875. (*Ibid.*)

[8] Enclosures "A" and "B," Whitney to Arny, August 19, 1875. (*Ibid.*)

[9] Enclosures "C" and "D," Whitney to Arny, and Hartwell to Whitney, both dated August 21, 1875. (*Ibid.*)

Apparently there was no disposition on anyone's part to ask Arny to withdraw his resignation. John Pope, in command of the Department of the Missouri, telegraphed Colonel Gregg on August 30: "Arny is relieved. Order the commanding officer Fort Wingate to take possession and charge of the Navajoe Agency and to perform the necessary duties of Agent for the Navajoes until Arny's successor is appointed, qualified, and appears at the Agency."[10]

By a curious turn of fate the end of Arny's Indian Office career coincided with the start of Thomas Keam's venture into Indian trading. With his brother William as clerk, he was licensed on August 31, 1875, to trade with the Hopi Indians. His trading post was in the canyon that ever since has been identified by his name. Willi and Lehman Spiegelberg secured his five-thousand-dollar bond.[11]

At Defiance Agency, the Navahos began to show impatience. Refraining still from violence but at no pains to conceal their hostility, the chiefs ordered Cicilia Arny to pack her belongings in a wagon and, with Miss Cook and other white women there, leave the reservation.

Such were the circumstances at the agency on the evening of September 9 when Major William Redwood Price rode in from Wingate accompanied by a corporal and two troopers. Not at all pleased to see them, Dr. Whitney bristled when the Major told him he was there under orders to take command. He would recognize no such orders, Whitney replied. Governor Arny had left *him* in charge, and he would not step aside until the Governor instructed him to do so. Major Price coolly answered that he did not recognize Whitney in the matter at all, but if Whitney chose to resist he would take the agency by force.

Loyal still to Arny, Whitney refused to co-operate. A military ambulance and wagon were put at his disposal, therefore, and on September 13, under Price's orders, he departed unwillingly for a rendezvous with Arny at Bacon Springs—later the site of Coolidge, New Mexico. Arny arrived there a week later with a cavalry escort furnished him by Colonel Gregg. His resignation had been accepted by the Interior Department before his departure from Santa Fe, but it was necessary for him to return to Defiance a last time to straighten the muddle of his accounts and officially turn over the agency to Major Price.

10 Enclosure "B," telegram from Pope to Gregg, in letter from Arny to Smith, October 11, 1875. (*Ibid.*)
11 *N. A., Ledgers of Traders.*

When he reached Defiance with Dr. Whitney on September 23, Arny decided he would not see the Major until it suited him and went into seclusion in one of the adobe buildings. Accustomed by now to this sort of behavior, Price the following day had an orderly deliver a message to Arny saying he was ready—at Arny's "earliest practicable convenience"—to receive and sign papers for the agency property.

"As the main trouble with the Indians seems to have arisen from a misunderstanding as to what was their property and what was yours," Price said, "I desire to be informed at once in writing what belongs to you. I believe I can then with very little trouble find what belongs to the Government."

Arny emerged the following day and consented to assist Major Price in taking an inventory. Ledgers were consulted, warerooms inspected, and lists of Arny's personal things, or those he claimed as his, were compared with lists of agency orders, furnishings, and supplies. A dry, dusty business. In the end, Price and Arny were locked in disagreement.

"I told him," Arny reported later, "I did not feel authorized to transfer anything to him, especially as he had already seized it.

"He then took my private property, and refused to give a receipt to me for it."

Weeks and months passed, and the Indian Office was forced into a long, inconclusive investigation, before anyone could decide what belonged to Arny and what rightfully should remain for the Navahos. Arny, meanwhile, hurried off to Albuquerque where a grand jury was about to hear criminal charges he had brought against the squaw men.

To prosecute these "wicked white men," Arny enlisted the services of U. S. District Attorney Thomas B. Catron, and swore out affidavits that were entered as complaints at the October session of the federal District Court.

Lorenzo Hubbell, then at Fort Wingate, was one of eleven witnesses summoned for the October 14 hearing. No court record of testimony was made and the files of the Albuquerque newspapers of that date, which might have reported the hearing, have been lost. There is nothing, either, to indicate whether any of the defendants were present, though probably they were not, as warrants for the arrest of three of them were issued when indictments were handed down on October 16.

Some light is cast on the nature of the complaints, however, by

ARNY AND THE SQUAW MEN

affidavits filed by Arny and two of the agency employees, F. M. Tanner and W. W. Owens. The latter, it will be recalled, was among those swept out in Arny's 1873 housecleaning; Owens evidently had since regained a position of grace.

Thomas and William Keam had been known to him personally for the last several years, Arny declared in his statement, and he had reason to believe that neither of them was a citizen of the United States. More than two years ago "they were discharged as employees at the Navajo Agency in consequence of their promiscuous cohabitation with Navajo women."[12]

Arny believed that "Thomas V. Keames after his discharge departed the Reservation and left a squaw and two children, and William Keames persisted in cohabiting with a squaw . . . and remained on or near the Navajo Reservation to the present time" and that "on several occasions I as Agent . . . ordered him to depart . . . as he was there in violation of the law and . . . he defied me."

Arny then told of Thomas Keam's outrageous conduct in Washington, when he spirited the chiefs away and returned them drunk and in no condition to meet the President of the United States.

"Since that time I have every reason to believe that . . . Thomas V. Keames has consorted with William Keames, Anson C. Damon and Daniel Dubois and informed the Indians that he, Thomas V. Keames, was to be their Agent, and excited them to rebellion against the Government . . . .

"And I further state that . . . Thomas V. Keames and the other parties . . . have represented to the Navajo Indians that there was no such act as the late act of Congress in regard to the distribution of annuity goods and rations and that it was but by an order of my own as Agent that the goods were distributed to the heads of families instead of to the Chiefs and heads of bands and that it was but by my order . . . that they were required to work . . . .[13]

". . . in consequence of these statements all of the Navajo employees were compelled to cease work and leave the Agency and a portion of the white employees through fear left the Agency."

12 A copy of this affidavit is included as enclosure "G" in Arny's letter to Smith, September 14, 1875. (National Archives, Records N. M. S., Letters Received. 1875.)
13 "Section 3 of the Act of June 22, 1874 . . . provides that able bodied male Indians receiving supplies pursuant to appropriation acts should perform useful labor 'for the benefit of themselves or of the tribe, at a reasonable rate, to be fixed by the agent in charge, and to an amount equal in value to the supplies to be delivered." (Felix S. Cohen, *Handbook of Federal Indian Law*.) In this instance Arny was right, and in his counsel to the Navahos, Keam was wrong.

Thomas Keam told the Navahos that when he was appointed agent they would not have to work for their annuity goods, Arny continued. And finally, he had found Daniel DuBois drunk and defiant in one of the agency buildings, and later—evidently in Santa Fe—"I saw William Keames furnishing whiskey to some Indians and . . . the whole party were drunk."

Tanner and Owens said they were acquainted with the defendants and that William Keam, Damon, and DuBois "have no fixed place of residence" and since last March "have been in the habit of frequenting and roaming the Navajo Reservation." And these three "by a course of systematic misrepresentation and intimidation excited the Navajo Indians to opposition to the Agent and employees of the Agency and also to arouse in [the] Indians a spirit of hostility to the Government and dissatisfaction with the policy of the Government towards them."[14]

Reviewing these charges with evidence offered by the witnesses, the Grand Jury on October 16 found no grounds for action against Thomas Keam and charges against him were dropped.

Indictments were issued against the other three. William Keam was indicted on charges of selling liquor to Indians and sending a seditious message to the Indians. Damon and DuBois were indicted only on the second charge. The cases were scheduled for trial at the April, 1876, term but were postponed until the fall, when they were again continued.[15]

Arny's successor, Alex Irvine, reported in June, 1876, that Thomas Keam was operating a trading post one mile south of the agency and just outside of the reservation line; he was separated from his Navaho wife, who, with their children, had returned to live with her Navaho kinsmen. William Keam was still living with his Navaho wife and operating his brother's trading post at Keams Canyon. "Both he and his woman make visits to this agency," Irvine said, "but never remain over one night on the reservation. DuBois lives about one half mile from the reservation and has a Navajo woman and three or four children. . . . I must report that since I have had charge of this agency I have had no reason to complain of any of these parties."[16]

Lorenzo Hubbell was working at the post trader's store at Fort

14 Affidavit marked "H," dated September 13, 1875, enclosed with Arny's September 14 letter to Smith.

15 Records of these cases are now on file in U. S. District Court, Santa Fe.

16 Letter from Irvine to Smith, June 6, 1876. (National Archives, Records N. M. S., Letters Received, 1876.)

Wingate. In October, venturing out on his own, he undertook to supply the Navaho agency with 100,000 pounds of corn. Thomas Keam and Henry Reed, the Wingate trader, were guarantors of his contract.

Finally, in the spring of 1877, hearings were held on the remaining indictments. On May 10, William Keam, Anson Damon, and Dan DuBois appeared in federal court before Judge Henry L. Waldo and pleaded not guilty. Judge Waldo found each of the defendants not guilty and the charges against them were dismissed.

Arny may have sensed the temper of the winds after appearing before the Grand Jury at the start of the litigation. In any event he wrote to Commissioner Smith on October 19, 1875:

"I would . . . respectfully suggest that a law be passed making it a criminal offense for a white man to cohabit with an Indian squaw unless he is married to her under the laws of the United States, and that when married they shall no longer live on the reservation."[17]

His suggestion went unheeded.

[17] *Annual Report, C. I. A., 1875.* Section 5 of the Act of February 28, 1891, "provides that for purposes of descent [in cases involving land allotment rights], cohabitation 'according to the custom and manner of Indian life' shall be considered valid marriage." (Felix Cohen, *Handbook of Federal Indian Law.*)

12

Thomas Keam: 1880-1882

As a WAGON AXLE without grease grates warning of impending breakdown, so the short new regime of Navaho Agent Galen Eastman was giving every sign of approaching disaster. The advance of the Atlantic and Pacific Railroad across New Mexico and into the plains of Arizona brought with it evils that Eastman was too lax or incompetent to control: an increase in traffic in guns and whisky and, with that, an upsurge in stock theft and general lawlessness. By early spring of 1880 military officers were frankly alarmed by the situation. Eastman's ineptitude, the contempt in which he was held by the Indians, cried out for change.

From his canyon ranch and trading post west of the reservation, Thomas Keam heard his name mentioned as the man the officers felt was best able to restore order. In April he was recommended as agent to replace Eastman by the commanding officer at Fort Wingate, Colonel L. P. Bradley, and by Brevet Major General Edward Hatch, commanding the Headquarters District of New Mexico.[1] From Fort Lewis in Colorado, Colonel George P. Buell, commanding, in June urged "in strongest manner the appointment of Mr. Kerns [Keam]

---

[1] Capt. Loud, Ninth Cavalry, HQ District of N. M., to Asst. Adjt. General, Dept. of Missouri, April 27, 1880, states in part: "General Hatch . . . directs me to forward his concurrence in the recommendation for the appointment of Mr. Thomas V. Keams to succeed the present agent of the Navajoes, which has been made by the Commanding Officer Ft. Wingate in letter referred to." Enclosure, with letter from Secretary of War to Secretary of Interior, June 19, 1880. (National Archives, Letters Received . . . 1880, #K959.)

Agent for the Navajoes, and especially that Mr. Eastman be not ordered to return."[2]

Before action on these recommendations could be taken, Galen Eastman was removed and on June 12, 1880, replaced by the veteran Frank Tracy Bennett, whose appointment was regarded as an emergency measure and temporary.[3] General of the Army William T. Sherman forwarded the letters recommending Keam to the War Department with the comment: "This [opinion favoring Keam] is superseded by the detail of Captain Bennett . . . but after a time Mr. Kearns [sic] should succeed him."[4]

Bennett remained at Defiance Agency one year, doing a respectable job. Eastman, meanwhile, assigned to special service with the Indian Office, returned to Washington and so effectively repaired fences that his reappointment as agent seemed assured. To forestall this, General Hatch again, on March 14, 1881, wrote to the Secretary of the Interior urging that Keam be given the position. When no answer was received, Hatch wrote a third time and in June received the Secretary's brusque reply :"I beg to inform you that your letter was referred by me to the Commissioner of Indian Affairs for report, and a copy of his reply, stating that serious charges against Mr. Keams are on file in his office, is enclosed for your information."[5]

The General, no doubt feeling puzzled as well as rebuffed, wrote a note on the back of the Secretary's letter: "Respectfully returned . . . with a request that copy of the charges against Mr. Keams be sent to me, and if not considered improper, the name of the person making them. Mr. Keams has been known so many years to officers of Army, favorably, it is singular he should have been guilty of any irregularities not known to the Army. I will state further that Mr. Keams has informed me his business engagements are such that he cannot accept the appointment, if given him."

Hatch's request for information was not acknowledged. The dos-

2 Asst. Adjt. Gen. William D. Whipple, Dept. of Missouri, to Adjutant General, Washington, D. C., June 17, 1880. (*Ibid.*, enclosure.)

3 Eastman had served as agent from April 26, 1879. Captain Bennett, relieved from duty with the Ninth Cavalry for this chore, previously had been the Navahos' second agent, serving from August 26, 1869, to February 3, 1871.

4 *Ibid.*

5 Secretary of the Interior to General Hatch, June 16, 1881. (National Archives, Letters Sent . . . 1881, #11997.) Commissioner Price's letter, enclosed, contained no specific charges against Keam, Price saying only that there were charges and "this office is in possession of information which shows that he is not a fit person to receive an appointment as Indian Agent." It is clear, however, that the resentment built up against Keam during the Arny regime remained strong.

sier of Keam's old opposition to Arny and his sinful behavior as a squaw man who dared expose the thieving and corruption of an Indian Office agent was not reopened.

In April and May, 1881, Captain Bennett was visited at Defiance Agency by a most perceptive guest, a man not usually given to acid observation. The visitor, Lieutenant John G. Bourke, temporarily detached from the staff of General George Crook to survey the Navaho country (assisted at Defiance by Navaho-wise Anson Damon), found, with apologies to his host, that the agency "is of adobe in an advanced stage of decay . . . it is a collection of old dilapidated mud, pig sties and sheep pens and nothing more."[6]

Galen Eastman, waiting now to take over again as agent, Bourke described as "a psalm-singing hypocrite whom the Navajos despised and whom they tried to kill.

"This Eastman had *on paper* a boarding school for Indian children, of which he wrote glorious accounts to the Sabbath-school papers and which I visited. It consisted of one miserable squalid dark and musty adobe dungeon, not much more capacious than the cubby hole of an oyster schooner; it was about 12x10x7 in height. No light ever penetrated but one window let darkness out from this den and one small door gave exit to some of the mustiness; Eastman reported that he had accommodations for *sixty children*, but I saw only nine (9) cottonwood bunks, in which, if he had made them double up, eighteen little children could be made wretched."

Bourke departed, soon to return, and in the meantime, on June 30, Eastman resumed the office of agent. His absence of a year he attributed to no failure of his own but to "military interference."

A storm was brewing between the agent and the man the Navahos wanted to replace him. Neither of them knew it, however, when Keam went to Fort Wingate in August and there met Lieutenant Bourke and his artist friend, Peter Moran. The latter had come out for the Snake Dance to be held that year at Walpi. They traveled from Albuquerque on the new railroad, finding it a slow, uncertain journey. Bourke, alighting at Wingate Station to walk through the rain three and one-half miles to the fort while Moran remained with their luggage, was welcomed by his friend, Colonel Bradley, the post commander. Bourke later wrote that "most comforting assurance of all received from him was one to the effect that the rattlesnake-dance would not occur until the 11th, and that Mr. Tom Keam was now

---

6 Bourke's comments appear in his diary entry for April 25, 1881. (Bloom [ed.], "Bourke on the Southwest, VIII," *New Mexico Historical Review*, Vol. XI [1936].)

in the post, where he was to stay all the next day and then start back for his home at Moqui Agency, reaching there in plenty of time for seeing this strange ceremony."[7]

The same evening, presumably in Keam's company, Bourke met Dr. Washington Matthews, then the post surgeon and noted later as an ethnologist and early authority on Navaho life-way and ceremonial customs. On August 7, taking leave of Wingate, Keam with Bourke and Moran rode to Fort Defiance where they were welcomed and evidently given lodging by the post trader, William Leonard, and his clerks, Sinclair and McDonald. The day following, according to Bourke, "Keam, Moran and myself, joined by Mr. Sinclair and two soldiers, Gordon and Smallwood, who had preceded us from Fort Wingate, started for the Moqui villages. Our drive of yesterday had been over forty miles; that of this day was to be over thirty, so it became necessary to leave early."

By late afternoon they were at the ranch and trading post of George M. (Barney) Williams. This was on the Pueblo Colorado Wash, evidently near the *anasazi* ruin the Navahos called *Kin Lichee* (Red House) and only a few miles east of Lorenzo Hubbell's Ganado trading post.

"With genuine western hospitality Mr. Williams insisted upon our taking up our quarters with him," Bourke relates. "Mr. Williams' ranch is of the Arizona order of architecture—a single-storied, long, low building of 'jacal' or palisade, filled in with mud chinking, and roofed with a covering of earth and brush. . . . Williams has built up for himself a thriving and lucrative trade with the Navajoes, over whom, in common with Keam and Leonard, he wields great influence. . . . One of the items of [his] commerce with the Navajoes was *crucibles*, for use in silver work; they also make for themselves out of the impure kaolin found in their country, the clay which they eat with the wild potato."[8]

Williams and his partner, a man named Webber, joined with them the next day, Bourke observing that "we were a large party to

[7] There is no certainty on the point but it appears that Keam's meeting with Bourke and Moran was previously arranged so that the trader might be their host and guide. Bourke's remarks here and following are from his *The Snake-Dance of the Moquis of Arizona.*

[8] The crucibles supplied by Barney Williams and those which Bourke says the Navahos made for themselves of kaolin, or white clay, would have been the utensils employed in melting coin silver prior to casting it in molds. John Adair quotes Roman Hubbell as saying that Atsidi Chon (Ugly Smith), an important early craftsman, was the first Navaho to make silver in the vicinity of Ganado. (*The Navajo and Pueblo Silversmiths.*)

impose upon Keam's hospitality . . . but the matter seemed not to give him the slightest concern. 'If you fellows'll take what I've got, without growling, why, you're welcome, and that's all there is about it.' And he added: 'I've got lots of grub and dishes, and a pretty fair cook, and plenty of blankets. What more do you want? You don't expect to find a Crystal Palace down at my place, do you?' "

While still fifteen miles east of the nearest Hopi villages, the party descended into Keams Canyon and were greeted at Keam's house by Alexander Stephen, a young scientist of unusual promise who lived with Keam and was more or less supported by him from 1880 until his death in 1894.[9]

Bourke looked about him to see how this young Indian trader—this Englishman—had built a home among the rocks and sand of an Arizona canyon. "Although his mode of life had necessarily many rude features, the fact that Keam still clung to the methods and mode of thought of civilized life was shadowed forth in the interior of his dwelling, which was tastily decorated with fine Navajo blankets, sheepskin rugs, Moqui pottery, and Smithsonian photographs.

"A set of shelves in one corner of the living room contained choice specimens of literature—Shakespeare, Thackeray, Dickens, Taine, and other authors, and also an unusually good representation of standard American and English magazines and newspapers.

"Chemical re-agents, test-tubes, and blow-pipes covered a table next the solitary window, and added to the tinge of refinement and education suggested by the books and *bric-à-brac*. A Liliputian flower garden claimed much of Keam's attention, and repaid his kindly care with a pleasing tribute of mignonette, candy-tuft, and aster.

"Other flowers in pots decked the windows of the bed and living rooms; the growth of these had lately been blighted either by the gases evolved during the process of assaying, or by the black flies

[9] Bourke refers to Keam's protégé as "a metallurgist and mining prospector" who had had considerable experience in Nevada and Utah. But Alexander Mc-Gregor Stephen, a Scot, is best remembered as an ethnologist. It was from his notes that Cosmos Mindeleff prepared the introductory chapter on Hopi traditionary history, for the *8th Annual Report of the Bureau of Ethnology*. Stewart Culin, in *The American Anthropologist* (N. S., Vol. VII) observed that after Stephen's death, "Mr. Keam preserved Stephen's numerous valuable manuscripts with jealous care, and erected a monument on his grave in the canyon." Watson Smith notes that "Stephen devoted nearly all his thirteen years of life in the Hopi country to a study of Hopi life, especially in its ceremonial aspects, and in pursuit of his knowledge he spent a great deal of time actually with the people, mainly on First Mesa, where he was respected and beloved. During his later years he kept a series of astoundingly rich notebooks, profusely illustrated." (*Kiva Mural Decorations at Awatovi and Kawaika-a*.)

alighting upon them and puncturing them with holes in which to deposit their eggs."

Keam's trading post and warerooms were separated from his house and farther down canyon, but on all sides Bourke found stumbling reminders of his host's occupation. "In every nook and cranny of the long low building bales of wool and sheep skins were packed, awaiting a favourable season for transportation to the eastern market."

And the atmosphere of this bachelor home was relaxed and comfortably informal. "The destinies of the kitchen were in the hands of a cook who understood his business, and whose two assistants were 'Garryowen,' a bright Navajo boy, who waited upon the table, and 'Mrs. Pinkham,' an old squaw, who faithfully brought the pitcher of goat's milk for our morning coffee.

"The water used from this ranch was obtained from three springs directly in front of the door, and was worthy of the highest praise for sweetness, coldness, and purity."

The Hopi agent, John H. Sullivan, called at Keam's house after breakfast and invited the guests to go with him to see the nearby ruins of Awatovi.[10] This they did, not returning until long after dark. Lorenzo Hubbell came from his home on the Pueblo Colorado to join the party and took them on to Walpi next day, to be joined there later by Keam who was detained in the canyon by business.

Early in 1882 there were renewed demands by the military for Galen Eastman's removal, and again Keam was recommended as agent. In the ensuing controversy Eastman felt that he was being victimized by the officers, but the true root of his trouble, he was certain, was Thomas Keam.

Confiding these thoughts to his brother-in-law, United States Senator T. W. Ferry of Michigan, Eastman allowed that his job was "no bed of roses" and if he could he would "swap it for an Inspector's,"

10 Keam's name for the ruin was Tolli-hogandi (the Singing House), which he told Bourke was a corruption of the Navaho word, *Atabi-ho-gandi*. Some ten miles southwest of Keams Canyon, Awatovi is located on the southern rim of Antelope Mesa, high above Jeddito Wash. Once one of the larger Hopi villages, it was chosen by the Spaniards as the site for a Franciscan church and friary. The church was destroyed during the Pueblo revolt in 1680. In 1699, Awatovi was partially reoccupied by the Spaniards, who again persuaded the natives to adopt Christianity. Angered by this defection, Hopis of the other villages, under the leadership of the mission-bred Indian, Francisco Espleta, sacked and destroyed the pueblo in 1700, killing all of the men and carrying off the women. It has been an abandoned ruin ever since. (John Otis Brew, *The Excavation of Franciscan Awatovi*.)

for which "I have tact and talent." But his tougher, more demanding duties as Navaho agent he would not quit yet—not under fire.

He concentrated his anger against Keam, as the leader of "the ring" or "junto" of squaw men who deviled him as they had deviled Arny. Keam's ambition to be the Navahos' agent was well known, Eastman said, hinting mysteriously that the trader somehow was linked with the murder of Agent James Miller in 1872.[11] Evidence of this he would not supply, as of course there was none; a seed planted in the Senator's mind should be enough.

As Eastman fretted over his insecurity, word of Indian trouble along the northeastern border of the Navaho reservation reached Santa Fe. Colonel R. S. Mackenzie, now commanding the Headquarters District, was not unduly aroused, but in February wrote to the assistant adjutant general of the Department of Missouri, urging certain precautions.

"I believe it would be well," he said, "to send four companies of Cavalry to Fort Lewis to look after the eastern edge of the Navajoe Country. I do not anticipate any general outbreak among the Navajoes, but their condition is not satisfactory and I am informed that they have no confidence in their present agent. I learn this from many sources but particularly from Professor Stevenson [James Stevenson, an ethnologist with the Smithsonian Institution in Washington and a good friend of Keam's] who has had the very best opportunities of learning the truth and who is, I judge, impartial."[12]

11 Letter from Eastman to Senator Ferry, January 24, 1882. (National Archives, Letters Received . . . 1882, #3817.) In his anger, Eastman writes almost incoherently: "The Hon. Commr. of Indian Affairs (who I believe to be the Peer of all his Predecessors) ought to know these facts in order to defeat such purposes and yet for me to be known in the matter too prominently would insure my joining company with the *three* Agents who have been murdered heretofore and whose bodies lie mouldering here—*as I*— (Agent Thomas & others at Santa Fe *know* about the 'Miller' matter) believe the victims of (the ring) *this man Keam's ambition*—to be Agent!" Circumstances of Agent Miller's death, well known to the Indian Office, curiously were not known to Eastman, who readily believed partisan rumors that Miller was killed by Navahos at the instigation of Keam. Eastman's implication that three Navaho agents had been murdered by Navahos is equally faulty. Capt. Henry L. Dodge, third agent to the Navahos before the tribe was moved to a reservation, was killed by Apaches in 1856. Maj. Theodore H. Dodd, first agent for the Navahos when they were moved to their new reservation in 1868, died of paralysis in January, 1869. Agent Miller, as related elsewhere, was murdered by two Wiminuche Utes, June 11, 1872. Otherwise, prior to Eastman's regime, Navaho agents retired quietly or were removed abruptly by a frequently embarrassed Indian Office. No Navaho agent ever was murdered by Navahos.

12 Letter from Col. Mackenzie to Asst. Adjt. General, Dept. of Missouri, February 10, 1882. (*Ibid.*, #7258.)

Stevenson probably had accurate information about the Navahos' discontent. As Keam's friend, however, he would not be impartial.

At Fort Lewis, where he commanded a token force of cavalry, Colonel Buell in March observed that whisky-sellers and cattlemen were causing serious trouble among the Navahos in the San Juan Valley. A cowboy had shot a Navaho "headman . . . for no cause whatever." A sizable clash was averted, but the Navahos—formerly dependent upon a few old caplock rifles—were now arming themselves with Winchesters and plenty of ammunition. The Indians were in no mood to be shoved around, and to prove it had burned the home of General Horace Porter, some fifteen miles east of the reservation's eastern boundary line.[13]

Instead of investigating the trouble personally, Colonel Buell remarked, Agent Eastman "simply sent a letter by an Indian to the San Juan Valley, addressed to no one in particular."

The Colonel recommended that Eastman be removed and that Keam be appointed in his place. He knew of no one better able to restore peace and order, and added that Keam was a man who "has lived many years among the Navajos; he speaks their language; he is known by almost every Indian in the tribe; he has their love and respect."

A copy of the Colonel's letter, written to his commanding officers of the Department of the Missouri, was secured by the Indian Office and forwarded to Eastman for his comment. If Buell's words were galling to him, however, the agent soon could expect worse.

In April a Justice Department inspector named S. R. Martin, after visiting Defiance Agency, reported to Washington that the Navahos had no confidence in Eastman: ". . . they say he has ten tongues— they would rather have no agent than the one they have got." Martin

13 Letter from Col. Buell to Asst. Adjt. General, Dept. of Missouri, March 13, 1882. (*Ibid.*, enclosure.) John Arrington recalls that it was not a head man but a Navaho of no rank who was shot. This occurred at Spencer's Store in Farmington when the Indian, who had been lounging at the counter, seized a bolt of calico and ran out of the door. The storekeeper fired a warning shot over his head, after which Tom Nance, a cowboy with the Two Cross Ranch on the LaPlata and noted as a bully and killer, shot the Navaho in the back, injuring him seriously. As Colonel Buell remarks, a large party of Navahos descended on the town in angry retaliation, fully prepared to destroy it. Further bloodshed was averted when Dr. John Brown, the town's physician, confronted the armed Navahos and, with the support of their chief, Kasti-anna, persuaded them to disperse. The home of General Porter, referred to by Buell, probably was located at a place in Gallegos Canyon known as *Hooshen'ih* (trading place) Springs, about halfway between the San Juan River and the future site of Dick Simpson's trading post.

added that Eastman's unpopularity was creating "a powder mine that may explode at any time" into a Navaho war.[14]

He did not know the trader personally, Martin added, but "all the military officers as well as all the white men and Indians without an exception . . . recommend Thomas Keam as a suitable man" to replace Eastman.

The letters of Colonel Buell and Inspector Martin were referred to retiring Secretary of the Interior S. J. Kirkwood, reaching his office on April 13. Before referring them to the Commissioner of Indian Affairs, Kirkwood scrawled a memo that said, in part: "I am of opinion it would be well to appoint a new agent but am not of opinion that it would be wise to appoint Mr. Keams. I think no action should be had until my successor [former Senator Henry Moore Teller, of Colorado] shall have taken his desk."

Eastman's superiors in Washington waited for his reply. On April 28 the agent made a blanket denial of all charges against his administration. Reports that a Navaho war was imminent, he said, "are as groundless and false today as they were last July or during 1880." Keam he dismissed angrily as "the favorite of certain of the military" interests that "heretofore controlled this and other agencies, as I believe, to their profit."[15] Colonel Buell's comments, based only on hearsay evidence, were an impertinent meddling in the affairs of the Interior Department. Eastman asked that Inspector Martin be removed from office, on grounds that Martin gave false evidence and violated the law by drinking on the reservation—in the presence of Eastman and his wife while at the agency, "showing us at the same time his flask, stating that it contained Gin, and that he had just partaken of its contents."

The tribe's grievance was due partly to the fact that annuity goods, guaranteed for ten years by the 1868 treaty, automatically were cut off after 1879. Since then, the Navahos felt, Eastman had made no effort to secure needed help for them. The 1882 appropriation for sixteen thousand or more Navahos was only $5,000, and this included

14 Martin's letter, to Brewster Cameron, general agent for the U.S. Justice Department, April 7, 1882, is enclosed with a letter from Atty. Gen. Benjamin Harrison Brewster to Secretary of the Interior S. J. Kirkwood. (*Ibid.*, #7256.) Brewster's comment on Martin's charges: "This letter is personal, but the gravity of the subject would seem to entitle it to serious consideration. Assistant Attorney General McCammon . . . vouches for the absolute veracity of the writer."

15 Letter from Eastman to C. I. A. Price, April 28, 1882. (*Ibid.*, #8721.) Enclosed are affidavits signed by James R. Sutherland, agency clerk, and E. J. Gynlay, agency storekeeper.

a year's salary for the agency farmer. This pittance was supposed to buy the tools and farming equipment the tribe needed to subsist itself.

More trouble for the agent was gathering. On May 12 a number of the chiefs met at the agency with the previously determined purpose, so they told Keam later, of seizing the agent and running him off the reservation. Keam advised the Secretary of the Interior of the situation as he knew it.[16]

"I have the honor," he wrote, "to state that 'Ganado Mucho,' the principal chief of the Navajo Indians, came to my house [in Keams Canyon] last evening and requested me to write you . . . .

"On the 12th inst. he with other principal chiefs of the Navajos visited their agency as before agreed on by them in council, for the purpose of taking their Agent, Galen Eastman, and placing him in a wagon [and] driv[ing] him out of their country, as they could tolerate him no longer.

"In council among themselves at the Agency, before proceeding to act, Ganado Mucho informed them of my having telegraphed a friend of mine in Washington [James Stevenson] to see you and inform you of their intention, and in a talk which lasted through the night, suggested they defer action until they heard what answer I received from Washington; this they all reluctantly agreed to, and subsequently in council with their Agent informed him of their intention. He told them he would write to Washington to have a man appointed in his place but he did not want to leave before some one was present to take over the position, so that he would not have to return among them again.

"They did not believe a word he said, and desire that a reply to this be sent to me, so that I can communicate the truth to them.

"Should they hear nothing satisfactory in eighteen days, they will place Mr. Eastman in a wagon and take him to the Rail-road as every Indian in the tribe hated him, but out of respect to the Government did not wish to injure him. With a good man as Agent in whom they could have confidence, who would go among them and give them good advice, most of their troubles and whiskey drinking could be prevented, and they urgently request you to take action in their behalf at once.

"If my influence with them can be of any service to the Department it is at your command."

16 Letter from Keam to the Secretary of the Interior, May 18, 1882. (*Ibid.*, #10078.)

The Interior Department reacted to Keam's letter with angry surprise. Teller, the new secretary, and Indian Commissioner Hiram Price, lacking firsthand knowledge of affairs on the Navaho reservation, felt it confirmed Eastman's charge that Keam was scheming to undermine Eastman's authority by turning the Navahos against him. They saw in Keam's phrasing an unmasked threat to an official of the Indian Office and, in that, an act of defiance aimed at themselves. Their sentiments were conveyed to Keam by one of Price's assistants, E. S. Stevens.

"Say to these Indians," Stevens replied frigidly, "that this office is convinced that villainous white men among them and near their reservation, have been for several years trying to influence them to disregard every request or command made by their Agent for their good, and have in every underhanded way, tried to weaken the influence of the Agent over them.[17]

"And say to them, further, that this office is also convinced that the efforts of the white men referred to are put forth, not for the good of the Indians, but for the basest purposes . . . .

"Tell them, too, that this office hopes they will not be so foolish as to listen to the infamous counsel of these bad white men, and that so sure as they attempt to injure the Agent or remove him from the reservation until the Secretary of the Interior says a change shall be made, they will be put down if it takes the whole Army of the United States to do it."

And Keam's offer of his services? "As you are understood to have considerable influence with these Indians . . . I think I may with confidence expect that it will be used to thwart the efforts of those who are evidently advising them very badly."

As clearly as Keam desired the appointment as Navaho agent, the Indian Office was determined he should not have it.

[17] Letter from Stevens to Keam, June 3, 1882. (*Ibid.*)

13

Keam and the Prospectors

FATE INTERVENED when Eastman needed help the most, to revive dimming interest in the murder of Merrick and Mitchell. The slaying of the two prospectors by Paiutes was shrugged off by Eastman in 1880 as none of his affair. The men died in what the agent chose to call the "land of death"—the region now known as Monument Valley; it was not then a part of the reservation and so actually not within Eastman's jurisdiction.

Less technical about boundaries, the military failed to see it that way. An Indian agent, they said, was responsible for what happened on his doorstep. The incident in 1880 had contributed to Eastman's temporary removal from office; now an accidental encounter renewed speculation about the unfortunate affair and Eastman seized upon this as a means for striking back at Keam.

What is known of Merrick and Mitchell, beyond their names and last few hours, is little indeed. Some time shortly before 1880 they entered the country northwest of the Navaho reservation, a silent and seemingly endless valley of sand and towering redrock buttes and pinnacles. This valley and the mesas rising as far to the west as Navajo Mountain was then a domain controlled by Hoskinini, or Handing Out War, the chief of a little-known but hostile band of Navahos. Sometimes associated with Hoskinini's people was a smaller group of Paiutes. The arid isolation of the region provided these Indians only rare contact with a few white men.

Somewhere in this valley of monuments, according to faulty legend, Merrick and Mitchell found a rich deposit of silver ore and brought out samples said to assay as high as eight hundred dollars a ton.[1] On their return to the vicinity, in January, 1880, some four miles south of the Utah line and near a butte now named for Mitchell, they were halted by a party of Paiutes.

Hoskinini-begay, son of the Navaho chief, has been quoted as saying that the Paiutes accused the prospectors of using water belonging to the Indians. More likely, with their advantage in numbers, they merely wanted the prospectors' guns and their horses and mules. In any case, the Paiutes opened fire.

Mitchell fell dead where he stood. His companion, although wounded, managed to make his way south for three miles until he could go no farther. He died near the valley monument now known as Merrick Butte.

This is all that Galen Eastman knew of the affair afterward—until chance brought to the agency one Philip Zoeller, offering information. A complete stranger, Zoeller turned up on June 19, 1882.

He was a Colorado man, a prospector, his home being in Pueblo County. About the same time that Merrick and Mitchell disappeared in Monument Valley, Zoeller and another party of prospectors entered the region. His party for some reason divided, and Zoeller made his way to Keams Canyon where for the last two years he had remained.

"I found his [Keam's] place to be closer to the locality I wished to prospect than any other," Zoeller explained, "but felt unsafe to enter again or return to Colorado alone."[2]

Zoeller told Eastman that for the past year he had worked at Keam's trading post and had been there in the previous summer when James Stevenson made the canyon a headquarters during his ethnological surveys for the Smithsonian Institution. He suggested that Keam and Stevenson were involved in a scheme to hold what was presumed to be a vast wealth of silver ore for themselves, keeping other prospectors out by arousing the Indians against them.

"Keam has told the Indians that if he (Keam) or two or three of his friends should go to this mineral locality—or Merrick Mine, it would

___

[1] It is not likely that the Merrick-Mitchell mine was in Monument Valley, as believed until now. Dana R. Kelley, formerly a geologist with the Atomic Energy Commission, spent three months at Kayenta in 1952 surveying the valley for mineral deposits. Dr. Kelly tells me that Monument Valley does contain uranium and copper, but has no gold or silver.

[2] Zoeller's statements are quoted from two affidavits: the first dated June 20, 1882, the second, August 4, 1882. (National Archives . . . Letters Received, 1882, #11725 and #14834.)

be all right and the Indians must do all they could for them and not molest them. But if a larger party, other than his friends, should go there, they were *bad*—thus giving the Indians to understand what their duty to Keam as their friend should be.

"I believe Stevenson, with others, to be greatly interested in the development of the mineral locality . . . solely for their own exclusive benefit, and especially anxious in keeping all others out."

Keam's desire to maintain good relations with Hoskinini would have caused him to discourage prospectors from entering Monument Valley. There is nothing of record, beyond Zoeller's affidavit, to indicate that Keam and Stevenson were greatly interested, themselves, in mining. Zoeller's animosity toward Keam, so evident here, perhaps stemmed from the trader's desire to prevent Zoeller from blundering into the valley and provoking Hoskinini's Navahos into another Merrick-Mitchell incident.

Keam went to Washington early in the present year, Zoeller continued, seeking appointment as agent in Eastman's place. Even before leaving, Keam had given the Navahos and Hopis to understand that he, rather than Eastman, was in authority over them.

"He frequently told the Indians that he acts under the authority of the General Government," Zoeller said, "and endeavors to make them believe that he has special authority over this whole section of country and more particularly over all the Navajos and their agent."

Again referring to the murder of Merrick and Mitchell, Zoeller said the prospectors outfitted at Keam's trading post before starting on their fatal trip, and Keam knew their plans and destination.

Not long after Merrick and Mitchell were killed, he continued, their pack animals and arms were brought in by Navahos and turned over to Keam.

"I firmly believe," he told Eastman, "that Keam has guilty knowledge—if he was not the instigator—of [their] murder."

Zoeller's story Eastman recorded and forwarded to Commissioner Price. For the present, he told the Commissioner, he was awaiting the return of his interpreter, Chee Dodge, and his agency farmer. Eastman had sent them off on a mission, a dangerous one he knew well: they were to enter the region of the Dead Men's Mine, find Hoskinini and his band, and establish "friendly relations." This was a task that Eastman had no wish to undertake personally. But to provide company for his two men—and in consequence making their trip more hazardous—he sent them out with two other prospectors, Jonathan P. Williams and William Ross.

When the party returned safely early in August, Zoeller, who was still hanging about the agency, somehow was reminded of a detail elaborating his previous story. Referring to Keam's supposed statement that any prospectors other than his friends were "bad men," Zoeller said the remark was made in the presence of two other white men and—most significantly—the Navaho chief Hoskinini and the Paiute chief San-a-pee, "who is reported to have aided in the murder of Merrick and Mitchell."

Williams and Ross then added their bit. They had encountered Hoskinini, they told Eastman, far off in his valley of red buttes, near the border of Arizona and Utah. The chief informed them that he and his Navahos had been advised by Keam that "he, Keam, was to be the Navajo Agent and was *then* the head of authority this side of Washington."[3] And further, said Williams, Hoskinini "told me that he had received from Keam the gun belonging to one of the murdered men—Merrick or Mitchell—taken from them at the time of the murder."

Hoskinini also told Williams that he and some of his band took all of the goods belonging to the prospectors to Keam's trading post. A mule brought in with the other things was held by Keam for ransom, Williams said, the trader refusing to surrender it until Mitchell's father paid fifty dollars to the Navaho who had taken the mule from the Paiutes.

Eastman forwarded this information to the Commissioner without recommending any sort of investigation or action; nor was any initiated in Washington, where the credibility of the stories attempting to link Keam with the murder of Merrick and Mitchell may have been questioned.

Soon afterward, Eastman advised Commissioner Price: "I have succeeded, through the personal effort of my farmer and interpreter, and at some risk to them, in establishing friendly relations with [Hoskinini's Navahos] and, by making the . . . Navajos responsible for their reckless neighbors' good conduct in future, I feel encouraged to hope that murders of prospectors and others in that heretofore land of death will be less frequent."[4]

Eastman's sanguine outlook might have been dampened in March, 1884, had he still been at the agency, but he was not. Eastman was removed as agent, without obvious pressure, and succeeded on Janu-

3 Affidavits of Williams and Ross, August 3 and 4, 1882. (*Ibid.*, #14834.)
4 *Annual Report, C. I. A., 1882.*

ary 1, 1883, by Denis M. Riordan. Saddled with the problems created by Eastman, Riordan himself was preparing to resign from the agency when he learned that two more prospectors had been murdered. Their deaths occurred in the vicinity of Navajo Mountain, Riordan was told—in any case, off the reservation and a tiresome distance from Defiance Agency.

The murderers this time were not Paiutes, but Navahos of Hoskinini's band. Their victims were men named Samuel Walcott and James McNally. Riordan decided to wash his hands of the affair, leaving it to his successor, John Bowman, to worry about.

Thomas Keam, meanwhile, had returned from Washington after interesting Secretary of the Interior Teller in a proposal to use his Keams Canyon buildings as an Indian school. Keam had been pleased with Teller's reception of his plan but his attention on arriving home was diverted by word of the recent killing of Walcott and McNally. The story was brought to him on May 31 by the Navaho chief Clee-e-cheen-beaz-be-ny, a trusted friend of nine years, who said he knew who the murderers were because in their own talk he had heard them tell of the affair.

Keam's Navaho informant then rode on to Defiance Agency, taking with him a note from the trader to Acting Agent S. E. Marshall. In his message Keam named two of the Navahos principally involved in the death of Walcott and McNally, and urged that they be punished.

"It appears to me to have been a cold-blooded murder, especially of the younger man," Keam wrote. ". . . I merely make this suggestion as I believe it to the interest of the Navajos and whites, some decided action should be taken, as I firmly believe if the murderers go unpunished it will not only have a bad effect, but will make travel in that and other parts of the reservation perilous." A copy of this note Keam enclosed with a longer letter on the same subject to Secretary Teller.[5]

Walcott, the older of the two prospectors, he wrote Teller, was killed with an ax. The Navahos "then tried to assassinate the younger [McNally] by attempting to shoot him in the back with his own rifle. Not succeeding in this, they surrounded him and fired several shots at him, he keeping behind his horses—of which they killed two. When he wounded one of the party with his pistol they took their

[5] Letter from Keam to Teller, June 5, 1884, and enclosure of Keam's note, May 31, 1884, to Marshall. (National Archives . . . Letters Received, 1884, #11520.)

wounded man away. When [McNally] made an effort to escape, they pursued him that night and ambushed and killed him the following day."

Waiting only for his term of duty to expire, Agent Riordan deferred action through the remainder of June; it would be unwise for him to do otherwise, he argued, until he could be assured the support of troops.

Bowman relieved Riordan at the end of June, and on July 3, 1884, the new agent wrote to Commissioner Price: "At once upon my taking charge of the Agency, I made the demand that the guilty parties should come in and surrender themselves. As they are distant from the Agency fully 175 miles, I gave them ten days time, and if they are not here at the expiration of ten days, it is my purpose to send the [Navaho] Scouts to make the arrest, and if they are not able to carry out my orders, then will call upon the military for help."[6]

The new agent was still confident of his ability to handle the situation unaided when, a few days later and under orders from Lieutenant Colonel R. E. A. Crofton, commanding Fort Wingate, twenty-five cavalrymen reported to him at Defiance and went into camp. Bowman regarded their presence without enthusiasm, observing that his Navaho scouts moved faster than the soldiers and were more effective. Already he had two prisoners to justify this belief: the chief himself, Hoskinini, and Tugi-yazzie, one of the accused murderers.

The latter was brought in on July 11 by the Navaho police. Hoskinini surrendered voluntarily, encouraging Bowman's mistaken belief that he was someone else, and submitted willingly when he was taken off under guard to Fort Wingate and locked up. Not until later did the new agent learn that Hoskinini had no part in the murder of Walcott and McNally, but offered himself as hostage to protect his son, Hoskinini-begay.

S. E. Marshall was a witness and Chee Dodge served as interpreter when Tugi-yazzie was led before Bowman to tell of his part in the affair. An agency clerk made these notes as Chee Dodge drew out the old man's story:

"I came to the camp of the Americans where the dead American was lying—the old man—and I said to the Navajos, 'My boys, what have you been doing here?' Hoskinini-begay and Dinet-tsosi and a boy were the Navajos. This is all I said to them, when I went a little distance away [and] saw Ba-leen-la-ki driving a herd of horses. I said

---

6 Letter from Bowman to Price, July 3, 1884, (*Ibid.*, #12891.)

to [him], 'My brother, I saw over here where some boys have killed an American.'[7]

"Ba-leen-la-ki and myself started back towards the Americans' camp. When near there we met . . . Hoskinini-begay and Dinet-tsosi and the boy, who had killed the old man, and there we sat a while, and soon three other Navajos came there.

"Then I told the boys, 'Let us go back towards our hogans and let this other American go'—so we sat there a while, and Dinet-tsosi and Hoskinini-begay said we had better kill the American [McNally].

"A short time after that the party split and the two Navajos [Dinet-tsosi and Hoskinini-begay] went together, and myself and Ba-leen-la-ki went away in another direction. We went a little piece, and us two were a little ways apart, and we were near the American.

"Then I heard three shots fired by Hoskinini-begay and Dinet-tsosi who killed three horses belonging to the Americans. After the killing of the three horses, I went a little ways walking along when I was shot by the American. Then I fell down, and then got up and ran away, but I fell down several times before I got entirely away."

Tugi-yazzie, with a scalp wound from McNally's pistol-shot, was confined at Fort Defiance until, a week later, Bowman's Navaho police brought in another of the murderers—Dinet-tsosi. The two prisoners were then taken by an escort of soldiers to Fort Wingate, where they joined Hoskinini behind bars.

Early in August Keam notified Bowman that Walcott and Mc-Nally were not killed in Utah, as supposed, but some miles directly north of Keams Canyon and at the northern base of Black Mesa, in Arizona. Bowman advised Commissioner Price of this on August 8, asking if he should proceed personally to the scene, or if Price felt the case should be turned over to the United States marshal of Arizona—the vicinity of the two murders still lying outside the boundaries of the reservation.[8]

Price's instructions, arriving in a series of departmental telegrams, were these: a military expedition would start at once from Fort Wingate—consisting of Troop K, Sixth Cavalry, under command of

---

[7] Tugi-yazzie said the murder of Walcott and McNally occurred about March 31. He answered vaguely when questioned about the location and for a time it was believed that the prospectors were killed near Navajo Mountain, Utah. The old man's statement was made July 12 and forwarded to Commissioner Price. (*Ibid.*, #13544.) In the transcript of his statement the names of Hoskinini-begay and Dinet-tsosi appear as "Ish-ka-ni-ne-be-gay" and "Ten-nai-tso-si."

[8] Letter from Bowman to Price, August 8, 1884. (*Ibid.*, #15296.)

Lieutenant H. P. Kingsbury; Bowman would accompany the troops and recover the bodies of the murdered men, if possible. He would arrest any Navahos he could find who were implicated in the affair and still at large.

Troop K camped within seven miles of Defiance Agency the night of August 15, and here Kingsbury received a message from Bowman urging him to make haste.[9] Feeling no sense of urgency, Kingsbury's cavalry leisurely traveled the intervening eighty miles to Keams Canyon in two days, where they were joined by Bowman and Chee Dodge. On the evening of August 18, Lieutenant Kingsbury and the agent met with Keam, who told them that Hoskinini-begay was camped with twelve Paiutes not far from the place where Walcott was killed. Two other Paiute bands were in the same vicinity, Keam told them, making a combined force of about forty Indians, all armed.

In the saddle from an hour after sunrise until sunset for the next two days, the cavalry, with Kingsbury and Bowman at their head, traveled seventy-three miles over viciously rough, wooded terrain. Their direction was nearly due north from Keams Canyon, across uninhabited wastes of Black Mesa, and finally down a precipitous switchback trail dropping some two thousand feet to the desert floor. Camp on the evening of August 20 was made a few miles south of the valley site of the later Kayenta. The men rested until midnight and then, hoping to surprise the outlaw band, Kingsbury broke camp. His troop rode until daylight, when "I struck the reported camping ground of the 12 Ute Bucks with whom Hosinini-begay, the murderer and his disaffected friend (both Navajos), were. From appearances they had not gone but a few hours."[10]

The Paiutes left no trail, and Bowman, despairing of finding them or the renegade Navahos, gave up the search but tried instead to round up the Indians' stock. Lieutenant Kingsbury back-trailed for twelve miles and went into camp for three days. He later reported that Bowman, meanwhile, "by search and inquiry discovered that all the stock belonging to the [Indians] had been run out of the country, and up into the mountains. On the 22nd he went out, dug up and brought into camp the remains of the old man, Mr. Walcott. He could not get the remains of Mr. McNally because the murderer

[9] This and subsequent information is found in Kingsbury's report to the Post Adjutant, Fort Wingate, September 1, 1884. (*Ibid.*, #18284.)

[10] *Ibid.* Hoskinini-begay's name was spelled "Osk-i-ni-ne-be-gay" by Kingsbury. Throughout his report he confused southern bands of Paiutes, affiliated with Hoskinini's Navahos, with Utes.

at large was the only one who knew where he lay on the mountain top."[11]

Walcott's body was taken back and buried at Fort Wingate, where Tugi-yazzie, Dinet-tsosi and the hostage chief, Hoskinini, were held in jail for about one year.

Troop K's return to the fort, like its outward march, was leisurely. For two days the cavalry rested at Defiance, awaiting three wagons of the cavalry train Kingsbury had detailed to transport Keam's trade pottery to the railroad at Holbrook.

11 Kingsbury, unfamiliar with this country, does not attempt to locate the place of Walcott's death and burial. Van Valkenburgh, however, quotes Sam Day II as saying the Navahos killed Walcott near El Capitan, or Agathla Peak, and the next day "trailed James McNally to a canyon near The Fingers, a sandstone projection standing apart from the rim of Black Mountain, and killed him there." Keam told Bowman that McNally covered a distance of thirty or thirty-five miles before his pursuers caught up with him, but fled in a northwest direction—which would have taken him away from Black Mountain.

14

Thomas Keam: 1884-1904

THOMAS KEAM was twenty-nine years old when he settled in the canyon with his brother William and began trading with the Hopis and Navahos. For him the year 1875 was mid-point in his life; the canyon would be his home for twenty-seven years more.

When Keam first saw the canyon that now bears his name is uncertain. Possibly in the 1860's, while serving with the First New Mexico Volunteer Cavalry, he passed that way.

His reasons for locating his trading post there are more easily determined. The canyon was sheltered and provided wood and pure water. More important, it lay astride a main trade route and formed the recognized boundary between the Navahos and the Hopis, whose three villages on First Mesa were only twelve miles to the west. By settling here, he was at once in the center of more than two thousand Indians of two tribes. The nearest white trader then was many miles to the east, on Pueblo Colorado Wash. This was a good place for a young trader who already spoke Navaho, would soon learn the Hopi language, and knew how to get along with Indians. Trading, however, may not have been uppermost in his mind when he went to the canyon.

"My main object in taking up a land claim here was to establish a Cattle Ranche," Keam wrote in 1886. Because the canyon was not then a part of any reservation he was able to file on 640 acres.[1] He

---

[1] Letter from Keam to Commissioner J. D. C. Atkins, February 11, 1886. (National Archives, Record Group 75, Letters Received, #5426, 1886.) His desert land claim remains something of a mystery since it could not be found on file at Pres-

intended to increase his holdings but was prevented from doing so when the Hopi reservation, created by executive order of President Chester A. Arthur, enclosed his "Ranche" in December, 1882.

A temporary Hopi agency was located at Trout Spring, fifteen miles northeast of Walpi, in 1874, but was abandoned the following year; Hopi affairs were handled thereafter from Defiance Agency until 1882 when Keam provided one of his canyon buildings for the use of Agent J. H. Fleming. A greenhorn sadly out of his element, Fleming was oppressed by his surroundings.

The agency, he said, "is in what is known as 'Kearn's cañon, famous for its springs. . . . With the high winds and rugged walls of the cañon on either side, one is reminded of some medieval prison-house. We are not trammeled by over civilization and the restraints of fashion. Our nearest post-office, except one at a Mormon settle-ment"—meaning Moenkopi—"is Fort Wingate, 120 miles distant. The surrounding country is an elevated plain, interspersed with barren mountains in the South and furrowed here and there with deep cañons."[2]

Fleming was even more depressed by the Hopis, whose customs Keam's protégé, Alexander Stephen, was then studying. He had not yet attended one of the Hopi dances, Fleming shuddered, but "The great evils in the way of their ultimate civilization lie in these dances. The dark superstitions and unhallowed rites of a heathenism as gross as that of India or Central Africa still infects them with its insidious poison."

The Navahos had a name for this place—Black Reeds Pointing Out, a reference perhaps to the reeds growing about the springs and lining the clear stream that then flowed level with the canyon floor westward into Polacca Wash. When Kit Carson camped in the canyon in 1863 his troops knew the site as Peach Orchard Spring, and it was only after Thomas Keam had been there a few years that traders and the military casually called it Keams Canyon.

cott, then the county seat. Establishment of the Hopi reservation in 1882 placed Keams Canyon in the southeast corner of a tract then comprising 2,920 square miles. The Navaho reservation, meanwhile, was enlarged with additions on the west (October 29, 1878) and east, south, and west (January 6, 1880). In 1883, before it was enlarged again the following year with additions to the north and west, the Navaho reservation contained 8,544 square miles. Navaho additions of 1878 and 1880 gave the tribe substantially more land than proposed by Arny in 1875, without requiring the surrender of the San Juan region. Boundary descriptions of these additions will be found in *Annual Report, C. I. A., 1878, 1880, 1883, 1884.*

2 *Annual Report, C. I. A., 1882.*

If the canyon reminded Fleming of a medieval prison, it would impress others as a pleasant oasis lying between high wooded plateau and the desert approach to the Hopi mesas. Curving east to west a distance of eight miles, the canyon's sandstone walls, varying in height from 150 to 350 feet, break off into huge boulders and talus. As it is relatively shallow, so the canyon is moderately narrow, averaging about 100 yards in width.

For the site of his trading post, Keam chose the sunnier north side of the stream, some two miles below the eastern head of the canyon. We have no description of this original post—one of the first in Navaho country away from Defiance Agency—but no doubt it provided living quarters for himself and his brother, and presumably for their Navaho wives. It was small, most likely, built of stone which lay abundantly at hand, and probably close by was a wooden stockade or corral.

Except for the next few years when he also maintained trading posts at or near Defiance Agency, Keam concentrated all his efforts on his canyon store. From the very beginning he prospered: wool and hides and Navaho blankets were brought to him from a radius of nearly one hundred miles. His pawn room glittered with a treasure of Navaho silver and turquoise. From the Hopis, by trade or purchase, came loom-work of the men weavers: sashes, kilts, and occasionally blankets. Shelves of his storerooms were loaded with Hopi pottery, baskets and woven plaques, a few rare *tabletas* used in Hopi ceremonies, and bright-hued kachina dolls. Havasupai and Apache baskets mingled with the rest, and from the ceiling beams hung Navaho saddles (high-forked fore and aft, the leather nail-studded), bridles and quirts, and rawhide lariats.

During his first six years in the canyon Keam depended for his supplies upon the Santa Fe contractors and government freighters, sending his wagons to meet theirs at Fort Wingate or, if he were lucky, at Defiance Agency. A trip one way in good weather might take five days, a month if arroyos were flooded or snow covered the land. In this high country winters were severe.

The summer of 1882 brought a crucial change: tracks of the Atlantic and Pacific Railroad advanced west from Gallup and then west from the Painted Desert towards the San Francisco Peaks and a raw new lumber town that would be named Flagstaff. In the wake of the road gangs the towns of Holbrook and Winslow sprang up, at once serving as supply centers for the entire territory, north and south. Now Keam's wagons cut a trail almost due south to Holbrook, only seventy miles away, taking two and one-half days for a journey that before required four or five. There was less chance of breakage or loss, and shelves that might be partly empty for weeks were now tightly stocked.

As his trade with the Indians prospered, Keam found it necessary to spread out, expand, and build more buildings. Soon after Lieutenant Bourke visited the canyon in 1881, Keam engaged in a building program that occupied him for the next six years. Besides his own home of four rooms, each fifteen feet square, there were his trading post, warerooms, blacksmith and carpenter shops, stables and wagon sheds, and several small buildings for friends, employees, and random tenants—all together a *hacienda* of perhaps twelve or fifteen structures. All were grouped close to his original site chosen in 1875, north of the stream and shaded now by a long row of cottonwoods.

A letter written by Keam in 1886 gives a fair picture of how his buildings appeared:

"They are all built of dressed stone, laid in adobe mortar, the walls averaging two feet in thickness. The roofs are constructed with ridge poles, joists and rafters of pine timbers, covered with boards, and overlaid with clay—an improved modification of the Mexican earth roof—essential to living in comfort in one story dwellings in this region.[3]

"For protection of the walls, all the roofs project over them about a foot and a half, and are surrounded with wide eave-boards in which numerous spouts are inserted to carry off the rain water. The rooms are all substantially floored with pine boards"—at a time when many dwellings had floors of pounded earth—"except the carpenter and black-smith shops . . . and the ceilings are from eight to eight and a half feet high. The interior walls are smoothly plastered and whitewashed. There is a large deposit of gypsiferous clay exposed on the mesa at a short distance from this place, which makes an admirable whitewash. This I have utilized, and at little cost keep all my buildings with white, glossy coats, both inside and out."

His own house, Keam said, "is also built of dressed stone with walls two feet thick; the roof, which is much higher than any of the other buildings is of shingles and the ceilings are ten feet high." Even under the hot sun of Arizona summer the house must have remained cool.

"The windows are large, the floors well laid with pine boards; the walls and ceilings are carefully finished and handsomely papered, and the floors carpeted. It is surrounded with a fine yard and paling,

[3] Letter from Keam to Atkins, cited above.

and in the garden in front of the house is a fountain supplied with excellent spring water brought through iron pipes and forced up by a hydraulic ram."

When Bourke visited Keam's home in 1881, as we have seen, he found in the shelves of good books, the racks of test tubes and chemicals, and the array of blankets and pottery a warm reflection of the personalities and tastes of the occupants. We may believe the house was filled with fascinating objects Bourke merely hints at, because Keam and his friend Stephen were knowledgeable collectors. Perhaps before Stephen's arrival in 1880, and certainly after that, Keam explored every foot of neighboring Antelope Mesa and—long before pot-hunting became illegal—dug into the ruins of Awatovi and lesser abandoned sites of the Jeddito Valley. The "Moqui pottery" Bourke saw in Keam's home undoubtedly included choice specimens from these ruins.

While exploring the lower reaches of Jeddito Wash with Stephen and their Hopi friend Polaki, Keam found an opening, or hole, in the rocks descending to a great depth and large enough to permit only one man to pass at a time.

Polaki informed them that modern Hopis never approached the place except with reverence, first scattering sacred corn meal on the ground. Entering the cavity, which for the Hopis may have had a significance similar to their mythical emergence upon earth from a dark underworld, Keam found the rock abutments covered with ancient petroglyphs.

Near this place they found also a cave in the rocks which Polaki told them the Hopis and Navahos both feared so much they would not enter it or pass close to its mouth. Keam and Stephen, of course, immediately made a search—and found the cave utterly empty except for the debris and droppings of a colony of porcupines.[4]

Another incident reveals Keam as a collector, this time of rare objects he soon felt compelled to surrender. Writing of Hopi kachinas, Jesse Walter Fewkes observed: "The worship of the horned A-lo-sa-ka is more strictly characteristic of the pueblo of Mi-con-in-o-vi [Mi-shongnovi], where this fraternity is probably more numerous than at Walpi. The images of A-lo-sa-ka were once in the possession of Mr. Keam (T. V.) for a few days, but at the earnest solicitation of almost the whole population of Mi-con-in-o-vi they were returned to the priests. At that time they were carried from Keams Canyon back to

4 This episode is related by Thomas Donaldson, quoted in Farish's *History of Arizona.*

the pueblo with a great ceremony, when a pathway of sacred meal was made for many miles along the trail over which they were borne."

The Alosaka, or Muy-ingova, is the Hopi Germ God or Two-Horned God, one of some thirty-six Hopi deities that are never, or almost never, impersonated in kachina dances or represented by images. Harold S. Colton notes that the Alosaka is one of the rare exceptions, in that he is impersonated at the time of the Wuwuchim ceremony in November.[5] Keam, perhaps with Stephen's aid, evidently found more than one carved figure of the revered Alosaka; and the priests of Mishongnovi, learning of this, begged him to restore them to the pueblo. If an altar boy should remove and sell some sacred church object to a foreign collector of antiquities, the situation would be similar.

Keam, unlike Lorenzo Hubbell and John B. Moore and a few other early traders, did not help the Navaho weavers of his region develop a pattern or style that might be identified with himself or his trading post. He did a large trade in blankets, however, and was well acquainted with problems and finer points of that craft.

A special-order blanket that he commissioned one of his weavers to make is an interesting example of the Navaho "pictorial rug"—a blanket which departs from the usual range of native design elements and instead is as faithfully representative of objects—such as a railroad train, a house, or a cow—as the weaver can make it. Moderately small, about three feet wide by four and one-half feet long, this blanket has a brown border and predominating inside colors of red, white, and blue. Symbols woven in the design are borrowed from the insignia of the Union Army: a United States flag with thirteen stars beneath an eagle, a five-pointed star, and the figures of two soldiers shaking hands. At the top, woven in orange yarn, are the letters "G. A. R."

Keam presented the blanket, soon before he left his canyon forever, to Lieutenant Joseph B. Loughran, with whom he had served in the First New Mexico Cavalry.

Washington Matthews once sought Keam's opinion while trying to determine when Navaho weavers first introduced the so-called two-

---

[5] "Alosaka, the god of reproduction . . . is thought of as gentle and kind and holds himself aloof. His home is in the underworld. . . . The headdress of the impersonator carries two horns that curve back. His hair hangs down his back. The only body paint . . . is a white line down the front of his arms and legs. For a costume he wears a white tanned buckskin. He wears moccasins and has turtle shell rattles tied on his legs. In his hands he carries deer horns and a wand." (Colton, *Hopi Kachina Dolls*.)

face blanket, an oddity of the craft distinguished by a front surface design entirely different from the design on the reverse side. During his first stay at Fort Wingate, from 1880 to 1884, Matthews said, he made a careful study of Navaho weaving, but he never saw a two-faced blanket until after he returned to New Mexico in 1890. For light on this matter he turned to an old friend.

"Mr. Thomas V. Keam . . . ," Matthews wrote, "is the Indian trader who has been longest established among the Navahoes, and is their most popular trader; he has dealt and dwelt with them, I think, for about thirty years, and he is an educated, intelligent, and observant man.[6] Had such blankets been even occasionally seen among these Indians prior to 1884, some of them would have been brought to him to trade and he would not have failed to observe their unusual appearance. In 1896 I wrote requesting Mr. Keam to get for me a two-faced blanket from his part of the country and asking him what he knew of the origin of the new blanket. In his reply, dated January 27, 1897, he says:

" 'As you suppose, it is only about three years since I first saw this work, and to date there are only a few who understand this weaving. The diamond or diagonal twill is undoubtedly copied by them from the Moki (Hopi), but the double or reversible weaving I believe to be of their own (Navaho) invention, as I know of no other tribe that does such weaving.' "

While in Washington in the spring of 1884, as related earlier, Keam met with Secretary of the Interior Teller and offered the use of his facilities in Keams Canyon for an Indian industrial school. Teller may have been interested, but nothing further developed until the fall of that year when Keam wrote to Agent John Bowman offering the free use "of three rooms at this place for school purposes during the winter." Bowman forwarded Keam's letter to Commissioner Price, pointing out that there was no school for the Hopis. He hoped that Price would "see fit to take advantage of a generous offer."[7]

A year passed in which nothing more was accomplished. Price was succeeded as commissioner by J. D. C. Atkins, and Keam renewed

[6] Washington Matthews, "A Two-Faced Navaho Blanket." *American Anthropologist*, N. S., Vol. II, No. 4 (1900). Amsden, in *Navaho Weaving*, traces the origin of the two-face weave back to about 1885, and cites the large Ganado rug of that type referred to in another chapter, as dating from that time.

[7] Letter from Keam to Bowman, September 19, 1884, enclosed with letter from Bowman to Price, September 27, 1884. (National Archives, Record Group 75, Letters Received, #18899, 1884.)

his proposal—this time offering to rent a building to the government that would accommodate twenty-four Hopi and Navaho children. In December, 1885, Atkins informed Keam that anything less than a boarding school for fifty pupils would not be practical. A few weeks later Keam replied that he had a building that would meet these requirements and was forwarding "accurate plans of my property in this Cañon, so that you may have a more definite idea of its situation, extent and adaptability for such purpose." Furthermore, said Keam, he had "asked my friends Colonel [James] & Mrs. Stevenson to call on you and explain the plans, they having visited here recently, and are well acquainted with all the details."[8]

In another letter to Atkins of the same date Keam pointed out that although the government had made no effort to teach the Navahos a trade, they were, as a tribe, "willing to work, and several have grown rich by their trades of silversmith, blacksmith, or saddler, which they have acquired from their contact with the few whites near them." His concept of an Indian school probably was mainly his own, influenced by suggestions made as early as 1871 by Agent James Miller; in any case, Keam had positive ideas on the subject.

"If practicable with every school," he said, "a carpenter and blacksmith shop should be established, and a few of the brightest lads taught trades, so that they could build houses, repair wagons, farming implements &c., now issued them by the Government, and when slightly broken, left to fall to pieces for lack of such facilities.[9]

"This will also supply to the Moquis, who while not so intelligent, are industrious, and being community dwellers are more dependent on each other. Living as they do on a barren rock seven hundred feet above the surrounding plain, half their time is lost in their journeys to water and their farms."

Keam admitted to some missionary work among his Hopi friends and, like so many missionaries, viewed his efforts with wistful optimism. "I have frequently told them of this," he continued, "and a number have decided to move to the valley, there build them[selves] houses, and being desirous to live like white men, they ask that lumber, doors, &c., be furnished them, as they have no means of obtaining such. . . . With encouragement in this way they would soon become a progressive people, and gradually move from the rock to the valleys below."

Rumors were about, Keam said, that the Navaho reservation soon

8 Letter from Keam to Atkins, January 2, 1886. (*Ibid.*, #1622, 1886.)
9 *Ibid.*, #1623, and enclosure, #14431.

would be extended farther to the west. The two tribes already occupied parts of the same (Hopi) reservation, and "any addition to this would not assist them in what they need most, a greater water supply for their large herds of sheep and horses. The Navaho like many other Indians will not seek to improve a spring; as long as there is a sufficiency for his herds he is satisfied; when from constant tramping of his herds and drifting of sand, it becomes partially covered and insufficient, he will move to some other place or take advantage of the white man's improvements . . . .

"Having lived among them so long I take some interest in them and have often explained the necessity of their improving their water supply. They fully understand it, and are willing to work, but like children require assistance in management.

"If encouragement in this way could be given them"—and Keam was thinking in terms of education—"it would wonderfully increase what is most needed by them, and also teach them it's to their advantage to be industrious."

With this letter Keam enclosed a petition signed by twenty Hopi governors or clan priests. "We live in stone houses upon the mesa top high above the valley," the petition began. "In bygone time we were forced to live here to be safe from our foes. But we have been living in peace for many years and we have been thinking."

They would wish to live in the good ways taught them by their fathers, the Hopis said, but some American ways were good too. Houses with doors and windows and board floors "were unknown to our fathers, yet they are beautiful, and we would like to have them . . . .

"We are also greatly concerned for our children. We pray that they may follow in their fathers' footsteps and grow up—good of heart and pure of breath. Yet we can see that things are changing around us, and many Americans are coming in this region. We would like our children to learn the Americans' tongue and their ways of work.

"We pray you to cause a school to be opened in our country, and we will gladly send our children."

Each of the signatories, led by Cimo—the Hopis' tribal chief—drew the symbol of his clan for his mark. The Orders of Masau, of Sun, of Katcina, and of Soyal were represented, as were the phratry or clans of *Kwa'-hii* (Eagle), *Pa'n-wa* (Mountain Sheep), *Ho'nau* (Bear), *Ka'ai* (Corn), *Ishawu* (Coyote), *Yo'ki* (Rain), and *Ho-na'-ni* (Badger). All of the seven Hopi villages were represented, an unusual expression of unanimity, especially in view of later disagreement and strife. And as evidence of their sincerity, these village and clan chiefs informed Keam in January that fifty Hopi children would be ready to enter school the day it was opened.

As negotiations continued and as plans for the school grew increasingly ambitious, Keam's plans for his own future in the canyon changed accordingly. His original offer to provide three rooms became, in two years, a proposal that the Indian Office take the major part of his property.

Early in February, 1886, Keam told Commissioner Atkins that the government might have thirteen of his buildings for a school, dormitories for boys and girls, and a storeroom. For use as a school farm he offered the Indian Office its choice of five fields in the canyon that he had under cultivation, amounting to twenty-seven acres. "At present" he would keep only his own house and trading post and about five other buildings or rooms needed to carry on his trading business. But these, too, he would be willing to give up "when the increase of pupils will render it necessary."

His hope in earlier years of turning to cattle ranching was nipped by the creation of the Hopi reservation, he explained. For this reason he was now willing to sell his property. "The price, $25,000, does, in truth, only barely reimburse me the amount I have invested."[10]

Through spring and summer, 1886, the terms were studied and threshed out. Atkins was unwilling to buy, but would rent—and he wanted not most of Keam's buildings, but all of them.

"My first proposal to rent part of the Trading Post buildings," Keam answered, "arose from a wish to help these Moki people. During my long residence here I have contracted sincere friendships with many of them, and I have seen their children grow up in ignorance around me. . . . To abandon all the conveniences of my Trading Post is certainly more than I contemplated, but I have considered the matter . . . and I accede to your proposal."[11] The rent he asked was $1,800 a year.

Commissioner Atkins, who evidently knew something about trading himself, remained silent, waiting. Keam's friend Stevenson represented him in Washington, calling several times at the Indian Office and finally, in November, telling Atkins that Keam would surrender all of the property for one hundred dollars a month. The offer was

[10] Letter from Keam to Atkins, February 11, 1886. (*Ibid.*, #5426.)
[11] Letter from Keam to Atkins, March 4, 1886. (*Ibid.*, #7443.)

accepted and a lease signed in May, permitting the school to open in the fall of 1887.

After transferring his property to the government on May 15, Keam moved two and one-half miles down the canyon and began building a new home and trading post at the location of the present Keams Canyon trading store. The Indian Office renewed its lease on the school buildings for a second year and then, after a special appropriation by Congress in March, 1889, offered to buy the facilities. Keam went to Washington and on July 13 signed a quitclaim releasing to the government "all that particular tract of land [known] as Keams Cañon" together with all buildings and improvements. He received in payment $10,000—less than half the price he had asked.[12]

Keam's optimistic hopes for the boarding school received a setback in December, 1890, when a conservative element at Oraibi decided the school was teaching too much of the white man's ways and refused to let their children attend. Violence was threatened and was only prevented by the arrival of the Tenth Cavalry from Fort Apache. Other villages remained peaceful and continued to look on the school with favor, but as soon as the troops withdrew, the dissidents at Oraibi resumed their rebellion.

By mid-June, 1891, Oraibi was fiercely divided between "hostiles" and "friendlies." Rumors spread that an attack on the school was planned by the hostile element and that Superintendent Collins would be killed for making attendance at the school compulsory. Troops were summoned from Fort Wingate, Indian trader C. H. Algert meanwhile riding into Flagstaff from his post at Tuba City with word that feelings were so high there might be a battle between cavalry and the pueblo of Oraibi.[13]

The *Coconino Sun* of Flagstaff reported in its issue of July 4 that the trouble reached a climax a few days before when "United States troops under command of Colonel Corbin arrived at the Oraiba village and found the Indians ready for battle. The sight of so many soldiers seemed to overawe them and . . . after a conference of about two hours Colonel Corbin succeeded in arresting the leaders and they are now enroute to Fort Wingate. . . . After four days' rest at Keams' Canyon the troops will be ordered to their respective posts."

12 Photostat copies of the quitclaim signed by Keam and other documents relating to it are in the files of the Hopi Agency at Keams Canyon.

13 For this brief, incomplete summary of the Hopi school revolt I have drawn upon the *Annual Report, C. I. A., 1883, 1895, 1896,* and files of the *Coconino Sun,* Flagstaff, Arizona, June 27 and July 4, 1891.

Oraibi's conservative leaders continued their opposition to the school, however, and troops were called back a third time, in the fall of 1894. Nineteen Hopi men were arrested and dealt with more harshly than the ringleaders of opposition had been before, being sent to prison at Alcatraz for one year. After their release the Oraibi conservatives ceased to threaten violence but stubbornly refused to send their children to school, on grounds that this conflicted with traditional Hopi beliefs. Bitterness over the issue finally split Oraibi in 1906, the conservative families packing up and moving away. On a high rock ledge of Third Mesa, eight miles to the north and west, the conservatives settled down and built the new pueblo of Hotevilla.[14]

The photographer Ben Wittick, who accompanied the Wingate troops on some of their campaigns and left an excellent pictorial record of New Mexico and Arizona in the 1890's, made a dozen glass-plate exposures in Keams Canyon at about this time. None of his photographs that survive, however, show the trading post Keam built down-canyon in 1887. The new post was smaller than the one it replaced, adequate but constructed with less concern for the future. This we know, thanks to the artist J. J. Mora, who one noon mingled out front with a group of Indians long enough to record its sun-drenched appearance and capture its atmosphere in a water color.[15]

A shoebox of a building, with flaming red walls of corrugated iron, it is set on a rough stone foundation perhaps forty feet long. Huge blocks of stone form three steps leading to the open door and dim store interior. Off to the left a sliding door is partly open on what must be the storeroom. Beyond that and forming the west end of the otherwise iron-sheathed structure is a stone-and-adobe office, or manager's room.

As fresh as Mora's water color was the impression of an eleven-

14 Van Valkenburgh notes that the Hopi name, *Hitvela,* or Skinned Back, "was taken from a spring . . . located in a low cave, so that one entering to get water often skinned his back." Youkeoma was the conservative under whose leadership the pueblo was built. Van Valkenburgh adds, "For two decades Hotevilla refused to send children to the school, and on one occasion the U. S. Cavalry was called out to round up the children hidden in the houses. The people also refused to allow their sheep to be dipped, and for this Youkeoma was banished to California." After the division of 1906, Oraibi steadily declined in population and now possibly may be removed by only a generation or two from final abandonment.

15 Mora's water color, dated 1906, is inscribed "To the Boss of the Ranch with remembrance of the best times ever"—the "boss" being Lorenzo Hubbell, with whom Mora was staying. The picture remains in the Hubbell collection at Ganado.

year-old boy when he climbed the big steps and first entered Keam's post a summer day in 1898. Allen, the lad's name was; his father was the new superintendent of the school. They had recently arrived from the East, taking two days by wagon to make the trip from Holbrook.

"Two things stand out vividly in my mind about the trading post," Allen wrote years later, when he was an old man. "One was the great amount of bolts of calico printed in bright colors that were stored high on the shelves behind the counter." And the other was on another day in the same hot summer when young Allen found himself alone in the post—"my eyes attracted by a movement among the bolts of calico.

"There suddenly appeared a huge snake, which I was sure was a rattler, common in that part of the country. I wasted no time in getting out of the post to find Mr. Williams, who was then in charge, to tell him of my great discovery. He just laughed and said, 'Don't you hurt my pal—he lives in the store all the time and catches the mice for me.' The snake was not a rattler but a harmless blow snake, also common about Keam's Canyon."[16]

Keam's house was a one-story building located near the trading post. "On one of my visits to Mr. Keam's place," Allen said, "I recall my father talking to a dapper, well-dressed, middle-sized man with sandy hair. I was told later that he was Thomas V. Keam and was to leave soon—possibly for England."

The last license issued to Keam permitting him to trade with the Hopis and Navahos expired August 24, 1898.[17] Keam may have continued trading for a short time after that and probably leased his post to another trader, for the store continued in operation and Keam remained in the canyon a few years longer.

Time shadows his activities after he ceased trading. In the fall of 1901, however, he was in Washington again, a Gallup newspaper reporting: "Thomas Keam is in the East trying to get capital interested in the leasing of a large mineral district in the Navajo reservation on which there is said to be valuable deposits of coal, copper and gold. The recent leasing of land in the vicinity of the Carrizo Mountains . . . has caused capital to investigate the rich mining section."[18]

16 W. R. Allen recalled these events of his boyhood in a 1959 letter to me from his home in Clayton, Missouri. Keam's manager may have been W. W. Williams, Mr. Allen wrote. Perhaps this was Bill Williams, trader son of the Jonathan P. Williams, who first appears in an earlier chapter. Bill Williams would have been twenty-eight years old in 1898.

17 *N. A., Ledgers of Traders.*

His interest was not in the Carrizo Mountains, but in an area midway between Lee's Ferry and The Gap, on the Kaibito Plateau just north of Mormon Ridge. Here, in the 1880's, probably with Alexander Stephen as companion, he had found rich deposits of copper. There is nothing to indicate whether he was able to interest a backer, but the region, now known as Coppermine, or Keam's District, has been successfully mined in the years since.

It may be that Thomas Keam felt the pressure of encroaching settlers and found the country becoming overcrowded. In 1902, after a flood raced through his canyon, cutting an arroyo forty feet deep and dropping the stream to that depth, Keam sold his trading post to Lorenzo Hubbell, Jr., and left the canyon for the last time. He returned to the family home at Truro, England, and there died of angina pectoris on November 30, 1904.

18 The *McKinley County Republican,* October 5, 1901. The first mining lease in the Carrizo Mountains was granted December 19, 1895, by Navaho Agent Constant Williams, to John P. Voorhies of Denver. The lease applied to a mile-square tract and was for a ten-year period. Voorhies sent a small party to mine the land, hoping to find gold or silver, but soon abandoned the project. A few years previously a party of geologists examined the same region under authority of the Indian Office and reported that no gold or silver could be found. In recent years, in the vicinity of Cove Trading Post, a uranium mine has been operated by Kerr-McGee Oil Industries, Inc.

15

Ganado

SLOPES OF SAND and sagebrush tilt gradually into the valley from all sides. Grass and green rushes and a few trees—a few cottonwoods, but not many—make the valley green until on the west it breaks into mounds and sand cones. These are of shapes and colors a furnace might leave when the fires have died out: ocher shades and yellow, blue and red and purple, pale green, white, and ash brown—these against a base soil quite red.

Through the valley the Pueblo Colorado Wash cuts an arroyo, not wide nor deep, and the river not red as its name suggests. Except sometimes, when it floods, the Pueblo Colorado is a thin, winding trickle of water, not a river or even a stream.

Late in the 1870's, when he was about twenty-four years old and the troubles created by Agent Arny were fresh behind him, Lorenzo Hubbell settled in the valley as an Indian trader. A photograph taken at the time shows him wearing rimless eyeglasses with rather thick lenses. Dark hair is parted just to the left of center and the mustache with little points curving downward is not yet mature. His frame is stocky and square, and he stands five feet, eight inches tall. The Navahos of the region have considered his appearance and named him *Nak'eznilih*, Double Glasses. Later, with respect, they will refer to him as *Naakaii Saani*, or Old Mexican.

Charles Crary, it is said, was first in the valley, operating a small trading post near Ganado Lake from about 1871 or 1872. Nothing further is known about him other than the certainty that he was

gone within four of five years.[1] The date and circumstances of Lorenzo's appearance here are equally undocumented, although it could
not have been before late fall of 1876. Presumably he came to the
valley from Fort Wingate, where some say he clerked for a trader
named Coddington. In later years Hubbell himself said he bought
his first post from a man named Smith, and it appears that he later
bought the post where he finally remained and homesteaded, from
a trader named William Leonard, in 1878.[2]

[1] Charles Crary's presence here, and nothing more, is mentioned by Clyde
Kluckhohn and Dorothea Leighton (*The Navaho*), by Van Valkenburgh, and by
Amsden (*Navaho Weaving*, pp. 173–74). Amsden gives Crary a partner named
Stover, who will appear later, and this probably is an error. Ganado Lake, orig-
inally a natural body of water but now retained by a dam, is located in the Pueblo
Colorado Wash about three miles east of the present Hubbell trading post. Since
until 1880 this region was not part of the Navaho reservation, the early traders,
not requiring licenses, cannot be traced through Indian Office records.

[2] As so many of his generation, Lorenzo Hubbell attached little importance to
dates and in his own references to such details quite agreeably contradicts himself
again and again. Late in life Hubbell recalled that he had worked "for a Mr.
Coddington, who operated a trading post at Fort Wingate" and that in 1876 he
"established my present post at Ganado." (*Touring Topics*, Vol XXII, No. 12.) In
1908, filing an affidavit in Phoenix in connection with a suit involving his homestead, Hubbell said that "from the year 1878" he was "the exclusive owner" of
his Ganado buildings. C. N. Cotton wrote on August 11, 1890, that the Hubbell
post at Ganado had been operated "continuously since early in 1878." (Report, to
accompany *H. R. 4001*, 56 Cong., 1 sess., "Rights of Settlers on the Navajo Reservation, Ariz.") Because Lorenzo was employed as issue clerk at Defiance Agency from
July 1 to October 1, 1876 (letter from Agent Alex Irvine to C. I. A. Smith, October
1, 1876, National Archives, Record Group 75), it appears unlikely that he could
have started trading at Pueblo Colorado Wash before late fall, 1876. In the same
Report accompanying *H. R. 4001*, Hubbell is quoted as saying that a year or two
prior to 1880 he had purchased his Pueblo Colorado property "from a man named
Williams." He possibly was referring to Perry H. Williams, who on March 31, 1877,
was licensed to trade at Fort Defiance and Washington Pass and was in this general vicinity for a number of years. Or perhaps he referred to George M. "Barney"
Williams, mentioned by Bourke as trading on the Pueblo Colorado Wash in 1881.
If we accept Hubbell's statement that he bought from a man named Williams,
that still leaves Leonard to deal with. Lorenzo's granddaughter, Mrs. LaCharles
Goodman Eckel, wrote in 1934 that Charles Crary sold his post to "Old Man
Leonard" in 1875 and that Lorenzo bought out Leonard the following year ("His-
tory of Ganado, Arizona," *Museum Notes*, Museum of Northern Arizona, Vol. VI,
No. 10). Other writers have accepted Mrs. Eckel's word for this, but none yet has
identified "Old Man" Leonard.
In the Southwest in that day, "Old Man" was an ubiquitous handle to apply to
any man in his thirties or older. My guess is that Old Man Leonard was William
Leonard, who soon after this time turns up as trader at Fort Defiance. There is
some evidence from the above that Hubbell came first to the vicinity of Ganado
Lake, traded there for a year or a little more, and then—probably in 1878—bought
the Leonard post, where he settled down. Finally, there remains some question
about the identity of the Mr. Coddington, for whom Hubbell said he worked at

No description of the buildings that Leonard sold to Hubbell has been found, but we can imagine that they were not impressive. A photograph from perhaps the late 1880's shows a remnant of the old Leonard place, a small stone and adobe building or two attached by a stockade of cedar posts to Hubbell's home. The location is a few hundred yards south of the wash and near the western end of the valley. Facing east, the house is a low, rambling affair sitting behind a picket fence and hitching rail. The roof is of tamped earth sloping easily to front and back from the center pole. An extension of the roof at front, supported by seven heavy posts perhaps ten feet apart, provides a porch shading the entire length of the building.

Navahos referred to the region as *Lu-ka'nt-quel*, Place of Water Reeds; the white man's designation of Pueblo Colorado, from the Spanish meaning Red Village, evidently was taken from the prehistoric pueblo ruin of *Kin Lichee*, or Red House, about ten miles to the northeast. Lorenzo filed a homestead claim on 160 acres here and sometime later, because of the postal confusion between this place and the town of Pueblo, Colorado, had the name changed from Pueblo Colorado to Ganado. This he did to honor his friend Ganado Mucho (pidgin Spanish for "Many Herds"), who lived in this valley and whose people promised Hubbell a large trade.

Ganado Mucho was sixty-nine years old in 1878, the sub-chief of all western Navahos, and head man of the Big Water Clan. It is told that his son, Many Horses, once dramatically saved Lorenzo from being put to death by the Navahos, and certainly the friendship between the two extended from Lorenzo's days at Defiance Agency when he was Spanish interpreter.

When Ganado Mucho later became head chief of all the Navahos, he was referred to by Agent Bowman as "very feeble in body and antiquated in his ideas . . . inclined to be friendly . . . and fair in all things, and a good talker."[3] That there was a sterner side to Ganado

---

Fort Wingate. In an earlier chapter we have seen that Hubbell was associated with Henry Reed, the Wingate-Defiance trader. The list of Fort Wingate traders (National Archives, War Records Division, Fort Wingate) does not include Coddington's name. This leads me to believe either that Coddington—perhaps the same Walter J. Coddington who was licensed to trade at Fort Defiance in 1880—was Henry Reed's manager at Wingate when Hubbell worked there, or that Coddington had an unlicensed trading post near Fort Wingate but off the military reservation. Other writers, including Mrs. Eckel and Ruth Underhill (*Here Come the Navaho!*), refer to a "Fort Wingate post" operated by a Coddington and Stover as early as 1869, and Mrs. Eckel says it was there that Lorenzo clerked in 1872.

3 *Annual Report, C. I. A., 1884.*

Mucho is clear, for Van Valkenburgh relates a Navaho story that the old chief and Manuelito in 1878 "led a wide program of extinction against 'ladrones' (thieves) and suspected witches in which some twenty are reputed to have been killed. One of these met his death in the doorway of the post [at Ganado Lake] and it was necessary to burn the building."

Albuquerque and Santa Fe were the largest towns nearest Ganado during these first years, and it was from them that Hubbell had to get his supplies. Until 1879, and before the Atlantic and Pacific rails moved west from Albuquerque in 1880–81, western freight moved by train only as far as Fort Dodge, Kansas. From there, Lorenzo once recalled, ox teams freighted over the Santa Fe Trail to Fort Union and then down into the Río Grande Valley. At Albuquerque the wagons were reloaded and hauled again by ox or mule team to the forts and western settlements—to Defiance Agency and Ganado.[4]

Lorenzo was well rooted at Ganado, though not yet making much money, when in June, 1879, he was married. His bride was Lina Rubi, daughter of Cruz and Tafoya Reyes Rubi, of Cebolleta, the small Spanish-American settlement in the eastern foothills of Mount Taylor. Their home in the early years was probably no more than a few rooms added to the post, as Lorenzo concentrated on his business.

The year following his marriage he opened a second trading post, on April 1, 1880, receiving his license to trade at Manuelito's Camp, located in the lower Chuska Valley and about forty miles east of Defiance Agency. His $10,000 bond was secured by Almarion M. Coddington and Elias S. Stover, both of whom gave their address as Albuquerque. Many Navahos lived in this region, which was known also as Manuelito's Spring, named for the tribal leader who was born here and died here in 1893.[5] Friendship between the young

4 The Santa Fe Trail, and Fort Union as a military post and supply base for the Southwest, fell gradually into eclipse when the railhead of the Atchison, Topeka, and Santa Fe Railroad reached Las Vegas, New Mexico, in 1879. When the Santa Fe line and Atlantic and Pacific met at Albuquerque and rails of the A. and P. two years later were extended into Arizona, traders could measure delivery of freight in terms of days rather than weeks or months.

5 Van Valkenburgh says that Manuelito was born about 1818 and that his death was caused by "measles which developed into pneumonia after treatments in the sweathouse and generous use of whiskey." A description of Manuelito's Spring by First Lt. W. C. Brown, during a water survey of the Navaho reservation in 1892, is quoted by Van Valkenburgh: "Here I found the largest collection of Indian farms seen on the trip, the camp and farms extending over an area about a mile long by one-quarter mile wide, with about ten to twenty families, according to the season."

trader and Manuelito also went back to Lorenzo's days as an employee at the agency, and this might have influenced him in opening the post.

Lorenzo had abandoned the store when Agent Bowman, referring to that place in 1886, wrote that in his judgment it "would be the best point for trade of any . . . were it not for the fact that the Indians who frequent that locality are of a very lawless disposition and no one has yet been found who was *brave* enough to keep a store there, any length of time, although several have tried it."[6] Hubbell did not renew his license at the end of the first year, although it is doubtful that his failure to do so was due to any lack of courage. In 1880–81 he may, rather, have found Manuelito's Camp too far removed from Ganado, the center of his interest, where he was still struggling to establish himself.

In the years following, Hubbell built or acquired a number of trading posts, most of them not farther than forty or fifty miles from Ganado. Among others these included two posts at Chinle, Black Mountain, Cornfields, Nazlini, Keams Canyon, Oraibi, and Cedar Springs—all in Arizona.

The Black Mountain Trading Post, in later times operated by Win Wetherill and Joe Lee, the latter a grandson of John Doyle Lee, is located about twenty-five miles west of Chinle. It stands, as Van Valkenburgh says, "like a fort on a small knoll in the broken lands of a cove of Black Mountain." The Cornfields post is ten miles below Ganado on the Pueblo Colorado Wash, and was operated for Hubbell, about 1896–97, by Charles Cousins. Nazlini Trading Post is almost midway between Chinle and Ganado, in Beautiful Valley. Cedar Springs post, one of the later stores as were those at Keams Canyon and Oraibi, is located on the Moqui Buttes road to the Hopi villages, about forty miles north of Winslow. Van Valkenburgh says that the Cedar Springs store was built in the 1880's by Jake Tobin, one of the first traders to settle in the valley south of the Hopi mesas.

As a main center of supply for his trading posts, Hubbell purchased a large warehouse and store at Winslow in the middle or late 1880's. The building still stands, though no longer owned by the family, distinguished by a massive front porch, large front windows, and stone block and adobe masonry. As he did in his home and in his office and rug room at Ganado, Lorenzo filled the Winslow build-

---

6 Letter from Bowman to C. I. A. Atkins, February 22, 1886. (National Archives, Record Group 75, Letters Received, 1886, #6219.)

ing with frontier relics and Indian artifacts, none of them for sale and many worthy of a place in a museum. The collection included ancient pottery, baskets, cavalry swords and old guns, leatherwork, kachina dolls, and a few paintings and drawings by his artist friend, E. A. Burbank.[7]

Lorenzo was a man of strong convictions; nothing about him was tentative, nothing he did was done part or half way. He did not smoke and once said that he had never tasted a drop of liquor, adding that "Liquor of any sort is, to use the popular Mexican expression, *buena por nada.*"

Manuelito, who in the last years of his life drank excessively and more than once was at Ganado when far from sober, served Lorenzo as an object lesson to other Navahos. His memory of the once-proud old man lying drunk on the ground near his store may have been partly cause of an angry dispute Lorenzo had, one day in 1897, with a company of Fort Wingate troops. Arriving at Ganado in the full heat of summer noon while on a march to Keams Canyon, the soldiers were invited by Hubbell to rest and have their noon meal in the shade of his trees. As they were eating, most of the men washed their lunch down with long pulls at whisky bottles which they carried in their knapsacks. Noticing this, Hubbell walked out to where the troopers were gathered and demanded that they discard the bottles in a large Indian basket he brought for that purpose. The company's captain furiously countermanded Hubbell's order—and then was forced to back down when Hubbell threatened to report the whole outfit for bringing liquor on the reservation. The bottles were collected and the contents dumped into the nearby wash.

On another occasion some years later, when visiting his friend Dan DuBois at the latter's place between Gallup and Zuñi, Lorenzo learned that Mexicans operating the nearby Piñon Springs Trading Post were making white mule whisky by the barrel. Even Dan DuBois, himself a formidable drinker and perhaps one of the Mexicans' best customers, had to admit that the Piñon Springs Indians were rapidly becoming besotted. Angered by what he heard and later saw,

---

[7] The Winslow store has been owned since about 1952 by Kyle Bales of Kansas City. When I last stopped there in 1959, most of the Hubbell collection of relics and artifacts remained intact. A suggestion of older days, seldom found in modern trading posts, was provided by a purchasable stock of wooden wagon hoops and steel plowshare tips. Lorenzo Hubbell, Jr., managed the Winslow store for a number of years, and as well owned trading posts (besides Keams Canyon and Oraibi stores) at Big Mountain, Dinnebito, Na-ah-tah Canyon, and Marble Canyon.

Hubbell arranged to buy the store and, with equally direct action, smashed the still and dumped out the mash.[8]

Lorenzo Hubbell's dislike of liquor was matched by his passion for gambling. "I suppose," he once said, "a man has to have some vices. . . . As a youth, I gambled at about everything that offered a gambler's chance; and, with the usual gambler's luck sometimes I won big stakes. Many a time I cut the cards for $30,000 at a single toss, and won or lost." In 1896, however, he quit gambling forever. "I lost $60,000 in a poker game and had to tell Señora Lina about it next morning. She was disgusted."[9]

In earlier days at Fort Wingate Lorenzo may have placed a bet on himself when he raced horses with a hardbitten cowpuncher who went by two names—Bill Cavenaugh and Snyder. Cavenaugh did not overawe Lorenzo then or later, when they met again on opposite sides in a range war, and Lorenzo freely admitted his own self-assurance. "At that time," he recalled, "I was an all round athlete, a foot racer, a wrestler, a fighter, and anything that came along."[10]

During the late 1870's the grazing land far south of Ganado was bloodily contested by cattlemen and sheep owners, the war spawning raiders, rustlers, and outlaws who made the towns of Springerville and St. Johns the center of the brawling activities. The situation prevailing at both places was described by the pioneer cattleman, James G. H. Colter:

"Julius Becker had a little store at Springerville, and the desperadoes used to come in every two or three months, and tell him to go out of the store, and they would take all the tobacco and clothes, and drink all the whiskey they wanted, and dance and have a good time, and keep the store about a day and a night, and then send word to Becker that he could come back and take charge of *their* store. . . . One time they got to fighting in Springer's store, and shot two of themselves. At one time they took possession of the country, and I went to Camp [Fort] Apache and the officer in command gave me three companies of soldiers, and came himself . . . and restored order after a fight in which several of the desperadoes were killed."[11]

8 Mrs. Edward Vanderwagen of Zuñi recalled this happening in 1918. Her husband operated the Piñon Springs post for Hubbell for a short time thereafter. Lorenzo sold the store about 1925.

9 *Touring Topics*, Vol. XXII, No. 12.

10 Hubbell wrote a short article of reminiscences of the range war for Farish's *History of Arizona*, VI.

11 *Ibid*. Formerly known as Round Valley, the town was named for Henry Springer, a merchant who moved to the valley from Albuquerque.

Order lasted a short while only, and the range war was at its height when Lorenzo Hubbell was elected sheriff of Apache County in 1882. He left his Ganado post in other hands, moving temporarily to the county seat at St. Johns, where he "took the side of the sheepmen, not because I favored them, but because the country was better suited for sheep than it was for cattle."[12] Reconciling the feud, he found, "was the same thing as trying to keep monkeys and parrots in the same cage." During the two terms he served as sheriff, Hubbell was shot at at least a dozen times and frequently at night, to protect his family, had to barricade the windows and doors of his home. While the cattlemen were nearly unanimous in wanting to dispose of Hubbell, lines between the two factions were blurred: each side had its share of outlaws and killers.

"When I came to St. Johns," Hubbell said, "I asked the storekeepers why they allowed the thieves to rob them.[13] I sent for guns and ammunition . . . the fight started in St. Johns . . . the first week seventeen of them were killed and eight of our boys. J. G. H. Colter [quoted above] was one of us. It was a rough fight and lasted a long time. . . . We had it all settled, we thought, and were getting on peaceably, when Huhning, Tee, and Smith, three of them who were elected to office by my efforts, turned around and wanted to put me out of office . . . on account, as they put it, of absence from the Territory. I was [at Ganado] inside the Reservation, and they tried to make out that this was absence from the Territory. . . . I refused to go out, and held the office. I was the strongest.

". . . The first war was ended in two weeks. These outlaws came in from Colorado and Texas. Cavenaugh, who went by the name of Snyder, was one of their leaders. They killed Colonel Hart, and wherever they went they left a trail of blood. . . . It stayed quiet for a year, and then it flared up again."

Cavenaugh was removed from action, after shooting an old German near Holbrook, when his gang fell to quarreling over a division of money stolen from their victim. Several of the men were killed and Cavenaugh was badly wounded.

Recalling this troubled period years later, Hubbell did not minimize his own part in helping to bring peace to the county or the personal danger in which he and members of his family lived. He made it clear, however, that he did very little shooting himself, but

12 *Touring Topics,* Vol. XXII, No. 12.
13 *History of Arizona,* VI.

"was, in fact, the man behind the guns." With no sense of false modesty he once said: "I went into politics in this Territory as one of the first and few men who had the courage to tell certain politicians that they were a lot of damned rascals. They took it and they feared me because they knew that truth and honesty are not afraid of man, beast, or devil."[14]

Near the end of his first term as sheriff, Lorenzo found it necessary to have someone he could depend upon to operate his trading business at Ganado and elsewhere while he was at St. Johns. Out of this need, in 1884, came his association with Clinton N. Cotton. It was a mutually rewarding partnership that lasted ten years and enabled Hubbell to divide his time, after his second term as sheriff, between Ganado and the Territorial Legislature, where he could keep an eye on the "damned rascals."

C. N. Cotton was a labor employer and telegraph operator for the Atlantic and Pacific Railroad when the partnership was formed. Although he had had no previous experience as a trader, he had an unusual aptitude that was soon widely felt. He is remembered as a hearty sort of man, tall, rawboned, and a chain-smoker of cigars. One old-time trader remembered that "whenever I walked in his store he would reach in a box and hand me a big bunch of El Araby cigars. He was friendly and well-liked, a very good businessman. He was always out for business."[15]

In a discussion of Navaho weaving the expression "Ganado blanket" is a still-current generic term referring more directly than not to an imprint on the craft made by Lorenzo Hubbell. Within flexible limits the term denotes a blanket of rather larger than average size, usually bordered in black, with a red background (although it may be blue or gray) and a predominance of cross-shaped or diamond design elements. A higher than usual standard of workmanship is usually implicit.

Just as he lived and entertained on an opulent scale, as he built his buildings like fortresses of massive stone blocks and adobes, so it was characteristic of Lorenzo to prefer, and to ask for, blankets

14 Ibid.
15 Interview with Charlie Newcomb. Hubbell has been quoted as saying his partnership with Cotton began in 1880, and again in 1885—but the year 1884 is generally accepted. Other writers have said that Cotton was a telegraph operator at Wingate Station when the partnership was formed, but Mrs. Edward Vanderwagen assures me that this is not so, that he was stationed at Guam, a rail camp long since abandoned, one mile east of Coolidge, New Mexico.

of generous size: nine by twelve feet—or even larger—although he would buy blankets much smaller. Quality of workmanship interested him more than quantity of blankets, and it was only after Cotton became his partner that the weavers of Ganado were called upon to produce more. During Cotton's first year at Ganado, according to George Wharton James, the number of blankets purchased amounted to no more than three or four hundred. Cotton thereupon "began to urge upon the weavers that they bring in more blankets of the better qualities and also that they make more of the common grades. Little by little they built up a good business."[16]

The bright aniline dyes that trader Ben Hyatt already had introduced at Fort Defiance appeared to Cotton as a means for increasing sales. James says that Hubbell objected to the use of these chemical dyes, but in the winter of 1886–87, "Mr. Cotton had his way and he succeeded in having one of the great dye manufacturers put up, ready for use, a quantity of aniline dyes." In the end, however, Hubbell's views prevailed. He discouraged the use of cotton warp and eliminated all but a small range of chemical dyes, the most common of these being red—a popular color which the weavers found difficult to achieve with native vegetable dyes—blue, and black. After the use of manufactured Germantown yarns disappeared, the weavers found that a black yarn carded and spun from the wool of their black sheep lacked uniformity of color. A strong black dye, therefore, became acceptable, at Ganado as elsewhere.[17]

The eastern artist, E. A. Burbank, following in the steps of George Catlin, Bodmer, and Moran, visited and worked among many of the western tribes, but perhaps the best of his work are the paintings and drawings he did of Navahos while staying with the Hubbells at Ganado. Over a period of several visits during the early 1900's, and as an accommodation to his host, Burbank faithfully reproduced, in small scale, fifty or sixty of the blankets Lorenzo selected as the best

---

[16] James, *Indian Blankets and Their Makers.*

[17] Amsden (*Navaho Weaving*) dates the use of Germantown yarn from 1880 to about 1910. Gladys A. Reichard (*Navajo Shepherd and Weaver*), who learned to weave on a Navaho loom while staying at Ganado, says that red bayeta was sold by the yard at Hubbell's Ganado post as late as 1920, but the last bayeta blanket, unfinished, was brought into the post in 1912. Prior to the advent of chemical dyes, Navaho weavers unraveled the bayeta cloth to obtain the desired strands of red yarn. Indigo, a staple item among annuity goods regularly supplied to the Navahos until 1878, remained in use through the mid-1880's at least, although it was generally displaced when traders began to sell the pre-dyed Germantown yarns and aniline dyes. All authorities agree that Hubbell did as much as any trader, and more than most, to improve the quality of Navaho weaving.

brought into his post. The small paintings were framed and hung on the walls of the rug room, where they were referred to by Hubbell's less talented weavers or by customers who wished to buy something "like" one of the good Ganado rugs of familiar design.

In prefacing remarks for a catalog he issued about 1902, Lorenzo warned against "cheap and gaudy blankets, loosely put together" and sold at "fabulous" prices. "I have," he said, "even at times unraveled some of the old genuine Navajo blankets to show these modern weavers how the pattern was made." However, "the old blankets are passing away, in the nature of things. I can supply genuine reproductions of the old weaves. What I tell you regarding these goods will be the truth, and you will . . . find the prices based properly . . . with no misrepresentations, no shams and no counterfeits."

Native wool blankets with gray grounds or blue and black striped grounds with red and white center and corner designs, Hubbell offered by the pound, from $0.75 to $2.50. His larger and better blankets, in sizes eight by nine and twelve by twelve feet, were listed from $40 to $150. *Hanolchadi*, or Chief blankets, with black and white stripes and corner and center triangular designs in blue, white, and red, were priced from $17.50 to $35. His "common coarse native wool" blankets were listed at $0.50 to $0.75 a pound. Old bayeta squaw dresses, even then becoming rare, were offered at $25 to $50, and Hopi squaw dresses of dark blue wool and diagonal woven borders, for $10.

C. N. Cotton saw commercial possibilities in Navaho silverwork while working in the Wingate Valley for the railroad, according to Van Valkenburgh, and with Lorenzo's approval, induced *Naakaii Daadiil*—Thick Lipped Mexican—a Mexican silversmith living at Cubero, to move to Ganado and, with other silversmiths brought from Mexico, to teach the craft to men in the Ganado region. The demand for Navaho silverwork then was negligible and scarcely more than that ten or fifteen years later when, in the same catalog, Hubbell offered concho belts and silver-mounted bridles or headstalls at $30 to $40, silver bracelets set with matrix turquoise at $2.25 to $10.00.

At this time or soon after, the Fred Harvey Company made an agreement with Hubbell to buy all of his Navaho blankets of the best or good quality, these in the main going to the Harvey Indian Room in Albuquerque's new Alvarado Hotel. Herman Schweizer, Fred Harvey's canny buyer, no doubt was responsible for this move.

The Hubbell Trading Post, Ganado. Lorenzo is seated in the foreground with the young Navaho woman. The large framed doorway opens into Hubbell's office, and the rug room is to the right. The store entrance is the first door beyond the corner of the building. At far right in this 1890's Wittick photograph is the large two-faced rug later owned by C. N. Cotton and now in the Gladwin Collection in the Museum of Northern Arizona. (*Collection of Mrs. Roman Hubbell.*)

The Hubbell wareroom (above) at Ganado displays harness, goat-skins, a perambulator, and a birdcage hanging from the vigas. Un-identified employees are seen among packages of flour, tobacco, coffee, and crackers. The scales at left were used in weighing wool. Below, the Hubbell living room shows Lorenzo's taste for ornament-ing his walls. Later the baskets were removed to hang in clusters from the ceiling. The man in the chair resembles Lorenzo's brother Charles. Both Ben Wittick photographs. *(Museum of New Mexico.)*

Tse-a-lee (Sehili) Trading Post, a remote post in the Lukachukai Mountains. Archibald Sweetland, the owner, is the large man seated beside the Navaho child. Ben Wittick made this photograph in the early 1890's. *(Museum of New Mexico.)*

Gallegos Canyon Post. The door at the left in this 1927 photograph leads to Dick Simpson's store; the ones at the right, to the wareroom and manager's quarters. *(Collection of Simpson's daughter, Mrs. Kenneth Wynn.)*

Oljetoh was John Wetherill's first post in Monument Valley, before he and Louisa moved to Kayenta. *(Collection of Sam Day II.)*

Cabezon Peak. Dick Heller's abandoned trading post, seen from the rear, faces the Heller home, across the road, now in ruins. This picture was made in 1958, when Cabezon was a deserted ghost town.

Uncle Billy Crane, at right, is shown at his ranch near Coolidge, New Mexico. Others in this Wittick photograph, probably taken in the 1890's, are not identified. *(Museum of New Mexico.)*

Anson C. Damon, at his place south of Fort Defiance. The rifle he holds, relic of his Civil War service, hung in 1960 on the wall of his son James Damon's Defiance home. In this skelter of Navaho blankets, concho belts, silver headstalls, and beads, Damon hung a brace of pistols, bayonet scabbards, a steel trap, and a pair of field glasses— along with his black campaign hat, assorted bottles, and kerosene lamps. Such cheerful untidiness suggests that this was his private den, not his pawn room. Probably taken in the 1880's. *(Collection of Mrs. Edward Vanderwagen.)*

Wool being delivered in Albuquerque in July, 1900, by Mexicans from Estancia Valley, using their own teams of oxen. *(New Mexico Stockman.)*

Hogback Post, New Mexico, one of the first in the San Juan Valley. Trader Wilfred Wheeler and his family are seen on the porch in this photograph, taken about 1922. *(Collection of Wilfred Wheeler.)*

Years later Schweizer recalled that "Mr. Hubbell was the premier Indian trader of them all, and did more to stabilize and standardize the Indian blanket industry than any one else. . . . We bought annually twenty to twenty-five thousand dollars in blankets [from him], and this was over a period of many years . . . his word was as good as his bond."[18]

Commenting upon this arrangement, Amsden observed, in *Navaho Weaving*, that the prices Fred Harvey paid "seemingly being somewhat higher than those prevailing in some other quarters, at first caused much adverse comment" among other traders, presumably. "But Fred Harvey insisted that the business needed greater stability of prices and standardization of quality."

No one person was responsible for the partial transition of the Navaho blanket from blanket to rug: efforts of many traders who sought a commercial outlet were combined in this, and the Navahos' own increasing preference for machine-manufactured trade blankets, notably from the Pendleton mills, was a strong factor. C. N. Cotton was one of the first to realize the potentials of a large eastern market for Navaho rugs, and his efforts in this direction, starting about 1890 and followed soon by the rug trade developed by the Hyde Exploring Expedition, and later by the Fred Harvey Company, probably were of greatest influence.

Lorenzo Hubbell's contribution to this development came early and was almost unique. Impressing upon others one facet of his personal liking for things done on a large scale, he encouraged "special order" blankets so large they could scarcely be used except as rugs in large rooms.

One of these, said to be woven about 1885, measures twelve feet by eighteen feet, two inches. A double-weave, or two-faced rug, it eventually was acquired by Cotton. For years the rug remained on the floor of Cotton's home in Gallup, but a table leg finally frayed a hole in it. Cotton sent the rug off to Coolidge, where his trader friend Berton I. Staples offered to have it repaired. Staples for some reason retained possession of the rug until his death in an automobile accident in the fall of 1938. Then, in part settlement of obligations owed to them, the rug was acquired by Mr. and Mrs. Harold Gladwin. It

18 *Santa Fe Magazine*, January, 1931. The opening of the Alvarado Hotel was noted by the *McKinley County Republican*, May 17, 1902: "The Alvarado at Albuquerque . . . finest railroad hotel in the Southwest, built at a cost of $125,000, was opened May 10 under the management of Fred Harvey. . . . One unique feature is a museum, where are displayed Indian curios valued at $75,000."

now forms a part of the Gladwin collection owned by the Museum of Northern Arizona.[19]

[19] M. L. Woodard of Gallup is my informant. The rug appears first in the background of a photograph taken at Ganado, probably in the late eighties. Another photograph of the rug, shown stretched at full length on a rack outside of Staples' Coolidge store, appears in Reichard's *Navajo Shepherd and Weaver,* (Plate XII, b). The Gladwin collection at the Museum of Northern Arizona, acquired in October, 1958, is valued by Director Edward Danson at $40,000. Lorenzo's son, Roman Hubbell, about 1937 commissioned what is still said to be the largest Navaho rug ever made. Guarded in the vault of the Bales store at Winslow, it measures twenty-two by thirty-six feet. Mrs. Doris Grace, an employee of Mr. Bales, tells me the rug was woven at or near Greasewood Trading Post, three women working for three years to complete it.

16

Hubbell and Cotton

SINCE THE EARLY YEARS of the seventeenth century, Canyon de Chelly was both gathering center and natural fortress for the Navahos. No count has been made of the number of times the Navahos were attacked or besieged there: a Spanish massacre of women, children, and older men in 1804 or 1805 gave name to Canyon del Muerto —one of De Chelly's three major connecting canyons; Colonel Washington's expedition in September, 1849, burned hogans there; again, in January, 1864, cavalry under Kit Carson and commanded by Captain Albert H. Pfeiffer and Captain Asa B. Carey cautiously penetrated the canyon gathering up prisoners for Bosque Redondo and destroying with fire and ax the Navaho cornfields and orchards.

In times of peace, most of the Navahos of the region lived in the piñon and juniper forests rimming De Chelly's deep chasms. When spring thaws livened the Chinle and other canyon washes, the rim families moved their sheep down to bottomland or out on the desert. Summer people in the canyon found the soil rich for corn and melons and some fruit trees. The area was populous, relatively prosperous, and had a rich potential for trade.

Van Valkenburgh says that a Mexican trader, remembered only by his Navaho name, *Naakaii Yazzie* (Little Mexican), operated a tent trading post near the west mouth of the canyon about 1882, and was driven out within a year by Agent Denis Riordan. Perhaps this is so. In any case, the first license to trade at Chinle was granted to Lorenzo Hubbell and C. N. Cotton, early in 1886.

Cotton first applied for the license, in his name and Hubbell's, on

213

January 26, 1885. Their ten-thousand-dollar bond was secured a few days later, and Agent Bowman twice wrote to Washington recommending that the license be granted. The partners said that five thousand dollars would be invested to stock the post and that Charles Hubbell and John W. Boehm would be employed as clerks. Months passed without action by Commissioner Atkins until Lorenzo finally wrote to Congressman C. C. Beam of Arizona requesting his intervention. The license was issued in the first months of 1886.[1]

Probably in the early spring of 1886, Hubbell and Cotton began operating at Chinle, taking over an abandoned stone hogan and adding to it a stone building of perhaps three rooms. A photograph of the post taken in 1906 shows that the building fronted to the east, projecting *vigas* supported a dirt roof, and the masonry was in Hubbell's preferred fortress style, though here the coursing of heavy stone was rather haphazard.

Trade at this place was a surprising disappointment. Hubbell and Cotton failed to renew their license after the first year, and the post fell into other hands. Each new owner changed or enlarged it. What remains of the original building now can be traced as a few vague walls in Camille García's modern Chinle store.[2]

A number of years later—probably about 1900—Lorenzo Hubbell, on his own, built a second post at Chinle. Several miles west of the original site and on a slight eminence east of the Chinle Wash, he built what at that time was the most impressive trading post on the Navaho reservation. Architecture was of Ganado style but on an even grander scale. Large blocks of dark red sandstone, carefully cut and faced, were used, the walls rising to an unprecedented two stories. The building reflected Lorenzo's belief, well founded but pre-

1 I could find no record of Little Mexican in Indian Office files, but would accept Van Valkenburgh's statement as correct. Correspondence relating to the Hubbell-Cotton license is dated from Cotton's January 26, 1885, letter through Lorenzo's letter to Beam, December 9, 1885. (National Archives . . . Record Group 75, Letters Received, 1885: #2394, #26179, #6956, #8960.)

2 The 1906 photograph, too faded to reproduce, is owned by Mrs. Charles Cousins, whose husband traded at Chinle at this time. Camille García assured me that Hubbell's original building developed out of the old hogan and was the first permanent trading post in that region. A succession of traders followed Hubbell and Cotton at Chinle, and it is likely that many of them occupied this building. Among them were Michael Donovan, licensed April 3, 1886, at Chinle, and March 7, 1887, at Chinle Valley, about twelve miles to the north; Washington P. and Thomas J. Lingle, January 23, 1888; Bernard J. Mooney and James F. Boyle, February 21, 1889; and John W. Boehm, July 6, 1889. (*N. A.*, *Ledgers of Traders.*) The neighboring Sam Day post, famous years later as Cozy McSparron's Thunderbird Ranch, is described elsewhere.

mature, that tourists would flock to see Canyon de Chelly if only accommodations for them were provided. The second floor of his trading post, which measured some 107 feet long by 35 feet wide, was composed of eight guest bedrooms opening on a long hallway, a large living-dining room for guests, and the manager's quarters.

Almost half of the building at ground level was given over to the trading store, the remaining space divided into two large associated rooms. Ceilings were ten feet high, the walls fourteen inches thick and, on the inside, plastered smooth with adobe.

Tourists arrived at discouragingly long intervals, and the few who came usually were seen in summer only. An exception was the visit of Fr. Anselm Weber of St. Michaels and the interpreter Frank Walker, accompanied by Miss Josephine Drexel and Sister Agatha, in December, 1902. As related by Wilken in *Missionary to the Navaho*, the small party "enjoyed the trader's usual warm hospitality. While there it was a novelty to watch Don Lorenzo pay out his own money 'chips' for blankets, and then observe how the Indians purchased their own supplies with this scrip." The following morning, a Sunday, mass was celebrated "on the dining table at the far end of the huge Hubbell hall."

Sam Day II worked here as clerk for Lorenzo, off and on as he was needed, and also in these years was employed to drive Hubbell in a high-wheeled open automobile about the reservation. The few roads that then existed were incredibly rough, but Day's memory of their long trips together are of Lorenzo's either talking untiringly or stretched out asleep in the back, oblivious to the bone-jarring bumps. Others who worked for Hubbell at the new Chinle post included Mike Kirk and Leon H. (Cozy) McSparron.

"Not many tourists came to Chinle in those days," Camille García once recalled, "—no cars and bad roads." Lorenzo gave up hope of making the post pay and about 1917 sold it to Cotton. In 1920, García went to work for Cotton at the former Hubbell store and remained three years.

"In 1923," García recalled, "Cozy McSparron and I and Hartley T. Seymour bought out all three stores at Chinle. The details of who owned what at that time are very complicated. Seymour was C. N. Cotton's son-in-law. We closed down the old Hubbell place and it has been falling into ruin ever since." The post now stands as a forlorn shell, roof and second floor gone, only the walls remaining.

If our civilization were to pass away and if a century from now a new race of men were to poke among the ruins of Hubbell's Chinle store and his buildings at Ganado, a natural conclusion would be that these were nineteenth-century fortresses built to withstand siege. And nothing could be farther from the truth. No fear of attack, but something in his Spanish heritage caused Lorenzo to build on a massive scale. His one concession to possible threat was to discourage thievery by sinking iron bars across his windows.

His Ganado buildings form a large square, the store and house at two corners, a great stone barn at a third, and employees' quarters elsewhere, enclosing a wide center yard. A gate of iron rods forms the one entrance into the yard on the long east wall of buildings running from store to barn. High in the barn walls wide openings for ventilation are laced with a picketing of three-inch poles. Walls of these buildings are a foot and a half thick, the stone dark red and quarried from this valley. Ceilings, as at Chinle, are about ten feet high and supported by ponderous *vigas* twelve to fourteen inches in diameter.

Two benches, each formed of three stone slabs, flank the doorway to the post, an old oxbow suspended in the top of the thick door frame. The store is long, narrow, and dimly lighted; a huge wareroom opens off at one side, Lorenzo's office and rug room at the other.

To relieve the mass and bulk and gloom of these surroundings, Lorenzo indulged his taste for ornament. In office and rug room he covered the floors with rugs from the Ganado looms, the colors red and blue predominating. Oil paintings, Burbank's red chalk drawings, and framed photographs of political friends—among them three Presidents—he hung from the walls.[3] Running out of floor and wall space, he looked to the ceilings. Between the *vigas* he suspended, bottom side up, baskets collected from all the Arizona weavers. In the rug room, at one end often piled shoulder deep with stacks of folded blankets, Lorenzo let his zest for frontier objects break free. Leaving no inch of adobe plaster bare, he festooned the room with Plains Indian beadwork, buckskin bow and arrow cases, buffalo-hide shields painted and dripping eagle feathers; with a gun rack and a score of old rifles, old saddles and saddlebags; a buffalo robe flung in a corner and a mounted buffalo head hung from the wall; with ancient pottery, modern Hopi pottery—and modern branding irons, among them two of his own "coffin" brand.

About 1900, Lorenzo abandoned his original adobe house, replac-

[3] As a Republican state senator and on private business, Hubbell visited Washington a number of times. He was on good terms with William McKinley and William Howard Taft, and regarded Theodore Roosevelt as a personal friend.

ing it with a new home constructed in the northwest corner of his quadrangle. It was low and unpretentious with a screened porch running the length of the front. No frills here, but the same solid touch toward largeness. The front door opened into a living room forty feet long and fifteen feet wide. He wanted no hallways, so off this room and flanking it he arranged five bedrooms, each dominated by a massive bedstead of carved dark wood or ball-and-tube brass.

At the far end of the living room, where the family dined, he built a door into an open but walled, flowering patio. Across that, another door led into a building of two rooms. One of these, according to Mrs. Dorothy Hubbell, was used at meal-time by the several men who worked on the place. ("There were anywhere from four to fifteen, depending upon the season's work.") After Lorenzo's death this became the family dining room.

The living room had as its focal point a wide stone fireplace projecting from the center of the long east wall. Furnishings and ornaments were an extension of the same decorations burdening walls and ceilings of his rug room and office. Navaho rugs again covered the floor, the largest measuring about eight by fifteen feet. Bookcases placed in the room corners contained his library of perhaps five hundred volumes. Government reports and technical works he shelved in the rug room, but here were the books for family pleasure: among them, the complete novels of Alexander Dumas, John Ruskin, Mark Twain, all of Bancroft's historical works, full sets of Charles Dickens, Edgar Allan Poe, and Nathaniel Hawthorne; a fifteen-volume set of the works of Lord Lytton, scores of western novels, George Catlin's two-volume *The North American Indians*, and Twitchell's six-volume *Spanish Archives of New Mexico*.

In a region known for its easy hospitality, the Hubbell home at Ganado became famous as a free haven for literally hundreds of visitors, from lonely lost souls of no rank or name to President Theodore Roosevelt. Generous to a fault, Lorenzo would not let his guests pay for anything, whether they came by invitation or strayed his way by accident or out of curiosity. He had a large capacity for liking people, all kinds of people. Henry Coddington once recalled that "it was nothing for him to entertain one hundred and fifty people at his place at a time—Indians, Mexicans, bull-whackers, Eastern tourists, anthropologists, archaeologists, ethnologists—he was the most hospitable man in the world!"[4]

[4] Resident of Gallup, Henry B. Coddington is the son of Joseph Henry (Harry) Coddington, who at this period owned the old Home Ranch Stables on Coal Ave-

Lorenzo himself once admitted that he held open house to all comers and "spent tens of thousands of dollars feeding and entertaining people from every part of the United States and even from abroad."[5]

In August, 1913, Theodore Roosevelt and his sons Archibald and Quentin were guests of the Hubbells at Ganado, and with Lorenzo went to the Snake Dance at Walpi. A correspondent for a Gallup newspaper accompanied the party and noted that before the final ceremony Roosevelt was admitted to the kiva of the Snake clan. ". . . we could hear a few chants being sung," the correspondent wrote, "and then the Colonel came out with a broad smile, declaring 'It beat the *first* degree in the Blue Lodge.'"[6]

Again in the summer of 1915, Roosevelt returned to Ganado. His visit that year was recalled afterward by a Colorado woman, then a girl and staying at the Hubbells' with her father and mother: "How familiar the house looks and the office where Don Lorenzo used to talk politics with Dad by the hour—good Republicans that they both were—me sitting on the floor listening in.

"That summer of '15 was high lighted by a rush trip Teddy Roosevelt made to see Don Lorenzo and to take his youngest boy to see the Snake Dance. They went by auto but Dad and I went by wagon with grub, etc."[7]

After his second term as sheriff of Apache County, Lorenzo had been elected to the Territorial Assembly. He served in that branch of the legislature until Arizona was admitted to statehood, in 1912, when he was elected state senator. Excitement over Theodore Roosevelt's effort that year to regain the presidency, on the Bull Moose ticket, may have influenced Lorenzo in 1914 to seek election as United States senator. He campaigned vigorously throughout the state. Arriving in Tombstone from Nogales one day in July, his presence was noted by the *Tombstone Prospector*: "State Senator J. L. Hubbell and Hon. Joseph E. Morrison [a former U. S. Attorney for Arizona] . . . spent the night here in conference with the leaders of the two

---

nue in Gallup. Henry's father and grandfather, Alfred Walter Coddington, had such a serious falling out that the grandfather's name was never mentioned and Henry knew virtually nothing about him. For this reason he could cast no light on which of his father's relatives was associated with Hubbell in the early Fort Wingate days. In 1915, Hubbell employed a W. J. Coddington as bookkeeper at Ganado.

5 *Touring Topics*, Vol. XXII, No. 12.
6 B. D. Richards, in the *McKinley County Republican*, September 5, 1913.
7 Letter from Ruth Collins Bagwell to Mrs. Roman Hubbel, August 10, 1958.

wings of the Republican party. The distinguished party are on an 'oil pouring' expedition. . . . Mr. Hubbell is a warm personal friend of Theodore Roosevelt and at the present time is entertaining some of the younger Roosevelts [at Ganado]. . . . Last year Mr. Hubbell sold $60,000 worth of Navajo blankets, and is the leading dealer in that commodity in America."

In November the Democrats swept the state. Lorenzo accepted his defeat philosophically, but friends say that he invested a small fortune in the campaign and this, with ensuing business reverses, was a financial turning point from which he never fully recovered.

Lorenzo's friendship with Roosevelt appears to have originated about the time a land dispute threatened to wipe out his homestead at Ganado. When boundaries of the Navaho reservation were extended westward by executive order, January 6, 1880, Lorenzo's 160-acre homestead, previously outside the reservation, was engulfed. Litigation was started to suspend his trading license, remove his buildings, and deny his claim to the property. The case dragged on for years, even beyond 1900 when a petition entered by Hubbell and Cotton based on "prior rights" won approving action in Congress. Hearings on the case required Lorenzo's presence in Washington, and subsequently he was forced to make special trips to Phoenix to appear at the United States Land Office. The patent for his homestead finally was issued October 17, 1917.[8]

Although the era of the automobile had arrived, the mud ruts and sandy arroyos of the reservation retarded progress at all seasons and especially in winter. Nevertheless, everyone was becoming transporta-

---

8 The most pertinent documents in this case are "Rights of Settlers on the Navajo Reservation, Ariz.", 56 Cong., 1 sess., *House Report No. 411*, and an affidavit of Hubbell's appearance June 1, 1908, before the Register and Receiver, U. S. Land Office, Phoenix. The 1880 reservation extension also affected Anson Damon, who then homesteaded just south of the old reservation line near Fort Defiance. Notified that he had no right to the land and must cease trading there, Damon wrote to Commissioner Atkins, July 6, 1886: "I beg leave to call your attention to the fact that one C. N. Cotton is trading with the Navajos at Pueblo Colorado—within the limits of the Reservation without a license and upon unsurveyed land that was settled upon several years before I settled upon my place. Also one Thomas V. Keams is conducting a trading store at Keams Canon—within the limits of the Moqui Reservation—without a license. . . . Why, if these men are permitted to continue in trade under the same circumstances that I claim the right, should the privilege be denied me? I most earnestly protest against such seeming unjust discrimination." (National Archives . . . Letters Received, 1886, #18803.) Damon was prevented from trading, at least for a short time, but remained on his homestead and his prior claim to it was upheld in the same action by Congress that supported Lorenzo Hubbell's rights at Ganado. Thomas Keam escaped this litigation, but after 1889 was required to hold a license at Keams Canyon.

tion minded. Lorenzo responded to the changing times by inaugurating a stage and freight line—horse drawn—in the spring of 1915. At the Gallup starting point he placed his son Roman in charge. Each morning at seven o'clock a stage left town for St. Michaels, passengers paying a fare of four dollars: for one dollar more they could hold their seats and ride on to Fort Defiance. Other stages were added for more distant points: Ganado, Chinle, Keams Canyon and Oraibi.[9] Mrs. Dorothy Hubbell has recalled that as late as 1920, Lorenzo owned sixty-six freight horses. Upsetting the winter schedule, conditions could be so bad that it might take the stage ten days to travel the fifty-five miles between Ganado and Gallup.

The years, with changes they brought, were beginning to tell. Lorenzo was nearing sixty when his wife died, on July 13, 1913. On the crown of a cone-shaped hill close to the family home she was buried, her grave near that of Lorenzo's old friend, Many Horses. Her passing did not bring an end to the once exuberant hospitality of her husband, but quietened it. More and more Lorenzo depended upon his sons, Lorenzo, Jr., and Roman, gradually relinquishing to them responsibilities of his ten or twelve posts. He could reflect that the Hubbell name was pre-eminent still, but other traders were crowding in, new posts were mushrooming across the reservation, and their competition was felt.

Several of the larger trading firms and one or two wholesalers were tightening their grip on the eastern side of the reservation by operating or supplying strings of trading posts and thereby slowly encroaching on areas where Hubbell once was unchallenged. To meet this situation, Lorenzo opened a trading supply house of his own in Gallup, in February, 1914, turning it over to Roman's management. Lorenzo, Jr., meanwhile, continued to run the Winslow store and look after the Hubbell posts on the western side of the reservation. With less to occupy him, Lorenzo traveled about restlessly, coming often to Gallup, where he could remain only a day or two, staying usually at the Page Hotel or with the C. N. Cotton family.

Hearing that his old friend Dan DuBois was ailing and in trouble, Lorenzo went to see him one day in 1922. Then eighty-four years old, as near as he could tell, DuBois was holed up in a crumbling hovel at his place in Coyote Canyon, thirty miles south of Gallup. Sur-

---

[9] Hubbell advertised the new stage line in the April 29, 1915, issue of the Gallup *Independent*. The fare from Gallup to Ganado was $10, to Chinle, $15; Keams Canyon, $20; and Oraibi, $25. In late years the passenger service was discontinued, but Mrs. Roman Hubbell said the freight line was maintained until 1945.

rounded by his family of all ages and sizes and dubious numbers, Dan protested to Hubbell's inquiries that all was well with him. Except for an old bullet wound or imbedded arrowhead giving him a twinge now and then, he never felt better in his life. Not fooled, Lorenzo could see that Dan was existing on an outer fringe of poverty. Although his own resources were not nearly what they had been, he quietly arranged to look after the old man's affairs.[10]

Hubbell on another occasion had come to his rescue. Hodge once wrote that "one time at Fort Wingate Dan became completely spiflicated and lay on the ice in an arroyo. Being bitterly cold, Lorenzo feared that Dan would freeze to death, so he took him home. In a temporary repentant mood Dan afterward said that it might have been better if he had been left there to die."[11]

Lean times fell upon Ganado in Lorenzo's last years. The lavish entertainment and hospitality so freely offered in the past were now possible only rarely and then on a smaller scale. The drain upon his resources to keep his large business afloat was constant and severely felt. A day came when Lorenzo in old age was embarrassed for money.

"Four or five years before he died," Henry Coddington has recalled, "my father met Hubbell one winter day in Gallup. It was snowing and blowing and my father was surprised when Hubbell said, 'Coddington, I'm broke.'

"That same day Hubbell met some Eastern people in town, whom he had entertained many times at his home in Ganado. They said to him, 'Let's get together for dinner tonight at El Navajó'—the Fred Harvey hotel—and Hubbell said all right, he would be there.

"When my dad told me this story he nearly cried. He said, 'Along about six that night I went over to the hotel and took a seat where I could see what was going on. All of them were sitting there with Lorenzo at the table. When they were through they pushed back their chairs and stood up. And do you know what those goddam sonsofbitches did? They walked off, leaving Lorenzo to pay the bill!' "

Lorenzo Hubbell is buried on the crown of the hill near his home, his grave beside the graves of his wife Lina Rubi, Many Horses, his two sons, and a daughter, Adele Hubbell Parker. The headstone marks the date of his death, November 12, 1930.[12]

10 The Gallup *Independent*, March 23, 1922.
11 Frederick W. Hodge, *Old Dan DuBois*. This biographical sketch appears to have been privately printed in a limited edition, with no publisher's imprint and no date. I obtained a copy of it from Mrs. Edward Vanderwagen of Zuñi.
12 Lorenzo Hubbell, Jr., died in March, 1942. Roman Hubbell died October 14, 1957.

When Cotton and Hubbell ended their partnership in 1894, the agreement was friendly and they remained good friends in the years following. In Gallup, Cotton founded the wholesale establishment of C. N. Cotton Company and prospered from the start. His timing was propitious. Gallup just then was realizing its fortunate position as a supply center for Indian trade, serving the region within a hundred-mile radius. Cotton's store was the town's first big wholesale house to take advantage of the situation, and Cotton, himself personally well liked, soon was supplying nearly every trader in the area.

His astuteness is illustrated by his obtaining exclusive regional control of two items basic to the Navaho trade: Arbuckle's coffee and Pendleton blankets. To most Navahos of that time, any coffee or blanket under another name was either counterfeit or an inferior substitute. The trader who was even dimly aware of his Navahos' preferences—and most of them were keenly aware—naturally must stock his shelves from Cotton's warehouse.

Charlie Newcomb, who was one of these traders, once said that Cotton paid the Arbuckle's distributor seven cents a package, or seven dollars for a case of coffee. Newcomb would pay Cotton eight dollars for the case and sell it, at Hans Neumann's Guam post, where he then clerked, for ten dollars.

"Pendleton blankets came in two grades," Newcomb recalled. "A fringe made the difference between a shawl and a robe. It used to cost us seven dollars for a robe and eight dollars for a shawl, and I suppose Cotton made a dollar profit either way. And he sold worlds of them—the Indians wouldn't buy anything else."

Cotton was probably the first person in the Indian trade to make a concerted, well-planned effort to develop an eastern market for Navaho rugs. George Wharton James said that about 1897 he wrote, for Cotton's use, "the first illustrated and descriptive catalogue of the Navaho blanket ever issued."[13] Amsden, in *Navaho Weaving*, observed that Cotton "worked vigorously" in creating an eastern market, and added: "He got hold of a mimeograph outfit and directories of various eastern cities, and proceeded to circularize the 'whole country,' as he phrased it. He featured three grades of merchandise. First came the rugs, the better specimens of blankets being put into this category. . . . Next grade was the saddle blanket known among traders as 'dougies' (*Di-yu-ge*, Navaho for a soft, fluffy weave). Sad-

13 James, *Indian Blankets and Their Makers.*

dle blankets cost the trader seventy-five cents each, shoulder blankets
. . . two dollars. Mr. Cotton says he loaded up, foreseeing a better
demand and higher prices when his mimeographed message should
have done its work."

Apart from increasing Cotton's own well-being, the economy of
the Navaho tribe benefited as well, and increasingly so as other traders adopted Cotton's strategy and, in many cases, worked to improve
the quality of Navaho weaving. Navaho Superintendent Reuben
Perry noted in 1906 that during the previous year the Navahos "derived in the neighborhood of $1,000,000 from their sheep, goats, and
cattle and the sale of blankets. Excellent blankets are being made,
and the prices received for them and the wool have been good."[14]

Government contracts were another large factor in Cotton's business. In 1905 his firm was awarded eight contracts totaling $156,261
for supplying feed, oats, and salt to the Navaho, Hopi, and Zuñi
reservations. The following year Cotton bid successfully on five contracts totaling $207,900 to supply feed and oats to the Indian schools
of Santa Fe and Albuquerque.[15]

In 1914, Cotton filed an amendment to his company's charter with
the State Corporation Commission, increasing the firm's capital stock
from $100,000 to $500,000. A year later, having outgrown his already
large quarters located in the center of town directly adjacent to the
railroad, Cotton ordered work started on an addition to his building.
The Gallup *Independent* of May 13, 1915, commented that "when
this new part . . . is completed, Gallup will have one of the largest
business houses in the Southwest."

Not entirely content with the wholesale side of trading, Cotton
returned briefly to direct trade with the Indians. Sometime after 1911
he bought the Round Rock Trading Post from S. E. Aldrich, and in
1914 was reported as controlling a trading post at Zuñi. His interest
in the former Lorenzo Hubbell store at Chinle, as we have seen,
lasted from about 1917 until 1923.

During his later years Cotton diverted much of his time to other
interests. He served Gallup as mayor for one term during the first
world war and usually spent the winters at his home in Los Angeles.
While wintering there in 1913, he and S. E. Aldrich attended a meet-

14 *Annual Report, C. I. A., 1906.* Commissioner Cato Sells observed in 1913: "The
blanket industry among the Navajo Indians of Arizona and New Mexico is perhaps the most profitable of the native industries. The actual number of Indians
engaged in this industry is unknown, but it is estimated that between $600,000 and
$700,000 worth of blankets were produced during the year." (*Ibid.*, 1913.)

15 *Ibid.*, 1905–1906.

ing of the executive committee of the National Highway Association —a group of dedicated persons who then were planning a transcontinental automobile highway. Surveys for a route (later to become U. S. Highway 66) already had been carried from Los Angeles as far as Williams, Arizona. Cotton and Aldrich, quite naturally, were desirous that the new dirt road should not bypass Gallup, and Cotton spoke actively for his town.

One stunt which he helped to organize was a motorcade in the spring of 1913 from Gallup to Albuquerque. The distance then was about 160 miles, and such road as there was was traveled mainly by wagons. Four cars left Gallup at four o'clock one morning in May, reaching Albuquerque seventeen hours later. Charles L. Day drove one of the cars, and among the seventeen men making the trip were the young traders Frank Mapel and William Bickel. Cotton and C. C. Manning, a fellow trader, met the automobiles on their arrival, having preceded them by train.[16]

The days of the horse and of the old-time Indian trader were nearing an end; both were in their last race, and it slowly became clear that this would be a dead heat.

[16] The *McKinley County Republican,* May 9, 1913. The Gallup men making this trip were delegates to a New Mexico Good Roads Association meeting held in Albuquerque to advance the cause of the transcontinental highway. In the fall of that year, Cotton's son Jack drove a Ford automobile in a road race between Gallup and Winslow, Arizona. Jack Cotton was first in a field of seven to cover the 235 miles, averaging twenty miles an hour.

PART THREE

"Our first thought of course is to get them to weave for us
and for us only, all the fine rugs they possibly can. . . . But it
is also our mission here to buy any and everything the Navajo
has to sell; his wool and pelts, his farm produce when he has
any, the surplus of his flocks, herds of cattle and horses. . . .
And it is also our purpose to sell him in turn, all his supplies,
groceries, dry goods, clothing, wagons, harness and saddles,
everything in fact that he has need for."

—John B. Moore, in "The Navajo," a catalog issued from the Crystal Trading Post,
New Mexico, in 1911.

17

Wingate Valley and Zuñi

TRADE ROUTES of the Southwest could be as errantly haphazard and changeable as the course of a dry wash. In common with the region's larger rivers, however, the major trade routes remained reasonably constant, determined secondarily by men after concessions to nature's topography.

Enclosed for all of its length by mountain slopes or redrock mesas, Wingate Valley is a hundred-mile link in one of several ancient trade routes from the Río Grande to California. Starting approximately at the malpais or lava beds south of Mount Taylor in New Mexico, Wingate Valley curves northwestward to the Mesa de los Lobos and then drops off into Arizona and vanishes in an open plain below Fort Defiance. Antiquity of the valley and its centuries of use by prehistoric traders are attested, for nearly its full length, by countless *anasazi* ruins and in them the presence of trade wares: pottery and non-indigenous beads of seashell and turquoise.

A southern cutoff equally timeless and travel-worn trails eastward from Zuñi Pueblo to present-day San Rafael. Over this cutoff the Coronado expedition traveled in 1540; the route was followed again in 1849 by Colonel John M. Washington's troops, returning to Santa Fe from their punitive campaign against the Navahos. A myriad of others who passed this way memorialized themselves by carving their names or initials on El Morro—Inscription Rock.

Spanish and Mexican traders dominated the region for almost two hundred years. Until the 1860's they were unchallenged, playing the marauding Apaches and Navahos off against the Pueblos, selling

227

firearms and firewater impartially to both sides, often in exchange for stolen horses or captive slaves. Spanish-Indian settlements of Mount Taylor's eastern foothills, Cebolleta most notoriously, harbored many of the gun-slave traders. Zuñi was their favorite market place, and under the traders' influence the pueblo, eager for trade, tolerated a limited presence of the enemy people. Agent James Calhoun, pausing briefly with Colonel Washington's command in 1849, observed the situation accurately when he said: "While at Zuñi, I saw several Mexican *traders*, who hailed from various places, all however, on *our* side of the supposed boundary line between the United States and Mexico . . . .

"So long as these wandering merchants are permitted a free and unrestrained access to the wild and roving Indians of this country, just so long are we to be harrassed by them, and their allies, the various bands of robbers . . . whose agents these merchants may be— It is through the medium of *these traders* that arms and ammunition are supplied to the Indians who refuse submission to our authority— These traders go where they please without being subjected to the slightest risk."[1]

Occupation of the southwestern territories until recently held by Mexico was still so new, the United States military establishment still so weak, that Calhoun believed the Mexican traders presented an immediate danger. Not only did these "traveling merchants" provoke bloodshed among the Indian tribes, but also they stirred conflict in the old Spanish settlements "by attempting the impression that the Government of the United States are unable to hold possession of this country." This the traders did, said Calhoun, by spreading rumors "that the Mexican Government, *at this time,* has twenty-five thousand troops marching, or ready to march into New Mexico."

By fall of 1849, Colonel John Munroe had succeeded to the military governorship of New Mexico. The situation was unimproved on November 2 when Calhoun, no alarmist, wrote to Indian Commissioner Medill: "The constant and unrestricted intercourse of traders with the Indians of this territory is, perhaps, the greatest curse upon it, and so exceedingly pernicious is it, I have ventured to suggest to Governor Munroe, the propriety of extending by *Order,* the Laws of Congress in relation to trade and intercourse with Indian tribes, over this territory, as a military measure, offensive and defensive, called

---

[1] Letter from Calhoun to C. I. A. Medill, October 15, 1849. *Official Correspondence.*

for by the war demonstrations of the wild tribes. He has taken the subject into consideration."

Somewhat earlier, Calhoun had recommended the establishment of a military post in the vicinity of Mount Taylor, where the "Navajoes and Apaches are exceedingly troublesome. . . . Not a day passes without hearing of some fresh outrage." In consequence, Governor Munroe stationed a company of dragoons at Cebolleta, on the eastern approach to Wingate Valley. This outpost offered the sole protection to the Wingate trade route until the post was abandoned with the garrisoning of Fort Defiance, in the fall of 1851, near the western end of the valley. Troops at Defiance were augmented briefly when a tent camp was created some forty-five miles to the southeast at Ojo del Oso, or Bear Spring, in August, 1860. First called Fort Fauntleroy, the camp was hastily renamed Fort Lyon when the officer for whom it was first named joined the Confederate forces at the outbreak of the Civil War.[2]

Two weeks after the nation plunged into war the troops stationed at Fort Defiance were withdrawn for duty in the East. Abandonment of Fort Lyon in 1862 left much of the western territory of New Mexico, and all of the Wingate Valley, undefended. The situation was soon remedied, however, with an order from Brigadier General James H. Carleton, commanding the Department of New Mexico, to establish a new fort "near the head waters of the Gallo," in "the valley of the Aqua Azul." Even before anyone in Santa Fe knew where, exactly, this was, the new fort was named Wingate—honoring Captain Benjamin Wingate, who died of wounds received in 1861 during an encounter with Confederate forces at the Battle of Valverde.

A location for the fort was chosen October 22, 1862, by a board of three officers appointed to the task by General Carleton. The site they selected was the "Ojo del Gallo [which] rises in a valley at the foot of the eastern spur of the Zuñi mountains. . . . By the present road it is 23.55 miles [west] from Cubero. The valley of the Ojo del Gallo is about nine miles long, north and south, and has a mean

2 Fourteen miles east of present Gallup, Ojo del Oso—called *Shashbitoo* by the Navahos—was a spring frequented by Navaho war parties traveling the Wingate Valley. It was here that Col. Alexander Doniphan, commanding the Third Missouri Volunteers, and Narbona, Zarcillas Largo, and other Navaho chiefs signed the Treaty of Bear Springs in 1846. Regular troops of the Fifth and Tenth Infantry were withdrawn from Fort Fauntleroy at the outbreak of the Civil War and replaced, until summer, 1862, by three companies of the Second New Mexico Volunteers. Fort Defiance was abandoned permanently by its military garrison on April 25, 1861.

breadth of about seven and a half miles."[3] An abundant supply of piñon wood for fuel, spring water "of remarkable purity," and "gentle slopes" close by the plain's bottom, affording "gramma grasses in plenty," all recommended the location.

So urgent was the need for defense against Navaho raiders that four companies of the First New Mexico Volunteers were ordered to proceed at once to Ojo del Gallo. Arriving in mid-November, when a frost covered the gentle slopes each night, they erected hut shelters. A labor as well as a fighting force, these green recruits, commanded by Lieutenant Colonel Francisco Chávez, toiled through the winter and the next summer building the fort.

Original plans and drawings of old Fort Wingate have been removed from the War Department files and presumably are lost. With a little imagination, however, added to a few surviving scraps of evidence, one may form some idea of the appearance of the fort.

"It is to be surrounded by a defensive stockade," wrote the trio of officers who chose the site, a stockade "whose north and west sides are flanked by the enclosure containing the magazine, and the south and east sides of the corral and stables." Further than this we have only a list of specifications:

> 9,317 feet of adobe wall, 13 feet high, two feet thick (walls of buildings).
> 1,800 feet of adobe wall, 8 feet high, 1 foot thick (walls surrounding officers' quarters).
> Buildings to have earth roofs.
> Defensive stockade: 4,340 feet long, 8 feet high.
> 1,500 *vigas*, 25 feet long, for roofing.
> 1,000,000 feet of lumber.[4]

Wingate's small garrison of volunteers—Companies B, C, E, and F, commanded by Chávez—patrolled from the Río Grande to the Gila River. They were too few in number, however, spread too thin, and based too far to the east to affect measurably the Navahos' redoubled

---

[3] The Board of Officers selecting old Fort Wingate's site consisted of Capt. Henry R. Selden, Fifth Infantry; Asst. Surgeon Joseph C. Bailey, Medical Dept., U. S. Army; and First Lt. Allen S. Anderson, Fifth Infantry. Their report to General Carleton, referred to here and following, was dated November 4, 1862, from Los Pinos, New Mexico. (National Archives, War Records Division, Fort Wingate File #1251.) Ojo del Gallo first was shown on the Miera y Pacheco (Domínguez-Escalante) map of 1776. Fort Wingate's site appears as "Ojo de Gallo Hay Camp" on the 1860 J. N. Macomb Map of New Mexico and Arizona. Later, the Spanish-American village of San Rafael, three miles south of Grants, was built a mile west and slightly north of the ruins of the old fort.

[4] *Ibid.* Specifications of old Fort Wingate, enclosed in letter from Lt. Anderson to General Carleton, November 16, 1862.

raids upon pueblos and widely separated Spanish-Anglo settlements. In June, 1863, in reprisal, Colonel Kit Carson launched a war of attrition against the tribe wherever found. His orders from General Carleton were to bring all Navahos of all ages as prisoners to far-off Fort Sumner, on the Pecos. A campaign of relentless pillage and burning, on a smaller scale foreshadowing Sherman's march through Georgia, forced the Navahos to their knees.

Fort Wingate became a receiving station on the Navahos' "long march" to the Pecos. A few military wagons and a few horses, were issued for those too old or too young, too sick or lame, to make the 300–mile journey on foot. By 1865 perhaps three-fifths of the Navaho tribe—8,491 men, women, and children—were gathered at Bosque Redondo on a reservation forty miles square and shared with Mescalero Apaches in poverty, filth, and hunger. Most of them had passed by way of Fort Wingate.

The fort in the valley of the Ojo del Gallo was abandoned with the Navaho Treaty of 1868, and a new Fort Wingate established, on July 22, at Bear Spring, the former site of Forts Fauntleroy and Lyon, sixty-five miles to the west. Here the Navahos came on their return from the Pecos to their newly created reservation.

From Mount Taylor to the Arizona line, Wingate Valley lay nearly dormant for the next ten years. A few cattle ranchers moved into the valley, a stage line was run from Santa Fe through the valley to Prescott, Arizona, but as a trade or war route the region was in eclipse.

Some trade, it is true, was conducted with the Indians by Uncle Billy Crane, who ranched in the deep grass and redrock country east of the new fort. Crane did not fancy himself as a trader, however; he preferred to raise hay and supply beef to the quartermaster at Wingate. A veteran of Carson's campaign against the Navahos, he settled in the valley in the early 1870's and maintained a stage station for the Prescott coaches. Uncle Billy might have been unknown to later generations had not the Atlantic and Pacific Railroad selected the vicinity of his ranch for a construction camp when the rails reached that far west in mid-March, 1881. The coming of the iron horse not only rejuvenated Wingate Valley, but utterly transformed it.

Bacon Spring, the contemporary place-name, was soon forgotten when the construction crew began referring to their sprawling, brawling tent camp as Crane's Station. The division point on the railroad, Crane's Station mushroomed a mile northwest of Billy Crane's log cabin and corrals. Despite the proximity, the identification with

Uncle Billy was of short duration: in March, 1882, Crane's Station officially became Coolidge, honoring—or so someone intended—the person of T. Jefferson Coolidge, a director of the railroad.

In progressing this far, the Atlantic and Pacific spawned such railside settlements as Grants and Mitchell (later named Thoreau, for the sage of Walden Pond, and regionally pronounced Thooroo or sometimes Throo). Advancing west, the railroad spun out the web of its tracks until in 1883 the rails joined at Needles, Arizona, with the California Southern. Lying in the wake were the raw desert or mountain camp towns of Gallup and Holbrook, Winslow, Flagstaff, and Williams. In 1884 the writer Charles Lummis first stopped at Coolidge and found it "the only town of one hundred people . . . between Albuquerque and Winslow." Even then, the people of Coolidge had visions of their tarpaulin tents blooming into a thriving city of wood and brick.[5]

Overshadowed by Coolidge, the tents and railroad shacks of Gallup then offered so poor a show that that town could raise only dust in a man's throat. Troops of Fort Wingate, fourteen miles distant, mingling with Indians, ranchers, and cowboys, found their fun instead in the saloons of Coolidge. Of these, according to Van Valkenburgh, there were fourteen, all "catering to the riffraff that followed on the heels of the new railroad. Outlaws and drunken Navajos purchased intoxicants openly. Eventually a series of killings terminated in the execution of seven outlaws."

Irving Telling describes an occasion when the town's justice of the peace, John B. Hall, sent off a frantic, incoherent wire for help to the officers at Wingate. Desperadoes had taken over the town, stolen a wagonload of beer from the railroad company, and paralyzed any semblance of civil law.[6] It seems that when the Wingate troops were not engaged in tearing Coolidge apart, they were being summoned there to keep others from doing the same thing.

"On this or an earlier occasion," Telling relates, "the Atlantic and Pacific threatened to recall 'the whole of the construction gang of several hundred men' [and] to level the town unless stolen barrels of beer were returned."

Not the lawlessness of Coolidge but the development of coal mines directly north of Gallup eventually spelled the end of the former town. In 1890 the Atlantic and Pacific moved its division headquar-

[5] Irving Telling, "Coolidge and Thoreau: Forgotten Frontier Towns," *New Mexico Historical Review* (July, 1954).
[6] *Ibid.*

ters and personnel to Gallup. Coolidge's decline was hastened by a fire a few weeks afterward that destroyed all buildings but the depot and Harvey House, one of the first of the Fred Harvey hotels. Billy Crane, now serving as postmaster, may have been only mildly surprised when the name of the ghost town reverted, in 1896, to Crane's Station. Even this did not last. The railroad distinguished the forgotten town by naming it Dewey, in 1898, for the naval commander at Manila Bay—and two years later changed the name again, to Guam. So it remained, after Uncle Billy's death in 1904, until the last trace of the once-brawling tent camp vanished in the 1920's.

Nothing much was left of Guam but the old depot when Hans Neumann came to the valley in 1899. With a partner named Johnson, of whom nothing is known and who departed soon, Neumann staked out a site forty feet north of the tracks for his Guam Lumber and Trading Company. He was not a stranger to the region. John Arrington recalls that Neumann came to New Mexico alone and with little more than a pack on his back. In the late 1880's or early 1890's he built a small trading post, of stone and with his own hands, on the Escavada Wash north of Chaco Canyon. How long he remained there is not certain, but he could speak Navaho with some fluency when he appeared at Guam. The Guam store, enlarged as time went on, Neumann built with adobe clay, timber from the Zuñi Mountains, and stones borrowed from nearby *anasazi* ruins.

East and west of Guam, other traders established posts in Wingate Valley. All were drawn by the railroad. Among them, contemporaries of Neumann, were Robert C. Prewitt, who came from Durango, Colorado; Charlie Fredericks of Navaho Church Trading Post near Gallup; James C. May of Fort Wingate; and the traders employed by the Hyde Exploring Expedition to manage their railroad siding post at Thoreau. Whether it was Richard Wetherill or one of the Hyde brothers who chose this name is uncertain, but from 1898 to 1902, Thoreau was a busy terminal point for the Hyde company's Chaco Canyon freight wagons.[7]

Al Wetherill, a younger brother of Richard, traded at Thoreau for

7 Van Valkenburgh says that the site originally was a sawmill and rail-tie camp named Mitchell. "The vicinity of Thoreau," he adds, "was important in the development of Navajo silversmithing as a commercial business. . . . Herman Switzer [Schweizer] encouraged a local trader to manufacture silver for commercial distribution by Fred Harvey, Inc., on trains and in Fred Harvey Houses." Not Thoreau, but more accurately, the region of Smith Lake, some twelve miles to the north, is known for the high quality of its Navaho silverwork. One of the best of the early craftsmen here was a Navaho named Charlie Largo.

a short time with W. S. Horabin, a Hyde employee. When Al moved on to become postmaster at Gallup, his partnership was taken by A. B. McGaffey of Albuquerque. The trading firm of Horabin and McGaffey, outlasting the Hyde Expedition, remained at Thoreau until about 1913.

Thoreau lay only a few miles east of Guam, and for this reason a certain competitiveness existed between Hans Neumann and his neighbors. Both of the posts operated lumber camps in the nearby Zuñi Mountains, and in addition to the Navaho trade of the valley, Neumann operated a trading post for Zuñi Pueblo, at Pinehaven.

Lewis L. Sabin and Charlie Newcomb, boyhood friends back in Manchester, Iowa, came west as young men, found jobs as clerks for Neumann, and later became successful traders on their own. Years later they both described Neumann as a somewhat saturnine "Dutchman," a chain-smoker of cigars who would not rise in the morning before clamping last night's cold cigar butt in his teeth; a gray-haired man standing five feet, ten inches tall, choleric on occasion, always strict and critical, a shrewd trader, a man basically honest and fair in his dealings with Indians.

Neumann's honesty, like a coin, had two faces. His principles would not allow him to cheat a Navaho but never prevented him from trying to outsmart a competitor, especially if the other trader were as experienced as himself. John Wetherill was operating the Ojo Alamo post for the Hyde Expedition, Lew Sabin recalled, when "one time at Guam, Hans Neumann got three or four cases of bad lard. If you scooped out a spoonful of the stuff it stretched like taffy —you could pull it across the room. Mr. Neumann told me we would get rid of it somehow, but I wasn't to sell it to the Navajos.

"John Wetherill came down from the Chaco about that time, riding a freight wagon and needing supplies. He brought blankets, hides and pelts to trade with us for groceries. He spent a morning loading up his wagon, and among other things he took the cases of bad lard.

"Of course, John picked it out himself—we didn't exactly sell it to him. I remember John sitting up there on the wagon box as he drove away, and the Boss standing in the doorway watching him go. Mr. Neumann was a serious man, not given to saying much or joking, and he just stood there watching John go, chomping a cigar up and down in his mouth. Then he turned to me, not even smiling, and said, 'Lew, it was a good sale, wasn't it?' "

As inevitably as its engines spewed cinders and smoke, the railroad and its wake of settlements brought saloons and the problem of the drunken "railroad Indian." Close to Fort Wingate but off the Navaho reservation, Neumann stocked a supply of liquor for Wingate officers who found his rug room at Guam offered greater privacy and quiet than the bars of Gallup. Shortly before he left for the Mexican border war, a Wingate lieutenant named John J. Pershing was one of this convivial group. Sometimes the officers brought their wives, and on such occasions the card games and drinking usually did not last through the night.

Sunday, generally a quiet day at the fort, was the day when the officers' wives might appear. Lew Sabin recalled this circumstance a bit grimly, years afterward, because as their husbands played cards, the Wingate wives whiled away the day pretending interest in Neumann's rug collection. And it was Sabin's duty, with the help of a Navaho boy named Smiley, to attend to the ladies' languid but persistent curiosity. The cost of Navaho blankets was not high—but neither was the pay of a lieutenant or captain, so sales were few.

"The blanket room was large," Sabin said, "and to enter it there was a step down from the store. But Neumann often had as many as a thousand blankets stored away, stacked to the ceiling in piles and covering the floor so deep there was no need to step down. On these Sundays, Smiley and I showed rugs by the hundreds. Each one we had to open up, spread out, and then fold up again. Smiley expressed my idea exactly one day, after the officers and ladies had gone away, when he said, 'Jesus Chli, Sabin—no good—all soldiers here!' "

Neumann paid fifty cents a pound for the common blankets, Sabin recalled, and as much as a dollar and a half to two dollars a pound for good Germantown weaves. Herman Schweizer made periodic calls at Guam for the Fred Harvey Company, "and told Neumann he wanted swastika designs in the rugs. We were one of the first trading posts to produce rugs, in any quantity, that included this design."

Riding the caboose of a freight, Sabin and Charlie Newcomb took their earnings to Gallup every few months and found the town always receptive. On the main business street—Railroad Avenue—"there was mud up to your horse's belly, and maybe fourteen or fifteen saloons. Most of them didn't have a key to the front door, gambling was wide open around the clock, and it was a dull night when someone wasn't hurt in a fist fight or knifing. Soldiers over from Fort Wingate were pretty thick, and some of them were pretty tough."

The Palace Saloon, operated by the Morello brothers, was a two-story stone structure at the corner of Third Street. For a time the

Palace advertised itself and perhaps was regarded as "the finest and largest in the city." But only a block away Pete Kitchen's saloon challenged and soon overshadowed the Palace by keeping the bar and faro tables going full blast at street level while luring a more respectable family trade to the upstairs Kitchen's Opera House; here townspeople could enjoy Calico dances and traveling melodramas such as "Uncle Tom's Cabin" or "Ten Nights in a Barroom."[8]

Gallup's saloons still were running wide open, but the town was beginning to achieve decorum, a few years later, when King Albert of Belgium, during a tour of the United States, announced that his special train would stop in Gallup so that the royal party might experience the flavor of the Wild West. Peter Paquette, then the Navaho agent at Fort Defiance, co-operated to the extent of sending nine Navahos to town to welcome King Albert's arrival. More or less under the commanding eye of Pete Price, an old medicine man, the Navahos' safety actually was entrusted to Charlie Newcomb.

"Their job," Newcomb has recalled, "was to perform a *yei-bi-chai* dance for the king. My job was to take care of them and see that while they were in Gallup they had proper lodging and meals.

"Well, of course the whole town turned out to meet the train. When it finally pulled in the king and his party came out on the back platform, there were speeches and so on, and my Navajos gave their dance. When it was over, King Albert called Pete Price up to the platform and presented him with a fine gold medal about as big as a flapjack. Pete was a handsome old man with gray hair and a gray moustache, tall and erect. He made a pretty proud figure as he stalked over and accepted the medal.

"Pete took the medal home with him, all wrapped up carefully in a bundle. His hogan was north of Defiance. But I might as well admit it, Lew Sabin had the medal almost all of the time after that. Lew was trading at Defiance then and straightaway old Pete brought the medal in for pawn. Every so often he would redeem it for a short while, and then back it would come for credit and hang another year in Lew's pawn room."

Hans Neumann's post, only twenty-two miles to the east, suffered as the Wingate Valley trade more and more was drained off by the traders and wholesale houses of Gallup. When Neumann was forced to cut down his operation at Guam and let his help go, Sabin in 1912

---

[8] The *McKinley County Republican,* January 25 and February 8, 1902.

joined trader William M. Bickel at Fort Defiance. Newcomb, after working a short time for C. C. Manning in Gallup, became manager of Manning's Naschiti store. In 1913 Neumann sold the Guam post and sawmill to Horabin and McGaffey of Thoreau. Soon afterward he traded for a short time at Fort Defiance and then settled in Gallup, where he spent the remaining years of his life as manager of the Gallup Merchantile Company, a wholesale house founded by Charlie Weidemeyer.[9]

With Neumann's departure from the valley, the region once known as Bacon Springs—then Crane's Ranch, then Coolidge, then Dewey, and finally Guam—reverted to grassland inhabited only by a few Navahos. Thus it remained until 1926 when Berton I. Staples came west from Vermont and succumbed to the green sweep of the valley and its picturesque red cliffs. He settled down a mile west of old Guam, building a trading post—"a sort of pueblo style palace"— using for the foundations the same stones that Hans Neumann years before had borrowed from the very much older *anasazi* builders. With no thought at all to the locality's past names, but with a Vermonter's admiring nod to the man then in the White House, Staples renamed the place Coolidge.

The Staples trading post, if it may be called that, probably could have been conceived only by an imaginative Easterner: certainly no other trader in the Southwest up to that time, even in moonshiny dream, blueprinted such an establishment. Faintly resembling the restored Palace of the Governors in Santa Fe, which today no longer resembles its old self, Staples' building had a long running porch of upright posts and horizontal *vigas* separating two adobe rooms each measuring twenty-five by fifty feet. An extension of the open porch and a third room of the same grand dimensions were added, to the east, with funds and encouragement provided by the Harold Glad-

---

[9] The sometimes bewildering interweaving of trader interests and associations is never more clearly illustrated than here. William Bickel was a native of New York City who first was licensed to trade at Zuñi, 1906–1908. After selling out to Mark F. Bennett, he traded at Defiance, hired Sabin as clerk in 1912, and shortly afterward sold the Defiance store to Hans Neumann. Neumann in turn sold out to Sabin, who then formed a partnership with Bickel in the Bickel Company— which operated several trading posts in Arizona until bought out in 1929 by Albert Hugh Lee, a great-grandson of John Doyle Lee, and Clarence A. Wheeler. Bickel also owned an interest in Weidemeyer's Gallup Mercantile but dropped out in 1913, about the time the wholesale house was taken over by Gregory Page, owner of Gallup's Page Hotel. Neumann, by all accounts, was an able manager for Page, but after his death Page sold the company to the Ilfelds of Albuquerque. Sabin built the Tse Bonito Trading Post, a few miles south and east of Window Rock, Arizona, in 1932, selling out in 1957 to Rev. Howard Clark, a missionary.

wins. From their Gila Pueblo headquarters at Globe, Arizona, the Gladwins came to Wingate Valley for archaeological research, based their operations at Staples' post, and with Staples in complete accord with their enthusiasm, induced him to add this wing to his building as a museum. The building then had a frontage of about 185 feet and a depth of some 70 feet. There is no general agreement concerning the exact number of interior rooms, but five rooms at least were reserved for visitors; the occupants could warm themselves at eleven fireplaces, and there were two patios opening at the rear and remembered for their profusion of tall summer hollyhocks and other flowers.

Space reserved in these unusual surroundings where the Navahos could trade—the store, in other words—was a room measuring twelve by sixteen feet.

Staples was the first president of the United Indian Traders Association formed at Gallup in 1931. He perhaps had a keener appreciation than some of the old traders for the true qualities of Navaho craftsmanship in weaving and silverwork. He was not a dilettante, nor was he an Indian trader in any of the basic terms we have considered. His knowledge and judgment of Navaho weaving, according to Amsden, was sound. Whether he contributed anything to this craft as a trader is another matter. After his death in 1938, his place at Coolidge was best remembered for the interesting personalities— artists, writers, and Hollywood actors—who for one reason or another stayed with him summer after summer as paying guests. Among these visitors were Alma Wilmarth Ickes, wife of the Secretary of the Interior, who wrote *Mesa Land* at Coolidge; Malvina Hoffman, the sculptor and writer of *Heads and Tails*; Gladys Reichard, who wrote *Spider Woman* here; and the novelist and short story writer, Gouverneur Morris.

A year following Staples' death, the Coolidge trading post was bought by Charlie Newcomb. After his youthful and hard-earned experience with Neumann at Guam and Manning at Naschiti, Newcomb operated the famous old Crystal Trading Post, near Washington Pass, from 1919 until 1936. A fire destroyed the Coolidge post about 1955, and since then Coolidge has been only a half-remembered place-name in Wingate Valley.

As related frequently by historians of the Southwest, Spanish contact with the Zuñi Indians first occurred in 1539 when Father Marcos de Niza and Esteban, a Barbary Negro, reported discovery of the "golden" cities of Cíbola. Francisco Coronado, setting out from Mexico City the following year, led an expedition to Cíbola for purposes of exploration, conquest, and plunder. After a minor skirmish with Zuñi warriors near the mouth of the Zuñi River, Coronado inspected each of the six pueblos, which capitulated to his troops, and was disgusted to find that they neither contained nor were built of precious metal. Forty years afterward, Francisco Sánchez Chamuscado identified the villages with the name Cuñi. In 1583 the name Zuñi was first applied by Antonio de Espejo. Both names were Spanish corruptions of the Keresan word *Su'nyitsa*, of unknown meaning.[10]

Franciscan missions were established in 1629 at two of the pueblos, Háwikuh and Halona, but were abandoned during the Pueblo Revolt of 1680, when the priest at Halona was murdered. Villagers of all six pueblos of Cíbola took refuge on the summit of Toaiyalone (Corn) Mesa, remaining there until 1692, when they were persuaded by Don Diego de Vargas to return to the plain and submit again to the rule of the church and the crown. Present-day Zuñi Pueblo dates from that year, built over the next years on the site of old Halona and spreading to the north bank of the Zuñi River. South of Gallup by some thirty-eight miles, the pueblo occupies the nearly treeless plain of a red-earth valley. Enclosing the valley to the north are tall mesas of alternating bands of red, pink, and pale yellow sandstone.

Mainly because of its position at the crossroads of ancient trade routes, Zuñi Pueblo became an important trade center for a mixed and usually mutually hostile population residing near or flowing through the Wingate Valley. The pueblo's eminence as a market place was established by generations of Spanish and then Mexican traders of the wandering, pack-mule sort; following the American occupation of New Mexico in 1846, Mexican traders continued to display their wares at Zuñi, but were increasingly beset by encroaching waves of Yankee traders. Not the first of these, but the first to trade at Zuñi with official sanction of the Indian Office, were James H. Whitenton, whose license was issued January 3, 1871, by Colonel Nathaniel Pope, and Andrew Napier, who was licensed the following month to trade at Zuñi, Acoma, and Laguna.[11]

The French trader, Auguste Lacome, a Taos veteran who was last seen among the Navahos and, before that, ranging the mountains and plains of northeastern New Mexico, turns up again in 1872 licensed to trade at Jemez and Zuñi. No man to stay long in one place,

10 Van Valkenburgh, the authority for this, says that the Spanish name Cíbola "derived from the native name *Shiwona* . . . the name of the whole Zuñi domain."
11 *N. A., Ledgers of Traders.*

Lacome again drops from sight only to reappear, in 1878, living at San Luis, Colorado, and in 1880, at Red River in the mountains north of Taos, each time long enough only to renew his permit to trade at Zuñi. Without a Calhoun to record his wanderings, Lacome becomes almost a spectral figure and vanishes entirely, at least from the files of the Indian Office, after 1880.

After Lacome came the Burgess brothers, William and John, who traded at Zuñi in 1877 and again in 1880. The length of their stay at the pueblo is uncertain, but without question their presence marked an epoch: the end of the wandering trader and the advent of the nailed-down counter and shelf.

Reserving a possible prior claim to the Burgesses, it is certain that Douglas D. Graham put his horse and pack mules out to pasture and opened a trading store at Zuñi in March, 1881. He never roamed far, it appears, until he sold out in 1898 to Samuel T. Toner. A resident of Gallup, Toner previously had traded at Zuñi in 1892–93; he operated the Graham store for less than a year when Graham bought it back and soon after sold again, to a former partner, James W. Bennett.

From this time forward a small legion of traders moved in upon Zuñi, operating from three or four posts permanently established at the pueblo and transferred from one owner to the next. Among the early arrivals were George and Mark Bennett, brothers of James; William G. Buchanan, of Albuquerque; Benjamin "Doc" Sylvester, of Gallup, who opened a second store at Nutria in 1902; the almost unremembered O. Acord; William A. Wray, who came out from Kansas City in 1903 and soon after sold out to Mark Bennett; the very durable Charles H. Kelsey, who bought out the James Bennett store, sold to the Ilfelds, and remained on as the Ilfeld manager; William A. Roberts, of Blackrock, New Mexico, whose store was destroyed by fire in June, 1908; Nathan Barth of St. Johns, Arizona; and, finally, Andrew Vanderwagen, who bought the Barth store in 1911.

As members of the numerous, aggressive Barth clan, Nathan and his brothers Sol and Morris were known through the territory both as traders and as stockmen. A fourth brother, Si Barth, drew unfavorable attention to all Zuñi traders in 1870 with his illegal traffic in arms and whisky. Si Barth's enterprise was observed first when a man named Ord, enjoying the hospitality of Fort Wingate, visited Zuñi and later was moved to write Brevet Major General G. W. Getty, commanding the Headquarters District of New Mexico:

"At Zuñi, which you know is a sort of neutral ground where Apaches, Navajoes, Moquies &c all go to trade, I found one Si Barth, brother of Sol, trading in munitions of war—I had already learned among the Apaches some of whom returned from Zuñi while I was in the White Mountains that Barth was at Zuñi & had everything including whiskey for sale. I seized some 10,000 percussion caps & about 40 or 50 lbs. bar lead, and I presume he had sold or concealed the guns which the caps & lead were to fit.

"The hostile Apaches I know visit that place to trade off plunder for arms, powder, caps &c and do get them."[12]

A year later, as already seen, brother Sol caused Pueblo Agent W. F. M. Arny to complain angrily when he (Sol) drew only a twenty-four-hour sentence in jail when convicted of a similar offense. Individually and as a family the Barths weathered such minor setbacks and gradually were purified: Louis and Sidney Barth, of the next generation, were licensed to trade at Zuñi in the early 1900's, and an Isaac Barth served New Mexico as a state senator in 1913.

If some evils common to the era of the wandering traders were continued by a few of their sedentary successors, the case of Andrew Vanderwagen offers an example of the more usual type: the trader whose concern for his own gain was measured at least equally with his concern for the Indians. As sometimes happened, Vanderwagen became a trader through circumstance. Born at Hallum, Friesland, in the northern Netherlands, he later received training in the Christian Reform church, at Grand Rapids, Michigan. In 1896 he came as a missionary to the Navahos at Fort Defiance, and two years later transferred to Zuñi.

Always strongly self-determined, the Zuñis welcomed Vanderwagen as a sincere friend, but amiably resisted all of his efforts to convert them to his religion. Finally, after several years, the Frieslander relaxed his missionary offices, accepted disappointment, and stayed on in the pueblo to trade with these stubborn people, whom he liked. A half-brother, Dick, several sons, and other members of the family operated the post and maintained the Vanderwagen name at Zuñi for more than fifty years after the Reverend Andrew's death.

Facing into an open, sun-baked plaza on the south side of the

[12] Letter from E. O. C. Ord to Getty, March 31, 1870. (National Archives, Records of the N. M. Superintendency . . . 1849–80. Letters Received, 1870–71.) Although he was evidently an army officer, Ord is not clearly identified in this correspondence, but he obviously was acting in an official capacity for the government.

pueblo's dividing river, Vanderwagen's store carried on a large trade in Zuñi commodities, the most important being pelts and hides and native wheat, corn, and bran. In exchange the Zuñis might barter for "just about everything"—from calico and groceries to saddles, plows, or wagons. Dena Vanderwagen, widow of Andrew's eldest son, Edward, has recalled that Zuñi women's preference for the bread of their own beehive-shaped ovens made it useless to stock "store bread" until 1920. And instead of bringing blankets, so common in Navaho trade, "Zuñi women would come in to trade small bags of bran or corn. We had very little Navajo trade, though Navajos came often to Zuñi and many Navajos lived only a short distance to the north of us.

"An almost total absence of Zuñi woven articles, as a trade item, was but one example of difference between the two tribes in their trade customs.

"Unlike the Navajos," Mrs. Vanderwagen said, "the Zuñis never depended much on pawn, and trading posts at Zuñi had little or none of it. No *seco*, or token money, was used here, although we did have it at our Piñon Springs store, for our Navajos.[13] Money was scarce, as everywhere. Zuñi men usually traded sheep or cattle, and when a Zuñi wanted to buy something expensive, like a wagon or pair of horses, he would enter a contract with a trader to supply a certain quantity of hay. Before 1900 the Zuñis traded for burros instead of horses, as horses were not really wanted very much at this pueblo until that time."

The sale of wool and hides, amounting in 1905 to $12,600, was the chief source of income for Zuñis in that year. Men of the pueblo otherwise earned $8,432 by working for the Indian Office on the reservation dam, $380 from the sale of wood, $81.75 from freighting, and $175 from the sale of hay. This cash income for a pueblo population of 1,514 persons, divided among five reservation traders, indicates the modest level on which the Zuñis and traders alike existed.[14]

The almost legendary Dan DuBois, a man so whimsical in his ways

13 Mrs. Vandenwagen's husband, Edward, at various times operated a number of trading posts, including the Outlaw Trading Post; Piñon Springs, near Cheechil-geetho; Church Rock Post, a few miles north and east of Gallup; and Mexican Springs Post, south of Tohatchi. After Andrew Vanderwagen's death, Edward's younger brothers, Richard and Bernard, operated the Vanderwagen post at Zuñi.
14 *Annual Report, C. I. A., 1905.* Undoubtedly the Zuñis had other means of earning money not included in this report. A few Zuñi silversmiths supported themselves through the sale of their work, although the craft—as with the Navahos—failed to reach a wide market for about twenty-five years. Edward Vanderwagen added modestly to Zuñi earning power when he helped to secure Zuñi workmen for the National Geographic Society's excavations at Chaco Canyon, 1921–27.

he defied pinning down by anyone, anywhere, inevitably turned up at Zuñi. In the last years of his life DuBois was seen more often at Zuñi than at Defiance. He lived then near Piñon Springs, a good friend of the Vanderwagen family, who regarded his eccentricities as no more and no worse than an aging mountain man was entitled to.

Zuñi trader Charles Kelsey, another of Dan's close friends, is authority for a story related by anthropologist Frederick W. Hodge, telling how DuBois—then living with the Utes—once led a Ute war party against the Cheyennes. The Utes succeeded in capturing a Cheyenne warrior and were engaged in burning him at the stake when the doomed one in agony cried out to DuBois: "For the sake of your mother's milk, kill me!" Dan responded promptly by shooting the Cheyenne cleanly between the eyes—this, as Kelsey is supposed to have heard it directly from Dan, being the one occasion on which DuBois ever killed a man.

Hodge, who met DuBois when he was excavating the ruins at Háwikuh, accepted the story with gentle skepticism, observing: "I was once informed by Frank Hamilton Cushing that Dan could boast eight notches in his gun. . . . That Dan knew no fear there can be no doubt, as the following episode will show—

"When the Hemenway Archeological Expedition, under the directorship of Cushing, was conducting excavations at and near Zuñi in 1888, Dan was employed as general utility man, looking after camp affairs generally, building a corral for the mules, and slaughtering a steer now and then . . . .

"It was during Dan's stay at Zuñi that we had an opportunity to observe something of his vagaries. He was ferocious when in his cups. On one such occasion he chased our little Alsatian cook, Eduard Haag, all around the camp and through the house . . . but Eduard succeeded finally in eluding Dan by seeking asylum under one of the beds.

"At another time, while I was writing in my tent, I heard a commotion close at hand. Stepping outside, I found Dan looking down the barrel of a Colt .45 held by his brother-in-law, Luberto. Dan was saying, 'Put it down; put it down, I tell you!' But Luberto, trembling of hand, was deaf to the command. A spade chanced to be leaning against my tent-pole. Entirely unmindful of the revolver still threatening him, Dan grasped the spade, and holding it aloft, brought it down on the head of Luberto, felling him to the ground. Dan picked up the gun and the affair was brought to a close, except for Luberto's revival a few minutes later. The cause of the difficulty was Luberto's claim that Dan owed him some money which he had come to collect. As Dan always paid his debts, I imagine that the claim was hardly substantiated."[15]

Dan DuBois was admitted to the Sawtelle Soldiers' Home, West Los Angeles, in 1923, and died March 13, 1925. Hodge says that it was C. N. Cotton who was instrumental in having the grizzled veteran accepted there; this no doubt is true, but also it is entirely possible that Cotton, who then had a home in Los Angeles, was acting on a suggestion by Lorenzo Hubbell.

[15] Hodge, *Old Dan DuBois*. Something of an eccentric himself, Cushing, an ethnologist with the Bureau of American Ethnology, worked for many years at Zuñi, joined the Bow, or warrior clan, and in 1882, in a letter to Navaho Agent Galen Eastman, referred to himself as "First War Chief of the Zuñis"—producing an effect we may guess may have been hilarious, as Cushing was serious and Eastman was entirely without humor. Cushing and Hodge (the latter headquartering at Zuñi from 1915 to 1923 while excavating Háwikuh for the Heye Foundation in New York) both rented living quarters at Zuñi from Charles Kelsey. The Kelsey buildings, adjacent to and fronting the same plaza as the Vanderwagen store, formerly were owned by trader James W. Bennett.

18

Cienega Amarilla, Crystal, Two Gray Hills

LEGENDS AMONG THE PUEBLOS of the Río Grande tell of chasing Navaho raiders as far west as the Chuska Mountains. Even Zia, small and unwarlike, sent out a pursuing war party when the raiders made off with Zia captives. Pursuit ended in the mountains, where it is said there was a great fight in the vicinity of Washington Pass.

Across the mountains and somewhat to the south, in a wide mountain valley, another fight over captive women and children took place in 1850. Van Valkenburgh tells of Mexicans coming to the valley with a cannon and plans for ambushing the Navahos. A renegade of the *Diné Ana'aii*—Enemy Navahos—who lived near Cebolleta and Cubero, led the Mexicans to the valley as a partisan. The ambush failed when the renegade turned informer on the side of his own people and the Mexicans were driven off. Van Valkenburgh says that the renegade was taken back into the tribe and signed the 1868 treaty as Delgadito.

A few years later, probably in 1858 or 1859, a sharp fight between Navahos and troops garrisoning Fort Defiance took place at the Haystacks, tall sandstone monuments rising in the lower valley. It is said that Navahos planned this as an ambush to rob the Defiance paymaster. The east face of one of the central haystacks still is scarred from scores of spattering rifle bullets, waist high to a man on horseback.

These encounters occurred at a place the Navahos knew as *Ts'i-hootso* (Mountainside Meadow), but referred to otherwise as Cienega Amarilla, the Spanish term recognizing the valley's onetime lush

245

growth of wild sunflowers. When the boundaries were drawn in 1868, Cienega Amarilla lay directly outside the reservation, the lower end of the valley south of Defiance Agency by eight miles.

Anson C. Damon was the first settler in the valley of whom there is any record. By his own account, he homesteaded one mile south of the reservation base line about 1875.[1] Here his Navaho wife, Ta-des-bah, bore him nine children, eight of them boys. At least three of the boys were given the spartan advantages of attending Indian schools in the East, but otherwise the children were brought up as Navahos and so regarded themselves.[2]

Himself the son of Irish immigrants, Damon was born at Calais, Maine, January 19, 1842. While still a youngster he ran away from home, reaching the California gold fields by way of the Isthmus of Panama. When the Civil War broke out, Damon—then nineteen years old—joined Company G, First Cavalry, California Volunteers. His son James believes that he saw little or no action during the war. By one means or another, however, he found his way to New Mexico, and on May 27, 1866, was enrolled as butcher at Fort Sumner, where for two years more the Navahos rounded up by Carson were to be held prisoner. It was while here that he married the Navaho girl, Ta-des-bah. After the signing of the 1868 treaty, Damon moved on to Fort Defiance as agency butcher. With him and his wife went two other Fort Sumner men: Perry H. Williams, who later also was an Indian trader, and Charles Hardison.[3]

1 Letter from Damon to C. I. A. Atkins, July 6, 1886. (National Archives, Record Group 75, Letters Received, 1886, # 18803; also, "Rights of Settlers on the Navajo Reservation, Ariz.", 56 Cong., 1 sess., *House Report No. 411*.)

2 The oldest boy, Ben, born May 4, 1869, and Charles went to Carlisle Indian School in Pennsylvania. James, the fifth son, born in 1880, attended Hampton Normal School in Virginia. As was customary at those schools where discipline was strict, the children were "hired out" during the summer. James recalled summers on a farm at South Deerfield, Massachusetts, "where I worked from 6 in the morning until 9 and 10 at night, and earned twelve dollars a week." All of the eight Damon boys, except Frank who remained single, married Navaho women. In later years, Ben and Charles were agency interpreters. Only James entered trading, and this for two years at the Divide Trading Post, east of present Window Rock, Arizona.

3 His headstone at a family cemetery on a hill south of Fort Defiance says that Anson Chandler Damon died October 19, 1925, at the age of eighty-three. Beside Damon's grave is that of his wife, Ta-des-bah, who died in 1913 at the age of sixty-three. James Damon took me to this burial plot in the summer of 1960, verifying his memory of dates as we moved among the family headstones. Fort Sumner information relating to Anson Damon, Williams, and Hardison is contained in a second-quarter report by Agent Miller to Superintendent Pope, March 17, 1871. (National Archives, Record Group 75, Letters Received, 1849–80.) Perry

The lower end of the Cienega Amarilla—referred to simply as "the Sinagee" by old-timers—was first homesteaded by Samuel E. Day, probably in 1882. From all accounts an aggressive individualist, Day also was a veteran of the Civil War. At sixteen he lied about his age and was accepted in the Eighty-first Ohio Volunteers, and upon discharge became a civil engineer. From the Black Hills of South Dakota, where he went about 1876, he moved to Iowa. There he married Anna Burbridge, a schoolteacher, and after a son, Charles, was born in 1879, brought his family by prairie wagon to Colorado.

Sam Day surveyed the first rail line to ascend Pikes Peak. On the strength of this he was employed by the government in 1880 to survey the first extension of the Navaho reservation. Two years later, still waiting to be paid for this work, he served the first of two terms as clerk at Defiance Agency and meanwhile settled his family in the valley nine miles to the south.[4]

"When my mother joined my father in this country we came to Coolidge by rail—that was the end of the line then—and by ox team to Manuelito," Sam Day II has recalled. "There was no road up here from Gallup, but there was a wagon road used by troops, south through this valley to Manuelito."

A Defiance trader named Caddy Stewart homesteaded half a mile west of his father's place, Day said, selling out about 1890 to the trader William Weidemeyer, who soon after sold to a Missouri trader named John Wyant. Between Wyant's property and the Day land another homestead was taken up by the trader Joseph R. Wilkin, who also freighted on occasion from Manuelito to the Round Rock post of Aldrich and Dodge.[5]

Not all of the Navahos regarded this settlement of the valley with favor. One in particular, a Navaho called Man with Worn-out Moccasins, became angry when the elder Day proposed to fence his land.

Williams was in charge of grain and "man on issue" at Defiance Agency until his discharge on May 4, 1871. Hardison was the agency's chief herder until his discharge on May 16, 1871.

4 Sam Day II, my informant, said his father "was up there [at Defiance] sixteen years as chief clerk while we lived down here on the homestead." In addition to Charles and young Sam, there was a third son, William, born in 1883.

5 William E. (Billy) Weidemeyer, like his brother John, was a native of Clinton, Missouri (the town that also produced veteran Chinle Valley trader Thomas H. Frazier). After leaving Cienega Amarilla, Billy Weidemeyer was licensed (1891–95) to trade at Fort Defiance, selling out in 1896 to Charles C. Manning. Manning in turn sold the Defiance store in 1906 to the Ilfeld Trading Co. Records indicate that Billy Weidemeyer also was licensed to trade at Zuñi, and in 1902 opened a trading store at Gallup.

"He told my father his bones would bleach right there if he built that fence," Sam Day II said.

"This happened when a bunch of Indians were gathered around. My dad turned to the crowd of Navajos and said he wanted ten men who would work for a dollar and a half a day, to build a stake and rider fence. Any objections? My dad fenced the whole forty-acre homestead with these Indians helping him. There was no trouble."

On another occasion, Day recalled, trouble did occur when a brawler named Mug Stevens moved in with John Wyant. Stevens chose a time when Joe Wilkin was freighting to Round Rock to "jump" his homestead. With Wyant's approval, Day said, Stevens tacked a notice on Wilkin's door telling him not to come back there or he and Wyant would kill him.

Upon his return, Day said, "Wilkin left his wagon sitting on the road and came over to my father's place and borrowed a rifle. He wanted my father to go with him as witness. Father said he was too busy—he could take Sammy, which meant me. I was about fifteen years old at the time. We came over the top of the hill and down to Wilkin's cabin. There was nobody there, but Wyant and Stevens saw us and came down. They both had rifles and they got behind posts of the division fence. Wilkin made me sit down behind a pile of grain and he went in the cabin and shot from a window. A splinter from a bullet grazed Joe under the left eye and in his left shoulder."

Shortly after, Day continued, Wyant and Stevens withdrew to Wyant's cabin. "Wilkin busted open a bag of coffee—there wasn't any other paper around—and wrote a note: 'Mug Stevens, do not let the sun go down on you in this country.' He gave it to me to take to Stevens, and Mug didn't let the sun go down on him. He headed out for Albuquerque right away."

Wyant and Wilkin patched up the quarrel, and as partners operated Wilkin's trading post until Wilkin sold his share in 1895 to William A. (Billy) Meadows, who for two years had been employed as Defiance Agency engineer and sawyer.[6] Meadows remained in the valley only three years and in the meantime, in 1896, built a new post in the mountains south of Chinle.

[6] It appears that Wilkin retained his partnership with Wyant for a few years after he started trading near Washington Pass. Wyant sold his interest in the Cienega Amarilla post to George U. Manning and went to Kansas. According to the *McKinley County Republican*, May 11, 1901: "John Wyant, the Cienega Indian trader, has sold his store . . . to George Manning . . . who will carry on the business at the same place. The ranch was bought by the Franciscan priests for the sum of $2,500."

Anson Damon—called *Chil-chee* by the Navahos, or Red Hair—traded sporadically at his place near Black Rock south of Fort Defiance. Ruth Underhill says that in 1869 he bought out a Defiance trader named Neale, and in 1878 his name appears as clerk for Romulo Martínez' post at Washington Pass.[7] In the late 1880's, Damon and Sam Day, Sr., entered a brief partnership when they operated a tent trading post at Chinle Valley, about ten miles north and west of Chinle. Damon's son James said the partnership ended in a dispute over money, and indicated that the ill-feeling that arose then between the Damon and Day families was never smoothed over.

The Days had lived at Cienega Amarilla only a short time when the advancing railhead of the Atlantic and Pacific, roughly paralleling the Río Puerco of the West, reached Ferry Station. Located seventeen miles west of Gallup and close to the Arizona line, this place at once became a freight terminal for trading posts to the north and west and for the Navaho agency. The station was a mile or two east of Manuelito, named for the Navaho war chief, where in 1882 a small trading post operated by a man named Brown was bought by Stephen E. Aldrich and James W. Bennett. Aldrich was a former cavalryman and veteran of the Apache campaigns. Bennett sold his interest in the same year to Elias S. Clark of Albuquerque and later traded near Houck's Tank, Arizona, and at Tuye Springs and Zuñi.[8]

Freight destined for the agency was hauled by wagon north from Ferry Station through Manuelito Canyon into the Cienega Amarilla and on to Defiance, a distance of about twenty-eight miles. Thomas Parker, a Mormon mule skinner, made this trip many times in the early 1890's when he freighted supplies to Aldrich and Dodge at their Round Rock post.

[7] Underhill, *Here Come the Navaho!*, 196. Neale may have been located outside the reservation, as his name is not included among the list of traders licensed to trade at Fort Defiance.

[8] *N. A., Ledgers of Traders*. In July, 1889, Bennett and Volney P. Edie formed a partnership in the latter's Tuye Springs (also *Tohgaii*: Hazardous Water) post, under the name of the Chaco Trading Co. The post was in the lower Chuska Valley, sixteen miles south of Tohatchi. Edie sold out in the same year. It appears that Bennett, who still maintained his store at Houck, ceased operating the post in December, 1892, to trade at Zuñi. He sold his Zuñi store in 1906 to Charles H. Kelsey. Charles Damon once owned a ranch near the Tuye Springs post, which is now operated under the name Tohlakai. According to Van Valkenburgh: "Years ago Tuye was an important Navajo rendezvous for both the Becente and Arviso outfits. There are old Navajo hogan sites which . . . as yet [are] undated, but seem to be of the early 19th century. Tuye took great importance when it was used as the landmark by the Navajos to designate the southeastern corner of the Treaty Reservation of 1868."

"I drove two eight-horse teams, loading 1,000 pounds to a horse," Parker has recalled. "I would freight up through the Sinagee to Round Rock until the weather got bad in December, and then I would go over and winter on the San Juan."

Parker remembered that in 1898 the Cienega Amarilla was chosen as the site of a Franciscan mission. A brave start was made under the humblest conditions. Always hard pressed for funds, Fr. Juvenal Schnorbus and his assistant, Fr. Anselm Weber, first occupied the stone trading post Billy Meadows had built in 1895 on the old Wilkin property. In time the mission buildings were enlarged, but only after Fr. Weber gave a lifetime of selfless effort in fighting for any cause that would benefit the common lot of the Navaho tribe.

Sam Day, Sr., sold his property in May, 1901, as a site for the mission school, to Rev. Mother Katharine Drexel, head of the Sisters of the Blessed Sacrament of Cornwells, Pennsylvania. Charles Day previously had bought the Billy Meadows trading post below Canyon de Chelly, and now the other members of his family joined him there. Sam Day II said that the post was situated on a mountain about twenty miles southeast of Chinle, known only by a Navaho name meaning the "Spring Where the Two Lay Together." In 1902, Sam Day, Sr., moved on and built a large log trading post at Chinle.

A post office was established in late summer, 1902, in the Osborne and Walker trading post at Cienega Amarilla and at the same time the place officially was named St. Michaels. John G. Walker, a half-blood Navaho and Thomas Osborne's partner, was appointed postmaster. Walker did not remain long in the valley, however, moving in 1905 to Tolchaco (*Tocliche'ekho*: Red Water Wash), Arizona, some twenty miles north and west of Canyon Diablo. Still later he was trading at Leupp, where in 1911 he anticipated a readiness of Navaho weavers to return to vegetable dyes—a readiness not realized fully until two decades later.

Demand for gaudy-colored diamond-dye blankets was going out of fashion, Walker advised the Indian Office. "The Navajos are going back to the natural colors, just as they come from the sheeps' backs, such as black, gray, white, brown and several intermediate shades. This is especially true in the western half of the Navajo reservation, where the natural colored gray blankets are produced in great quantities. What's needed more than anything else in the weaving industry is a good vegetable dye that will remain fast."[9]

9 Letter from Walker to Assistant Commissioner F. H. Abbott, August 18, 1911, reporting the volume of his trade in Indian products during the previous year.

George Washington Sampson, called *Hostine Bai*—Gray Man—bought the old Weidemeyer post at Cienega Amarilla in April, 1902, employing Charles Kyle as manager. Perhaps for the benefit of workmen then constructing a new building for St. Michaels, Sampson stocked the post with liquor. In any case this was a mistake, which may have had some bearing on the murder of Kyle and the burning of the store the following December.

A veteran trader, Sampson is said to have opened his first post at Sanders, Arizona, in 1883. Four years later he was operating the Rock Spring store north of Gallup, and in 1890 a third post at Tohatchi, which he sold in 1892 to Percy A. Craig. His other posts included Coyote Canyon, sold to Dan DuBois in 1902, Lukachukai, and Chilchinbito—twenty-five miles southeast of Kayenta.

Sampson was operating the latter post in 1911 when he expressed some of his firm opinions about Indian trading, in a letter to Assistant Commissioner F. H. Abbott:

"During my twenty-five years' experience," he wrote, ". . . I have often noticed that the [Navaho] flocks of sheep have not increased as they should have—and I believe this is due to the fact that they have been allowed to sell their sheep for cash, worthless turquoise and beads. Having thoroughly investigated this particular subject I firmly believe—the Navajo should not be allowed to trade his stock for anything but the necessities of life—which he can obtain from licensed traders."[10]

Other traders at Cienega Amarilla in the early 1900's included Joseph White and Julius Neubert, neither of whom prospered or remained long. Charles Day returned to the valley when his father in 1905 sold his Chinle post to Charles F. Weidemeyer, the son of Defiance trader John Weidemeyer. For a time the elder Days lived at Navajo, Arizona, and then joined Charles at the Cienega, a few miles

(National Archives, Record Group 75, Classified Files: #71406/11—910.) Walker said he had paid $2,996.82 for wool, $250 for silverwork, $3,570 for blankets, $784 for hides and pelts, and $540 for Navaho livestock. Camille García told me that about 1930 he and Cozy McSparron encouraged the Chinle weavers to return to vegetable dyes "and go back to their old designs. I bought about thirty-eight old rugs—some old Navaho and some old Spanish double serapes—and showed them to the Navaho women as examples of design and weave." Garcia said that Mary Wheelwright's efforts to reintroduce vegetable dyes—a trend which soon spread down the Chinle Valley as far as Wide Ruins Trading Post—came later.

10 *Ibid.* Letter from Sampson to Abbott, August 21, 1911. In the year just past, Sampson said his trade at Chilchinbito included $4,000 for blankets and $550 for silverwork. Also, he had taken 650 sheep "in exchange for the necessities of life—such as coffee, flour and sugar and clothing"—allowing from $1.50 to $2.00 per sheep.

west of St. Michaels, where Charles built the forerunner of the present Two-Story Trading Post.

The Days continued to make the valley the base of their activities, and in 1915 Charles Day operated his post in partnership with J. P. Petersen. The year following, Charles was stocking a new store near Round Rock. His venture there was brought short in 1918 when, near Chambers, Arizona, the car he was driving left the road, plunged over an embankment, and overturned four times. Charles was injured fatally, but Sam Day, Sr., riding with him, was unhurt, and lived on at Cienega Amarilla until his death in 1925.

A year or so after the shooting scrape in the valley left a bullet crease below his left eye, Joe Wilkin moved up into the Chuska Mountains. Here in 1894, near Washington Pass, with Elmer E. Whitehouse as partner, he built a new trading post that fared poorly. Joe Reitz replaced Whitehouse as Wilkin's partner in 1896, and in the same year Wilkin sold out his interest to John B. Moore.

Wilkin came down the eastern slope of the mountains into the Chuska Valley, where we will find him again presently, and Reitz remained one year more until Moore bought him out in 1897.

A native of Sheridan, Wyoming, and a tall, thin Irishman, Moore renamed the place Crystal; so successful was his operation that the name of his trading post became even better known than the famous old name of the pass.

Moore's Crystal store was located at a mountain spring of rare purity, on a high wooded plain some eight miles west of the pass itself. From the time of the Navahos' westward migration beginning in the second half of the 1700's, the mountain crossing was used by the Navahos and known to them as *Beesh-lichi'ii-bigish*, or Copper Pass. The craggy route emerges in our history when it was reconnoitered on August 31, 1849, and two days later crossed by the command of Colonel John M. Washington while on its expedition against the Navahos.[11] Lieutenant James H. Simpson, in his journal of the cam-

---

[11] In his journal for September 2, 1849, Lt. James H. Simpson notes: "The pass at the most dangerous point we found extraordinarily formidable. On the north side is a wall of trap, capped with sandstone, running perpendicularly up from the bottom of the defile to a height of about six hundred feet. . . . . The width of the pass at this point is probably not more than fifty feet, and barely furnishes a passage-way (a sidling one at this) for the artillery. . . . Colonel Washington informs me it is the most formidable defile he has ever seen. . . . In [his] honor . . . I have, on my map, called it Pass Washington." (31 Cong., 1 sess., *Sen. Exec. Doc. 64*; 31 Cong., 1 sess., *House Exec. Doc. 45*.) Van Valkenburgh observes that the name

paign, named the pass for the commanding officer, and on a stream near the site of Moore's future trading post "noticed towering pines and firs, also the oak, the aspen, and the willow; and bordering the stream was a great variety of shrubbery, the hop vine, loaded with its fruit, being intertwined among them. Flowers of rich profusion, and of every hue and delicacy, were also constantly before the eye."

Not the beauty of the place but its proximity to many Navahos recommended it as a trading center. Romulo Martínez, as previously mentioned, was licensed to trade there and at Fort Defiance in 1873, but probably waited several years before setting up his first trading tent or log hut at the pass. He was there, we know, in 1878, and remained until his license was revoked in 1881. Stephen Aldrich and Elias Clark had a trading tent at Washington Pass in 1884; others who may have traded there briefly were Ben Hyatt, Walter Fales, and Michael Donovan.[12]

Inaccessibility of Washington Pass, especially in winter when the rough wagon trails were blocked for months, probably was a major reason for the rapid succession of traders at that place. How severe this handicap could be was pointed out by Thomas Keam in 1884, when he learned that the Navaho agent considered the region ideally suited for a sheep ranch.

The mountain plain was very pleasant in summer, Keam wrote Secretary of the Interior Teller, "but entirely impracticable . . . in winter, as it is one of the coldest places on the reservation. [I] was told that eighteen inches of snow fell there on the last of April . . . whoever recommended [the sheep ranch] never visited the place in winter, when it is often covered with two feet of snow."[13]

J. B. Moore built a log trading post and house secure enough to withstand the winter storms; by freighting in large quantities of supplies in the fall, he managed to survive the long months of isolation.

John Arrington, who worked for Moore during the winter of 1908,

Cottonwood Pass "as shown on the maps"—for the same place—"is definitely erroneous. Chee Dodge states that the name refers to a location east of the pass. He further states that it originated from an incident in which some Navajos saw a party of Whites cutting a trail for their wagons through a dense copse of willows and cottonwoods."

12 Hyatt was licensed to trade at Washington Pass in 1882–83–84; Fales, in 1884–85; Donovan, in 1886. If they were actually there, it is possible that they operated from tents and only in the summer. Reitz and Moore received their license June 29, 1896, and after Reitz sold out, Moore was issued a license, as sole owner, June 28, 1897. (N. A., Ledgers of Traders.)

13 Letter from Keam to Teller, June 5, 1884. (National Archives, Letters Received, Record Group 75, 1884, #11520.)

recalled that Moore then had about sixteen Navaho weavers making rugs for him, and "would charge out the wool to them, knowing just how much they needed." During his first years at Crystal, Moore gathered about him some of the finest weavers on the reservation and, from designs which he had a large part in developing, established a recognizable "Crystal rug" that found a good market in all parts of the country.

Moore introduced variants of the Greek fret, both in rug borders and as interior design elements; a heavy cross-form appeared often in connection with a diamond pattern; red was a predominating color, but his weavers also favored black, blue, tan, or brown, and occasionally natural grays and whites. Over the years Moore built up a substantial mail-order business, sending out hundreds of elaborate four-color-plate catalogs in which the best or most typical of the Crystal rugs were illustrated, described, and classified according to quality. His "ER–20" rugs Moore catalogued as "first or special grade," and priced at ninety cents to one dollar a square foot; the "T–XX" rugs he referred to as "second or tourist grade" and sold by quality of the weaving, by size, or by the weight, from one to two dollars a pound.

With only slight variations in design, Moore's weavers departed from the usual practice and turned out the same rug patterns again and again. One of the most popular, and now regarded as possibly most typical of Moore's Crystal style, might be found in either the ER–20 or T–XX classification. This usually was the work of one of Moore's best weavers, Bi-leen Alpai Bi-zha-ahd, and incorporated another design element unique to Crystal: an elongated, angular "hook," usually repeated four times within the outer border.

His special-grade rugs, Moore wrote, "differ from all others in that we first buy the wool, select only the best and most suitable of it, ship it away, have it scoured and thoroughly cleaned, and shipped back. It is then spun into yarn and dyed in the yarn with a very superior and different dye too, than that used in the trade woven rugs . . . insuring even and absolutely fast colors."[14]

Moore elaborated on this when replying to a series of questions sent out by the Indian Office; in the year 1910–11, he said he paid his weavers thirteen thousand dollars for their blankets and only one thousand dollars in the same period to his silversmiths.[15] He then

[14] Quoted from *The Navajo,* Moore's 1911 Crystal catalog.

[15] Letter from Moore to Assistant Commissioner F. H. Abbott, September 2, 1911. (National Archives, Record Group 75, Classified Files 71406/11—910.) Charlie Newcomb, who managed the Crystal trading post for C. C. Manning for about two years and then bought Manning out about 1922, told me that when he first

added: "Fully seventy-five percent of the blankets bought by myself are made of the native wool carded and spun by the Indians, if not more. For a class of very special work, to meet the demands for perfect cleanliness and fast, even colors, I do furnish some special weavers with a wool, cleaned, spun and dyed, ready for the weaver to work up; but as above stated not more than twenty-five percent of my handlings are done of this material.

"Some other traders furnish limited quantities of the Germantown or other yarns in a similar manner, and all of us buy some Germantown or yarn blankets made by weavers from the yarns they have themselves bought and woven up on their own account. But with all this, fully eighty to ninety percent of the entire [reservation] blanket output is made of the native wool, more or less cleaned, carded, spun and dyed by the Indians themselves."

Native vegetable dyes were rarely used now, Moore said.[16] The Navahos never had a satisfactory red dye of their own but "for their red color . . . have been dependent upon the white man: first, the old time red 'bayetta' or flannels introduced by the Spaniards, raveled, recarded and spun . . . and later, the red [aniline] dyes sold by the traders to them. Practically all the blanket work of the present is done in the trade dyes now on the market and has been for years."

Moore said he had been led to experiment with dyes and native wool when he found that faulty colors and greasy yarn, only partly cleansed when washed in hard water and suds of the yucca root, produced a low-grade blanket. To improve the quality of Crystal weaving, he asked his weavers to supply him with a quantity of single-ply wool, thread, which he then shipped East to be washed and dyed. Upon its return he had it "worked up by weavers of known and proven skill only."

went there, he found "a lot of wool Moore had sent East to have washed and dyed. I think this was done for him in Wisconsin." Newcomb also found a number of Moore's catalogs, which he mailed out until the supply of some 2,000 was nearly exhausted. The catalog is now a collector's item.

16 Crystal weaving in recent years has reverted almost entirely to vegetable dye. Trader Don Jensen told me that when he went to Crystal in 1944, "maybe one in five rugs was vegetable dye. Now they are almost all vegetable dye." Des-bah-nez, seventy-three years old when I talked with her at Crystal in 1960, said: "I think I was the first one in this region to use vegetable dyes. I had been dyeing buckskins [for moccasins] and wondered how this dye would be with wool. I tried a little bit of wool at a time. This was about twenty years ago."—or about 1940. Des-bah-nez is a daughter of one of J. B. Moore's best weavers, Yeh-del-spah-bi-mah. Vegetable dyes of the Crystal area—yellow, light green, brown, tan, and Sienna red— are exceptional for their depth and richness of color. By comparison, vegetable dyes of the Chinle–Wide Ruins area are pale pastel hues.

Weaving, Moore said, was the Navahos' one industry—other than the sale of wool and hides—and he estimated that the value of all blankets then in the hands of traders and wholesalers was between $200,000 and $250,000. The trader's real problem, he said, "is not getting the blankets made, but getting them sold."

One of the best of the old silversmiths lived near Crystal, and that mountain region was moderately productive of good silverwork, but Moore's efforts were centered more upon weaving.[17]

"The little silver that I myself buy of the Indians is mostly sold back to other Indians and not one-half of it is marketed outside of the trade, and I think this is true of most traders."[18]

Some years before, probably about 1906, Moore had tried without success to find a market for silverwork. In one of his earlier catalogs he listed bridle heads "of heavy plates and conchas of silver so stapled or keyed to the leather as to entirely conceal it"—priced by weight at $1.25 to $1.50 an ounce. Concho belts were offered at the same per-ounce price. Silver bracelets, ornamented but without stones and weighing up to eight ounces, were listed at $1.25 an ounce; bracelets with turquoise sets were listed at $2 to $10. Squash-blossom necklaces, of eight to twelve ounces of silver, were priced not by weight but "according to wear and condition"—from $6 to $18.

Moore suggests, by "wear and condition," that his necklaces, and perhaps most of his other silver, were pawn, and we may believe that much of it was of excellent quality now worth many times the prices he asked. Nevertheless, the results from his mail-order samplings were so poor that he dropped his listing of silverwork when the 1911 catalog was printed.

A scandal for which he personally was not responsible caused Moore and his wife to leave Crystal a few weeks after he wrote the letter quoted here, in the autumn of 1911. He sold the trading post to Jesse A. Molohon, who had been his manager since 1908, and never returned to the reservation. The unfortunate circumstances of his departure do not blemish his name or his unique contribution as an

17 John Adair quotes Chee Dodge as saying that Beshthlagai-ithline-athlsosigi (Slender Maker of Silver), still living near Crystal in 1909, "was one of the best of all the Navajo silversmiths."

18 Twenty years or more would pass before a sizable tourist market would be developed for Navaho silver. Meanwhile, in 1911, Moore's purchases of blankets and silverwork corresponded, relatively, with the purchases of most of the other traders: Frank Noel, at Sa-nos-tee, reporting payments of $6,000 for blankets and $350 for silverwork; Joe Reitz and Ed Davies, at Two Gray Hills, $6,855 and $125; Olin C. Walker, at Red Rock, $10,417 and $397; Foutz and Black, at Mexican Wa-

Indian trader. If one were to choose six traders who did most to improve the quality of Navaho weaving after the advent of aniline dyes, Moore would have to be included.

Moore's Crystal blanket unquestionably influenced weavers of other localities, both in Moore's time and later. Whether Moore and his Crystal weavers deserve credit for the development of the Two Gray Hills blanket—as some authorities have claimed—is quite another matter, as we shall see.

Indian traders usually were as restless and rootless as the Navahos are commonly believed to have been. For every two traders who held on steadily, there were ten who roamed from one post to another, never really settling down. Joe Wilkin was one of these, and those who knew him said his fondness for poker and the faro tables of Gallup was, as much as anything, a cause for his wanderings.

In the spring of 1897, one year after he had sold out his interest at Washington Pass to J. B. Moore, Wilkin joined with the Noel brothers, Henry and Frank, to start a new trading post in the Chuska Valley. The place they chose was at the eastern base of the Chuskas, eighteen miles northeast of Crystal by airline—a good day's horseback ride by the mountain trails.

The partners set up a tent in a treeless valley on the Tuntsa (Big Tree) Wash, sheltered to the south by a low flat-topped peninsula of land that extended eastward several miles, its surface littered with the fallen walls and potsherds of an *anasazi* village. Rearing up between their tent and the first green slopes of the mountains were two rocky mesas distinctly reddish in color, a detail of minor curiosity since the partners named their post Two Gray Hills. Within gunshot of this place Colonel Washington's party camped in 1849 before ascending Washington Pass, and it was here, too, that Lieutenant Simpson recorded the shooting of Chief Narbona and six other Navahos. With no regard for the two red mesas or Colonel Washington, the Navahos called this place *Bis-da-clitso*, or yellow clay mound, a reference to an insignificant knoll north of Tuntsa Wash and slightly east of the trading post.

"From that time on I was a busy man," Frank Noel wrote in recalling that spring. "I had two big fine teams and two wagons and freighted most of our supplies in and out of Gallup . . . lumber to

ter, $5,420 and $500; Aldrich and Dodge, at Round Rock, $6,510 and $582; and Babbitt and Preston, at Tuba City—an exceptional case—$2,384 and $2,814. (National Archives, Record Group 75, Classified Files, 71406/11—910.)

build with and goods to trade with the Indians."[19] While his brother Henry and Joe Wilkin sun-baked adobes in forms eight by twelve inches, Frank "hauled rock for the foundation, lumber for floors, windows and doors, and roofing for the building—the tent being only a temporary shelter.

"After a while we had a building of two rooms—one big room which was the store proper, and a small room" for living quarters. "We moved in just before cold weather came."

Within a year Wilkin felt restless again and sold out his interest to the Noel brothers, moving north to build a trading post on Sanos-tee Wash.

Frank Noel, meanwhile, hauled in logs from the Chuskas and built a one-room log cabin close to the Two Gray Hills post. Here in the fall of 1898 he brought his bride, the former Mary Eliza Roberts, a pretty, full-breasted, and cheerfully devoted Mormon girl whose parents were among the first to take up farms on the San Juan at Fruitland. After the wedding Frank drove off with Mary perched beside him on a wagon seat, Frank geeing and hawing his team across the river ford and up the bluffs on the other side. An October moon lighted the desert that night. Halfway out from Two Gray Hills they stopped, and young Noel spread their bedroll on the sand and made camp. It was a short honeymoon, this wagon trip between Fruitland and her new log cabin home, but Mary made no complaint.

"As a general rule trade would be light until noon," Frank Noel wrote, "the busiest hours being from one to five o'clock, when we really worked hard. In the summer of this year [1899] we bought quite a number of sheep and some cattle. An Indian would come to the post and say he had sheep in the corral for sale and then I would have to call Mary from our room to stay in the store while I was out at the corral. She soon learned the prices of everything and with the Indians just pointing at what they wanted she was able to do a lot of trading without much talking."

The two-room post in which they started had been enlarged so that now they also had "a storeroom about twenty-five feet by fifteen, and a pelt and wool room." This last, Noel said, was a general storage room where they would "unload goods, price and mark them, and then put them . . . in the main store. A big door in the center of the trading post opened into the bull-pen, a space ten by twelve feet enclosed on three sides with a counter four feet high."

[19] Quotations here and following are from "Eighty Years in America," an unpublished manuscript written by Frank Noel in 1954.

Blankets brought in for trade at that time were of rather poor quality. Noel recalled that he paid from $2.50 to $4.00 for saddle blankets, and from $5.00 to $25.00 for blankets of average size.

Frank Noel sold his interest in Two Gray Hills in the spring of 1900, his brothers Henry and Hambleton Bridger Noel, who had recently come out from the East for his health, continuing to operate the post two years more until they sold out to Win Wetherill.[20] H. B. Noel stayed on with Wetherill a short time, and soon after, in 1904, the post changed hands again when it was bought by Wilkin's former partner, Joe Reitz.

Friends of Reitz say it was not his pleasure in trading that brought him back to the reservation so much as his wife's belief that desert air and isolation would be good for him. In Gallup he had been a wagon driver for a brewery—so agreeable an association with his favorite beverage as to make him regard life at Two Gray Hills with less than enthusiasm. Certainly he did not share the interest of J. B. Moore in the crafts of the Navahos. And not until Ed Davies came over the mountains in 1909 to join Reitz, and then bought the post three years later, did weavers of the Two Gray Hills region make anything but coarsely woven blankets of undistinguished design.

Davies was an Englishman with a few years' previous experience at Fort Defiance, where, under the eye of Frank Mapel, he clerked in the former Manning store later owned by the Ilfelds of Albuquerque. He had been owner of Two Gray Hills only a short time when George Bloomfield moved in five miles west, to a place in the foothills the Navahos call *Toh-ha-lene*, or water bubbling up, a name white men corrupted to Toadlena.

A tall, powerfully built, mild-mannered Mormon, Bloomfield was no stranger to the area. Originally from Ramah, he had surveyed the site the year before and helped to build the Toadlena boarding school. He returned now to buy and run a small adobe trading post started there in 1909 by two brothers, Merritt and Bob Smith. Competitors though they were, Bloomfield and Davies became good friends and then collaborators in improving the quality of their Navahos' weaving.

A year before his death in 1959, when he was retired from trading

---

[20] With the financial help of C. H. Algert, Frank Noel bought Wilkin's post in 1905 and renamed it Sa-nos-tee. Henry Noel dropped out of trading, and brother Hambleton went on to build trading posts at Teec-nos-pos and Mexican Water. From Two Gray Hills, Win Wetherill went out to Oregon and then returned to operate a trading post at Black Mountain. His last years were spent on a small ranch, or farm, on the eastern outskirts of Farmington, New Mexico.

and living as a missionary in Gallup, Bloomfield recalled that "there was no such thing as a Two Gray Hills rug when I bought the Toadlena trading post. The first rugs I bought were just common ones woven in natural wool colors of gray, white, black, and brown."

Design elements were crude, he said, the weaving coarse, the wool yarn often greasy and dirty. One negative factor distinguished the product: Navahos of the Toadlena–Two Gray Hills region showed an untypical, pronounced dislike for the color red.

The widow of Ed Davies was equally emphatic on this point. "Our Indians didn't like the reds. They wanted subdued colors, even in their dresses and shirts. When George Bloomfield first came out to Toadlena he put in a lot of red calico. But he couldn't sell it and had to ship it back."

Replying to the same questions that J. B. Moore and other traders were asked by the Indian Office in 1911, Ed Davies said that the yarn his weavers used was "all native wool carded and spun by the women. There is no natural dye used in this part of the country."

Moore had been gone from Crystal a year or longer when Bloomfield and Davies began encouraging their weavers to use cleaner and better wool, to spin a finer yarn thread, and to improve their designs. A nearly standard-size rug, about forty-eight by seventy-two inches, was developed. Natural wool colors of white, gray, and tan or brown were preferred—aniline dyes (except black) and Germantown yarn were ruled out. An outside black border about two inches wide, soon to incorporate a chindee path to let devil spirits out one corner, became a regional trademark.

Charlie Curley Ba-es-ah (ba-es-ah meaning "wife of"), her sister Police Girl, and Mrs. Taugel-clitso were willing to listen and the first to show promise. Bloomfield soon learned not to argue the merits of a rug with them in the trading post, where other Navahos cheerfully listened and later jeeringly repeated the trader's criticisms. When an audience gathered once to hear him advise a weaver, the woman suddenly became angry, snatched up her rug, and stamped out. After that, Bloomfield said, "When my best weavers brought rugs to sell, they came into my living room."

Mrs. Charles Herring, Bloomfield's daughter, remembers him down on his knees, often for as long as two hours, pointing out defects and discussing with the weaver how she could eliminate a "lazy line," correct a wobbly design element, or introduce design variations of multiplying complexity. Over at Two Gray Hills, Ed Davies did the same.

And both traders took snapshots of the best rugs as examples to show their other weavers.[21]

No overnight masterpiece of Navaho textile art resulted, but slowly there was improvement. Outside influences were felt, of course. Progressive and interlocking frets and hooks were borrowed from Crystal, as they were borrowed by weavers up and down the Chuska Valley. Gradually the simple diamond and cross forms with embracing frets multiplied—and then exploded into the fantastic crystalline imageries that star a winter-frosted window. And still the natural wool colors were used to the exclusion of all others.

A Two Gray Hills style, as such, did not emerge until about 1925, although by then the weaving of Mrs. Sherman Manygoats and several other women had achieved a sophistication rarely surpassed since. The late Stanley Stubbs of the Laboratory of Anthropolgy in Santa Fe believed that the Two Gray Hills style began "after 1915 and developed by 1925." These dates appear to be as close as anyone may come: in the Laboratory's vault is a Two Gray Hills rug bought about 1929 that is indistinguishable from fine rugs made in the area thirty years later.

The few design elements borrowed from Moore's Crystal rugs were absorbed in the early Two Gray Hills period of trial and error, and disappeared entirely in the second half of the 1920's. Since then Two Gray Hills weaving has remained basically unchanged, standing uniquely apart in design, color, and technique.

As this regional style emerged, so its value changed. George Bloomfield, who once paid one to three dollars a pound for a rug, lived to see Daisy Taugel-chee, a Toadlena weaver, receive eleven hundred dollars for a Two Gray Hills blanket measuring only thirty-three by forty-four inches.[22] It was a price that would have made John B. Moore blanch.

21 A photograph lent to me by Mrs. Jennie Noel Weeks, Frank Noel's daughter, shows four large rugs exhibited at the 1913 Shiprock fair, presumably hanging in front of Noel's Sa-nos-tee booth. Two of the four rugs show some Crystal influence.

22 As soft to the hand as a piece of cashmere, this blanket was purchased by Gilbert Maxwell of Farmington, a collector and wholesaler, in 1959. Daisy Taugel-chee cards and hand-spins wool from her own sheep, achieving what for others is impossible: a weft thread so remarkably fine that her work rarely measures less than 90 strands to the inch—a good machine operation. Her best weaving counts 110 threads to the inch. Traders who followed Bloomfield and Davies, including Vernon Bloomfield, Charles Herring, and Willard Leighton, were largely responsible for increasing the price of Two Gray Hills weaving. A good blanket from that region today brings from $250 to $500—sometimes considerably more.

19

The Arizona Traders

THE EARLIEST TRADERS in Arizona were wilderness-seekers: independent men of the Keam and Hubbell stripe, who waited for no one to point or break the way. As the country became more familiar, and as the hazards—as the frontiers—receded, the less adventurous, the less daring, moved in.

Across the 25,000 square miles of Arizona ranged by Navahos the traders who followed Keam and Hubbell chose trading locations on either of two principal routes of commerce and travel. Both of these trade routes had origins in an ancient past, both were "discovered" again by white men. The first was Jacob Hamblin's Mormon Trail, pioneered by him in 1873 from Lee's Ferry to the Little Colorado and then on to the San Francisco Mountains. The second route nine years later was marked out with the ties and rails of the Atlantic and Pacific Railroad, which in 1882 met the lower terminus of Hamblin's Trail at the lumber camp called Flagstaff.

Coincidence and topography made of these routes a natural, then a lawful, boundary, enclosing the Navahos north to south on the west, and east to west on the south. By the time the Indian Office finished redrawing the lines of the reservation (and perhaps the end is not yet), the old Mormon Trail approximately defined the Navahos' western limits; the railroad, following the valley of the Río Puerco of the West, more or less roped in the tribe on the south. Along these boundary highroads the Arizona traders settled in the 1880's.

Then, after a decade, they gradually fanned out into the interior, again drawn naturally to places most numerously inhabited by Indians. And naturally again the terrain of the country scattered them along old or ancient trade routes from north to south through the Chinle Valley and westward from Fort Defiance to the Hopi Villages.

Contemporaries and followers of Keam and Hubbell never rivaled those two in their unique importance to the Navaho people, though a few among them may have known greater financial rewards. Certainly the power of Lorenzo Hubbell and a measure of his influence were absorbed in the years of Hubbell's wane by the Babbitt brothers of Flagstaff.

No hint of the dynasty they founded was observable that day in 1886 when David and William Babbitt stepped off into Arizona. Travel-worn by their train journey from Cincinnati, Ohio, they alighted at Flagstaff on a raw day in February. Stained with soot and probably aching with cold and unsure of themselves, they could only bleakly survey the prospects of this tiny lumber town, squatted in a high saddle of the mountains. Just as bleakly, the town's string of dismal false-fronts, frozen in the mud of Front Street, could only stare back in mute and wooden unwelcome.

The town's cheeriest optimist would have detected nothing in this moment that promised much of good on either side. For all of his erect height and sober face, David Babbitt was only twenty-eight years old. His brother William was five years younger. Left behind them in Cincinnati, all they knew and now abandoned, was a small grocery store. They had sold it to finance their venture into the cattle business.

A few weeks after their arrival the brothers leased grazing land at the foot of the San Francisco Mountains and bought a herd of stock numbering twelve hundred head. The selection of this spread, by two admitted greenhorns, was first in a bewildering series of later business enterprises that typified the Babbitts' almost unerring bent for avoiding mistakes. Considering their small initial stake, their success was remarkably compounded of shrewd imagination, tough-mindedness, and hard work. Before the mountain valleys were free of snow, David and William were joined by their youngest brother, Charles, who was twenty-one, and "later recalled that, during his first five years in Arizona, he spent practically every minute on the range with the stock"—for an Ohio dude, an impressive performance.[1] A fourth brother, George, came out to Flagstaff the same year, and still later the fifth brother, Edward, followed the others. Edward stayed long

[1] The *Arizona Daily Sun*, Flagstaff, seventy-fifth anniversary edition, March 27, 1959.

enough to become the youngest member of the Arizona Territorial Legislature and then returned to Ohio to practice law.

Owners of the powerful neighboring cow outfits—the Hashknife and A-One-Bar spreads—smiled indulgently as the Babbitts laid on their C-O-Bar brand ("C" for Cincinnati and "O" for their native state), and referred to the newcomers as the "Boot Brand Outfit." As any old cowpoke could plainly tell, these Babbitts would be high-tailing back East within a year. But somehow it didn't work out that way. Surviving an Apache raid and a mixup in the Tewksbury-Graham range war, the Babbitts emerged strong enough to buy out the Hashknife and big A-One-Bar. Long before this, however, the brothers diverted a small amount of funds into a ramshackle wooden building in the center of Flagstaff, eldest brother David appearing on billheads as operator of the town's newest general store, and "dealer in Hardware, Stoves, Paints, Oils, Cement, Plaster of Paris and Hair. Guns and Ammunition. Also a complete line of Doors, Sash and Redwood Shingles, in carload lots."[2]

Two years later, in 1889, so magical was his touch, David's trade had expanded to the point that he was forced to build a new two-story stone and brick building—Flagstaff's largest— that under one roof accommodated a county courtroom and "opera house" as well as the enlarged store, now operating for the first time as the Babbitt Brothers Trading Company. The Babbitts' customers came from more than one hundred miles in every direction. They came by wagon or carriage, by train or by horse, mule, burro, or jackass. They represented a fair crosscut of northern Arizona: cowpokes and ranch owners, lumberjacks from the Ponderosa Pine sawmills, railroad hands and housewives, mule skinners, saloon-keepers and schoolmarms. And Indians, always and most conspicuously Indians: tall, blanketed Navahos, stockier Hopis and Havasupais; and sometimes a few Apaches, up from the Gila River country.

Shouldering their way in among this motley crowd were the reservation traders who twice a year or oftener came to Flagstaff to fill their wagons with fresh supplies from the Babbitt warehouse. Joseph H. Lee, a son of John Doyle Lee, was one of these—among the old-timers already regarded as a veteran. Contemporaries who knew him best could give no certain account of his past. Of a later generation, Amsden is one of the few bold enough to couple Joe Lee's name with a date, saying that Lee "went to Tuba City (of the Moencopi colony) in 1879"—but even this is doubtful. Albert Hugh Lee of Ganado, one of the old trader's grandsons, recalls that Joseph Lee "settled in Tuba City about 1874 or 1875" and farmed the valley below the Hopi village of Moenkopi before he became a trader.

Farming the Moenkopi Wash appears to have held Joe Lee's interest only briefly. The date is uncertain but probably before 1880, when in partnership with a J. C. Brown, he chose the high dividing point on the Hamblin Trail, forty-five miles south of his father's old ferry, and built The Gap Trading Post. It was a small store based at the foot of the red, jagged Echo Cliffs on the east side of Hamblin Wash, facing south.[3] Still later he operated a trading post at Blue Canyon, east of Moenkopi, but when he was there is not known. Presumably it was two or three years after 1881, which Paul J. Babbitt says is the year when Lee located on the Tokesjhay Wash to build the first Red Lake—or Tonalea—trading post.

Lee had been at Red Lake for about one year, according to Paul Babbitt, when the trader George McAdams "set up a small trading post in a stockade building, partly of stone, directly across Red Lake from the present trading post." In 1885, McAdams moved to a new location half a mile southeast of Red Lake and there operated another log and stockade post until he sold out, in 1888, to a trader named Dittenhoffer.[4]

The emergence of Dittenhoffer might go entirely unnoticed had his demise not followed so swiftly—and resulted in drawing the Babbitt brothers into the Indian trading business. Dittenhoffer's misfortunes were calamitous, but are simple to relate. First, and this was not exceptional, he was permitted to run up a large bill of credit with the Babbitts for supplying his Red Lake store. Soon thereafter he went further into debt by buying a new buckboard. So bright and smart was this conveyance that he had no trouble in persuading one of Flagstaff's flashier young belles to join him for a ride. This too would have been unexceptional had Dittenhoffer resisted an impulse to keep driving until he and the lady gained the intended privacy of Red Lake.

[3] Only the foundations, about forty by thirty feet, remain. After Joe Lee abandoned this post, a new store was built on the west side of the Hamblin Wash by a trader named Johnny O'Farrell. Trader Troy Washburn says that O'Farrell's post burned down about 1937 and was replaced by the third, and present, Gap Trading Post on the west side of Highway 89.

[4] Paul Babbitt, my informant, said that McAdams later became a Babbitt partner at Red Lake and traded there until about 1900. During the next thirteen years McAdams operated trading posts at Chinle, Arizona, and at Seven Lakes, Gallup, and Crownpoint, New Mexico.

One of the girl's devoted friends followed them there, William Babbitt later recalled, "and in a card game that ensued, the newcomer shot and killed Ditt. Naturally, we had to take over the business to protect our interests."

If the Babbitts entered Indian trading almost accidentally, their lukewarm interest at the start veered quickly to a more characteristic stance of aggressive enterprise. Charles Babbitt assumed active direction of the Red Lake post in 1890 and soon after took in Samuel S. Preston as partner and resident manager. The selection of Preston, as might be expected, was another judicious move; the Red Lake store began to prosper in a vast region where most other posts survived precariously for a few months or years and then seemingly vanished in the first big sandstorm.

Preston consolidated the brothers' gains at Red Lake in 1891 by constructing a new two-story building, and in the next few years the Babbitts looked deeper into Navaho country, north, south, and east, for new posts to build or acquire. At one time or another they owned the Apache Trading Post at Cibecue; the Babbitt and Roberts post, or Antelope Springs Trading Post, at Jeddito; the Conley, Favella, and Sharp trading posts, all at Keams Canyon; the Volz Trading Post at Canyon Diablo and Sunrise Trading Post at Leupp; the Western Navaho and Bell trading posts at Tuba City; the Babbitt and Steckel Trading Post at Tolchaco; Willow Springs Trading Post above Cameron; and Echo and White Mesa trading posts still farther to the north.

Nor were these all. In addition to the Red Lake store, the Babbitt Brothers Trading Company bought or built—and still owns—the Tuba Trading Post Company at Tuba City, Warren Trading Post at Kayenta, Cedar Ridge Trading Post north of The Gap and also on the Hamblin Trail, the Oraibi Trading Post at Oraibi (bought from the Hubbell family in 1955), and the Indian Wells Trading Post, at Indian Wells.

While building this small reservation empire, the brothers, more actively concerned with their cattle business and expanding retail operations in northern Arizona, delegated management to others. Most of the trading posts owned by the company were incorporated in 1923, according to Paul Babbitt.

"Prior to that time they were operated as partnerships, the manager usually having a partnership interest in the post. For example, before the Warren Trading Post was incorporated, H. K. Warren owned a one-third interest and Babbitt Brothers . . . two-thirds . . . also, John

P. Kerley owned a one-half interest in the Cedar Ridge Trading Post and Babbitt Brothers . . . the other one-half. Mr. Kerley also was a partner in the Tuba Trading Post and later on owned one-half of the stock after the post was incorporated."[5]

Sam Preston, first of the Babbitt partner-managers, was a native Kentuckian who came West with a government pack train in the middle 1880's to operate a small trading post of his own at Black Falls, on the Little Colorado. After taking over at Red Lake for the Babbitts, he parted company with them temporarily in 1894 to trade again on his own, first at Willow Springs. Preston was neither the first nor the last to trade with Navahos and Hopis at this place, but today the desert spring and its oasis of sheltering trees is abandoned, bypassed by a modern highway and all but forgotten. Van Valkenburgh suggests that Domínguez and Escalante may have been the first white men to stop at the spring, in 1776. Jacob Hamblin unquestionably made the spring a regular stopping place on his frequent trips to the Hopi country, and largely in consequence a small legion of Mormon pioneers paused there on their journeys south. Of these a few remained for a while to trade with the Indians.[6]

A bachelor through these years, and as lonely no doubt as any single white trader might be, Preston went courting in the summer of 1904. The girl of his choice, a girl of less than half his years, was Laura A. Williams, who at sixteen—four years before—had come bravely out from Missouri to be a schoolteacher for Navaho children at Blue Canyon. They were married in October. In February, 1905, Preston took

[5] Letter from Paul Babbitt to the writer, September 19, 1959.

[6] Many of my older Mormon friends remember Willow Springs as a place where they stopped, in the years of their youth, when setting out for new land to settle. The spring is located about sixteen miles north of Cameron, Arizona, and its trees are visible in a lower extension of the redrock Echo Cliffs, a mile east of present Highway 89. Approach by passenger car now is possible, first by a crossing of Hamblin Wash and then over a rough dirt trail. Van Valkenburgh notes that historically the region was once a Havasupai farming community. And further: "One mile south of Willow Springs on the rough and rocky road that runs to Moenave and Tuba City, are located one of the finest and largest series of inscriptions in the Southwest. These petroglyphs completely cover a number of large, smooth boulders for some 75 feet. It is said that these date from the 12th century until modern times and are still used as clan symbols for Hopis traveling to the Hopi Salt Mine in the gorge of the Little Colorado River. This is, according to Navajos who have descended the dangerous and long trail, not a mine, but a large cave in which salt crystals hang from the ceiling like stalactites. Further down the same trail and in the bottom of the gorge is found the little-known Blue Spring. This is said to be the greatest spring in volume in the Navajo country. It is indigo blue in color and runs a stream said to be some 3 feet deep." The Navaho name for Willow Springs is 'Apa'to, or "Lost Spring."

his bride by wagon to Tuba City. There the Babbitt brothers had bought out the trading post of C. H. Algert and persuaded Preston to take over as partner and manager. Between this year and 1917 when he finally sold out, Preston remained at Tuba City, rebuilding with stone Algert's original adobe store. Preston's post was a two-story octagonal building, a design borrowed from the post–Civil War architects of New York State's Hudson River school. The store remains today much as he built it, a curious and somehow pleasingly uncopied landmark in the Southwest.

Hopis from nearby Moenkopi Pueblo mingled with Navahos in the Tuba City store, but Navahos alone brought their handicrafts to Preston in trade. In 1911 Preston reported to the Indian Office that during the year just ended "we paid out to the Indians $2,384.50 for Navajo blankets and $2,814.64 for native [Navaho] silverware. The blankets are made by the women out of native wool carded and spun by them although a few blankets are made with the Germantown yarn. . . . We have never heard of them using native dye for their blankets as aniline dyes are always used." If he took any Hopi pottery or other Hopi crafts in trade, the amount was so small that Preston found it needless to mention.

At the same time, from the Babbitts' Red Lake Trading Post to the south, H. K. Warren reported spending $3,911.75 for Navaho blankets, only $150 for silverwork, and $434 for "other native work . . . [which] includes basket work done by the Paiutes to the amount of about $350 . . . the remainder . . . squaw belts etc., made of yarn furnished the Navajos by us for that purpose. . . . Coloring is all done with artificial dyes now with the exception of brown which is, as a rule, from brown sheep. In some cases however brown dye is used but not to any extent. The gray wool is of course the carding of black and white wool together."[7]

The Babbitt Brothers Trading Company, meanwhile, expanded far beyond the limits of the growing Flagstaff. As they moved into a new century, the brothers increased their cattle business until they owned ranches in California, Kansas, and Montana; maintaining their headquarters in Flagstaff, they opened department stores and supermarkets, acquired an automobile dealership and an ice plant. The Babbitt name appeared on drugstores, hardware and furniture stores, garages, and loan companies across the northern half of the

[7] Letters from Preston and Warren to Assistant Commissioner F. H. Abbott, reporting the volume of their trade in Indian crafts during the previous year. (National Archives, Record Group 75, Classified Files: #71406/11–910.)

state, in Prescott and Phoenix, in Holbrook and Winslow, at Williams, the Grand Canyon, and Kingman.

Charles, the youngest, lived long enough to see the early vision of brothers David and William develop into a complex family enterprise employing more than three hundred persons and doing an annual business of more than fifteen million dollars.

Jonathan Paul Williams, a frustrated seeker for gold, came upon the scene in 1882. A minor personality, Williams deserves brief attention if only because he involved himself in the lives of others more important, and managed—between forays in search of gold—to build the first trading post at Blue Canyon. This too happened in 1882, when he moved his family to Arizona from Watsonville, California. By wagon trail twenty-five miles east of Tuba City, the spot Williams chose was an unshaded sandy bottom along the Moenkopi Wash, closed in by canyon walls candy-striped in horizontal strata of pink and red and white sandstone.

In this submerged, remote wasteland of ruddy pinnacles and turrets, eroded spool-shapes and toadstool formations, the Navahos long before had detected traces of clay that was not red, ignored the obvious, and ever since knew this gorge as *Boh-koh'Doh't Klish*, or Canyon of Blue Clay. And now, with two boys and a small daughter to rear, Annie Williams, a dance-hall girl before she married Jonathan and accustomed to facing reality unblinking, saw it differently. All of her feeling for this lonely canyon was compressed into the moan: "It's such a God-forsaken deep *hole!* All I can see is the sky."[8]

The trading post Williams built with the help of his sons, Ben and Bill, was a small, rectangular building constructed of stone and adobe mortar. Supplies were freighted in from Winslow, three days by wagon to the south. Trade with the Navahos and Hopis was good enough —when he wanted it that way—but Williams at heart was a prospector, not a trader. More and more often he left the post in others' hands, wandered northward looking for gold, never found it but never ceased to believe that gold was there.

His search once led him to build a steam-powered skiff in which he navigated a stretch of the Colorado River; another time, he tried placer mining on the San Juan. Finally, after seven years of this, he abandoned Blue Canyon and any further pretense at trading and moved his family to Winslow. Off he wandered again, to the moun-

8 This is quoted from Elizabeth Rigby's "Blue Canyon," *Arizona Highways*, August, 1959.

tains of Mexico, following rumors of gold. There he died—killed, it is said, by Yaqui Indians.

Two of the Williams boys stayed on in Arizona: Bill trading at Red Lake, Ben moving a few miles farther north to Cow Springs. Here, according to Paul Babbitt, Ben "set up a small shack as a trading post on the north side of Cow Springs Lake." Forlorn enough, this lower end of Kletha Valley, but Ben's post was on the old Mormon Trail and so was in the way of travel, as well as a fair amount of trade with neighboring Navahos. A competitor soon appeared in the person of Frederick W. Volz, who came with a wagonload of trade goods furnished to him on credit by Lorenzo Hubbell. Volz pitched a tent on the opposite side of the lake and traded there for about two years— the length of time, Paul Babbitt has said, that Hubbell continued to back him.[9]

Volz moved down the Little Colorado about 1899 until he reached Canyon Diablo, at a point just north of the Atlantic and Pacific Railroad, where he built another post. His arrival coincided with a range war between the Navahos and white ranchers in which two cattlemen were killed. The conflict flared on all sides of him but only affected Volz personally when, to end the trouble, President Theodore Roosevelt in 1901 established the Leupp Jurisdiction, granting an additional twenty-four square miles to the Navaho reservation. The extension embraced the gorge where Volz' post was located, immediately subjecting him to Indian Office regulation. Before long he was at angry odds with Joseph E. Maxwell, the local agent, and although his license was not renewed after 1904 he continued to trade there for some time afterwards.[10]

From Red Lake and Cow Springs north to the Colorado, meanwhile, the great western corner of the Navaho country was virtually unsettled by whites. Mainly it was the domain of still primitive and warlike bands that recognized little more than the regional autonomy exercised by the old chief, Hoskinini. These Navahos already had demonstrated their hostility toward white men, and barred all traders from their lands. None knew this better than John Wetherill. Nearly twenty years before, exploring the region for *anasazi* ruins with his brothers, Richard and Al, John had learned of the risks

9 Paul Babbitt believes that Ben Williams started trading at Cow Springs about 1895. Volz was licensed to trade at that place in June, 1897. After Volz moved away, Babbitt says, the Williams family maintained Ben's small post for several years, "mostly during the summer and fall months of the year."

10 *Annual Report, C. I. A., 1905.*

taken by anyone who antagonized these western Navahos. Nevertheless, the vacuum created by the reluctance of other white men to test Hoskinini's patience was, for John Wetherill, irresistible.

A few years after the breakup of the Hyde Exploring Expedition led to his leaving the Ojo Alamo post, John scouted the San Juan country westward into Utah and Monument Valley. In 1906, with young Clyde Colville as partner, he put up a tent on Oljetoh—or Moonlight—Wash, close by the home camp of Hoskinini. A council with the chief followed, Wetherill pleading his cause so convincingly that he was permitted to stay. Louisa Wetherill soon afterward joined her husband in this loneliest of desert outposts and with unyielding fortitude helped John to survive tides of hardship that would have routed any couple less determined.

From their first tent camp, the Wetherills moved downstream one mile and built a post that would offer greater protection against the valley's raging sandstorms and winter cold. A faded photograph owned by Sam Day II shows their Oljetoh home to be large enough, and sturdy, but scarcely a place of beauty.

Long and low and humpy, the pitched dirt roof barely cleared the tops of the door jambs and windows. Walls were constructed of upright juniper logs unstripped of shaggy bark, combined with undressed stones set this way and that in adobe. Projecting *vigas* suggest a cabin-like interior, while three squat stone chimneys and one tilting metal stove pipe indicate how the six or eight rooms were heated. Log house joins stone store but projecting outward from the outside wall, as if to separate the two and afford the family some privacy, there is a tall, drunkenly angled, stockade fence. In the bare front yard, enclosing a poled crossbeam fitted with pulley and rope, rough planks salvaged from a crate hedge in the Wetherill well.

The solitary feminine touch in this otherwise ruthless setting is seen in the optimistic placing of several tree sproutlings, shielded by wooden frames from the teeth of Navaho ponies.

Friendship and trust the Navahos gave, but only with time. The Wetherills no longer were regarded as intruders, but still were the only white people in the region when, in 1910, they left Oljetoh and moved down the valley some thirty miles to Laguna Creek. Here, in a desert hollow known since as Kayenta, they built a new trading post and their permanent home. Their desert post office, they boasted, was farthest distant from a railroad of any in the United States.

Sharing some traits of his elder brother Richard, John was restless. Indian trading was his livelihood and, at this difficult place, an occupation that required a variety of skills. He was a good trader, perhaps one of the best from the Navahos' point of view, but in the eyes of some others almost a failure: he got along all right, but died poor. More than trading, however, John enjoyed exploring, as he always had since his youth at Mancos, when with his brothers he discovered the major cliff ruins of Mesa Verde. During his years at Kayenta he became known not only as a trader but as a knowing explorer, pack-trip master, and guide for all who came to this part of the Southwest.

There was nothing about John Wetherill that to the observer was heroic and little that was even colorful. He was an unassuming man of plain habits, plain talk, and plain shameless honesty. Slight of build, not tall, in his later years he appeared almost frail—and this was his only fraud. He had the strength of an ox. Whether hoisting flour sacks into a wagon, leading a pack train into the Utah wilderness, or climbing by foot the steep trails of Skeleton Mesa or Tsegi Canyon, he was nearly tireless when men half his age wilted with exhaustion. The hollows under his cheekbones and the melancholy droop of his mustache made him appear a melancholy man. But he was not; he had a puckish humor.

Gamboling around a campfire one night, at the end of a fatiguing trip as guide for Zane Grey, he convulsed his cook and trail hands—and an eminent Harvard archaeologist, who has recalled the episode—with a travesty of the tenderfoot novelist, swaggering in the firelight and flapping leather chaps, six-guns bouncing from his hips. Chaps and guns were borrowed for this bit of mimicry, as John's own garb for such a trip was a greasy leather jacket, cotton shirt, denim pants, and a pair of worn-out sneakers. Side arms he never wore, though with a rifle, like all the Wetherills, he was a good marksman.

Guests at the Wetherill home in Kayenta were numerous and fell into several categories. One included the tourists, writers, and artists who had the means to hire John Wetherill's services as guide. Among these were the wealthy Charles Bernheimer, who once engaged Wetherill and added the young archaeologist Earl Morris to his entourage, for a quasi-scientific tour of the Rainbow Bridge–Colorado River area. A second group of visitors was active in politics on a state or national level, and of these one most appreciative of the Wetherills' hospitality was Theodore Roosevelt. Finally, and probably for the Wetherills the most welcome guests, were the archaeologists and ethnologists, many of whom returned to Kayenta year after year. These included the same Earl Morris, as he grew older, T. Mitchell Prudden, S. J. Guernsey, and Alfred Vincent Kidder.

John frequently arranged pack trips for his scientific friends, taking all of them at one time or another to the great cliff ruins of Betatakin and Kiet Siel, nearly inaccessible in the depths of Tsegi Canyon. At *Shaa'tohi*—Sunshine Water—on the southern approach to the ruins, Van Valkenburgh says, Wetherill and Joe Lee built a trading post in 1915. This location, too, was in a deep canyon bottom, but the profusion of grass and nearby spring made it a favorite gathering place of the Navahos. In time the spelling of the Indian name was changed to Shonto.[11]

A measure of doubt surrounds the earliest days of the Shonto Trading Post, but Hubert Richardson says that he bought the store in 1917 or 1918 and several years later turned it over to his brother, C. D. Richardson. A succession of owners who followed included the Babbitt brothers, Harry R. Rorick, and Reuben Heflin. During their ownership the Babbitts built a dugway on the western approach to the canyon, giving access to a trail that leads to Inscription House ruin. Rorick, in his time, dynamited a road through the canyon's eastern face. The road allowed agile goats and Indian ponies to pass without great difficulty, but otherwise has since been damned by many travelers as the steepest, roughest half-mile in the United States.

The Navaho country was on the threshhold of change when Hubert Richardson came to Arizona in 1908 from Alvarado, Texas. Kind circumstance and his own longevity enabled Richardson in the next fifty years to participate in the Navahos' emergence from the nearly primitive to the white man's age of electronics.

No hint of this radical transition was apparent when Richardson joined his uncle, J. Higgins McAdams, at Sunrise Springs. Fifteen miles southwest of Lorenzo Hubbell's Ganado, the Sunrise store, as the young Texan first saw it, was small and far removed from civilization. A man in that part of the country who wanted to travel could fork his legs over a saddle or climb aboard a wagon—or walk. His choice was that simple and limited.

Richardson and his uncle soon parted, the younger man moving down the Pueblo Colorado Wash to team up with Edwin Jacob Marty, a Swiss, and build a store at Indian Wells.[12] Their partnership

11 Mrs. Anton Hegemann, whose first husband was the Shonto trader Harry Rorick, could not confirm Van Valkenburgh's belief that John Wetherill joined Lee in building the post. She was certain, however, that Joe Lee traded at the place from tents before the original store was constructed. The store and two adjoining rooms were built of stone.

12 The Sunrise Springs post was bought by the William Bickel Co. in the 1920's. Ownership was transferred to Albert Hugh Lee and Clarence A. Wheeler when

continued until 1913, when Richardson married and, the year following, went on to rebuild and trade from the old Jonathan Williams post in Blue Canyon. Since Williams' departure in 1889, the property had passed through others' hands. Vacant and slowly crumbling, the buildings after ten years were taken over by the Indian Office in 1899 with creation of the western Navaho reservation extension. An agency and school for Navaho and Hopi children were opened in 1890, sheltered in stone wings added to the old Williams post. C. H. Algert, already trading at Tuba City, built an adjoining stockade store during the early days of the agency, but within a few years abandoned it. In 1903, after the purchase of all Mormon holdings at Tuba City by the government, the agency and school at Blue Canyon were moved there and—until Richardson's arrival—the canyon was silent and empty for another eleven years.

A relocation of reservation roads bypassed Blue Canyon, increasing its already formidable isolation. Richardson maintained his canyon store, while branching out elsewhere, until 1921, when trade drained to a trickle and finally he was persuaded to lock the doors and give up. Blue Canyon has been deserted ever since.

The new roads made the difference between the old way and the new. Before long the roads brought the new automobile rattling and wheezing onto the reservation. The automobiles mired in mud, blew tires and gaskets, and ran out of water and gas, but on they came in increasing numbers. Highway 66, unpaved and hazardous, advanced across Arizona, paralleling the rails of the old Atlantic and Pacific—now the Atchison, Topeka and Santa Fe Railroad—spawning new trading posts and revitalizing a few of the older ones.

Gas pumps became as important as pawn rooms at Chambers (L. J. Cassidy, trader) and Sanders (Spencer Balcomb, A. C. Coon, and Hoske Cronemeyer, traders). A few miles off the new highway, but not too far north and on a road of their own, between Chambers and Ganado, William Lippincott and his wife, Sally traded with the Navahos, pumped gas, and dispensed hospitality to a new kind of western traveler—the touring sightseer. Their Wide Ruins Trading Post, built on the site of a major *anasazi* ruin called Pueblo Grande by the

they bought out the Bickel company in 1929. Earlier, Lee had bought an interest in the store, and Wheeler ran it for Bickel and Lee starting in 1925. Edwin Marty moved to Arizona from Gallup in 1908, buying the Eighteen Miles Spring Trading Post started by Freeman H. Hathorn in 1896. Hathorn later traded at Keams Canyon. The Indian Wells post was located on Teshbito (*Tsebitho'*) Wash, a fork of the Pueblo Colorado.

Spaniards and *Kin Teel* by the Navahos, formerly had been owned by Spencer Balcomb, Wallace Sanders, and Peter Paquette, the one-time Navaho agent.

Hubert Richardson was still operating the Blue Canyon store when a sway-back, one-track suspension bridge was erected in 1911 over a gorge of the Little Colorado. The bridge and a new dirt road meandering to it across the desert, north and south, were improvements of Hamblin's Trail, the spidery span obviating any further use of the old Mormon ford and its perilous chasm approaches. At this place, called Cameron, Richardson in 1916 built a small trading post.[13] North of Flagstaff by fifty-three miles, the Cameron store then was visited only by Indians and trade was confined to barter for Navaho wool, skins, rugs, and livestock.

"The Indians had many sheep and cattle in those days," Richardson recalled years later. "They had more of everything than they do now, maybe four times the amount of livestock. A family that owned six or eight hundred sheep was reduced to two hundred head. They couldn't live on two hundred head and the sheep were depleted until they were just about gone. But in the first years it was nothing to see 1,200 to 1,700 sheep in here at one time. The shipping points were Flagstaff and Winslow."

With his brother Dick, Richardson built another trading post at Kaibito, near White Mesa, and in the winter of 1916 opened a wholesale store at Winslow which eight years later was sold to Lorenzo Hubbell, Jr. Otherwise, in addition to Shonto, the brothers owned a trading post at Leupp, located west and north of Winslow on a bar in the treeless river bottom of the Little Colorado.

"We busted up stores," Richardson recalled, "along with the depression of 1922. I took Cameron, Leupp and Winslow, and my brother took Kaibito and Shonto. I went in partners with Stanton Borum of Flagstaff, who ran Leupp until he died in 1936."

Only the Cameron post remained in Richardson control past the

---

13 The place-name celebrates the memory of R. H. Cameron, a sheriff of Coconino County in the 1890's and later a member of the Arizona State Senate. Van Valkenburgh relates that near this place in 1898 Sheriff Cameron, "assisted by range-hungry stockmen, ejected Beeshlhagai Atsidi and his people from their hogans, forcing them to cross over to the eastern bank of the Little Colorado. The river was in winter flow, carrying a great deal of ice; many sheep were lost and the Navajos suffered greatly from exposure. Herbert Walsh of the Indian Rights Association took up the cause of the Navajos but with little immediate success." The old bridge at Cameron, it is said, was built at Senator Cameron's urging with funds taken from the Navaho tribal appropriation—without the wish or consent of the tribe. A new, wider bridge replaced the old span in 1958.

mid-century. Then, no longer a dusty, lonely outpost, Cameron became a tourist haven on Highway 89, the store's adjoining hotel and restaurant combining with a leased garage and filling station to reassure travelers to the Grand Canyon's southern rim that they were not venturing too far into the wilds. The old trading post was rebuilt: on one side, a modern grocery store—on the other, a curio shop offering tomahawks and feathered headdresses along with imported and brightly colored Tesuque pottery and Chimayo blankets and the most up-to-date Hopi and Navaho silverwork. Summer trade mounted into the multiple thousands of dollars, backing Hubert Richardson into a glass-and-wood partitioned office where, one day in 1957, surrounded by the clack of adding machines, he reflected:

"Navahos hereabouts never bothered much about silverwork. There was none any good this side of Manuelito or Crownpoint. But they always made good rugs—usually the storm pattern, in reds, blacks, and browns.

"The Indians started traveling in cars and pickups about 1930, and that was about the time the tourists started coming. When I built this place, I saw nobody but Navahos. Now it's 80 per cent tourist trade."

Once at Cameron there was a guest hogan, south and east of the old store. Not so long ago the hogan was torn down because tourists had to drive around it to reach the new island of gas pumps—no loss, really, as the Navahos already had ceased to use it.

20

Shipley and Perry

MEMORIES of Bosque Redondo, ever present and persuasive, were arguments for peace, although in some younger members of the Navaho tribe a wild strain remained close to the surface. In the 1890's and the decade following, the reservation was still an unhealthy place for a white man inept enough not to recognize trouble, or reckless enough to ignore or flout trouble when it arose.

In time separated by a few years, David L. Shipley and Reuben Perry, both agents for the Navahos, shared a common trouble largely of their own making. Both were very nearly killed by Navahos. Both in some measure owed their lives to the intervention of Indian traders who had nothing to gain from risking their own safety.

Shipley was an Iowa man, appointed in 1891 as agent for the Navahos and Hopis. His career at Fort Defiance, with two exceptions, was routine enough: he lasted about a year and a half. In the long, rapid succession of agents he stands out briefly because of his kettle penchant for calling the pot black and for his awkward brush with death in 1892.

He observed with distaste that among the Navahos, gambling was the prevailing vice and of their dances, one, the annual ceremonial *hish kohu*, a "heathenish" affair, was waning and soon would be a thing of the past. He attended but one of the Hopi dances and this, the Snake Dance, repelled him even more. "I can not but think," he said, "it is one of the evils that lie in the way of their civilization. The dark superstitions and profane ceremonies of a system as gross as that of darkest Africa still infects them with its poison."[1]

[1] *Annual Report, C. I. A., 1891.*

One might gather that Shipley in his personal life knew little of wrong-doing, and then only from a virtuous distance. This is not quite correct.

Sam Day, temporarily free of his duties as trader and serving at the agency as Shipley's clerk, soon discovered that Shipley had a small share of human frailities. For a full year Day kept this knowledge to himself and then, in some exasperation, complained to the Indian Office: "The first difference between us occurred in March, 1891 when he reported Henry F. Shipley, his brother, as Irregular Employe from Feby. 11, 1891 to March 10, 1891, employed to do office work when Henry F. Shipley had never been nearer [the] Navaho Agency than Iowa."[2] The brother remained on the payroll in the third quarter of the year, Day added, drawing $77.50 in pay.

Day also questioned Shipley's appointment of Emma DeVore as a teacher in the Navaho boarding school, asking if she and the agent were not related. "Upon his telling me that she was his wife's sister, I called his attention to the regulation requiring him to report such facts and he replied he didn't care a d—n. The Indian Office had approved her and that relieved him. I differed with him there."

When Day mentioned these and other matters to the agent, protesting that Shipley was paying one-half cent a pound above the market price for hay and corn, the agent warned him that an agency clerk should be less observant.

"Must a man who enters the Indian Service put away his identity and manhood and become a nonentity and lickspittle in order to retain his position?" Day demanded. "Or has he the right to have an opinion of his own?"

To these were added other complaints, from other sources, that Agent Shipley was profane and given to drinking more heavily than an Indian agent should, who by the book should not drink at all. In May, 1892, there was an investigation of Shipley's affairs. While it was found there was some truth in the charges, the Indian Office did not regard the evidence as serious enough to remove Shipley. He was still in a position, therefore, to embroil himself with Black Horse and his outfit in the fall of that year, at Round Rock Trading Post.

Some fifty miles north of Fort Defiance's cool timberland and meadows, the country is treeless moonscape. This is a place of desert valleys and spectacular redrock buttes, parts of it sooted with black

2 Sam Day's complaints against Shipley were addressed to Commissioner T. J. Morgan, in a letter dated March 8, 1892. (National Archives, Record Group 75, Letters Received, 1892, #9639.)

volcanic ash, other parts encrusted with fallen trunks of trees for centuries lying petrified in amber stone.

Lukachukai Creek cuts a dry wash through one of these valleys equally distant by about six miles from the Lukachukai Mountains to the east and Round Rock Mesa, a place sacred in mythology to the Navahos, on the west. Blocking the northern portal to the valley are Los Gigantes Buttes, towering cathedral-like spires and buttresses.

Close to the wash and on the slight eminence of a sand hill in the center of the valley, Stephen E. Aldrich, of Manuelito, in 1890 built a small rock and adobe trading post. He named his store for Round Rock Mesa and installed as his partner and manager the onetime agency interpreter, Henry Chee Dodge. Charles Hubbell, brother of Lorenzo, soon became a clerk.

Aldrich also was the builder, with his partner Elias S. Clark, of the Sehili post, located high in the mountains about twenty-five miles to the southeast. The partners built Sehili of logs, about 1885. It was now owned by Archibald S. Sweetland.[3]

Sweetland may have been at the mountain store when David Shipley stopped at Sehili with a small party one day in October, 1892. The agent's destination was the Round Rock Trading Post, where he expected to enroll children from the region for the boarding school at Fort Defiance. Accompanying him was Chee Dodge. At Sehili, Shipley divided his party into three groups, to inform the Indians of his coming and his purpose. He sent two Navaho policemen into Black Horse's region in the Carrizo Mountains; his interpreter, Frank Walker, he sent with two policemen to Canyon de Chelly; his own group, including Chee Dodge, his industrial school teacher, and three policemen, proceeded to Round Rock.

The size of Shipley's police escort might indicate he expected a less than cheerful welcome from the Indians whose children he wished

3 A year after he and Aldrich built the Sehili Trading Post, Clark sold out his interest in the Manuelito and Sehili stores to Sweetland. Sweetland became the sole owner of Sehili about 1889. In the summers, when the Navahos brought their sheep from the lowlands up into the mountains, the post did well. But trade dwindled away to almost nothing with the deep snows of fall and winter. Sweetland put up with the seasonal handicap as long as he could and finally abandoned the post on November 14, 1892. (N. A., Ledgers of Traders.) Thomas Parker, who once freighted for Aldrich and Dodge, told me that before Aldrich and Clark opened the Sehili post, they operated a trading post one winter and summer in 1882 or 1883 at Black Salt, five miles due west of Crystal. Parker was in his eighties when we met, at his home near Crystal in 1960, blind, nearly deaf, living with a Navaho wife. Van Valkenburgh preferred the spelling "Tsalee," and gave also the Navaho spelling, "Tsehili," meaning "Where Water Enters a Box Canyon."

to take off to school. In any case, opposition did appear, and quickly, when Black Horse rode up to the Round Rock post with a number of his well-armed followers. Not a chief, but one of the most influential head men of the northern part of the reservation, Black Horse was the sort of man whose presence dominated nearly any group he entered. Traders who knew him say he stood an inch or two over six feet.[4] He was remarkably articulate, dynamic, and filled with prejudices which, already reaching to the heart roots of most Navahos, he was gifted, with oratory, to bring boiling to the surface.

As many of the two factions as could find standing room crowded into the trading post, Shipley opening a council that soon locked in heated argument.[5] His quota of children from this area was thirty-four. He spoke of what already had been done at the boarding school for the children's advancement. Resistance on the part of the parents would be abusing the confidence and generosity of the government that since Bosque Redondo had treated them well. He reminded Black Horse of the Navahos' past offenses, crushed by the soldiers "when from starvation they were compelled to surrender as prisoners of war in 1862 and 1863." All of this was true enough, but salt to wounded Navaho pride; and now his words became threatening.

"I assured them," he said later, "to what their opposition would lead and the punishment that would surely follow if they disregarded my instructions."

Black Horse replied in kind. He knew well the crowded quarters of the boarding school, the sickness of children forced to go there, the bad food. He would not permit children from his region to be taken, and any who had been taken, the agent must turn over to him. His anger flaring as he spoke, Black Horse said the school must be closed, the agency should be abandoned entirely, and traders should be driven from the reservation. In turn, he became threatening. If the agent persisted in this matter of the school, the Navahos would kill him.

"He worked on his followers to such an extent," Shipley said, "that they rushed on me, and very violently overpowered me."

Shipley and one or two of his Navaho policemen were dragged out

---

[4] H. B. Noel, while trading at Teec-nos-pos, knew Black Horse well and was on reasonably good terms with him. "He lived up in the Cove area," Noel told me, "and was a real devil to get along with. I took care of him once when he was sick. When he talked at meetings, his words carried weight. He hated white men."

[5] Shipley described the affair in messages of November 2, 3, and 6, 1892, to Commissioner Morgan, from which his remarks quoted here are taken. (National Archives, Record Group 75, Letters Received, 1892, #40407, #40408, #39851.)

of the post and beaten, the agent receiving a broken nose and bruises and one of his policemen a clubbing over the head. The agent no doubt would have been killed on the spot if others had not intervened.

"A very powerful friendly Navajo," the agent said, "assisted by my police, the trader Chee and his clerk, Mr. Hubbell, succeeded in tearing me away from them and getting me on the inside of the trader's store again."

The door was locked, and from behind iron-barred windows the men inside prepared for a siege. Badly outnumbered, they had for defense only two Winchester rifles, two revolvers, and fifty rounds of ammunition. They could hear members of Black Horse's outfit yelling outside that they would kill the agent and all the others in the store. Sometime later in the day one of the Navaho policemen succeeded in getting away without being seen and started back toward the agency for help. Those inside settled down to wait, Agent Shipley fearful that at any moment the store would be burned down around them. Aside from the nearly fireproof construction of the building, this was made entirely impossible when a hard, continuing rain set in, wetting down everything but the anger of the besiegers.

"The Indians were frantic and chided themselves for not having killed me and the rest of the party when they had the opportunity," Shipley said. "We were subjected to this very uncertain suspense for nearly thirty-six hours, with the Indians continuing their threats throughout the entire time. I was compelled to make all sorts of promises to this gang of thieves and murderers in order to partially pacify them."

Shipley did not afterwards disclose what promises he had made, but evidently they were sufficient to divert Black Horse's people from further violence. The siege of the trading post, by now half-hearted, was ended with the arrival of Lieutenant Brown and ten soldiers, summoned from Sehili where they were found by the Navaho policeman who had escaped.

The agent and his party were allowed to return to Fort Defiance— but they returned without any of the children Shipley had expected to take back. Shipley requested that the Indian Office support him in this affair and help him to bring Black Horse in for punishment, but nothing further was done and the episode presently was forgotten.

After his replacement as agent in 1893 by Lieutenant E. H. Plummer, Shipley dropped into obscurity but evidently did not leave the country. Eight years later he turned up in Gallup, where he applied for a license to trade with the Navahos. The license was granted April

28, 1905, and then, for no reason mentioned in the Indian Office records, was revoked the following month.[6]

An abler man than Shipley, certainly a more durable one, Superintendent Reuben Perry came as close to death at the hands of his Navahos—the incident occurring at Chinle, Arizona, late in October or early November, 1905. The trader who interceded for him was Charles Cousins, a young man whose early background in some respects parallels that of Thomas Keam.

The son of Scotch-English parents, Cousins was born and reared in India. After serving in the British merchant marine, he came to the United States, joined the First New Mexico Militia, and later saw action in the Geronimo campaign with C Troop, Sixth Cavalry. He was discharged at Fort Wingate in 1896, and, liking the country, went into trading. His first position was manager for Lorenzo Hubbell's post at Cornfields, located in the valley of the Pueblo Colorado Wash about ten miles southwest of Ganado. Then for a time he worked in Gallup for C. N. Cotton. About 1903, after his marriage to Lucie Randolph, he worked for Stephen Aldrich at Manuelito. In early 1905, Sam Day sold his trading post at Chinle to Charlie Weidemeyer of Fort Defiance and at Weidemeyer's request Cousins went to Chinle in the spring to run the post. It was the only trading store operating at Chinle at that time.[7]

Lucie Cousins remained in Gallup for a few weeks that spring while her husband got settled at Chinle and then started out by stage to join him. Snow blocked the road at Fort Defiance, forcing her to stay there nearly a week, as guest of the trader Monroe Holloway and his wife.

"When Mr. Holloway thought the snow had melted enough for us to get through," Mrs. Cousins has recalled, "he found an Indian with a team and wagon who would take me to Ganado. It wasn't far

[6] Shipley's license was canceled May 15, 1905. There is no ledger entry, as in a number of similar cases, to give the reason. (*N. A., Ledgers of Traders.*)

[7] When Cousins went to Chinle it was with the understanding that, should he wish, he could buy a part ownership and eventually become sole owner. He did not accept this offer, however, and after a few years left Chinle to work for Weidemeyer at Mariano Lake and then at Fort Defiance. In 1909 he built his own post at Whitewater, twenty miles south of Gallup. This post, no longer standing, he sold in 1925 to Charlie Davis, and moved nearer to Zuñi. The post he built there is now operated by his son Tom. The part her husband took in the Chinle episode was related to me by Mrs. Lucie Cousins during two interviews at her home at Cousins Trading Post, in February, 1959. Another version of the same affair appeared in the Gallup *Independent*, September 29, 1957. Mr. Cousins died in 1940.

—perhaps forty miles—and after leaving early in the morning we arrived at the Hubbell place at nine o'clock that night.

"Lorenzo Hubbell came out to meet me. First thing, he asked where we were going. When I said to Chinle, he told me we couldn't possibly get there. Melting snow and rain had filled the Colorado Wash so we couldn't cross it, and the washes and roads beyond were impassable.

"He asked me if I was Charlie Cousins' wife and when I said yes, I was, he said, 'You aren't going any further. You get down from that wagon and stay with us.' He took me into the house, where I met Mrs. Hubbell, and showed me a room.

" 'That's your room,' he said, 'and you make yourself comfortable. We get up early here'—I found this was true, he was always up and busy by six o'clock—'and if you hear us stirring, don't bother. Sleep as late as you like.'

"Another week passed and then Mr. Hubbell thought it was safe for me to go on. He had a Mexican who worked for him take me up to Chinle."

The post her husband operated was built in 1902 by Sam Day, Sr. The location was a treeless level space at the mouth of Canyon de Chelly, one hundred yards or so south of the wash. From logs square-hewed and cemented with adobe, Day built the trading post sixty feet long and twenty feet wide, facing east toward the canyon. Covering the log walls was a pitched roof of corrugated iron. Windows were of standard size, the sills only three feet from the ground, and, of course, were protected by iron bars. Connecting with the store and the wareroom and rug room, at the north end, were the owners' quarters, a single log room with a flat roof, the roof timbers on the east side projecting about five feet to support a porch shade of brush. A year or two before he sold the post to Weidemeyer, Day increased the living quarters by adding a small wing projecting eastward at right angles to the main building.[8]

Charlie Cousins had been an Indian trader for almost nine years, but in the fall of 1905 could count less than eight months' acquaintance with the Chinle Navahos. He was, therefore, still something of a

---

8 Three photographs of the Day post were made by Day's good friend, Ben Wittick, about 1890. One of these, reproduced in Amsden's *Navaho Weaving* (Pl. 85b) is incorrectly identified as "the present García store." Camille García occupied the original old Hubbell post, about a mile to the west. After a succession of owners, the Day store became famous among tourists as Cozy McSparron's Thunderbird Ranch.

stranger to these Indians, and on terms of less than mutual trust, when the sudden arrival of Superintendent Perry nearly provoked an uprising.

Perry came to Chinle on various matters of agency business, driving his own buckboard and without an escort. The only safeguard he had taken was to slip a pistol into a coat pocket. Uppermost in his mind was a report that Tol Zhin, a Chinle Navaho, had raped a Navaho woman while she was herding sheep. Tol Zhin was instructed to surrender himself at the agency, but so far had refused. Perry was here now, personally, to arrest him.

A mile west of the Cousins trading post and separated from it by low sand hills, Perry stopped his carriage at the field matrons' cottage close by the old Hubbell building now occupied by an agency farmer named Speicher. Miss Verda Clapham and Miss Joanna Speers received him there. As field matrons, far from civilization, it was their lonely, hard task to look after the sick and teach such Indian children as could be cajoled into their classroom.

Cousins first learned of the Superintendent's presence when a Navaho horseman rode up to the trading post and in great excitement asked him to come quickly—some of the Indians were "going to kill Mr. Perry."

At the matrons' cottage Cousins found fifteen or twenty Navahos milling in an angry mob around Perry's buckboard. They had dragged him from the seat and now seemed on the point of beating him to death. Two Indians holding Perry's arms to his sides continued to hold him as Cousins approached. Through a yelling clamor the trader was able to piece together the Superintendent's stutter of what was happening.

These were friends of Tol Zhin. Hearing that Perry had come to arrest him, they had swarmed down on the agent, first to protest that Tol Zhin was innocent and then to demand that Perry pardon him. They wanted also the promise of immunity for themselves. One of this band, Winslow, grabbed a bridle of the superintendent's team when Perry mounted the buckboard to drive away, and then when Perry shouted his refusal to their demands and started to draw his revolver, another—Dlad—pinioned his arms and pulled him to the ground. As for the rest—Cousins could hear and see for himself.

The Navahos assured Cousins that they would hold Perry until Tol Zhin was pardoned. Sensing their mood, Cousins told the Superintendent: "I was a soldier, so if you want to make a fight of it, say the word. But it will be our last one."9 He told Perry there were several hundred other Navahos in the vicinity, most of them armed, who would be drawn in by the first sound of gunfire.

Perry saw the reason of this, as he said a few days later, and so "was compelled to grant their request" to pardon Tol Zhin.[10] The Navahos released him, and he was allowed to return to Fort Defiance. Since then, Perry added, "I have learned through other Indians that they said they were anxious that I should have fired a shot at them so they would have had an excuse for murdering me."

He had learned something more, Perry said, almost as an after-thought, in his report to Commissioner Leupp. Tol Zhin was not guilty of rape, "but had endeavored to have carnal intercourse with this woman"—leaving it to the Commissioner to ponder the distinc-tions, legal and social, between intercourse and rape. If Perry at first had been mistaken, however, the difference to him scarcely mattered. Furthermore, the Indians who had assaulted him, with a few rene-gade friends from the Black Mountain region, were a bad lot, known for thievery and encouraging whisky-sellers to come on the reser-vation.

All was quiet for a day or two afterward, and then trouble erupted in two places at once—at Chinle, where Cousins' post was broken into, and at Sam Day's ranch at Cienega Amarilla, where two thousand or more Navahos gathered on November 6 for a *yei-bi-chai* dance.

At Chinle someone forced his way into the post at night, broke the glass in the pawn counter, and scooped up a hatful of silver and tur-quoise jewelry. Cousins had no clue that would identify the thief or thieves, until perhaps a week later, when he noticed that a Navaho lounging in the store was wearing one of the stolen bracelets.

When Cousins asked the man where he had gotten the bracelet, the Navaho replied that he won it in gambling. That might be so, Cous-ins said, but nevertheless it was pawn that had been stolen from him, and so it must be returned.

9 Lucie Cousins supplied these quotations, asserting that she remembered her husband's account of the affair clearly.

10 Perry notified C. I. A. Francis E. Leupp by telegram of the attempt on his life, November 4, 1905, on his return to Fort Defiance. Two days later he submitted a report of the affair, not mentioning the intercession of Cousins. Direct quotations are taken from related correspondence (National Archives, Navaho File 121: let-ters and telegrams of Superintendent Perry, Commissioner Leupp, Acting Secre-tary of War Oliver, Secretary of the Interior Hitchcock, S. M. Brosius, Second Lt. G. A. McElroy, officer in charge of prisoners at Alcatraz Prison, and First Lt. C. Y. Brownlee, assistant surgeon, Post Hospital, Alcatraz. A summary of the case also is contained in the *Annual Report, C. I. A., 1906*).

No, the Indian said, turning slowly to spit on the bull-pen floor, it was his now; he would not give it up. Several other Navahos came into the post, all of them wearing jewelry that Cousins recognized as the stolen pawn. They, too, refused to surrender it on Cousins' demand. In the casually open way in which the Navahos revealed the stolen silver, almost insolently they made it clear that this was the ultimate moment for any new trader—the moment that Cousins' manhood would be tested.

Cousins walked out from behind the counter, locked and bolted the door, and, returning to his position behind the counter, placed a revolver in front of him.

"You will all stay in the store until the pawn is given back," he told them.

A few of the Navahos wore side arms. They looked at Cousins without speaking, and for a time no one moved. The morning hours passed and other Indians came to the post and knocked on the door. Cousins let them in, one at a time. At noon there were about twenty-five Navahos locked in the trading post. The place was quiet; scarcely anyone moved about or said anything.

Lucie Cousins, blithely unaware that anything was wrong, came to tell her husband that his lunch was waiting. He asked her to go back into the house, lock herself in, and keep away from the windows.

"I've got a varmint by the tail," he told her, "and I don't know how to turn it loose."

The afternoon dragged on in quiet, leaden silence, the smoky air in the cramped quarters of the post fouler by the minute. As November's early dusk closed in, Cousins lit an oil lamp, but it seemed only to deepen the shadows. Then, and it was now nearly five o'clock, sounds outside were heard and there was a pounding at the door. Again Cousins opened it—and looked into the faces of a young cavalry officer and the Navaho Welo, a head man of the Fort Defiance area. In the darkness behind them, dimly visible, were the forms of a number of horsemen.

And so Cousins let loose his hold on the varmint. This was a part of Captain H. O. Williard's K Troop, Fifth Cavalry, from Fort Wingate With them, besides Welo, were several other Navaho head men who were volunteers for the assignment that brought them here. They had come to arrest the men who had roughed up Superintendent Perry.

Winslow was found and taken in custody, as was Tol Zhin, who had not participated in the assault at all but, on Perry's second thought, was not to be pardoned (for non-rape) after all. Four others wanted by the troops were not found then: Dlad, Tsosi-begay, Dinet-lakai, and Ush-tilly.[11]

Before the soldiers left with the two prisoners, most of the stolen pawn was recovered and given back to Cousins. And afterwards, when he was asked how many troops appeared at his door so fortuitously, the trader wagged his head. "I don't know—but if you would have asked me then I would have counted forty for every man, it was such a relief to have them there."

Soon after Perry's return to Fort Defiance, and just before things were coming to a head at Chinle, the large gathering of Navahos on the Sam Day place gave some cause for concern. Anticipating a large supply of whisky at the *yei-bi-chai*, Perry on November 6 advised Commissioner Leupp that he would need troops to enforce order.

"The rough class of Indians from Chin Lee and the Black Mountains will be in attendance," he said, "and some believe that at the close of the dance will endeavor to make some trouble."

His request for troops was answered with the prompt dispatch from Wingate of Lieutenant Lewis with a small detachment of cavalry. At Cienega Amarilla, Lewis found no sign of disturbance and was assured by Day that there would be none—that Perry's fears were caused by his unhappy experience at Chinle. On November 9, Lieutenant Lewis reported that the final night of the dance was postponed until the fifteenth, his presence there was no longer needed, and he was returning to his base. Arriving at Fort Wingate on the fourteenth, Lewis again reported there was no likelihood of trouble.

In Washington, where he received by wire the substance of Lewis' report, Acting Secretary of War Robert Shaw Oliver outlined the developments in a telegram to Secretary of the Interior E. A. Hitchcock. He concluded with the remark that "Agent [Perry] thought that renegades might come in and try to break up dance. Others who ought to know consider this very unlikely. Affair is yet a matter for agency police to settle. Full report of Lieut. Lewis by mail."[12]

11 Often there is a wide discrepancy in the spelling of Navaho names. I have taken, for the most part, the spelling used in the official Indian Office correspondence. In Perry's letters the names of the seven Navahos eventually taken prisoner appear as Winslow, Tol Zhin, Gladhy, Tsosa Begay, Denet Lakai, Ush Tilly, and Do-Yal-Ke. Wilken, relying mainly on Fr. Anselm Weber's notes, gives another version of this episode, naming only six of the seven prisoners: Winslow, Linni Dlad, Tsossi ni' Biye, Dinelgai, and Doyaltqihi. (Robert L. Wilken, *Anselm Weber, O. E. M., Missionary to the Navaho.*)

12 Telegram from Acting Secretary Oliver to Secretary E. A. Hitchcock, November 14, 1905. (National Archives, Navaho File 121, #91614.)

Perry was unable to share his calm point of view. The final night of the dance drawing closer by the hour, he sent an urgent message to Fort Wingate. He must have troops, he said. The situation at Cienega Amarilla was more than his Navaho police could handle. Lieutenant Colonel George H. Paddock, Wingate's commanding officer, ordered Captain Williard and K Troop to proceed to the Day ranch.

A setting sun briefly painted the nearby Haystacks on the evening of November 15—the night Perry feared. Through the early hours of darkness, before the dancing began, in a campfire ring composed of hundreds of silent, blanketed Navahos and their wagons and horses, the tribe's best orators spoke in seemingly endless pleas for peace and order. Black Horse, on this occasion firmly on the agent's side, was one of the speakers; Chee Dodge was another.

"Black Horse and several of the headmen have made talks before you, tonight, but they were not strong enough," said Chee Dodge. He spoke at length of the evils of whisky, "for it will destroy you." He warned of punishment if the Navahos disobeyed their agent; he warned of traders who told Navahos that their agent "is no good." Such men, said Chee Dodge, "are lying to you, there is no truth in what they tell you in regard to the agent. The agent is the best friend you have."[13] There was much more, and it was oil on roiled waters. From boyhood, Chee Dodge knew where power lay and how it was exercised.

Shortly before midnight the dancing began, and it continued until daybreak. No incident occurred to mar the affair or alarm anyone, even though Williard's cavalry had not arrived and would not until later that day, November 16. With a finger to the wind, Perry the same morning wired Commissioner Leupp: "Several thousand Indians attended dance which closed this morning. Controlled them through head men. Believe imminent danger avoided. Indians continue to discuss trouble. With moral support of troops believe difficulties can be settled peaceably.[14]

Captain Williard, on arrival, offered his services in bringing in the ringleaders of the assault on Perry at Chinle. Eight influential leaders of the tribe offered to assist. Among them were the widely respected

[13] Excerpts from Chee Dodge's speech, November 16, 1905. (*Ibid.,* #94947.) Dodge was a unique person: politician, diplomat, and realist. Much told and remembered about him is romanticized myth. He is a figure deserving some writer's careful research.

[14] Telegram from Perry to Leupp, November 16, 1905. (*Ibid.,* #91826.)

Peshlakai, or Silversmith, Atsitty-yazzie-begay, Bish-klan, Bechi, Welo, Hosteen Tsosi, Hosteen Dilawishe, and Nosh-gully.

Tol Zhin and Winslow, who were arrested at Chinle, as already noted, were brought in on November 19. A few days later, Dinet-lakai either surrendered himself or was brought to the agency. And then, early in December, Dlad, Tsosi-begay, and Ush-tilly, who had been hiding out in the vicinity of Crystal, gave themselves up to Peshlakai.

Superintendent Perry, meanwhile, on November 30 recommended to Commissioner Leupp that the six Navahos be confined in a military prison: Tol Zhin, Dinet-lakai, and Dlad for two years, the other three for one year. He did not then, or later, present formal charges against the men, and Tol Zhin's offense—as Perry already had admitted in effect—was refusal to be arrested for a crime he had not committed. Collectively, Perry said, "these parties belong to what is known among the tribe as the most vicious, criminal and worthless clan among their people, and . . . are guilty of the greatest number of crimes and misdemeanors committed by the Navajoes."[15]

At a council with a number of the tribal head men on December 8, Perry was informed that a man named Do-yal-ke, who two or three years before was said to have threatened the life of Superintendent Burton, of the Hopi school, was an instigator of the episode at Chinle. Perry ordered Do-yal-ke's arrest, and the Indian was brought in on the nineteenth by several of the head men. It was recommended that his sentence in prison be two years.

Informed that the prisoners were behind bars at Fort Defiance, Commissioner Leupp recommended to Secretary of the Interior Hitchcock that the Navahos be sentenced, for the terms Perry suggested, to hard labor in Alcatraz Prison. It would not be necessary to charge the prisoners formally with any specific crime, nor bring them to trial, the Commissioner believed. He explained: ". . . the offending Indians are not only non-citizens, but among the most ignorant and lawless people with whom the Office has to deal. . . .

". . . The removal of the ringleaders . . . to a remote point would be surrounded with an atmosphere of mystery likely to be very impressive to those who remain at home. . . . All . . . will have very interesting stories to tell their friends of [what] they have seen, and of other wonders . . . and these will go a long way toward quenching any further desire to defy the authority of the government."[16]

Citizens or no, the pleasures of *tourisme* or no, Leupp was not quite

15 Letter from Perry to Leupp, November 30, 1905. (*Ibid.*, #97168.)
16 Letter from Leupp to Hitchcock, December 13, 1905. (*Ibid.*, #12169.)

unaware that these Navahos were being denied certain fundamental rights of law.

"I appreciate the fact that from a strictly technical point of view such a treatment of offenders is anomalous; but, for that matter, so is the reservation system under which the Navajos have been brought up to the present time."

Two wrongs might make, if not right, then—to Leupp's mind, at least—a certain sense. "At the worst," he continued, "what I have here recommended would be but a logical evolution from the existing situation."

Secretary Hitchcock concurred, and with the co-operation of the War Department the seven prisoners were removed from Fort Defiance and, on January 10, 1906, delivered to Alcatraz Island. The damp climate of San Francisco Bay, so different from the dry Arizona air, was part of the logical evolution: three of the Navahos entered the prison hospital with respiratory ailments, said to be minor.

The case was not to go unnoticed, however. In April, 1906, the Indian Rights Association intervened. An investigation of the whole affair was proposed, and in the meantime S. M. Brosius, agent for the association, suggested that the prisoners "should be removed without delay to a dryer climate."[17]

Perhaps to forestall public exposure of its extra-legal action, the Indian Office, which at the outset had insisted upon "hard labor in a military prison" as most likely to produce Leupp's desired "atmosphere of mystery," swiftly softened in its position. Superintendent Perry, as before, indicated the way. He recommended that the prisoners be removed to "a post which is not a prison" somewhere in the Southwest. He observed that "prison life is so different from their free outdoor life that it will have a bad effect," and recommended shortening the two-year terms of the principal offenders.[18]

"But the Indians must understand," he added, "that such a request is made by the Indian Department and not by the Indian Rights people."

In August, 1906, the seven Navahos were taken from Alcatraz to Fort Huachuca in the southeastern corner of Arizona. With records of good behavior, Winslow, Tsosi-begay, and Ush-tilly were released to Fort Defiance on October 20, 1906. Tol Zhin, Dlad, Dinet-lakai, and Do-yal-ke were released in June, 1907.

[17] Letter from Brosius to Leupp, May 8, 1906. (*Ibid.*, #40779.)
[18] Letter from Perry to Leupp, July 18, 1906. (*Ibid.*, #68024.)

21

The San Juan Valley

THE RIVER BEGINS as a clear rivulet, from springs and brooks in the San Juan Mountains of Colorado. From Arboles to the Four Corners the river swings a thin arc across the northwestern tip of New Mexico, running silty and shallow. Past Bluff, Utah, the channel cuts deeper, and below Mexican Hat enters the tortuous gorge of the Goosenecks. Some fifty miles beyond and not far above the Crossing of the Fathers, the waters merge with the Río Colorado.

Some say that Juan María de Rivera named the San Juan River for himself when he first saw and forded it, probably in 1765. Other Spanish explorers knew it as the Río de Nabajóo, and thus it appears on the map Miera y Pacheco drew to accompany the diary of Father Escalante. Either way, Pacheco had in mind the confluence of this river and the tributary Animas as site for a presidio, or settlement, for the pagan, unco-operative Hopis. The Moquis, he advised the king of Spain in 1777, should be moved "by force from their cliffs" and resettled in this valley, to provide "a rich and strong province" adjoining or united to Spanish New Mexico.[1] Nothing, of course, came of the idea.

---

[1] A native of Burgos, Spain, Bernardo Miera y Pacheco settled in El Paso del Norte in 1743, held title as engineer and captain of militia of El Paso, and from there led five campaigns against the Apaches. Moving to Santa Fe, he was appointed *alcalde* and military captain of the frontier of Pecos and Galisteo. After accompanying the Domínguez and Escalante expedition of 1776, he wrote to the king of Spain, October 26, 1777, advocating that presidios be established for the Hopis at the "Valle de Timpanogos," in the vicinity of Utah Lake, and "at the junction of the River of Nabajóo with that of Las Animas, along the beautiful and exten-

Other than Pacheco's proposal for the Hopis, little specific reference to the San Juan Valley is found in Spanish records. We may still be sure, though, that the valley was well known to Spanish traders and explorers, who named the river's tributaries: Piedra, Los Pinos, Las Animas, La Plata, and Mancos. The San Juan itself historically has been regarded as roughly a boundary separating the Navahos, on the south, and the three bands of Southern Utes—the Wiminuches, Capotes, and Moaches—who ranged north of the river from Sierra Abajo to the mountains above Taos.

One hundred years after Rivera, American settlers moved into the upper valley, about 1865 building fifty houses in the vicinity of modern Aztec, on the Animas. Who they were and what happened to them is not known. The Utes and Navahos possibly made them unwelcome. In any case, their houses were abandoned and they were gone by 1868.[2]

The Hendrickson brothers, William and Simeon, rode their horses up the valley in 1875. They avoided difficulty with the Indians and "saw no white men along the San Juan." From Animas City in Colorado they had followed Mancos Creek through Mancos Canyon to the San Juan and then turned eastward, passing Pacheco's chosen spot for a Hopi presidio. The following spring they returned with friends and at a place the Navahos call *Toh'tah*, they built the first house on the site of future Farmington.[3] With the vanguard of settlers who followed was Benjamin Keene McGalliard. Originally a resident of Trinidad, Colorado, McGalliard lived in Parrott City before coming to the San Juan in the fall of 1876. Here, at the mouth of the Animas, he built and operated the valley's first trading post. He remained only a short time, moving in 1877 to Animas City.

Settlement of the valley in 1876 resulted from an executive order

---

sive meadows which its margins provide for raising crops, together with the convenience of the timber, firewood and pastures which they offer." Pacheco found precedence for his proposal in the large number of *anasazi* ruins in the region: "There still remain in those meadows vestiges of irrigation ditches, ruins of many large and ancient settlements of Indians, and furnaces where apparently they smelted metals." The "furnaces" certainly were not for reducing metal ore, but probably were burned-out subsurface kivas. Pacheco's letter, quoted here in part, is translated by Herbert E. Bolton in *Pageant in the Wilderness*, and Herbert S. Auerbach in "Father Escalante's Journal with Related Documents and Maps," *Utah Historical Quarterly*, Vol. XI (1943).

2 *Annual Report, C. I. A., 1868.*

3 John Arrington is my informant. The Navaho word *Toh'tah*, meaning among, or between, the waters, applies to present Farmington, between the Animas and San Juan.

by President Grant, opening to public domain this region which three years before had been set aside as a reservation for the Jicarilla Apaches. No agency had been built, however, and the Jicarillas remained far to the east, unhappily divided between the agencies at Abiquiu and Cimarron. Adobe and log houses were raised in Farmington and downriver twelve miles, at Fruitland, where the valley is broad and level, the Mormon families of Benjamin T. Boice and Jeremiah Hatch settled in early spring, 1878. Other Mormons joined them or settled two miles east at the place John Moss named Olio.

And why Olio? Moss, who was not a Mormon and who wanted to open a post office in his small store, was informed by post office officials that first the unnamed community needed a handle. Moss turned to his dictionary and found Olio: "any mixture, a hodge podge, or potpourri"—because here were Mormons, Gentiles, Navahos, and Utes.

The Indians were friendly to them, but to be sure they were safe, the Mormons at Fruitland built the semblance of a fort on the Walter Stevens ranch. "It was made," according to one account, "of large Mexican adobes, with no windows or doors on the south or west [and] faced the east and north in an L. . . . It contained about nine or ten rooms with a large dugout . . . in the front. . . . This fort housed the Stevens families and when the [Luther C.] Burnhams and others came to the valley they were all made welcome there until they could get established in homes of their own."[4] The fort never was used defensively.

Albert Farnsworth, also a Mormon, came to Fruitland about 1884 and opened a small trading post. Farnsworth was liked by the Navahos, and apparently his post did well. Neighboring Olio, meanwhile, was less able to justify its whimsical name, as more families moved in from Utah, and in the 1890's Olio was changed to Kirtland, for the early Mormon town of the same name in Ohio.

Eight miles west of Fruitland a high barrier of scaly rock narrows the valley to its river bed. Seen from distant hills or the air, the formation resembles the backbone of some reptilian monster caught in the earth's crust. The head of the Hogback, as it is called, rests near the fossilized seashell beds of The Meadows, above Waterflow; the spiny tail disappears in the desert twenty-five miles to the south, above Bennett's Peak. A natural cut or gap through the Hogback allows a narrow passage for the river and the road to Shiprock.

---

4 Mrs. Arthur Tanner, "History of the Settling of Fruitland and Kirtland," unpublished manuscript. Mrs. Tanner is the daughter-in-law of trader Joe Tanner.

In the river bottomland, at the eastern foot of the barrier, a man named Hank Hull built one of the valley's first trading posts.[5] Twice, as the river changed course, the store was moved to higher ground. Hull himself moved away, about 1900, when he sold the Hogback post to his nephew, Harry Baldwin. The Navahos did not lament Hull's departure but may, in fact, have hastened it. Old people of the valley remember a pastime of the younger Indians: perching in the rocks high above the post, they waited for Hull to come out; seeing him, they aimed their rifles to place the shots close but without hitting him. It is said that Hull became a nervous, irritable man.

A shooting of serious import occurred near the post about 1894. A man named Welch, who worked for Hull, was irrigating his land when he quarreled with a Navaho and was killed. The affair divided the valley settlers against the Navahos, nearly one thousand of the Indians, all armed, gathering under Chief Kasti-anna between Hull's store and Kirtland. Clay Brimhall, one of the Mormon residents of Fruitland, rode his horse through The Meadows to Durango, where he telegraphed to Fort Wingate for troops. The entire valley was tensed and ready for war when two days later a company of cavalry arrived and went into camp on the sand bluffs south of Fruitland. Even then the situation was dangerous. Sheriff Al Dustin spoke with the troop's commander, asking for time before the cavalry moved closer. Dustin then persuaded the Navaho who killed Welch to surrender, and the man was taken under arrest to Wingate. A week or ten days later the Wingate troop rode out of the quiet valley.[6]

The Hogback post again was the cause of a large gathering of Navahos—this time peacefully—when Joe Tanner celebrated his buying the store from Baldwin by giving a two-day feast and "sing." Nearly every Indian in the valley rode in by horseback or wagon.[7] It was a

[5] The year when the Hogback post was built is uncertain. An old board from Hank Hull's original trading counter is marked in ink or paint with the date September 19, 1871. The Wheeler family believes that this establishes the year Hull started trading on the river bottom. I would regard this doubtfully. Others in the valley acknowledge the Hogback store as "one of the oldest," but believe that Hull did not appear on the scene until the 1880's.

[6] Interview with John Arrington. There is disagreement over Kasti-anna's background, some saying he was a renegade Apache, others that he was half Apache, half Navaho. Arrington says that Kasti-anna had no Apache lineage, but was half Laguna and half Navaho. His home was in The Meadows above Waterflow, a place also referred to as Ute Pasture.

[7] The Gallup *Independent,* August 3, 1916: "Joe Tanner who recently bought the Baldwin trading post, gave his opening celebration Saturday and Sunday. . . . There was more than 1,000 Indians in attendance and races, chicken pull, etc. were in progress all the time. The big dance in the evening was well attended."

glorious beginning for Tanner's short term of ownership; a year later the post was sold to Wilfred Wheeler and Albert Hugh Lee, the former becoming sole owner in 1918.

Located one hundred yards outside the reservation's eastern line, the Hogback post once was a favored market place for Navaho livestock. Wheeler has recalled that his warehouse might still be filled with the spring wool clip when the Navahos in the fall came to sell him their cattle, sheep, and horses. It was not uncommon for a Navaho family to drive in 200 or 300 head of sheep or as many as 150 head of cattle. Nor was Wheeler's trade entirely with the Indians. One of his good customers between 1917 and 1920 was Ben Wetherill, son of John and Louisa, who "used to bring a string of mules over, regularly, from Kayenta. He would load the mules here and then drive them all the way back." Ben's trail was a dusty one—by way of Teecnos-pos, Mexican Water, and Dinnehotso—and long: about one hundred miles.

Other early traders in or from this part of the valley included Alison F. Miller and two Englishmen, Ed Thurland and Dick Simpson. Miller was one of the first settlers of Farmington, operating a general store and the town's first post office. In 1888 he was issued a license to trade with the Navahos at a place they called *Sai ha'atiin*, or Sun Coming Out, and which white men knew as Sulphur Springs. Near Ford's Butte, in the Chuska Valley, the store should have done well. Navaho hogans and cornfields were numerous and the people prospered, owning many sheep and horses. After a year, however, Miller sold out, and his successor, Stephen A. Booten, remained only until May, 1891.[8] The post then was abandoned.

Ed Thurland was a quiet man of whom little is known or told. After coming to this country from England, he settled near Waterflow in the late 1890's, operating a small trading post at The Meadows. It is said that he joined the Mormon church, and after Kasti-

---

[8] Ford's Butte rises east of Shiprock-Gallup Highway 666, facing the larger and more familiar Bennetts Peak, named for Major Frank Tracy Bennett, agent to the Navahos in 1869–71 and 1880–81. No trace of the Miller-Booten store remains, but in recent years the spring has been improved and a concrete catch-basin built for Navaho livestock. Miller's license, issued October 24, 1888, named W. N. Wallace and Milton Virden as clerks. Booten, who came from Houck's Tank, Arizona, was licensed to trade at the springs from November 30, 1889. (*N. A., Ledgers of Traders.*) John Arrington recalls that Miller's post "was on the old freight road from the Hogback. We used to camp there when I was a kid driving cattle. The water would collick the horses, but if you dipped it out and let it stand it was all right. Miller got into a fight with a Navaho there and troops were called before the trouble was over."

anna's death married his widow and helped in bringing up her Navaho children.

Dick Simpson, who became one of the best known of the valley traders, was not a quiet man. Slightly under six feet tall, and slender, he was "always a great favourite with the ladies," a man "proud and determined even to rashness, kindly and generous to a fault, very excitable."[9] Besides this, he at various times had four wives, two of them Navaho women; he drank "heavily" in the opinion of friends who themselves were heavy drinkers; his drinking and his generosity led him to dissipate a small fortune. The Navahos knew him as *Hosteen Ya-hay*, or Mr. Talk.

Simpson was thirty years old, experienced only as a bank cashier and stockbroker, when he reached the San Juan, by way of Albuquerque, in 1893. For three years he farmed and raised sheep at Olio, then sold out to build a trading post in Gallegos Canyon. This heads on the south bank of the San Juan two miles east of Farmington. The canyon is said to have derived its name, first as Cañon Giago, when a Mexican scout of that name was killed near the canyon mouth in 1859 by Navahos.[10] Simpson's post was down the canyon fourteen miles, on the north side of the Gallegos Wash. Before his arrival there, the place had been headquarters for the Kansas–New Mexico Land and Cattle Company—also called the Carlisle Cattle Company—a rough frontier outfit continually embroiled in range disputes with the Navahos and any others who came on the unfenced land. It is told that seven Mexican sheepherders were killed by cowboys in the 1880's, the shooting taking place on the old Farmington-Gallup road where it climbs a hill a few hundred yards south of Simpson's store.[11]

In acquiring the Gallegos land, Simpson fell heir to the large barn and corrals abandoned a few years before by the Carlisle outfit. These he maintained, building his L-shaped adobe trading post across the road, facing east, and near it a well-house for his stock and a three-room dwelling for himself. The store was of average size, twelve by twenty-five feet, with the usual high counters facing the entrance and enclosing the bull-pen. Opening off the store were two warerooms and an office for his manager. Across the rear of the building were

9 Letter from Dick Simpson's younger brother, Cecil Simpson, July 25, 1945, to Mrs. Kenneth Wynn of Farmington, Dick's daughter by his third wife, Annie Mae Youre.

10 Frank D. Reeve, "A Navaho Struggle for Land," *New Mexico Historical Review*, Vol. XXI, No. 1 (1946).

11 Interview with Kenneth Washburn, of the Gallegos Sheep and Mercantile Company.

quarters for his help, always three to five people, who assisted in the store or ran his stock. Walls of the low building were the thickness of two adobes, or about ten inches. The sloping flat roof was of packed earth. Adjoining the barn Simpson built a granary, blacksmith shop, and guest house, for it was a rare day or week when travelers did not stop and ask for food and lodging.

"There was a lot of travel on the road in those days," Kenneth Washburn once recalled, "and Simpson liked to have people stop overnight with him. He liked to have a lot of people around."

The dirt road then was the main highway to Gallup or to Albuquerque by way of Chaco Canyon, and also for travelers to Durango and other towns in Colorado. The road continued to be used until the early 1920's when more direct, modern highways left it unused and forgotten.

"In the winter," Washburn said, "people traveled right down the wash to the mouth of the Gallegos. In the summer they cut east of the wash up over the hill, where you can still see wagon trails." Either way, the roads emerged near the river ford at Corkins' Crossing. "When the river was in flood it sometimes took a week or two to get across. You would often see a lot of wagons camped on the south side, waiting for the water to go down. If a man was in a hurry to get home to the missus, of course, he could unhitch his horses and ride them across, come back later for his wagon. But in those days no one was in a hurry and time didn't mean much."

Simpson traded for horses when he first came to the Gallegos, but soon gave that up in favor of sheep, which he owned in large numbers. Responsibility for the livestock usually fell to his manager—for some time, Lester Setzer, whom the Navahos knew as *Klinch chugee*, or Stud Horse. Setzer moved on to open a post of his own farther east, his place being taken by Joe Hatch, a son of the Mormon trader Ira Hatch. Young Hatch was still clerking for Simpson, however, when a question involving sheep arose during one of Simpson's long sessions with the bottle. Finally, Hatch has recalled, after the last bottle was gone and after a week's confinement, Simpson emerged to stand blinking in the doorway "and saw thousands of sheep grazing over the hills across the wash. He called to the man who was running the place for him then, and said: 'All those sheep out there will use up our water. Find out who owns them and buy them.' The manager told Dick the sheep were his already. He had bought them while Dick was on his bender."

The quality of weaving in this region had not yet declined, and

Simpson did a large trade in good blankets. One of his best weavers also was his wife, Yana-pah, who was among the first of the Navahos to introduce a *Yei* design in her blankets. It is said that she did few of these, however, limiting the design to a single large figure of one of the mythical Navaho deities.[12] After Yana-pah's death in 1912, Simpson married Annie Mae Youre, also a Navaho but not a weaver.

From his family in England, Simpson occasionally received large sums of money which, added to the income of his trading post, enabled him to go into a number of enterprises which were not always successful. In 1921 he bought the Aneth Trading Post, but sold it five years later to Bob Smith, who had been his manager.[13] About the same time he organized the Simpson Mercantile Company, a wholesale trading house, in Farmington. John Wetherill was one of the outlying traders who bought extensively from the firm. Simpson Mercantile eventually was acquired by Willis Martin and reorganized as the Farmington Mercantile Company.

Simpson became a naturalized citizen and returned to England only once, in 1919, called by his mother's illness. And at least once, it appears, some members of his family came to see him, Kenneth Washburn recalling that "there's a story that his people came over from England, and he met them in Denver. Wouldn't let them come any farther because he didn't want them to see his place here.[14]

Events stirring to the west and north, in the vicinity of Tuba City, presaged interesting developments for the San Juan Valley. Conflict

12 Mrs. Kenneth Wynn told me that Yana-pah wove only four *Yei* blankets, one of which is now in her possession. Measuring 4'4" by 6'5", the blanket has a black and red border. The large *Yei* figure, filling the central area, is predominantly tan against a gray background. Amsden pictures an almost identical *Yei* blanket (*Navaho Weaving*, Pl. 53; see also p. 106) as done by "the wife of an Indian trader" near Farmington who "did a thriving business, turning out one *Yei* blanket after another." I think Amsden unquestionably referred to Yana-pah, and perhaps was mistaken about the number of *Yei* blankets she made. Amsden elsewhere notes that Simpson "recalled selling indigo in his trading store until 1905, when the demand, which had been failing for some time, ceased to justify its continuance. He bought the dyestuff in lumps from an Eastern supply house, selling it at two or three dollars a pound. A bit could be broken from the lump and sold by weight to the customers."

13 The same Bob Smith, with his brother Merritt, built Toadlena Trading Post in 1909. Their younger brother, Taylor (Pat) Smith was killed by Navahos at Tucker's Store in 1918, as related in another chapter.

14 Simpson was born May 17, 1863, at Park Cottage, Devises, a town in Wiltshire, England, the third child in a family of four brothers and one sister. His father was owner of the daily Wiltshire *Gazette*, which later became the London *Gazette*. At the age of sixteen Dick Simpson left school to become clerk in the Wilts &

over water rights and land use for some time had troubled Navahos and Mormons in the Tuba City–Moenkopi area. In 1896, Navaho Agent Constant Williams querulously noted that the government had taken no action on his "repeated recommendations" to drive the Mormons out.[15] Shortly thereafter action was taken by the Indian Office to include the Mormon land in a western extension of the Navaho reservation. In November, 1902, the government began apportioning $45,000 to nineteen Mormon families remaining near Tuba, and by early the next year all had moved away. Thus closed the book on the pioneer colony founded through Jacob Hamblin's efforts in 1875.

A number of the dispossessed, traveling by foot, horseback, and wagon, came to the San Juan at Fruitland and Kirtland. Among them was a stiff, black-frocked, white-bearded patriarch—Joseph Lehi Foutz, husband of three wives and father of thirteen sons and sixteen daughters. Their arrival in the valley was not quite so overwhelming as this sounds, as Joseph's first wife, Amanda, and her children had returned earlier to Ogden, Utah.

Family records say that the Foutz clan originated in Germany, where the name appeared variously as Pfauts, Pfouts, Pfauss, and Pfaus—all deriving from the ancient German word *Faucher,* which means spitter, or "one making sounds of rage, like the snorting of an angry bull."[16]

Joseph Lehi was a strict disciplinarian and, when occasion arose, could snort like a bull. Of medium stature, he was totally unafraid of any man. Once when freighting in Arizona he came upon a stranger's wagon mired in mud. A second stranger arrived on the scene at the

Dorset Bank at Devises, later moving to a branch of that bank at Bath. After transfer to the Shaftesbury branch as cashier, he resigned in November, 1890, to become a stockbroker in London, but the change was not a success and he came to the United States in 1892. His first marriage, to Ellen Clarke of Folkestone, England, ended in separation, Ellen later dying aboard ship en route to India to visit relatives. His second (common law) and third marriages, while at Gallegos Canyon, are related here. Simpson sold the Gallegos store in 1927 to the Progressive Mercantile Company and moved to Farmington. Here he married Helen F. Gage of Durango and operated a small grocery store until his death April 15, 1945.

15 *Annual Report, C. I. A., 1896.*
16 For information relating to the Foutz family I have relied upon unpublished family genealogies prepared by Grace Foutz Boulter, Mary Foutz Corrigan, and Alice Parker Foutz; also upon interviews with Eva Foutz Noel, daughter of Joseph Lehi by his third wife; his sons, Al and Hugh; and his grandson, Russell Foutz. In the Boulter-Corrigan genealogy it is noted that "during the years when polygamists were being persecuted, Joseph Lehi was able to evade the officers as a fugitive. He spent one year in Old Mexico. When he returned from there he brought with him Susan Judd, who was his third wife. He jokingly remarked that he would just as 'lief' be hung for a sheep as a lamb."

same time and made no sign of stopping to help. Joseph jumped to the ground, peeled off his coat, and challenged the second man—who was larger than he—to raise his fists and prepare for a beating. His bigger opponent warned him of his disadvantage, to which Joseph replied, 'Even so, I can whip any man that is small enough to pass up a fellow traveler in this kind of trouble." He then proceeded to do so. Afterwards the two together helped the first man out of the mud.

A friend and exploring companion of Jacob Hamblin, Joseph moved his family from Utah to Arizona in 1877, spending one season operating Lee's Ferry and the trading post on the Colorado. From there the Foutzes moved south to Moenkopi, and then settled at Moenave, where Joseph bought the former home and land of John D. Lee. It is said that while the family was here and before moving to the San Juan, Joseph traded for a time at Tonalea. The home at Fruitland was Joseph's last. He died there in March, 1907, as six of his sons were beginning unusual careers as Indian traders.

Junius, or June, Foutz, the eldest of these sons, had worked for C. H. Algert at the latter's Tuba City post, and so now was the natural leader of his younger brothers, Alma, Hugh, Jess, Leroy, and Luff. Together, and with their sons later, they at one time owned or operated twenty trading posts in New Mexico, Utah, and Arizona.[17] The range of their interests and holdings, probably unmatched by any other family of traders, owed its start, if indirectly, to Algert.

Though not a Mormon, Algert had thoroughly identified himself with the Mormon community at Tuba City. When the Mormons were removed from Tuba in 1902–1903, Algert followed his friends to Fruitland and established the C. H. Algert Company, a wholesale trading store housed in a two-story building constructed of brick, adobe, and cement. He remained in control only a few years, moving to California after selling out to June and Al Foutz and their brothers-in-law, Bert and Sheldon Dustin. Each of the four partners paid four thousand dollars for his interest and the firm was reorganized as the Progressive Mercantile Company, with merchandise valued at about ten thousand dollars.[18]

---

[17] These posts included: in New Mexico—Beclabito, Tocito, Sa-nos-tee, Smith Lake, Burnham's (Teec-tso-secad,) Bisti, Whitewater, Pinedale, Shiprock Trading Company, Sheep Springs; in Utah—Aneth; in Arizona—Red Rock, Teec-nos-pos, Red Mesa, Dinnehotso, Piñon, Sawmill, Wide Ruins, and Hunter's Point. Sons of the six brothers who have maintained the family name at some of these posts are Russell Foutz, son of Al; Munro, son of Hugh; Ed, son of Luff; and Clay, Philip, and Keith, sons of Leroy Foutz.
[18] Interview with Al Foutz.

Under Foutz-Dustin management Progressive Mercantile soon justified the optimism of its name. "We bought our supplies from salesmen or directly from the Ilfelds' Gallup Mercantile Company," Al Foutz has recalled. "A round trip to Gallup by wagon took eight to ten days, and we had teams on the road nearly all the time—six-horse teams with wagon and trailer."

Within a short time the partners were supplying half of the trading posts in the region. As suppliers they were in strategic position to move in when a promising area for a new post opened up or a trader at an established post decided to sell out. Al Foutz's son Russell once explained the firm's usual procedure: "When Progressive Mercantile bought a trading post, the partners would find a young married man to run it for them and give him a one-fourth interest in the store." More often than not the young married man was a member of the family, either son, half-brother, or nephew. In this way the firm bought H. B. Noel's Teec-nos-pos store. Al Foutz managed it for a short time and then turned it over to his sons, first to Edwin L. Foutz and then to Russell. Also the owners of Progressive Mercantile might buy a trading post in their own names, individually, or with outside partners. Thus, in 1927, Dick Simpson's Gallegos store was bought by Al Foutz, Corlis Stolworthy, Ace Palmer, and Sheldon Dustin. Al Foutz later bought out the others and gave the management and a half-interest to his son Russell.[19]

Other sons of Joseph Lehi Foutz, although not partners in Progressive Mercantile, did well as traders. Jess Foutz, with a man named Sante Bowen, built Tocito (Warm Water) Trading Post about 1913, first trading from a hogan, which later was incorporated in the post's east wing and wareroom. Seven miles northwest, Jess and another partner, John Walker, bought the Sa-nos-tee post, which Frank Noel had sold to Progressive Mercantile. Hugh Foutz bought the Beclabito post, on the road to Teec-nos-pos, and later bought Sa-nos-tee.[20] Le-

19 After buying Simpson's post the new owners abandoned Simpson's buildings and located a new post one and one-quarter miles to the north—where better water was found—naming it the Gallegos Sheep and Mercantile Company. Kenneth Washburn bought a one-third ownership in 1949. In 1958, Washburn said that 95 per cent of the Gallegos firm's business came from running 600 head of cattle on about 35,000 acres of land.

20 Beclabito Trading Post, located on the northeast slope of the Carrizo Mountains, was built by Billy Hunter in 1911. In building the store, H. B. Noel once told me, Hunter used lumber which was washed down the San Juan in the flood of that year. Hunter sold out to an old-time freighter named Biffle Morris, who in 1924 sold to Hugh Foutz. Russell Foutz bought the post in 1953.

roy Foutz once owned Burnham's Teec-tso-secad post and Bisti, and was a partner in the Sweetwater post.[21]

Eventually, Progressive Mercantile moved from Algert's original building in Fruitland to a building owned by Willis Martin in Farmington. The Charles Ilfeld Company bought an interest in the firm and in 1941 took over sole ownership.

The eastern valley country drained by Largo Canyon and the Chaco was a center of a Navaho population so old that archaeologists still are fitting together the fragmentary pieces of its history. In spite of an early westward movement of the people, many families still remained when white settlers moved into the region. Never a part of the reservation, the early traders therefore left little or no record of themselves and at this distance their names are shadowy.

Little is known, then, of Frank Townsend, except that "he was one of the oldest traders in the San Juan country" and operated a small post on the west side of Largo Canyon at its junction with the San Juan River.[22]

A trader named W. B. Haines in 1884 ired the foreman of the Carlisle Cattle Company by luring Navahos to his store—somewhere on the Gallegos.[23] Nothing more than this, of him. Was he related to H. L. Haines, who in 1887 carved notice in the cliff behind Pueblo Bonito, in the Chaco, that his store was "10 miles down canon"? Neither of these men, probably, was kin to John Roger (Doc) Haynes, who came to the Largo in the early 1900's to mix medicine with trading and ranching. A protégé of Doc Haynes, Jim Counselor once observed: "He had an old place three miles north of my post, at the second big rincon. Doc treated Mexicans, Indians, a few whites for whatever ailed 'em. He had ever' damn thing—sheep, mules, cattle, Indian ponies—but he wasn't a rancher, he was a trader."[24]

21 Teec-tso-secad (Big Trees Along the Wash) was built on Brimhall Wash by Roy Burnham about 1927. More commonly known as Burnham's, the post is located thirteen miles east of present Highway 666, midway in the desert between Beautiful Mountain and Washington Pass. A large portion of this book was written at this place in the summer of 1960. Roy Burnham once told me that he started trading in 1918–19 at Tsaya, where he bought out the Blake brothers. He sold Tsaya to his brother-in-law, Corlis Stolworthy, before building Teec-tso-secad.

22 Interview with Jim Counselor. John Arrington recalls that on Townsend's letterhead was this frank statement: "Frank Townsend, Indian Trader. Trader in Sore-back Horses, Scabby Sheep, and Sandy Wool."

23 Reeve, "A Navaho Struggle for Land," *New Mexico Historical Review*, Vol. XXI, No. 1 (1946).

24 Jim Counselor worked for Doc Haynes for a time in 1919. Before that, Coun-

Trubey Canyon heads in the Cíbola Mesa and cuts eastward to enter the Largo. At this place, Van Valkenburgh says, "a settler named Rogers . . . operated a small trading post for the Navajos and Jicarilla Apaches in the 1880s." Henry Trubey, for whom the branch canyon was named, had a small post here also, operating it with his brother John. When the Trubeys came to the Largo is not known, but Jim Counselor said that they were there before 1919.

Traders who came to the region at this time or later included O. J. Carson, of Carson's post on the east fork of the Gallegos; Stokes Carson, who built the original Huerfano store, eight miles south of the present Bloomfield-Cuba highway; and Wilfred L. and Jim Brimhall. Wilfred, better known as Tabby Brimhall, built the Blanco Trading Post, at the north road entrance to Chaco Canyon, and his brother Jim built and operated Nageezi, a few miles farther east.

Across the mesas and valleys to the southwest, on the outer fringe of the San Juan, other posts were built for the Chuska Valley trade. Of these, the post most remote from the San Juan was Brimhall's Store, built by Alma James Brimhall, an early settler in Fruitland and father of Tabby and Jim Brimhall.

Farther north in the Chuska Valley, Thomas C. Bryan and Charlie Virden in 1880–81 built the Naschiti Trading Post, one of the first to occupy the eastern slopes of the Chuskas. The store's name derives from Badger Springs, which rises in the vicinity of the store on Salt Springs Wash. Bryan, a tall Irishman, was known to the Navahos as *Bekin-de-giz*, a reference to his flattened and twisted nose. Virden was Bryan's brother-in-law and an early settler of Farmington. John Arrington says that Virden also built a small trading post south of the San Juan near the mouth of La Plata River, sometime between 1882 and 1884, but abandoned it a year later. The Naschiti post was sold

selor built his first trading post at the junction of the Escrito, South Largo, and Largo canyons. In the early 1920's he helped Bill Lybrook (nephew of R. J. Reynolds, tobacco merchant) to build a massive stone house and trading post at Lybrook's, on the Bloomfield-Cuba road. Counselor built the post that still carries his name, under a new owner, a few miles south of Lybrook's, in the winter of 1931–32. In the years immediately following, Counselor's post was frequently used as field headquarters for archaeologists and paleontologists visiting from the East. The surrounding region, Van Valkenburgh notes, is rich in "old Navajo defensive sites with watchtowers and breastworks in association with hogans. . . . According to tree-ring data, these hogans date from 1720–60 and seem to have been occupied by Navajos and refugees from the Rio Grande and Acoma. Four miles southwest [actually northwest] of Lybrooks is an important Navajo citadel site located on an isolated and high crag commanding the entire Chaco Canyon region."

by Bryan in 1902 to C. C. Manning of Gallup, who, as related elsewhere, employed Charles Newcomb as his manager there for a number of years.

In badlands east and slightly north of Naschiti a man named Hunter built Bisti Trading Post, probably in the early 1900's although the actual date is unknown.[25] Bisti's formidable surroundings may have had something to do with the rapid succession of its owners.

Again near the Chuska foothills, at the foot of fingering tablelands dotted with the ruins of *anasazi* farming villages, John L. Oliver built a small post about 1904. Just south of Captain Tom Wash, the place first was known to white men as Crozier, but the name was changed to Nava when the post tradership succeeded in the winter of 1913–14 to Arthur J. Newcomb.[26]

Four years younger than his brother Charles, Arthur Newcomb came to New Mexico from Iowa about 1911. He worked first for C. C. Manning's Gallup store and then for about two years at Fort Defiance for George U. Manning. In his years at Nava, Newcomb built up one of the most successful trading businesses in the Chuska Valley. The fine quality of his blankets resulted in part from circumstance—his post was in the region of the Two Gray Hills weavers—and from his efforts, and his wife's, to maintain high standards of weaving. One of their best weavers was not a woman but the medicine man, Hosteen Clah. Mrs. Newcomb became his trusted friend and through Clah's influence and assistance was able to reproduce a nearly complete series of Navaho sand-paintings.

Valley traders to the Navahos were not long in learning of the traditional enmity between the Utes and Navahos. The early traders

[25] Of the old-timers in the valley only H. B. Noel and Joe Wynn, who once owned Bisti, could say with certainty that it was Hunter who built the post. Noel also identified Hunter as "a cattleman who ran a small bunch of cattle in that area," but was not sure whether he was the same as the Billy Hunter who started Beclabito.

[26] Van Valkenburgh says that the Navaho name for this place is *Bis deez'ahi*, Clay Pointing Out. Mrs. Franc Newcomb, when widowed and living in Albuquerque, told me that she had heard Navahos speak of it as *Pezh-doclish-dezii*, literally translated as Trader at the Blue Point. ("Most of the mesas there are red or gray, but at our post the mesa was good pottery clay—blue.") The nearby wash is believed to have been named for Captain Tom, Navaho employed as policeman at Fort Defiance in 1894. (*Annual Report, C. I. A., 1894*.) Oliver sold his store about 1911 to Charles Nelson, who in turn sold to Arthur Newcomb. Crozier, or Nava, also appears on some maps as Newcomb's, or Drolet's—the last for J. M. Drolet, who with Paul Brink of Farmington bought the post from Newcomb about 1943–44. Drolet later sold his interest to Brink and moved to California.

learned also that long before their arrival trade between these tribes, under a temporary truce, was not uncommon.

Father Escalante in 1776 found buffalo as far west as the Green River in Utah, and early accounts tell of Utes trading buffalo robes and elk hides for Navaho horses and blankets. In 1870 a party of Moache Utes left the Cimarron Agency to trade with Navahos at Abiquiu; the Capotes then were mostly in the vicinity of Tierra Amarilla, although Sobeta's band mingled with lodges of the Wiminuches near the San Juan, reported at various times that year as being camped on the Animas, La Plata, and Mancos.[27] The Utes were well armed, as were the Navahos, with muzzle-loading rifles and Colt revolvers.

Valley trade with the Southern Utes and the allied Jicarilla Apaches was an occasional affair of wandering pack trains until the two tribes were placed upon reservations. For some years yet these Indians would have agencies but no land they could call their own. Abiquiu Agency was established in January, 1850, for the Wiminuches and Capotes, but as far as traders were concerned it little mattered. Except when they appeared briefly for rations of food, blankets, and gunpowder, these bands were roaming to the west and north near the San Juan. The Moaches and Jicarillas were loosely confined to the Cimarron Agency, north and east of Taos, until in 1873 the Jicarillas were divided between Cimarron and Tierra Amarilla Agency—which had replaced Abiquiu in June, 1872. None of the Indians remained for long at one place and reports were frequent of quarrels and killings when they encountered wandering Mexican traders.

Moses V. Stevens appears to have been the first officially recognized trader to the Capotes and Wiminuches, receiving his license in September, 1869. Presumably, in contrast to previous Mexican, French, and American traders who came and went with mule-trains, Stevens set up a temporary trading post at Abiquiu. Four years later, when the Capotes and Wiminuches were told they must draw their annuities at Los Pinos Agency on the Uncompahgre River, Isaac Gothelp, a resident of Saguache, Colorado, was licensed to trade with them there. Again in 1874, with Otto Mears as partner, Gothelp traded with the Southern Utes at Los Pinos.[28]

27 *Annual Report, C. I. A., 1870.*
28 *Ibid., 1873.* Stevens was licensed for one year only. Gothelp was licensed to trade at Los Pinos Agency, June 10, 1873. With Mears as partner, the license was renewed for a second year, June 1, 1874. (*N. A., Ledgers of Traders.*) The Los Pinos Agency on the Uncompahgre served the Tabeguache and Uncompahgre Utes, and should not be confused with the Southern Ute agency established in 1878 on Los Pinos River and also called, in the early years, Los Pinos Agency.

When Cimarron Agency was abandoned in July, 1878, the remaining Jicarillas were moved to a base at Tierra Amarilla, and the three bands of Southern Utes were established on the first reservation created for them, with headquarters at present Ignacio, Colorado, on Los Pinos River. The agency site was selected in June, 1877, and the first buildings were erected that summer. Some months after the Utes were moved there, grumbling because their agency was not on the San Juan, President Rutherford B. Hayes signed an executive order, February 7, 1879, establishing the reservation limits. Agent Henry Page reported in the following year that his charges owned many sheep, goats, horses, and cattle, but stubbornly refused to become farmers. They much preferred, he said, to hunt over the 864,000 acres of their land.[29] In other terms, their reservation was a narrow strip of mountainous land 15 miles wide and 120 miles long, in the extreme southwestern corner of Colorado, separated from the San Juan and the Navahos by one to twenty miles.

Joseph Clarke of Leavenworth, Kansas, in May, 1879, became the first trader licensed to the new Southern Ute agency. He was succeeded the following year by Will F. Burns of Animas City, who was joined by John H. Burns as partner in 1882. Also in that year George M. Drake of Dumont, Colorado, was licensed to trade at the agency. Drake operated his post until April 16, 1885, when he sold out to Edward Schiffer of Durango.[30]

The Utes, like the Navahos, roamed in all directions beyond their reservation limits. In 1885, however, the "partly civilized" Moaches shared the eastern part of the country with the small band of Capotes, while the more warlike Wiminuches preferred the western region extending from the Mancos to the Sierra Abajo. Few of them could speak more than a few words of English, they continued to resist all efforts to make them farmers and held tenaciously to their buffalo-hide lodges and traditional ways as nomadic hunters.[31]

The Jicarillas, meanwhile, fared less well. While at Cimarron Agency they had been in continual conflict with neighboring Mexican and Anglo landowners, who regarded them as thieving, shiftless, drunken marauders. Three times a reservation for them was created; twice the land set aside for them was withdrawn and restored to the

[29] *Annual Report, C. I. A., 1873.* In the previous year Page reported that the Wiminuches, Capotes, and Moaches based at his agency numbered 1,307.

[30] *N. A., Ledgers of Traders.*

[31] As buffalo disappeared from the scene, the Utes made tipis of heavy canvas duck. Frank Pyle recalled that a band of Wiminuches, under Chief Mariano, camped in twenty or thirty canvas lodges at Mariano Springs as late as 1930.

Navahos at Chinle. The group posed in front of Sam Day's post was photographed about 1902 by Ben Wittick. The man with spear at left, wearing the skin of a mountain lion's head for a cap, is Dinet-tsosi, arrested in 1884 for his part in the murder of prospectors Walcott and McNally. Seated, holding a muzzle-loading rifle, is Naakaii Nez (Tall Mexican). To the right of him, holding spear and bow and with an arrow case of mountain-lion skin, is Hosteen Kliz-ini (Black Man). At far right, feet apart, stands a Navaho called The Gambler. The woman seated at far left is the wife of Tse-nun-eskai (Man with Trimmed Hair), a tribal chief in the days following the Navahos' imprisonment at Fort Sumner. Sam Day II identified those named above. *(Collection of Sam Day II.)*

The Spiegelberg brothers, Santa Fe contractors. Solomon's grandson, George A. Spiegelberg, identifies the group, left to right, as Emanuel, Lehman, Solomon Jacob, Levi, and Willi. Others believe that Willi, youngest of the brothers, may instead appear second from the left. Photographer and date unknown. *(Museum of New Mexico.)*

Traders at Shiprock Fair, 1912. Bottom row, left to right: uniden-
tified government employee, Arthur Newcomb, Superintendent
William T. Shelton, Joe Tanner, Louisa Wade Wetherill, John
Wetherill. Second row: "Old Man" Hawley, Frank Mapel, Mrs.
Edith Mapel, Crownpoint Agent Samuel E. Stacher, George Bloom-
field, Mrs. Ed Davies, Ed Davies, Mary Davies. Third row: Herbert
Redshaw (government employee), Alma L. (Al) Foutz, Olin C.
Walker, Will Evans, John Hunt (Bluff City, Utah), unidentified
government employee, unidentified man. Top row: Sheldon Dustin,
John Walker, Jess Foutz, Ike Goldsmith (Sheep Springs Trading
Post), Bert Dustin, Frank Noel, Fonnie Nelson, June Foutz, Bruce
Bernard, unidentified government employee. Members of this group
were identified and the names cross-checked, by H. B. Noel, George
Bloomfield, and John Arrington. *(Collection of H. B. Noel.)*

Crystal weaving at its early best. John B. Moore is shown with Bi-leen Al-pai Bi-zha-ahd and one of her superior "ER-20" grade rugs. Note the characteristic hook elements and the central cross and diamond patterns. Photograph by Sim Schwemberger in Moore's 1911 catalog, *The Navajo*.

Navaho women and their children are pictured at the 1913 Shiprock
Fair. The Chuska Valley blankets hanging in the background contain design elements developed from Crystal patterns and later
greatly refined by Toadlena–Two Gray Hills weavers. *(Collection of
Frank Noel's daughter, Mrs. Jennie Noel Weeks.)*

Black Horse (Bi-leen-kla-zhin) and Tayoneh, a headman of the Ganado region. This Sim Schwemberger photograph made at Crystal, probably in the early 1900's, is from J. B. Moore's 1911 catalog, *The Navajo*.

Bi-joshii, Navaho medicine man, leader of stubborn resistance in the Beautiful Mountain Uprising of 1913. *(Pennington Studio, Durango.)*

Traders' booths at Shiprock Fair. Navaho horsemen gather to hear a speaker, standing between the booths of John Wetherill and Clyde Colville, of Kayenta, and Frank Noel, of Sa-nos-tee. Probably taken in 1912. *(Collection of H. B. Noel.)*

public domain. Numbering fewer than eight hundred people, they were a tribe dispossessed, homeless, and unwanted.[32]

When Tierra Amarilla Agency was abandoned in 1882, the Jicarillas were shuttled nearer to the San Juan and, very briefly, to their own reservation. An agency of sorts was established for them at a place called Amargo, seven miles east of present Dulce, New Mexico, on the Amargo Arroyo. In this high timberland the Jicarillas also were assigned their first trader, a man named Ed Vorhang—who soon after dropped from sight. Presumably he left the region in August, 1883, when the Jicarillas were told to pack up and move once more.

The famous Navaho "long march" to Fort Sumner was being repeated, in diminished scale, by the Jicarillas. Leaving Amargo on August 20, 747 Jicarillas began a journey of five hundred miles to the Mescalero Apache reservation in southeastern New Mexico. Again, this enforced march was made mostly afoot and lasted forty-seven days. Six of their number died of smallpox before reaching the Mescalero agency near Fort Stanton. Here the others were confined until, in the fall of 1886, homesick for their mountains, they walked away. The starving vanguard camped near San Ildefonso Pueblo in November, defiantly refusing to return to the Mescaleros and demanding to be placed on their own reservation.[33] Their appeals were favorably received, and by May, 1887, they were permanently located on a reservation twelve miles wide and thirty-two miles long, adjoining the Southern Utes and Navahos, south and east of the San Juan.

Until their own agency was established at Dulce, the Jicarillas shared both the agency and the agency traders at Ignacio with the Utes. Here they brought in trade their livestock, wicker baskets, moccasins, buckskins and peltries, beadwork, bows and arrows, and quiv-

32 By treaty of December 10, 1873, the first Jicarilla reservation was established "north of the San Juan in New Mexico and east of the Navajo reservation." No effort was made to move the Jicarillas to this vaguely described land, and the reservation was abolished March 25, 1874, by executive order of President Grant. The land was restored to public domain by executive order July 18, 1876. (*Annual Report, C. I. A., 1874–75–76–77.*) A second Jicarilla reservation of 307,200 acres was created by executive order, September 21, 1880. (*Ibid., 1883.*) An agency was provided at Amargo, and the tribe was based here from December, 1881, to August, 1883, when the Jicarillas were moved to the Mescalero Apache agency. The Jicarilla reservation was abolished at this time, and the land returned to public domain by executive order of May 14, 1884. (*Ibid., 1884.*) Finally, in May, 1887, the Jicarillas were moved to their present reservation of 416,000 acres, established by executive order, February 11, 1887. (*Ibid., 1888.*) for the first few years the Jicarilla agency was operated jointly with the Southern Ute agency at Ignacio, Colorado, and then was moved to Dulce, New Mexico.

33 *Ibid., 1883–84–85–86–87.*

ers made of mountain lion skin. The value of their crafts amounted to no more than two thousand dollars a year, but to a poor tribe it was better than nothing.[34]

Among the traders at Ignacio during this period were Thomas J. Roush of Logansport, Indiana, who was first licensed in April, 1886, and sold out in 1889 to James E. Schutt of Durango; William W. Weir of Durango, who succeeded Schutt in 1892, and in turn was succeeded the following year by George H. Kraus, also of Durango; and Henry L. Hall of Dulce, who bought out Kraus in 1897.[35]

A western extension of the Southern Ute reservation led to the establishment of a new agency at Navajo Springs in 1896–97. Located in the wide valley west of Mesa Verde and near the southern foot of Ute Mountain, the agency buildings, of adobe with corrugated iron roofs, were scarcely completed before they were abandoned for lack of sufficient well water. The agency then was moved to Towaoc, on the lower eastern slopes of Ute Mountain—rising from the valley like a recumbent giant, its head to the north. Early traders called it Sleeping Ute, apt enough, though to the Utes themselves it was known as *Wee-so-gar-um*, or Soapweed Mountain. In the valley several miles east of Towaoc a trader named Bob Bryce built one of the first posts in the area in the late 1880's. The store later was bought and operated by Louis Ismay, as the Ute Trading Company.

In these years and later the Jicarillas and Utes knew many traders. Three men, however, overshadowed all the others. First of the three was Oen Edgar Noland, a tall, slender Missourian.

From Saguache, in 1873, Noland worked his way down to the La Plata, freighting by ox team from Alamosa to Durango, then working as a logger for a sawmill in the mountains at Thompson Park, east of Mancos. About 1881 he married Callie Mitchell, daughter of the family with whom he boarded. Indian trade appealed to him, but he wanted to make it on his own and not as another man's clerk, and his savings were hardly more than the price of a saddle. With nothing to offer as security he obtained a ten-thousand-dollar loan. The lending agency held a life insurance policy taken out by Noland in that amount and naming the firm as sole beneficiary.

Noland's Store was constructed on the north bank of the San Juan, within rifle-shot of the Four Corners. It was an L-shaped building,

[34] In 1896 the Jicarillas owned "a large number" of horses, 3,000 sheep, and 600 goats. During that year the traders purchased over 1,500 of their wicker baskets, paying from fifty cents to eight dollars a basket. (*Ibid., 1896.*) The tribe's income from baskets and beadwork in 1906 was $4,000.

[35] *N. A., Ledgers of Traders.*

back to the river and facing north: built of cottonwood logs, a large store in one wing, living quarters in the other. At the west end of the store he later added a huge wareroom built of dressed stone, the interior walls plastered white. The walls were pierced with loopholes in event the place had to be defended. Logs and planks supported a sloping dirt roof. Noland freighted in supplies from Mancos, and in 1884 or 1885, in this half-store, half-fort was ready for trade.[36]

Trading with Utes and Navahos, Noland at first was regarded with suspicion, as an unwanted, interloping white stranger. Several times incidents arose in which a lesser man would have panicked and done something foolish. Noland kept his head and restored quiet without threatening to use his rifle. The Indians responded by giving him their respect, the Navahos calling him *Ba'dani*, a word meaning "son-in-law" and implying friendly kinship. Several years later, as the trade continued to increase, Noland and his father-in-law, Stanley Mitchell, built a second post five or six miles downriver. Again the store was situated on the north bank of the San Juan, near the mouth of Mc-Elmo Creek, a place Noland called Riverview, but which came to be known as Aneth.

While operating the Riverview post for Noland, Mitchell became involved in a quarrel and had the misfortune to kill a Navaho. Mitchell took refuge at the Four Corners store, to which the Navahos laid siege for a week. Noland's arguments and appeals did nothing to quiet the Indians' demands that he surrender Mitchell to them. The affair would have ended with more shooting had Noland not succeeded in getting word to Fort Lewis, asking for troops. The arrival of a small force of cavalry restored order and the Navahos dispersed. Soon afterward, Noland turned over management of the Aneth, or Riverview, post to Pete Guillet, who bought the store a year later when his brother Herman came out from Missouri to join him.[37]

The construction of the new agency at Navajo Springs induced Noland to sell his Four Corners store and build another post at the

36 The actual date when Noland's Store was built is uncertain, as it occupied land not then a part of the Navaho reservation and Noland did not need a license. The 1884–85 date is given by Ira S. Freeman (*A History of Montezuma County, Colorado*) and probably is close. The store is no longer standing, but was described to me by Mrs. John Ismay, whose father, Joseph Heffernan, bought the post about 1908. Other traders in this Ute-Navaho region of the San Juan, between 1890 and the early 1900's, included Jim Holly, Billy Carlisle, Joe Lee, Jr., and Monty Morland.

37 The Guillets sold Aneth to their half-brother, Sterl Thomas, about 1890. Shortly after, Thomas sold out to A. J. Ames and Jesse West. There has been a succession of owners ever since. Ames and West also bought Noland's Four Corners store when Noland moved to Navajo Springs.

new agency. It appears that he remained there only a short time but continued trading in the Towaoc area. In the early 1900's, with O. S. Crenshaw as partner, he bought the Bauer Mercantile Company of Mancos and spent the rest of his life in that town.

Oen Noland already was on the San Juan when Frank Pyle was born at Lost Canyon, between the Dolores and Mancos rivers, in 1887. Pyle's closest friend in boyhood, as later, was a Wiminuche called Jack House, whose Ute name, *Dah'ma tuc-it,* meant "A Man Who Can Stop (or Hold) the Sun." Jack House was a son of Acowitz, the Ute whose words about the ancient ones led Richard Wetherill to the discovery of Cliff Palace in 1888. Frank Pyle and Jack House played together as children, then hunted together, and together ran stock from Dove Creek to the San Juan. By the time he was a young man, Pyle would catch himself thinking in the Ute language.

After cowpunching for a few years, on his own and as a hired hand, Pyle became assistant and then head stockman for the Ute Mountain reservation, in charge of three thousand head of Ute cattle. The job ended in the killing drought of 1917–18. Scores of animals died, and finally an inspector for the Indian Offce ordered that the cattle remaining must be sold. Pyle filed on a homestead of 640 acres north of Dolores and for two years ran three hundred head of his own cattle. In 1919, with Jim Belmear as partner, he bought Joe Tanner's trading post on Tanner Mesa, which rises in lower Mancos Canyon immediately north of the New Mexico line in Colorado. Navahos who summered on the mesa offered a meager subsistence for the post. Pyle and Belmear finally abandoned it in 1923.

Near the base of Tanner Mesa, meanwhile, Pyle built a second store—Mancos Creek Trading Post—which he operated until he sold out in 1926 to Dan Tice of Farmington and Sam Walker of Cortez.[38] After another interval, when he again ran cattle, Pyle in 1932 bought the old Ute Trading Company, where in the first years he took in 47,000 pounds of wool annually.

Pyle's friendship with Jack House continued, perhaps became even closer in later years when Pyle became chairman of the Approval Committee and adviser to the Ute Tribal Council. Once the two went to Washington together to testify before an Indian Affairs Committee of Congress on a Ute rehabilitation program. When he retired from

[38] Interview with Frank Pyle. The Mancos Creek post was financed by T. H. Akin of Dolores, who continued as Pyle's partner until Pyle took sole ownership in 1925. The original building was one and one-half miles west of the present store, on the old road from Shiprock to Cortez.

trading, Pyle continued to live at Towaoc, giving all of his active time to the interests of the tribe. Since Thomas Keam, perhaps only one other trader—Emmet Wirt—worked as hard and unselfishly for the Indians.

Emmet Wirt, like Pyle, backed into Indian trading after starting as a cattleman. From a farm in Cass County, Missouri, he came to New Mexico in the mid–1880's, while still in his teens. After working for a logging outfit near Chama, he moved to the San Juan and signed on as a cowhand with the Carlisle Cattle Company. With Largo trader Frank Townsend and fellow hand Frank Allen, he once traveled to Fort Wingate to take delivery of sixteen or eighteen head of cattle. These they brought back to the Gallegos—white-faced bulls, the first Herefords to reach the San Juan country.

It is said that Wirt told the foreman of his outfit to withhold his pay, drawing only enough for an occasional spree in town or to renew his supply of ammunition.[39] A time came when Wirt asked for the full amount owed to him and was told he would have to wait: the company just then was embarrassed for money. Seeing that this word was final, Wirt packed his belongings in a saddle roll and proceeded to cut out of the Carlisle herd enough good steers to balance the debt. Alone, he drove the cattle to Pueblo, Colorado, leased grazing land, and began supplying fresh beef to the Pueblo markets.

The price of beef slipped, or perhaps Wirt tired of town living. Anyway, he drove his remaining steers south to the Jicarilla reservation, knowing that the agent in time would take the beef as rations. Wirt settled at Amargo, about 1890, and opened a trading store. When the Jicarilla agency was moved from Ignacio to Dulce, he moved with it and remained at Dulce as trader, and probably the Jicarillas' best friend, for the rest of his life.

A big man and a woolly individualist, Wirt was not given to starting or backing away from a fight. The story is told of a day in winter when Wirt found himself in an angry dispute with another white man. The cause of the row has been forgotten by those who witnessed it; it is only remembered that Wirt was encased in a heavy overcoat, that before he could reach his revolver, his adversary stabbed him with a knife, wounding him seriously. After that Wirt was never known to wear any sort of coat. Instead, if the weather was cold, he wore buckskins under his trousers and shirt.

39 J. Denton Simms, "Emmet Wirt, Pioneer Extraordinary," in *Pioneers of the San Juan County*, Vol. III (1952). Simms gives Wirt's date of birth as February 7, 1868.

Emmet Wirt never became wealthy. The Jicarillas, never prosperous and more often dirt-poor, were loyal customers and that was all. For reasons of his own, however, Wirt had no wish to leave Dulce. The occasion for which he is best remembered resulted from the depression of 1907. When the agency funds had been exhausted, no more money was provided from Washington; food supplies diminished until rations were issued only twice a month, and then only to those too old or too sick to work. Through the winter of panic there was starvation on the Jicarilla reservation. Hunger reached such an acute point that the Jicarillas boiled and ate their moccasins and buckskins. When these were gone, they shredded bark from the juniper trees to chew on the moist inner membrane.

Throughout this period of distress, Wirt extended credit as long as his supplies held out. When his supplies were gone, he used up his savings to buy more. Even when his savings were gone, it never occurred to him to move away. When he died, in 1938, he was buried at Dulce.

22

Cabezon

A MOUNTAINOUS BREAST with dome-shaped nipple, Cabezon Peak stands alone in the Río Puerco Valley. The volcanic plug is the largest of a series extending northeastward in a lava flow from Mount Taylor. An ancient landmark visible for miles, it was most familiar to the Pueblo Indians of Jemez and the Río Grande, and to the *Hoolk'idnii Diné,* Rolling Hill Navahos, of the Torreon region. Later it was known, too, to Spanish travelers from Santa Fe who made it a fixed compass point on trails west and north. In the early 1870's, two generations before the Navahos moved away, Spanish-American sheepherders and farmers moved in.

Where the curve of Cabezon Peak meets the level of the valley, the Puerco cuts a winding course. Here, north of the river and north of the peak, the families with names like Cháves and Sandoval and De Mastes built a town of adobe houses, a town of one street, a dusty road rising in gentle grade from east to west. They called it La Posta.[1]

1 The brothers R. H. and E. M. Kern camped about fifteen miles northeast of Cabezon (Spanish for "big head") Peak on August 23, 1849, while accompanying Col. John M. Washington's expedition against the Navahos. In his report of that expedition, Lt. J. H. Simpson refers to the volcanic landmark as the *Cerro de la Cabeza,* and in these words: "A mile further, and we were upon the high land dividing the waters of the *Rio de Jemez* [also Río de los Vacas] from those of the Rio Puerco—an extensive prospect of the valley of the latter, with the accessories of some high isolated mountain peaks, bursting unexpectedly upon us from this point. Among the peaks are to be noticed the *Cerro de la Cabeza.*" By this name Cabezon Peak is marked on E. M. Kern's 1849 map of the expedition's route. It is not marked by either name, nor shown, on R. H. Kern's 1851 "Map of the Territory of New Mexico." I believe the peak was overlooked by cartographers

For a longer time than the oldest Navahos remember, Cabezon Peak marked their tribe's eastern boundary. And while many Navahos already were gone from this region, into the Chuska Mountains and beyond, enough of them remained in the valley to provide a large share of La Posta's trade. Much of this trade flowed into a store operated by two men of German rather than Spanish origin: Kisenbach and Haberland. When they built their trading post there and why they sold it are not known, but in 1881 they did sell—on a plan of term payments—to two young partners who, like themselves, were strangers to this land.

Richard Ferdinand Heller, native of Prague, Czechoslovakia, came to Albuquerque by way of New York in 1879, when he was fifteen years old. In Albuquerque's old town he worked in the store of Edward Spitz, his brother-in-law, making friends with John Pflueger, another clerk. Three years later Dick Heller and John Pflueger had saved enough to make the first payment on the trading post at La Posta. On May 15, 1889, with the note to Kisenbach and Haberland paid off, they signed papers of co-partnership.

In this Spanish-Navaho community, where Anglos generally were not made welcome and others in their place might have failed, they prospered. They accepted calmly and then overcame the initial hostility towards them and filled their store with all of the things these people wanted most. A contemporary list of their stock is, for that remotely placed little settlement, unusual. The inventory includes the staple items: flour, lard, sugar, green coffee in hundred-pound sacks (customers roasting the beans in ovens at home and then grinding them), and canned goods. On their shelves were bolts of calico, fine muslins, Spanish lace, cards of fancy buttons, and spools of bright silk ribbon. High-top shoe laces—always black—were either displayed on a shelf or hung from a rack. For men, there were jackets, shirts, trousers, and sombreros; for women, there was a wide choice of rainbow-hued *tapalos*, or shawls. And in the main store and adjoining sheds were heavy-duty items: axes, shovels, saddles, harness, wagons, and hay and grain for livestock.

Dick Heller and John Pflueger continued in the trading business together, buying large numbers of sheep and cattle which they ran through the Puerco Valley, until Heller bought out his partner in

---

generally until the 1881 U. S. Geological Survey "Map of Northwestern New Mexico" marked both Cabezon Peak and La Posta—although "Cabezon" is shown on both the 1860 J. N. Macomb "Map of New Mexico and Utah," and an 1869 "Military Map of the United States" (U. S. Engineers Dept.).

1894. The extent of their trade, ten years after taking the post over, is indicated by a small newspaper story appearing in the Albuquerque *Morning Journal*:

"Messrs. Pflueger and Heller's wool clip consisting of 40,000 pounds arrived yesterday from Cabezon, in the north Rio Puerco district, and was sold on Railroad Avenue to the highest bidder, the same being . . . A. J. Crawford. The sight was an imposing one, the wool being loaded on seventeen wagons . . . drawn by 67 horses."

The distance was not great, about seventy miles, but even in good weather a wagon train leaving Cabezon at four o'clock in the morning would not reach Albuquerque until seven o'clock at night. Often there were long delays, when the roads were muddy or the Río Grande running too high for the wagons to ford. To meet the latter contingency, Dick Heller for years depended upon Narcisco Zamora, who had a flatboat tied up near Bernalillo and, for a good fee, would ferry the wagons across the river.

Wool and hides and Navaho blankets from the Torreon area the wagons carried, in later years being taken directly to the warehouses of Antonio García and Company and the Louis Ilfeld Company. There are stories, no doubt exaggerated, that on the return to Cabezon one of the wagons would be filled with gold and silver coins.[2] Silver dollars and gold pieces were used by Dick Heller at his Cabezon store, but never paper money. Most common in his trade with the Navahos was his own tin scrip, or *seco*, which was made for him in Albuquerque.

Navahos and Spanish natives, both, herded the trader's livestock, which at one time numbered 16,000 sheep and 2,000 head of cattle. The spread was one of the largest in the Puerco Valley, Heller one of the valley's most prosperous landowners. The Navahos called him *Peschi-wo* (Gold Tooth), all of them in the valley south of Starr Lake giving him their trade.[3] His name was widely known, a reputation for his adventures with women grew about him, but he remained a bachelor until he was forty years old.

Young Jake Meyer, an Albuquerque merchant, warned his fiancée about Heller's reputation when she told him she would go to Cabezon

[2] Sometime after he bought out his partner, Dick Heller became his town's first postmaster, and the name was then changed from La Posta to Cabezon.

[3] Located north of Chacra Mesa and just east of the Continental Divide, Starr Lake Trading Post was built in the late 1890's or early 1900's by Albert Starr. Cabezon lies thirty-five miles to the southeast. Starr sold his post in 1913 to George and Albert P. Blake, who in turn sold to Richard Frankel, a partner, in 1917–18. The Navaho name for this region is *Chech'il da Lichee,* or Red Oak.

to visit a sister. She should not go, he told her. But she, Beatrice Gonzales, smiled sweetly and said she would not let Heller's presence there interfere with her trip. Born in Corrales, the great-granddaughter of Capitán Juan Gonzales, she was a young lady of fiery pride and independence. After all, her illustrious ancestor had come into possession of the Alameda land grant of 89,346 acres in 1712.

Arriving in Cabezon, Beatrice Gonzales dutifully went straight to the home of her sister, Mrs. Teresa Sandoval, and then, of course, to Dick Heller's store.

"He was very, very handsome," she said years later. "He introduced himself to me at once and then gave me a box of chocolates. He was nice to me."

When Beatrice returned to Corrales soon after, she took with her another gift, a diamond solitaire.

"I wore it on a ribbon around my neck and under my dress, so that my mother wouldn't know. She did not know that I had promised myself to Mr. Heller until the day and the moment he came for me."

They were married on August 4, 1904, in Bernalillo, and the next day Heller took his bride back with him to Cabezon. The home he brought her to was the largest in that village of 150 families—a low, rambling adobe house of eleven rooms, the walls two feet thick, the ceiling *vigas* a foot or more in diameter. In a number of the rooms there were corner fireplaces, and the furnishings, for that simple place, were elegant. The house was near the east side of town and on the south side of the town's one road, directly opposite and facing Dick Heller's store.

Centered in a group of low adobe buildings and open front livery sheds, the store itself was different enough from others in the town to be interesting. A pitched roof, sheeted with corrugated iron, made it —after the Catholic church—Cabezon's tallest building; as a vagary, perhaps, a dovecot under the roof's peak at front offered twenty-four openings, with perches beneath for Heller's collection of birds. Below this and extending outward toward the road was a raised wooden porch, balustraded, the roof supported by four turned columns; descending from the porch, not across the front but at both sides, were short flights of broad steps. Iron-barred windows flanked the wide center doorway giving access from the porch to the single, large room of the store.

Small as it was, remote as it was from the nearest large community, Cabezon was a familiar stop for nearly fifty years on stage routes and wagon trails westward from Santa Fe and Albuquerque. Many of the travelers, among them cavalry troops from Fort Wingate, rested or warmed themselves in the Hellers' hospitality. The Wingate and Gallup route followed the Chico Arroyo to the small Spanish hamlet of San Mateo and soon after forked—the southern and longer road emerging west of present Grants, the more direct north road coming out near Chaves, or present-day Thoreau. Another road roughly followed the Puerco Valley south, winding almost aimlessly to touch the settlements of Guadalupe, Salaza, Juantafoya, and Cebolleta.[4]

Circumstances of time, place, and opportunity that allowed Dick Heller to prosper slowly changed, in his later years, to all but ruin him. First, as new roads were built, travel on the old roads dwindled until Cabezon seemed almost an island cut off from the rest of the world. Then the Navahos began to move away, family by family, moving farther west year by year, until the big trade he once had with the Indians was reduced to almost nothing. Finally, about 1927 when irrigation dams in the valley were washed out, the Spanish natives started moving away too.

Never a big stream, but carrying more water than now, the Río Puerco cut a deeper and deeper arroyo, the water table went farther down each year. Grama grass, once stirrup-high, withered to stubble. The valley no longer could support large herds of cattle and sheep, and the herds were sold. As the water level sank lower, the fields of corn and beans and melons thinned brown, the crops died.

The golden years gone, ruin facing him, Dick Heller died on March 22, 1947. At his death his ledgers showed more than seventeen thousand dollars in accounts unpaid by his Spanish and Navaho trade.

Cabezon outlived Dick Heller by about one year. His widow stayed on until 1948, keeping the post office open for the handful of remaining families. Then they too moved away, and Mrs. Heller, after bricking in the doorway of the store and boarding the windows, followed them. Once deserted, its adobe buildings crumbling under wind and rain and the looting of vandals, Cabezon slipped into empty silence —a ghost town.

4 These old trails, now scarcely used, are marked on the 1881 U.S.G.S. map referred to above. A third wagon road, much traveled in the 1890's and 1900's and approximating Col. Washington's route in 1849, went northwestward toward the Chacra Mesa, then through Chaco Canyon and nearly due west to the Chuska Mountains. In the vicinity of the Tsaya Trading Post this road crossed the north-south road, by way of Gallegos Canyon, from Farmington to Gallup.

PART FOUR

"I met General Scott in Gallup. It had been raining and snowing for about a week. The General's car got stuck in the mud at China Springs and from there on he rode horseback. We followed him . . . with the jackass battery . . . and escort wagons . . . as best we could. Arnold was the trader at To-hatchi. We took all his food, paid five cents a pound for dressed hog. That night we camped at Charlie Newcomb's store. At Noel's place [Sa-nos-tee] we heard that the Indians refused to come down. General Scott had us build many camp-fires, so's they would think we were in there strong. The troops got the scours from the piñons Charlie Nelson gave them."

—*U. S. Deputy Marshall J. R. Galusha,* personal recollections, Albuquerque, September 19, 1959.

23

Some Exceptional Cases

ANY PURSUIT man engages in seriously—whether sport, business, the arts, or war—builds from a framework of basic rules. So in Indian trading certain attitudes have been basic to a trader's survival. Among these a trader's attitude toward personal danger has been important, an occupational reality often present and never distant. The stricture is crystal clear: a trader may feel fear from his hair roots to his toes —but never, never, can he let an inward quaking take control.

Lorenzo Hubbell once told of an episode that occurred at Ganado, soon after he started trading there, in 1878.

For Lorenzo the critical moment came when a brawny Navaho, ignoring the trader's demand for payment, walked out of the store with a bag of flour. Smaller than his adversary, Hubbell vaulted the counter, caught the man outside with a fierce grip on his hair, and spun him to the ground. Grasping the fellow by one ear, ignoring an audience of some seventy-five Navahos who seemed to have been forewarned that the new trader was to be tested, Hubbell twisted on the ear until the Indian carried the flour back into the post and set it down exactly where he found it.

Hubbell then addressed the Navahos outside: "Come on any of you who think you can steal from me. I'll twist the ears of any Indian who wants to try it." His challenge was not accepted. He realized, Hubbell said later, that if he had allowed the Navaho to get away with the flour, "every Indian in the country would storm the post to carry off anything they might lay hands upon."[1]

1 "Fifty Years an Indian Trader," *Touring Topics,* Vol. XXII, No. 12 (1930). A

Trouble of this nature was predictable at every trading post in the Navaho country until a new trader gave convincing proof that he was unafraid—or was driven off. The danger of such tests' developing into anything as serious as shooting was rare, however, and few traders were murdered by Indians before the early 1900's. From that time onward a graph of the death rate among traders would correspond with the increasing consumption of liquor by Indians. Between 1901 and 1934 more than twenty traders were murdered, and in all but one of the cases the circumstances were remarkably similar.

The over-all pattern of these slayings showed that the murderers usually were drunk, their motive was robbery, and personal animosity against the trader over some slight or wrong was not a factor. In nearly every case the trader was attacked when he was alone and after sunset. A not uncommon practice was to burn the trading post down around the trader's dead body in the hope of destroying damaging evidence.

An exception to the pattern so soon to establish itself was the murder of trader D. M. Smith in 1893 or 1894. Smith became involved in a drunken gambling row at his Defiance Station trading post, and was killed. His personal involvement in a dispute before his death is the exceptional factor.[2]

The future was more accurately forecast the night of July 22, 1901, when people in the vicinity of Fort Wingate Station were startled to see the John Woodgate trading post, two miles to the northeast, burst into flames. Even at that short distance, the building was a flaming ruin before anyone wishing to help arrived on the scene. From the debris rescuers pulled the partly consumed body of Alexander S. Mor-

---

modern variant of the episode shows how little the situation has changed. Trader Kenneth Bradshaw, after only a few weeks at Burnham's Teec-tso-secad post, New Mexico, was challenged by Peter Hogue, a Navaho, in February, 1960. With a silent audience of his Navaho neighbors watching, Peter insisted upon coming around behind the bull-pen counter—violating a traditionally recognized trading post rule. Bradshaw first warned the young Indian, who was his own size, and then knocked him down. In the ensuing fight the trading post door was battered down, a telephone ripped from the wall and hurled, by Peter, and presently Peter ended, on all fours, in the dust outside. At no time did the onlookers make any move to join the melee. "They had no idea of interfering," Bradshaw told me. "They just wanted to see who was the best man." Bradshaw said he had been expecting some such trouble because an incident invariably was forced when a trading post was taken over by a new trader. "The Navahos want to see if you are afraid of them. Any trader moving to a new place knows that. He will have a fight on his hands, or a showdown, sooner or later. The only question is—and he never knows—who will he have to fight with, and when."

2 Annual Report, C. I. A., 1894.

rison, who had been Woodgate's post manager. An autopsy performed by the Fort Wingate surgeon showed that Morrison had died not of burns but from a bullet which passed through his head just back of the ears. The store was known to have contained a fair amount of pawn silver, but most of this was found later among the charred beams. Not found was some thirty dollars in silver which Morrison jingled in a sack a few days before his death.

Two Navahos who had been observed at the store the night of the fire, both drunk, were held for a week in Gallup jail on suspicion of murder. Questioning of the two brought out that neither was in the vicinity of the post when the fire started, and they were released. Morrison's death has remained a mystery.[3]

Winter-evening darkness had settled over the valley of Cienega Amarilla when, on December 12, 1902, flames roaring up from another trading post were detected. A small building owned by George W. Sampson, the post was constructed entirely of lumber and burned as quickly as a bonfire of dry pine. When employees of St. Michaels School arrived—and they had only one mile to come—the roof timbers were ablaze on the ground. Details fitted together within the next few minutes were reminiscent of the Morrison affair.

Among the still-burning ruins was found the headless body of Charles Kyle, Sampson's manager. And according to the *McKinley County Republican* of December 20, "a few bones were found near by, but no other trace of the head. The feet had apparently been burned off. There was a cut or break in the back of the body three inches long, also a blue mark on the breast."

No autopsy was made, nor was one needed to show in general the cause of Kyle's death. Again, there were indications that the trading post had been robbed, and again there was nothing definite to lead to the murderer.

Among other similarities, the cases of Kyle and Morrison, like that of Smith, occurred in the vicinity of Gallup. In some other respects different, the fourth slaying occurred many miles to the north, on the San Juan River in Utah.

The trading post here was the old Four Corners store built by Oen Noland and operated now—this was late 1909 or early 1910—by Joseph Heffernan, originally a New York State man whose people came out

3 In reporting this episode, the *McKinley County Republican*, July 27, 1901, observed that Morrison, twenty-nine years old, was an Englishman who had come to the United States fifteen years before. He was unmarried, lived alone at the trading post, and "had no enemies and neither drank nor gambled."

to Parrott City, Colorado, in 1876, Heffernan bought the trading post about 1908 from a man named Johnson and as his manager employed Charles Fritz, a bachelor who lived at the place alone.

For Fritz the end came as return for a simple kindness. When two Navahos appeared at his door one evening saying they were without money and hungry, the trader invited them into the house adjoining the post, asked them to sit down, and fed them. As the pair walked out into the dusk, preparing to leave, one remembered his leather gloves, which he had forgotten and left on the table. Fritz and the Indian went back into the house together, Fritz leading the way. When Fritz's body was found later, lying face down on the floor, a bullet hole in the back told part of the story. The rest was pieced together after it was discovered the store had been robbed, and finally when one of the two Indians was caught south of the San Juan and at his trial at Salt Lake City was sentenced to ten years in prison.[4]

The element of almost complete surprise usually weighed decisively against the trader, but not always, and all attempts at robbery were not successful.

In a steady, winding climb from Ganado, a dirt road cut through sand and sagebrush eastward past Kin Lichee toward a distant summit forested by tall Douglas firs. Before the road reached the big trees, however, it passed through a lower covering of smaller piñon and juniper. Close to the road and in this almost shadeless setting, C. C. Manning of Gallup built the Cross Canyon Trading Post. Some twelve miles east of Ganado, the post commanded a far view of the pink and white cliffs forming the lower escarpment of Chinle Valley to the west; more in its favor, practically speaking, the post was encircled by and had a large number of Navaho hogans to draw upon for trade.

John E. Owens, Manning's manager, was assaulted there by a Navaho named Chis-chili-begay, wielding a revolver, on January 12, 1915. Son of Curly Head was bent on murder, but was subdued before accomplishing his purpose and was arrested. Records of United States District Court, Prescott, Arizona, show that the Indian appeared on September 8, 1915, before Judge William H. Sawtelle. Convicted of assault with a deadly weapon, Chis-chili-begay was sentenced to serve a year and a day in the state penitentiary at Santa Fe.

When the Navaho came up before the parole board in December,

---

[4] Details of this incident were told to me by Mrs. John Ismay, daughter of Joseph Heffernan. Mrs. Ismay and her husband were then operating the Ismay Trading Post, southwest of Cortez on the Colorado-Utah line.

Lorenzo Hubbell was in Santa Fe to plead in his behalf. The clerk's notes, briefly jotted, give the salient questions asked by the board and answered by Hubbell:

Q.—Do you think he would attempt to escape were he given work outside the walls, and had given word he would not?

A.—Am positive he would not try to escape.

Q.—At what was he employed previous to his getting into trouble, and by whom.

A.—He was not employed, as he had stock of his own to take care of.

Q.—Of what character were his associates?

A.—Good.

Q.—Did he drink to intoxication and make the saloon his head-quarters?

A.—No.

Hubbell's advocacy helped in some measure, as Chis-chili-begay was released from prison before his sentence was out, on June 29, 1916.[5] Lorenzo almost always was a reliable judge of Indian character; in this instance he made a mistake and unquestionably regretted it later.

A successor to John Owens at Cross Canyon provided the motive for murder a few years afterwards. Frank Dugan, sent out from Gallup by Manning to operate the post, baited the trap in mid-January, 1922, when he stored an unusually large shipment of flour in his warehouse. Word of this accumulation of riches spread quickly; on the evening of January 18 the Cross Canyon buildings were seen in flames. Frank Dugan at first was reported missing.

Sam Day II, a deputy United States marshal since 1898, along with his other varied pursuits, was not far away and so naturally was asked to investigate.

"At the time this happened I was living at Kin-na-zhin, between Klagetoh and Wide Ruins, where I had a little store," Day recalled. "Just before, I had been up to see my folks at St. Michaels for New Year's and on the way back passed the Cross Canyon store. It was cold and the wind was blowing and my wife was with me with our little baby in her arms. My brother Bill was working for J. L. Hubbell at Ganado, and after the fire Bill sent word that they wanted me to help.[6]

---

[5] Case No. 3679, State Penitentiary, Santa Fe. John Owen's assailant had the same name as the Navaho who murdered Richard Wetherill in 1910, but the two men were not related.

[6] Sam Day related the story to me during one of four interviews at Karigan's

"It was snowing the day the Cross Canyon post was set on fire, and was still snowing a little bit in the evening when the Navahos came to do it. On that same day there was a big powwow or ceremonial going on ten miles south of Ganado, and these Indians had come up from there. They had three wagons which left tracks in the snow.

"They got Dugan to come out of the store to get them some hay. Some years before, Dugan had lost the lower part of an arm in an accident and he wore a hook on that arm.

"When he was getting the hay, one of them hit him with the reach of a wagon that had been broken in two.[7] Dugan was hit across the back of the head, enough to kill him, and when he was down, he was hit two or three times more on the head. They dragged him from where he fell, outside, and laid him over the top of a bale of hay just inside the hay shed. Then they robbed the place and set it on fire.

"The warehouse was a tin shack with wooden beams—two by sixes. The flour had been stacked in the warehouse on a platform. At one end of the platform there was a barrel of empty pop bottles. Only a few of the bottles on top had cracked from the heat of the fire. Next to the barrel was a box of rice, and only the rice on top was brown from heat.

"But the flour was gone. And it hadn't burned—it couldn't have. The Indians who killed Dugan stole the flour, taking it away in the wagons. They took the flour and some other things from the store to an empty hogan near Black Mountain and hid it there and sold it. I learned this later from Navahos living in that area, who also turned over to me some strings of beads still carrying the Cross Canyon pawn tickets."

Four Navahos suspected of having a part in the affair were arrested near St. Michaels and taken to jail in Gallup. And late in March, Sam Day brought in two more suspects—one of them the same Chis-chili-begay who had attacked John Owens seven years before. When the Indians were being taken from Gallup to trial at St. Johns, Arizona, the following November, Chis-chili-begay escaped. With deputies fol-

---

Trading Post north of St. Michaels, where he was then living. His account corresponds generally with stories of the murder printed in the Gallup *Independent* of January 19 and 26, March 30, and November 16, 1922. Day recalled that 12,000 pounds of flour was stored at the post.

7 A wagon reach is a coupling pole running beneath the wagon from the rear axle to the forward transverse bar, giving the frame greater strength. The Gallup *Independent*, January 26, said that Dugan was struck with an oak doubletree "on the back of the head. . . . This evidently knocked him out, but they kept on beating him for some time."

lowing on his trail, he made his way to the hogan of an influential Navaho named Yellow Policeman, who lived near Klagetoh and was reported to have given information that led to Chis-chili's arrest.

"The man who killed Dugan was Chis-chili," Sam Day said. "He and Yellow Policeman [who was either not arrested or not held] belonged to the same clan and were instigators of the murder. Before the murder, Chis-chili had his sheep one-half mile from Cross Canyon. The night of the murder he moved them to where he lived—at Natural Bridge, halfway from here [St. Michaels] to Fort Defiance"

The Gallup *Independent* reported the encounter at Yellow Policeman's hogan, referring to the Navaho as Yellow Scout: "Chis chile entered . . . and emptied two revolvers in an attempt to kill Yellow Scout, but succeeded only in wounding him slightly. Chis chile then threw both pistols at his victim and walked away. Yellow Scout then procured one of the pistols he had taken from the Dugan store, it is said, and fired, wounding Chis chile in the abdomen. It was believed by all Indians thereabout that he was so seriously wounded that he would die in a very short time. Both of the wounded men are in the hospital at Ft. Defiance."[8]

To the best of Sam Day's memory, and his memory here may have been faulty, "a young Indian named Da-kai, which means 'light complected,' spent twenty-four years in Leavenworth" for the murder committed by Chis-chili-begay. "I had absolute proof that there were nine men connected with [it], but couldn't get any convictions and they went free."

Curt Cronemeyer was among the early traders who came to the Wingate Valley–Zuñi region in the early 1880's. There is some evidence that Cronemeyer located first in the vicinity of Cheechilgeetho and then, with the advent of the Atlantic and Pacific Railroad, moved across the line into Arizona to build another post one and one-half miles from the rails and a deserted whistle-stop and blind siding called Allantown.[9]

When he was a small boy, traveling with his father from Cienega

8 The Gallup *Independent*, November 16, 1922. The Fort Defiance Indian Hospital informed me, on my request for the medical record, that the files were "stored in another location" and in any case, "no information, no matter how far in the past, can be given regarding any patient in a hospital without the signed consent of the patient."

9 Cheechilgeetho is located some thirty miles southwest of Gallup in high, pine-forested country. Van Valkenburgh says that Cronemeyer, "with a man named Chambers, was the first to open a trading post in the region" and some time later moved to Allantown.

Amarilla to Zuñi to get cartloads of wheat, Sam Day II recalled that they always stopped on the way at Cronemeyer's store. Cronemeyer he remembered as "a big, hefty Dutchman, about five feet, ten inches tall and must have weighed about two hundred pounds."

In later years Cronemeyer employed a red-headed assistant, a middle-aged German legally named Charles A. Brewer—but who preferred to be called McDonald, and so was known. It is said that when Brewer first came to Gallup looking for work, the coal mine operators were not employing Germans. Red Brewer took the name Mc-Donald and told his companions to consider him a Scot.

The association of the two men was a short one, Day remembered, not lasting more than three or four months. "Red McDonald," said Day, "was in his fifties and could drink more whisky—and walk straight—than any man I ever saw. Cronemeyer drank beer, but I never saw him drunk."

Cronemeyer was married to, or at least part of the time lived with, two Navaho women, and by them had two or more children. He was a good trader, solid and steady, and in Gallup, where he did his banking and bought his supplies, he was known to be at least well-to-do. It was noticed, then, but not with surprise, when Curt Cronemeyer's wagons rolled into town one day in June, 1915, heavily loaded with wool. Even before he left town, the word got around that in disposing of the wool about thirteen thousand dollars had changed hands. Most of the money Cronemeyer left at the bank, where it was heard—and later repeated outside—that he was taking three thousand dollars back to Allantown to buy cattle. Usually he preferred to do business by check, but this time he took cash.[10]

Besides his own, the telephone nearest to Cronemeyer's trading post, and on the same line, was twenty miles west at Houck, a windy spot in the Río Puerco Valley named for an early settler, J. D. Houck. The valley soil was rich enough to sustain a number of Navaho farms, but otherwise little was there besides a small railroad station. And it was in this station that Houck's one telephone sometimes rang, but not often.

On Friday evening, June 25, the telephone rang. It was eight o'clock, which would mean the sun had set half an hour before and the last color was now draining out of the sky, leaving the valley in dusk. The station agent answered the call, according to a Gallup

[10] The Cronemeyer-McDonald case from this point forward is based on files of the Gallup *Independent*, July 1, 15, 22, and August 26, October 7, and December 30, 1915. Quotations used here are from this source.

newspaper report later, to hear at the other end of the wire a voice that was weak and uncertain. It merely said, 'We have been shot. Come quick, quick, quick.' No other sound could be heard over the phone."

Two men employed at the Houck station started at once on horseback for Cronemeyer's store. Because of the darkness and because they were not sure of the way and twice were lost, it was after midnight when they reached there.

"They found both Cronemeyer and McDonald dead in the store," the newspaper account continued. "McDonald lay behind the counter, face downward and Cronemeyer lay face down on his bed. Cronemeyer had been shot through the hand and through the abdomen with a high power pistol or a rifle. McDonald had been shot twice through the breast. One bullet struck in his left breast, [and] taking an upward course passed through his neck, breaking it, and passed up into the head and out through the right eye.

"A few trading checks and a box of soda crackers lay on the counter where McDonald fell, as if he had been trading with someone at the time he was killed."

It appeared that only Cronemeyer, almost sixty years old but still in rugged health, could have reached the telephone; after his cry for help he evidently managed to get as far as his own room and his bed.

"Evidence about the room and house show that Cronemeyer had his rifle in his hand after he had been wounded . . . as it was covered with blood. Drops of blood and tracks on the outside of the building show that he had walked around the house once or twice after being wounded. One shell was empty in the rifle."

Twenty-four hours after the shooting the two bodies were placed in the baggage car of a Santa Fe local and taken to Gallup. Only one clue was found giving any indication who might have committed the crime. The footprints of a lone man—so far apart as to show he was running—led away from the store. Sheriff's deputies followed the tracks eastward as far as Schuster's Springs, and there the trail was lost.

The double funeral reminded some townspeople of Gallup's garish yesterdays, when troops from Wingate quarreled and fought with miners and cowboys in the gambling halls and saloons that never closed. Burials then were cheap, fast, and lacking in ceremony.

"A large cortege of friends and acquaintances of the deceased were present to pay their last respects," the Gallup *Independent* commented. "This was the first double funeral held in this town in many years. It was the first time that two hearses were used."

The size of Cronemeyer's estate, deflating from a first estimate of $100,000 to its actual $44,000 value, was no deterrent to the search for suspects. A Navaho living near Allantown was arrested within a week of the slaying and, failing misearably to give an account of himself, was held for the fall grand jury. Soon afterward a second Navaho believed to have been implicated was locked up in the jail at Holbrook. Jurisdiction in these cases was awarded to the courts of Apache County, Arizona, when it was found that Cronemeyer's trading post was not on the Navaho reservation and across the line from New Mexico.

Even with two suspects locked behind bars a feeling persisted that the real murderer had not been caught. A reward of $1,800 was posted in August, offered by the state of Arizona and administrator of the Cronemeyer estate, and the search continued.

Jail-cell talk and barroom gossip led Deputy Andy Romero of Gallup off on a surprising tangent. Late in August, Romero was in El Paso, Texas, engaging in quiet discussions with a Mexican detective named Varile, and finally offering an inducement of three hundred dollars for Señor Varile's co-operation. The money was not wasted.

While the sheriffs and their deputies of Gallup and St. Johns were out combing every hogan and summer brush shelter in the vicinity of Allantown, Victor Huizar (or Wizar) and Blas Lozzano spent the days after the murder quietly playing cards in a Gallup saloon, two or three blocks from the police headquarters and jail.

In one friendly game of seven-up Victor Huizar had the luck to win a pistol—the same pistol his friend Blas had sold the day before to a fellow Mexican national. Soon thereafter, Huizar and Lozzano left town. But not before Huizar pawned two revolvers—his own and the Lozzano gun won in the card game. Both pawn tickets bore Huizar's true name, and this was a grave mistake because these were the weapons that killed Curt Cronemeyer and Red McDonald.

Huizar was arrested in El Paso, Lozzano at Isleta Pueblo on the Río Grande, and both were brought back, first to Gallup and then to St. Johns. Here they were put in jail to await trial.[11]

Dan DuBois, coming from his home near Zuñi, was one of many witnesses when hearings were held in December at St. Johns to establish the legal heirs to Cronemeyer's estate. Isaac Barth was there to represent some relatives who had turned up in Germany, but DuBois,

---

[11] Disposition of these cases is something of a mystery. Merle W. Heap, clerk of Superior Court at St. Johns, informs me that the last entry in the court file is a motion to set aside the charges of murder.

among others, supported the claims of Cronemeyer's son and daughter and their Navaho mothers. The dead trader's paternity was recognized, and Peter Paquette, Navaho Agency superintendent, was appointed as the children's guardian.

The year 1918 was a time of restlessness and fear, of sickness and of death. Hot summer winds dusting across the Southwest seemed to carry the seeds of epidemic, sparing neither town-dwellers nor Navaho families in the most distant, isolated hogans.

By early October, nineteen persons in Gallup were reported dead of Spanish influenza within three weeks. Out on the reservation, Indian Office Inspector W. S. Coleman found the epidemic out of control—"in some instances whole families were stricken with the disease and died. Reports of hogans with several dead bodies in them have been made . . . Many of the Indians were treated only by the medicine men. . . . No estimate has yet been made as to the number of fatalities."[12]

Pressures building up in this atmosphere may have caused more than the usual drinking at a *yei-bi-chai* dance that July, about fourteen miles northeast of Chaco Canyon and near Tucker's Store. John Arrington, then a government stockman operating from a station on Kinnebito Wash, had come over to police the sing. He encountered what seemed only routine trouble.

One big Navaho had had too much to drink, Arrington recalled later. "He wandered over to Tucker's place—Ralph Tucker and his wife and the boy, Pat Smith, were there then—and made a real nuisance of himself. It got so bad I finally put handcuffs on him and threw him into the warehouse in back."

The Navaho was released some hours afterward, but only after promising to pay Tucker for the dozen new brooms he had destroyed by breaking the handles in a crack in the warehouse door. Once quiet was restored, Arrington went back to his place on the Kinnebito, and the Tuckers prepared to take a few days off and go in to Albuquerque. Pat Smith, who was eighteen and the youngest of four Indian trader brothers, would take care of the post in their absence.[13]

---

12 The Gallup *Herald*, October 12 and November 16, 1918.
13 Ralph Tucker, a native of Pennsylvania, built the trading post about 1915. Arrington remembered Tucker as a tall, rather solemn man, bald, and with a big nose. "The Indians called him *Jay-sho*, which means Buzzard, but Tucker always thought it meant American Eagle." The store was located some six miles north of Pueblo Pintado, a Chaco ruin, at a place the Navahos called *Tse-daa'tohi*, or "Spring from the Rock." Tucker rebuilt the store after it was burned but died

Early in the morning, a day or two afterward, Arrington was awakened by old Hosteen Tso-begay pounding on his door.

"Pat wants you," the old man said.

"What's the matter?" Arrington asked.

"Oh—I don't know. The store is burned, I think."

"Where's Pat?"

"I don't know. Pat wants you."

At Tucker's Store, what remained of it, Arrington found young Pat Smith far beyond needing anyone. The charred, blackened walls stood roofless around his body, which lay on the floor.

Arrington rode on to Pueblo Bonito where he left his horse with Ed Doonan, the Chaco Canyon trader, and proceeded by car with sheep rancher Ed Sargent to the agency at Crownpoint. From here a message containing the report of Pat Smith's death was directed to authorities and friends in Gallup. Late that night the group gathered at the burned-out store included Arrington and Sargent, both of whom had returned with Agent Samuel F. Stacher, and the traders C. C. Manning and Frank Mapel and Sheriff Bob Roberts, all from Gallup, and Pat's brother, Bob Smith, who came from his Starr Lake trading post.

"We found out that the Navahos had moved their sing a few miles down the valley," Arrington said, "and we knew that they were drinking. It was long after midnight—almost daybreak—but we decided not to wait. We got into two cars and drove right down among them."

A Navaho named Comanche, an Indian policeman who had worked before with Arrington, separated himself from the others and told the white men where they would find Pat Smith's murderers. One, a Navaho called Luis Chávez, was asleep in a hogan; the other, Augustine, was hiding in the canyon.

Confessions, signed by the pair at Crownpoint before they were taken on to jail in Gallup, indicated that Luis Chávez killed young Smith in a room adjoining the store while his companion waited outside.[14]

Following the usual pattern, the two Navahos bided their time until Smith locked up the store for the night and retired to the living

---

soon later, and his widow sold out to Ed Sargent and Bob Smith, who financed Lester Setzer in operating it. Under this ownership the post became known as Setzer's Store—until Arthur Tanner bought it, about 1939, moved it ten miles east, and renamed it Pueblo Alto Trading Post.

[14] Full text of both confessions, in places contradictory as Chávez attempted to make Augustine an equal partner in the affair, was printed in the Gallup *Herald*, July 20, 1918. The murder occurred the evening of July 17.

quarters. He arose from a chair where he was reading when Chávez called to be admitted, and unlocked the screen door. The Indian made a pretense of wanting to buy something and demanded credit, but Smith, again settling down in his chair, told him he would have to come back the next day. Those were probably his last words. Chávez circled behind him and hit him on the back of the head with a pistol. The blows that killed Smith were struck with a broken chair arm as he lay unconscious on the floor. Oil obtained from the warehouse was splashed through the room, the body covered with magazines and newspapers, and then Chávez and Augustine dropped matches in the oily pools and fled.

Augustine, even though he admitted he had helped in carrying the oil and starting the fire, was released some weeks afterward. Chávez was tried for murder at Bernalillo in February, 1919, and sentenced to a term of twenty-five to thirty-five years in the penitentiary at Santa Fe. He died there on April 8, 1928.[15]

Courts and juries in some parts of the Southwest frequently took a lenient view of murder. Certain distinctions should be made, however, between the legal and the popular attitudes. The people, as distinguished from juries and courts, generally were not in favor of murder, and rather frowned on it.

There was neither widespread approval nor astonishment, then, over the jury's verdict when Clyde Byal was brought to trial at San Juan County Court in Aztec for the attempted murder of trader Ed Doonan.

An extension of the same restiveness that hung everywhere like a fog that summer of 1918, the shooting occurred at Doonan's Chaco Canyon store the evening of September 29. The store and connecting living rooms, originally built by Richard Wetherill in 1899 as a guest house for the Hyde Exploring Expedition, stood at the southeast corner of the ruins of Pueblo del Arroyo. The front door facing east, opened into a small yard fenced off by a low stone wall.[16]

Hearing someone outside call his name, Doonan came to the door and stood there a moment, silhouetted against the lantern light at

15 This information was supplied by Warden T. M. Woodruff, by letter, January 28, 1959.
16 Having previously obliterated all trace of the nearby Wetherill buildings, the National Park Service, custodians of Chaco Canyon's great pueblo ruins, started demolishing this last landmark in the summer of 1960. In its final years, as the Park Service was erecting California ranch-style bungalows to replace the old stone buildings, the old store was converted into a museum by archaeologist Gordon Vivian, who made his home in the living quarters.

his back. Not more than ten yards away, just beyond the yard wall, he perceived the shadowy forms of two Navahos, and then light glinting on the steel of a rifle barrel.

The Indians' first shot struck Doonan in the right shoulder, turning him around. As he stumbled back into the house, to get his own rifle, his married daughter, Rose, came running from another room. Snatching up a blanket from a bed where her baby lay, Rose knocked the lantern to the floor. A series of shots were then exchanged in darkness, one of the .25–.20 slugs glancing off a wall and striking Rose in the arm as she knelt over her baby. Handicapped by his own wound and the darkness, Doonan knew that his shots were wild, but—as suddenly as it started—the firing ceased and the two Navahos rode off.

The next morning Doonan was taken to a hospital in Albuquerque, with Rose and her baby, by Doonan's son, who had been working in a cow camp north of the Chaco. The trader recovered within a few weeks, John Arrington recalled, but Rose and her brother, stricken with influenza, died while he was in the hospital.

"The case bothered me," Arrington said. "Two government marshals worked on it for about a month, but didn't get anywhere and left. I talked one day with an old squaw who told me that Clyde Byal and his brother were the men we wanted."

Twelve miles west of Chaco Canyon, on the Kin Biniola Wash, Arrington found and arrested Kee Byal. "At first he lied back and forth," Arrington said, "but finally he told what had happened. He said he held the horses that night at Doonan's store while his brother Clyde did the shooting. Later on I sent old Comanche, the Navaho policeman, down there and he brought Clyde in."

Watching the court proceedings in Aztec, Arrington was dazzled by the performance of the defense attorney, J. M. Palmer, who first presented Byal as the image of virtue and then browbeat a witness—who thought differently—into abject silence.

"Palmer had him *peoned* until he didn't know," Arrington recalled. Kee Byal testified that he was present when his brother fired at Doonan, but the jury chose not to believe him. Three bullets of unusual .25–.20 caliber recovered from the walls of Doonan's house were introduced in evidence. It was suggested that they had been fired from Clyde Byal's .25–.20 rifle, but several of the jurymen refused to go along with such a notion, and Byal was given his freedom.[17]

17 Jurors were chosen, testimony was heard, and the divided verdict was returned in one day: October 28, 1919. Judge Reed Holloman presided. An interesting sidelight developed when Chis-chili-begay, released from prison after less than

The jury's equivocal handling of the Clyde Byal case, popularly regarded with disfavor, almost certainly determined the outcome of events after Wally Kimmel was murdered. When Arrington quit as stockman at Kinnebito in 1920, he was succeeded by a man named John Tyler, and Tyler in turn was replaced within the year by Kimmel. The cause the new man gave for offence, if any, is not known; but near Kinnebito station, one day, he was shot and killed by a Navaho named Platero.

A group of armed men arrived at some point on the trail as Deputy Sheriff Westbrook was taking Platero to jail. Too far outnumbered to protest, Westbrook surrendered his prisoner. Platero was taken back to Kinnebito station and was hanged by a rope in a barn until he was dead. The body was cut down, taken to a high point in rocks above the wash, and was left there hanging from a cedar tree.

There is little that anyone can remember of Sloppy Jack Lewis' personality or behavior that could arouse resentment; among those who knew him well it is said that he had no enemies.

Named plain Frank Lewis when he was born in Paris in 1866, he was brought home to the United States while still an infant. At some distant date he moved to the Southwest and for all of his adult years was known in the vicinity of Gallup as an Indian trader and, from about 1915, as the owner of the post at China Springs. Located on high ground in a sheltered cove of rocks, China Springs was the scene of an ambush of United States cavalry by Navahos in 1863.[18] Nothing further of measurable interest occurred there until Lewis' time, although the post was on the main road between Gallup, five miles to the south, and Tohatchi.

three years for the murder of Richard Wetherill, threatened—because Clyde Byal was his son-in-law—to kill Arrington and other witnesses for the prosecution. Court records at Aztec show that a contempt order against Chis-chili was filed May 13 1919, charging him with intimidating witnesses, but for some reason a warrant was not served.

[18] Van Valkenburgh quotes an old Navaho's version of the encounter in these words: "We found out that more soldiers were being sent to Fort Wingate near Bear Springs. Some Navajos had been there and spied on them. A band collected at Many Arrows [China Springs]. They hid behind the rocks—all in a line and not far behind. A troop of soldiers came up the road, and the Navajos all shot at once. Chaali Sani shot the soldier captain right in the middle of the back of the neck and the bullet came out through his eye. Other soldiers, which we called Those Who Shoot From the Side, were shot down. Some got away on their horses." When the China Springs post was built is uncertain, but Frank Mapel operated it in 1911, selling it the same year to J. J. Phillips. Early Gallup newspaper items refer to the place variously as China Springs and Chinaman's Springs.

Charlie Newcomb has recalled a time in February when, starting from Naschiti with his wife and his brother Arthur, his 1918 vintage automobile bogged to the hubs in mud and had to be abandoned. A Navaho in a wagon took them on to China Springs, and here, after traveling forty miles in three days, nearly frozen and starved, "the Lewises and their daughter Mitzi gave us a royal welcome . . told us to come in and get warm.

"Mrs. Lewis set about fixing some food (We hadn't eaten in two days). She poured out some hot coffee and then—I'll never forget—hoisted a jug to her shoulder and put something in the coffee to stiffen it a little."

There was no extra bedroom, but blankets were found and the Lewises insisted that their guests stay overnight.

"I heard Lewis get up at 5 o'clock," Newcomb said, "so I got up too—and found him outside pounding dough in a big iron tub, fixing to make bread. Everyone called him Sloppy Jack because, well, because he was sloppy, I suppose. He was a big, middle-aged man, sort of fat. But there was nothing sloppy about his hospitality, or about the way he made bread . . . everything just as nice and clean as your own kitchen."

As most traders did, Lewis heated the store in winter with an iron stove placed in the bull-pen. At one time or another, undoubtedly in the evening or early morning when no one was around to observe, Sloppy Jack dug a hole in the floor directly beneath the stove, dropped in a bag of silver, and covered the opening with a thin stone slab. He may have been pleased with himself for devising this simple cache for his money. Perhaps it was a holdover from a time when his mother may have sewed up the family fortune in a mattress. It was a curious thing to do, nevertheless, especially since the banks in Gallup were only a few miles away.

No one knows how long Sloppy Jack had been burying his money under the stove, and we might guess that he happily belived that no one knew of the hiding place. There is no question at all, though, that he shared his secret with others the night of April 23, 1921. His wife and daughter were in Gallup because of Mitzi's illness, and Lewis was alone.

"The store which he conducted was a typical trading store of the West," the Gallup *Independent* reported five days later, "constructed partly of adobes and partly of lumber. People in Gallup and the mining camps saw the fire reflecting in the sky, and went out to see what it was. They found the store building in a mass of flames. There was no one near the place."

Days afterward, it was remembered that on the afternoon of the fire Lewis and a San Juan Navaho who was drunk had argued violently. The Indian, who insisted that Lewis take some worthless bauble in pawn, finally was driven from the store. Not willing to end it there, the Navaho caused a disturbance among the horses in the trader's corral—until Lewis came out with a gun and fired a few well-aimed shots over the man's head.

"After the fire subsided some," the *Independent* story continued, the onlookers "began raking the cinders and found the body of the unfortunate trader lying in the bedroom wrapped in a blanket. The verdict of the coroner's jury was that the man had been murdered, the body wrapped in a blanket, saturated with kerosene, and set on fire. . . .

"A long wire lariat was used to drag out the charred body . . . which was all but consumed by the fire. There were no signs of bullet holes."

Lewis, it was learned later, but not until much later when his murderers were indicted, was killed with blows from a wooden club and an ax. It became known also that on the same evening, as was his custom, Lewis had dropped a bag of money under the stove, and although the stone slab was neatly in place after the fire, there was no trace of the bag or the money.

The San Juan Navaho with whom Lewis had quarreled was brought to Gallup under arrest, was questioned, and released. The Indian had positive proof that he was not in the vicinity of China Springs when the trader was killed.

In the months that followed, trader Mike Kirk of Gallup and Frank Walker, an agency interpreter from Defiance, questioned more than twelve Navahos living between Gallup and Tohatchi. Their efforts were beginning to appear entirely hopeless when suddenly one day a few words spoken put them directly on the trail of three Navaho suspects. The men were arrested and jailed. As usual, the motive for murdering Lewis had not arisen from animosity. They had simply wanted his money.

The defendants—Noki Dena, Cha-cha-begay, and Noco Yazzie—appeared in Gallup court and, one year lacking a day after Lewis' murder, were found guilty and sentenced to hang. A motion for a new trial was denied, but defense counsel's motion for appeal was granted. Arraigned before the state Supreme Court, the defendants pleaded guilty, and all three were sentenced to serve from forty to fifty years in the state penitentiary.[19]

Other traders died in much the same way after 1921, including old Charles Hubbell, killed in the 1930's at a post in Arizona. An always present factor was the isolation—many times, the extreme isolation— of the trader from the nearest white settlement. Because the hazard was shared in common and the danger rarely one that arose from provocation, the possibility of sudden, violent death was a calculated part of a trader's life.

[19] Case No. 456, records of Gallup County Court. The Supreme Court sentences were handed down October 1, 1923.

24

Teec-nos-pos

HIS LOOKS belied his age. He was twenty-six years old and perhaps appeared five years younger when he applied for work with the Hyde Exploring Expedition. His name, Hambleton Bridger Noel, was entirely too heavy for such slender shoulders. But he had found his own way into Chaco Canyon and was frank about presenting his best, and at the moment only, assets: a head of wild corn-colored hair crying for cutting, a thin hungry face, a pair of good blue eyes, and a grin that could make you smile. Richard Wetherill, the Hyde company manager, took a liking to him and he was given a job.

H. B. Noel was a native of Essex County, Virginia. He was working for the Baltimore Traction Company (streetcars) when it was discovered he had lung trouble. To remedy that, he came to New Mexico in the summer of 1899 and joined his older brothers, Henry and Frank, at Two Gray Hills.

Winslow Wetherill, who had been working at Tiz-na-tzin, one of the Hyde Expedition posts twenty-five miles northwest of Pueblo Bonito, bought out Henry Noel in 1902. Hamp Noel stayed with Wetherill at Two Gray Hills about six months and then, his health much improved, applied at Chaco Canyon for a job. The Hyde Expedition had been engaged in archaeological work in Pueblo Bonito and was now launching into a fabulous trading business.[1] Young Noel was employed to run cattle in the Chaco, and then as a freighter.

---

1 Tiz-na-tzin was one of the oldest trading posts on the reservation. Located on Coal Creek Wash midway between Tsaya and Bisti, it was first operated by Old Man Swires, of whom practically nothing is known. John Arrington believed that

As a Hyde company freighter, Noel sometimes drove a four-horse team the long distance from Two Gray Hills to Albuquerque, going by way of Chaco Canyon and Cabezon, where Dick Heller's trading post prospered. The trips he looked forward to were those in the fall that took him to Albuquerque for the annual territorial fair. In those years the fair borrowed from the Wild West shows of Buffalo Bill and Pawnee Bill. Half of the excitement was provided by the Hyde Expedition, which usually brought about two hundred Navahos into camp at the fairgrounds, where they put on dances and took part in the parades and performances of bronc riding, roping, and marksmanship. The other half of the spectacle came with the mounted drills and simulated war maneuvers of cavalry sent over from Fort Wingate.

Noel left the Hyde Expedition to work a short time at Tohatchi for Lorenzo C. Haskell, and then moved on to clerk for the C. C. Manning store at Fort Defiance.[2]

"We didn't deal in the goods then that the trading posts do today," Noel has recalled. "Trade was mostly in coffee, flour, and calico. The men would come in wearing calico pants with garters around their buckskin leggins at the knee. There was a can of free tobacco on the counter—we furnished the brown papers too—and the Navahos rolled their own cigarettes and the air in the bull-pen got blue with smoke."[3]

The winter he spent at Two Gray Hills in 1902 with Win Wetherill, he remembered as one of the coldest he had known. Snow lay on the ground and the sky was threatening more, one afternoon, when "a Navaho woman came to the post and said her husband was bad sick —would I get Mrs. Cole, a missionary woman, and come to their hogan?[4] Mrs. Cole was at Toadlena, about six or eight miles west and up

---

Swires built the post in 1878, but this date might be early by several years. In any case, Swires, then an old man, was still there in 1895. Win Wetherill was clerking for the Hyde Expedition in 1900 when he operated the store. Soon afterward the post was abandoned with the demise of the Hyde Expedition. It was rebuilt and operated by Harvey Shawver of Farmington. John Arrington's brother Paul worked there for a time, as did George Blake, who then moved on to rebuild the old Tsaya post. After Shawver, the store was operated by Bert McJunkins. It no longer stands. A detailed account of the Hyde Exploring Expedition appears in the author's book, *Richard Wetherill: Anasazi*, and so only passing reference to the Hyde company's activities is made here.

2 A native of Bayard, Iowa, Haskell held a trader's license from 1898 through 1908. (*N. A., Ledgers of Traders.*)

3 Much of this chapter is based on a number of interviews with H. B. Noel at his home in Fruitland, New Mexico, in 1958–59.

4 Mrs. Henrietta Cole was in charge of a small Methodist mission, then located close to the Two Gray Hills post and north of the Tuntsa Wash. The mission was

where the Chuskas begin. It was snowing when I started out on horseback, but soon it got worse—blew up a driving blizzard that blinded
me. I couldn't see anything at all, just put my head down on the
horse's neck and gave him free rein to pick his own way. The horse
probably couldn't see any better than I could, but got me there after
dark. Mrs. Cole wouldn't go back with me that night so I stayed over
and we went in the morning. She was a pretty good doctor—anyhow,
the Navaho recovered."

In 1905, after securing the approval of Superintendent William T.
Shelton of Shiprock Agency, Noel chose the most improbable location
on the eastern side of the reservation to build his own trading post.
He loaded a wagon with trade goods and headed his team across the
all but trackless desert west of Shiprock and into the northern foothills of the Carrizo Mountains. His destination—a cottonwood-lined
canyon on T'iisnasbas Creek—was in country controlled by Black
Horse, known for his unfriendly feeling toward white men. Ten years
before, Black Horse had driven out two other men who came with a
similar purpose.[5]

John Wetherill, with Clyde Colville as companion, quite knowingly
took the same risk in March, 1906, when on the western side of the
reservation, under conditions almost identical to those now facing
Noel, he argued with tough old Hoskinini for permission to trade
at Oljetoh.

Alone, the Navahos of the region aware of his coming and waiting
for him, Noel sat on the wagon seat, driving for the Carrizos. He went
unarmed and would have made a simple target, now in the foothills,
or later, at a council he held with the Indians when he reached the
cottonwood canyon. Several hundred Navahos gathered there to de-
bate whether they wanted this small, unafraid white man to build a
trading post and settle among them. The talk lasted most of the day,
Noel going to his wagon for flour, coffee, and a few muttons to give
to the women that they might cook a feast in the late afternoon.

Clah-chis-chili (Left-handed Curly Man) spoke for Noel, telling
the Navahos he believed this man would treat them fairly. It was in

opened in 1898, and Mrs. Cole was appointed field matron two years later. She
was no longer there in 1909, but Mrs. Ed Davies said the Navahos still spoke of
her with respect, using the name *Esth-than-nez-tso,* or Tall Heavy Woman.

5 "Everybody made a living the best way he could in those days," Noel told me.
"A dollar looked as big as a house. Joe Hatch and Ed Thurland went to the Chuska
Mountains about 1895 and started to build a store. Black Horse called a meeting
and gave them until daylight next day to get out. They didn't argue the point,
and got out." Joe's father was Ira Hatch, a Mormon missionary to the Paiutes who
married a Paiute woman. Joe was one of their children.

Noel's favor that some of them already knew the trader at Sa-nos-tee —Frank Noel—his older brother, who was always honest with them. Opposing any suspicion they held, and any prejudice against another white man on the reservation, Clah spoke of the advantages to them of having a trading post here.

Time, of course, was a value of no importance to Navahos, but time plus distance plus rain or snow and cold was a thing of meaning. When they needed trade goods or had wool and sheep and hides to sell, a post here would save them long and hard miles of travel.

Clah was persuasive. But in the end the decision probably was made on the basis of Noel's kinship with the Sa-nos-tee trader, a good man, and on his own appearance: to these Indians he looked still scarcely more than a boy, but steady and unafraid. They said they would trust him, agreeing that he could build his post.

Noel lived in a hogan near the head of the canyon while the Teec-nos-pos (Cottonwoods in a Circle) store was built close by. But in spite of the Navahos' saying they would trust him, Noel found it difficult, in the first months, to trust the Navahos. There was not another white man within thirty miles.

"I knew I was up against it, but didn't want trouble," he once said. "A drummer sold me an automatic-loading, high-powered Remington rifle. I took the Navahos out and we shot at rabbits, or at pieces of rock high up in the canyon. After a lot of this shooting and letting the Indians see how I could shoot, I hung the rifle up. I put it on the wall back of the counter in easy reach and where they could see it. But I never had to take it down in a hurry. There was never any trouble."

Clah-chis-chili continued to befriend him. "He was a tribal judge, broad and squat, and he looked like a Ute," Noel said. This was as it should be because Clah's father once went up into Utah and bought three Ute girls for three blankets. He brought them back to Teec-nos-pos region where he lived and later married two of the young women and gave the third to his brother. Clah was one of the offspring.

A strong feeling of enmity existed between Navahos and the Jicarilla Apaches, Noel said, and consequently there was no intermarriage between the two tribes. Similarly, a Navaho would not marry a Ute woman; but it frequently happened that a raiding party of Navahos brought Ute and Paiute children back as slaves, and when the girls reached adolescence, they might marry into the Navaho tribe. In earlier years there was considerable intermarriage between San Juan Navahos and Mexicans living in the vicinity of Cuba and

Cabezon. Occasionally a woman from one of the Pueblo tribes would marry a Navaho.

Two years after he came to Teec-nos-pos, Noel built a second trading post about thirty miles farther west, on high plateau land south of the San Juan, calling it *Naakaii-toh*, or Mexican Water. This was empty country of redrock mesas where few white men had ever been.

"The post was open only a short time," Noel said, "when a Navaho came in with a pack train to sell me wool and blankets. His daughter—a girl maybe seventeen or eighteen years old—stood off to one side, not speaking a word. But she watched me steadily, every move I made, until I couldn't help being curious. I asked the man why his daughter looked at me that way. He said this was a very big experience in his daughter's life. I was the second white man she had ever seen. The first, a prospector, she saw when she was a child, and then from a long distance."

The freight wagons of John Wetherill, coming first from Oljetoh and later from Kayenta, when he moved there in 1910, were slow harbingers of civilization. Across the northern part of the reservation they made a track that appears on old maps as the Wetherill Trail, skirting the Carrizos and descending to Teec-nos-pos. Here, by prearrangement, the Wetherill wagons were unloaded and filled again from Noel's wareroom to return with goods and supplies needed at Kayenta. Noel then filled his own wagons with the freight from Kayenta and took it on for credit to the Wetherill account at the Progressive Mercantile wholesale store in Fruitland.

Navaho women in his region were exceptionally good weavers and before 1905 developed a serrated-outline design for their blankets that was peculiar to the region. Noel was convinced that a Mrs. Wilson, who might have been a missionary and who certainly lived somewhere on the San Juan, influenced the style now identified as Teec-nos-pos weaving. This he learned from the weavers themselves, since Mrs. Wilson was no longer in the country when he went there.

George Wharton James describes one blanket he found in Noel's collection, said to be unusual for both its design and the fact that it was woven by a man. The predominant colors were red, green, and white, two zigzag lines running through the center from top to bottom resembling lightning. James tells that he wished to purchase the blanket, but no offer he made "could shake, in the slightest, Mr. Noel's determination not to part with it."[6] Then as now, no limit be-

[6] A curious story that James tells in connection with the blanket may be apocryphal. Noel refused to sell the blanket (Fig. 143 in James's *Indian Blankets and*

yond the weaver's taste determined the choice of a blanket's colors, which could include various tones of green, blue, red, white, black, and purple. Four-ply Germantown yarns supplied this color range fifty years ago as the aniline dyes do today.

Word of troop movements on the reservation always spread rapidly and so it was, even in his isolated canyon, that Noel had forewarning of trouble in the fall of 1907. This resulted from several orders issued by Superintendent Shelton which met with widespread disfavor; among these was his order that Navaho children of certain areas henceforth must attend boarding school at Shiprock.

Byalille, head man of a clan and an influential medicine man then living in the Aneth region north of Teec-nos-pos, met the order with open defiance. Having no desire to repeat David Shipley's role in the incident of Black Horse's rebellion in 1892, Shelton called for the support of troops. Captain H. O. Williard with two companies of cavalry numbering about seventy-five men, started on a two-day march from Fort Wingate.

"Clah-chis-chili and three or four Indians came to see me at Teec-nos-pos, to tell me there might be trouble," Noel recalled. "Clah came as a friend, warning me that if the troops attacked, Byalille's outfit would cross the San Juan, rob my store, and with the supplies go to Hoskinini's country to hide out. He didn't say so directly, but Clah wanted me to know that if this happened, Byalille's people would burn my store and probably kill me.

"Williard's cavalry came to my brother's place at Sa-nos-tee and then at night went on to Shiprock. Just before daylight they surrounded Byalille's camp near Aneth and took fifteen or twenty prisoners. I was not there, but Indians who were told me about it later. One of the Navahos came out of his hogan with a rifle, went up behind a fence, and shot at one of the troopers and missed. The troops then opened fire and killed this man and one other Navaho. I don't think the soldiers had any casualties."[7]

Their Weavers), but agreed to let James borrow it so that he might have it photographed.

[7] Byalille was taken from his hogan before the shooting started. The horse of one of Williard's men was killed, but otherwise the attacking force, including Troops I and K, Fifth Cavalry, and a few Navaho police, suffered no losses. Paralleling the Reuben Perry case of 1905, the Indian prisoners were not brought to trial. Shelton recommended that Byalille and a man named Polly be sentenced to ten years' hard labor in prison, and that seven others be sentenced to two years. Commissioner Leupp concurred, and the nine prisoners were taken to Fort Huachuca.

Noel said he believed that Clah's warning was well grounded and that his trading post might have been burned if Byalille's camp had not been caught so completely off guard.

Praised and criticized for his administration of the agency, Shelton was a hard disciplinarian, a stubborn man who would tolerate no opposition to his methods.

All Navahos were unruly children, Shelton believed—magnifying the gleam of a reasonable premise—and so the rod was applied frequently. An empty jailhouse was a sign of laxity, so the agency police worked overtime and the jail scarcely ever wanted for tenants. All of his moments were not so stern, however, and the annual Shiprock Fair, which he started in 1909, benefited the Navahos, first by enabling the traders to exhibit and sell the best of their crafts, then by encouraging their skills in animal husbandry and agriculture.

But even the annual fair could bring out Shelton's autocratic tendencies, and the fair of 1911 provided an example.

"The fair was held during late October," Noel recalled, "but before the opening the weather was bad, raining hard off and on for about a week. All of the traders brought the best of their blankets and silverwork, camping on the river bottom among the cottonwoods just east of the old wooden bridge. The exhibit booths were set up in a large rectangle, on slightly higher ground, where the agency buildings are located today.

"When the river rose that night we moved and camped on Bruce Bernard's hill—a crowd of us huddled together like castaways on a tiny island.[8] In the morning I went down to the exhibit grounds where my horses were tied and found them in water up to their backs, stretching their necks up to keep from drowning.

"We wanted to move the exhibits, but Shelton told us we couldn't —we had to stay right there. I had five thousand dollars' worth of Navaho silverwork and blankets which I stood to lose, but Shelton told me I couldn't move it.

Again, as in the Perry case, the Indian Rights Association protested the extralegal handling of the affair, so effectively that the prisoners were released in March, 1909. (60 Cong., 1 sess., *Sen. Doc. 517*, "Report on Employment of U. S. Soldiers in Arresting By-a-lil-le and Other Navajo Indians.")

[8] One of the best known of the San Juan traders, Bruce Bernard about 1909 bought Robert Stuart Baker's Shiprock Trading Post. The store then was located just west and at the foot of the hill Noel speaks of. Another trading post, operated by Walker and Hubbard, just below Bernard's store was bought by Will Evans soon after 1911. Much enlarged, the Evans post is now operated as the Shiprock Trading Company by Russell Foutz. Bruce Bernard moved his post to the top of the hill about 1917–18 and ran it until his death in 1952.

"During the morning Harry Baldwin, eight miles east of us up at the Hogback Trading Post, called on the telephone and told my brother Frank that the river was cresting and water already was up around his door.

"Frank and the rest of us packed up our exhibits—just defied Shelton, who still didn't want us to move—and pulled out to higher ground. If we hadn't we would have all gone beautifully broke.

"The river crest hit Shiprock a few hours later, swept away the San Juan bridge and the exhibit booths, and filled the bottomland to the eaves of the houses. It was the worst flood in the valley's history."[9]

[9] Noel sold the Naakaii-toh post several years after building it, and sold Teec-nos-pos in 1913 to Bert Dustin in order to go into ranching at Fruitland. Owned in recent years by Russell Foutz, Teec-nos-pos was destroyed by fire in the spring of 1959. It was rebuilt the same year a few miles east and north of the original site.

25

Beautiful Mountain

BEAUTIFUL MOUNTAIN is one of the cloud-gathering taller peaks of the Lukachukai range, southwest of Shiprock Agency by thirty-five miles. A rider approaching its foothills from the east and across the valley, is first aware of change as the flatly undulating desert forms into humpy brown sandhills. These progress in taller waves upon each other until rock outcroppings appear; in turn the outcroppings mount higher until they merge with pink sandstone cliffs.

A canyon forms, a mile wide at the mouth, shallowing out into a broad and greening valley that narrows gently as it ascends. Quite as beautiful as the mountain it drains, the valley is shaded by cottonwoods and patterned in rectangles by Navaho cornfields.

Always in sight above, always withdrawing, the mountain's crest touches 8,340 feet. From piñon level, far higher than cottonwoods will grow, the mountain builds upward in three rocky terraces, the intervening slopes green with scrub fir. One thin trail for a horseman mounts the third and highest terrace. Here, near the top, the slopes break against a vertical serrated palisade of brown rock. Above this collar the mountain's crown pulls inward to a peak, a dark cap of fir trees.

In camp near the summit a small band of Navahos went into hiding in the fall of 1913, and for more than two months defied all efforts of the United States government to dislodge them. Referred to since as the Beautiful Mountain Uprising, their revolt was led by the medicine man Bi-joshii. It was the last time in this country that a large force of troops was used against Indians.

Among those drawn into the affair, and eventually suffering from it, was Frank L. Noel, whose Sa-nos-tee trading post became the mediation point for Bi-joshii's people and various agents of the government.

Frank Noel's store was a small building of stone and adobe set among cottonwoods and facing, across a wide clearing, a group of log sheds, a plank barn, and string of corrals. Lower than the desert plateau, and at the eastern foot of Beautiful Mountain, the post was down on the sandbar of a wide arroyo cut by Sa-nos-tee (Surrounded by Rocks) Wash.[1]

Dinét-sosi-begay, well knowing Superintendent Shelton's edict against plural marriages among Navahos, and perhaps seeking favors or revenge, touched off the trouble. To Shiprock Agency one day in September, 1913, he brought a story that Hatot'cli-yazzie—a son of Bi-joshii and medicine man in his own right—"had three wives, two of them young women whom he had taken within the last year or two."[2] And further, he said, this same Little Singer but recently returned from a visit with Utes at Ignacio, brought with him whisky in bottles, and tried to force the stuff into the mouth of his third wife. Shelton directed that Hatot'cli-yazzie and his wives be brought to the agency for questioning. Navaho police were unable to find Little Singer, said to be far off at Black Mountain, but managed to bring in the three women.

---

[1] According to Hugh Foutz, Sa-nos-tee was built by Will Evans for Joseph Wilkin, probably about 1899 or 1900, after Wilkin sold his interest in Two Gray Hills to Henry and Frank Noel. Evans stayed on for a time to run the store for Wilkin. In the spring of 1905 Wilkin sold to Frank Noel, who operated the post under the names Little Water and Sa-nos-tee until he sold to Paul Brink about 1922. In recent years the store has been owned by Hugh Foutz and his son Munro.

[2] Report of Superintendent Shelton to C. I. A. Cato Sells, December 5, 1913. (National Archives, Record Group 75, Classified Files, 120395–13–121, 146247–13–123, 150298–13–175, San Juan.) For the story of the Beautiful Mountain uprising I have drawn upon some 100 letters and telegrams in these files; equally helpful have been interviews with Frank and H. B. Noel and J. R. Galusha. After reading an early draft of this chapter, Frank Noel supplemented the material I then had with his own notes on the surrender negotiations between General Scott and Bi-joshii, and also made available to me his own unpublished manuscript, "Eighty Years in America." While visiting my home in Farmington, Charlie Newcomb recalled the night that General Scott's advance party camped at his Naschiti store. I have made some use of the files of the Gallup *Independent*, November 27 and December 4, 1913, and of the *McKinley County Republican*, November 28, 1913. Wilken, in *Anselm Weber, O.E.M., Missionary to the Navaho*, 181–89, gives an excellent account of the uprising drawn mainly from the notes of Fr. Weber. Davidson B. McKibben's account, "Revolt of the Navaho, 1913," *New Mexico Historical Review*, Vol. XXIX, No. 4 (1954), is based largely upon National Archives material cited above, and contemporary newspaper files.

On September 17, when Shelton was absent and in Durango, old Bi-joshii, with Little Singer and nine other men, rode into the agency like a hailstorm, freed the three women by armed force, and went off with them. One of Shelton's police who tried to stop them was disarmed and quirt-whipped over the head. Three days later, reporting the incident to U. S. District Attorney Somers Burkhart, in Santa Fe, Shelton said it was necessary to make an example of these Navahos. He asked that warrants be issued for their arrest.

Bi-joshii and his people went into camp, above Frank Noel's Sa-nostee store, on Beautiful Mountain; by mid-October Shelton had warrants charging Bi-joshii and eleven of his men with various offenses, including riot, horse-stealing, deadly assault, stealing a government revolver, and flourishing arms in a settlement. The old medicine man made it clear, meanwhile, that he would not surrender and he and his people would fight before submitting to arrest. On October 16, Commissioner of Indian Affairs Cato Sells telegraphed Shelton that, at the latter's request, he had asked the Justice Department to send a United States marshal to the scene. He urged Shelton, who was then forming a citizens' posse in Farmington and Aztec, to "proceed with care and good judgment" and to "use sufficient force but to avoid unnecessary violence."

Preliminary discussions towards a peaceful solution were held at St. Michaels Mission on October 18, when Fr. Anselm Weber met with Chee Dodge and Superintendent Peter Paquette of Fort Defiance Agency.[3] After this talk, Fr. Weber, Chee Dodge, Peshlakai, the agency interpreter Charley Mitchell, and Black Horse, went into the Lukachukais in search of Bi-joshii's band. They found Hatot'cli-yazzie, whom they then believed to be the leader of the revolt, at a big squaw dance and asked him to come in for a council at St. Michaels. The Navaho agreed but insisted that regardless of what might be said there, he would not surrender to Shelton.

Eight days later a group including Fr. Weber, U. S. Marshal A. H. Hudspeth, Shelton, Paquette, and Chee Dodge, waited at St. Michaels for the Indians to come in—and waited in vain. Indian Supervisor William R. Rosenkrans, then in Gallup, wrote Commissioner Sells on October 29 that the Navahos decided not to go to St. Michaels when they learned that Shelton and Hudspeth would be there.

3 Shelton said he telegraphed Paquette asking him "to get Chee Dodge, a half-breed Indian . . . to use his influence" in persuading the Navahos to surrender. Shelton added that he learned later that Chee Dodge was "peeved" with him—a gentle understatement—because "of an idea he had that I was too strict with the Indians."

349

Peshlakai and Charley Mitchell in the week following made contact again with the Navahos, this time with Bi-joshii instead of his son. The old man agreed to surrender on November 13—but changed his mind before that date arrived.

The affair took a more menacing turn at the end of the first week of November when newspaper wire services, after the first account of the trouble appeared in the Farmington *Enterprise*, sent out exaggerated stories of a threatening Navaho revolt and the stories appeared in client newspapers across the country under scare headlines. On November 7, Shelton wired Commissioner Sells that he had been warned in a message from Peter Paquette that Bi-joshii was on his way to Shiprock to ask for a complete pardon—and if the pardon was not granted, his Navahos would attack the agency.[4] Shelton asked permission to employ citizen posses for protection.

Commissioner Sells telegraphed Shelton the next day to use force if necessary, but to be careful. He advised the superintendent that Secretary of the Interior Franklin K. Lane had instructed Inspector James McLaughlin to proceed at once from his station at Devils Lake, North Dakota, to Shiprock Agency, and upon arrival there act as the Indian Office's personal mediator and representative. A former agent for the Sioux, Major McLaughlin was a veteran in negotiating such disputes.

Members of Bi-joshii's band were coming almost daily to Frank Noel's trading post, their movements between their mountain camp and the store unhindered. Noel thus found himself between two seemingly irreconcilable forces, friendly to both disputing sides, the person each side used for communicating with the other. From this rather unhappy position the trader could resolve the trouble in its simplest terms:

They were guilty of no wrong, Bi-joshii's people told Noel. Shelton, in fact, was the offender against peace by having the three wives of Hatot'cli-yazzie arrested and held prisoner at the agency. The Navahos had done no wrong either, they felt, in coming to the agency and setting the women free. They hated and feared Shelton and under no condition would surrender to him.

Shelton, for his part, maintained that Bi-joshii's people were well aware that plural marriages were not sanctioned by the government. He had acted properly, Shelton said, in having the women brought

---

[4] Paquette soon after notified Shelton that his information was incorrect, and Bi-joshii had made no such threat.

to the agency. By coming with guns, roughing up his policeman and threatening other agency employees, and running off with the three women prisoners, Bi-joshii's people were guilty of riot and violation of lawful processes.

Relying upon information he received from Frank Noel, and on the same day that he learned Major McLaughlin was coming to his aid, Shelton telegraphed the commissioner: "Situation unchanged. . . . Received reliable information that majority of gang will fight to finish. Every precaution has been and will be taken to handle situation with least trouble and expense."

Fr. Anselm Weber, having tried once and failed, thought he would try again to arbitrate the differences before it was too late to prevent bloodshed. The Franciscan priest was known by name, if not by person, to nearly all Navahos. His fifteen years at St. Michaels were a remarkable achievement in missionary work—not because he won many converts to his faith, but because his efforts to help the Navahos in their immediate, daily troubles were so effective as to deserve their trust and friendship. On November 8, therefore, he made plans to go to Sa-nos-tee and, if possible, arrange a council between Shelton and Bi-joshii's band. He was accompanied to Noel's trading post by Frank Walker and several influential head men of the tribe. In the presence of Frank Noel and another trader, he met with Bi-joshii's people during the next two days, and earnestly advised them to give themselves up.

Shelton remained away, which may account for Fr. Weber's partial success. Two members of Bi-joshii's band, At-do-la and Clah-begay, least persuaded of the wisdom of the medicine man's course, surrendered to Shelton at the agency. On November 15 they were taken to Santa Fe by United States Deputy Marshal J. R. Galusha. When they appeared before federal District Judge William H. Pope on November 19, they were found guilty of unlawful assembly and sentenced to ninety days in jail. Judge Pope stayed execution of sentence, however, and soon after dismissed the charges and set them free.

Meanwhile, Major McLaughlin arrived at Shiprock and was met on November 13 by Shelton and Anselm Weber. Two days later the Franciscan friar returned to Sa-nos-tee with the Major for still another conference with Bi-joshii. Nothing that either of them could say was to any purpose, however, and by eight o'clock that night McLaughlin was back at Shiprock reporting failure.

The renegades, now numbering about fifteen men, "absolutely refuse to surrender," he telegraphed Secretary Lane. It would be unwise to attempt their arrest with civilian posses, but "Marshal [Hudspeth] has concluded to apply for U. S. troops to make the arrest, which I also recommend and Superintendent Shelton concurs, to insure the arrest without bloodshed. . . . I recommend sufficient force to over-awe the recalcitrant band. . . . I recommend prompt action."

He would greatly regret to use force, Secretary Lane telegraphed back the following day, "and this must be the last resort. Is it not possible to starve the recalcitrants out? Have they water where they are, and food? How much ammunition have they? Could we not sur-round them and keep them from getting food or water? . . . I am not favorable to the use of troops if this can be avoided."

Nothing less than a battalion of troops would be effective, Mc-Laughlin replied. Bi-joshii's band was entrenched on the mountain six miles northwest and above Noel's trading post, with enough food, water and ammunition to withstand a siege. From a military point of view, the Major added "their camp cannot be reached by the regular trail from Noel's store, which is through a narrow, tortuous gorge between high rimrock walls with numerous large rocks overhanging the trail, behind which defenders can shelter themselves and prevent any body of men from reaching their camp from that direction. They can only be successfully reached by coming over the mountain and approaching their camp from the northwest or southwest. It would require 500 men to surround their camp and in my judgment they cannot be starved into submission . . . and while all the Navajo ex-cept these fifteen are friendly and exceedingly anxious that they sur-render, they, at the same time . . . would furnish any of this lawless band with subsistence and ammunition if demanded by them."

The aging veteran of Sioux campaigns may have been too easily shaken by his aged Navaho adversary. Bi-joshii, the Major reported seriously, was threatening the life of the trader named Walker, whose post was fifteen miles northwest; the old devil also was threatening that he would burn the agency sawmill six miles south of his camp and would kill the white people working there. Unless troops were ordered out promptly, McLaughlin said, further delay would only result in bringing other Navahos to Bi-joshii's support.

Major McLaughlin's arguments were persuasive enough. Secretary Lane on November 18 requested the War Department to dispatch troops, and at the same time asked Major McLaughlin to remain and report to the commander. This was to be Brigadier General Hugh L. Scott, then on Mexican border patrol, commanding the Second Cav-alry Brigade at Fort Bliss, Texas. General Scott's orders were to proceed from El Paso to Gallup and there await the arrival by train of Troops A, B, C, and D of the Twelfth Cavalry, then stationed at Fort Robinson, Nebraska.

Superintendent Shelton meanwhile advised Commissioner Sells that he had directed the sawmill employees to withdraw to the safety of the agency. Also, he "suggested to trader Walker [that he] close up his store and bring all white people there off the reservation."[5] He said he was trying to arrange for a few white men to go to Frank Noel's Sa-nos-tee post for protection. Shelton added that Noel and his family would remain at Sa-nos-tee because otherwise their departure would "arouse suspicion and might do harm." And as further evidence that he believed the winds of his little storm were about to blow up a gale, Shelton requested permission to employ extra night guards to protect the agency.

With the telegraph wires humming and the news services and the War Department alerted, what now of old Bi-joshii and his dozen followers? Shelton forwarded to Sells the latest message received from Frank Noel.

"Things have taken a turn for the worse here," Noel wrote. "After their talk with the Inspector the Link Gang went up to their camp and moved higher up on the mountain.[6] They openly say they are not going to Santa Fe or even to Shiprock. Hosteen Nez' brother has gone back to them and now says he is going to stay with them. All the In-

---

[5] Frank Noel told me that Olin C. Walker heeded Shelton's warning, closed his Red Rock store, and brought his family in to Shiprock. Walker built Red Rock post about 1908. Located just within the eastern boundary of Arizona, the store is sixteen miles southwest of Shiprock pinnacle. Walker's original store was forty by twenty feet, with two adjacent warerooms. Eighteen-inch walls were poured— using a mixture of adobe and stone. Ceilings were of old pueblo-style construction, some of the heavy beams measuring a foot thick. Willis Martin bought the post in 1918, Roswell Nelson, son of Charles, going there as manager and, later, part owner. The Navaho name for the store's location is *Tse-liche-daskan,* a reference to the redrock haycocks and mesas of the region. The people of the sawmill, according to Noel, "were all Navahos, except Mr. and Mrs. James Ayres, who with their son Willard lived at the sawmill and operated it for the government. During the trouble they came down to Sa-nos-tee and stayed with me until Bi-joshii and his people were taken away."

[6] The reference is to the two-hour conference McLaughlin and Fr. Weber had with the Indians on November 15. H. B. Noel told me that Mrs. Joseph Wilkin, while living at Sa-nos-tee before his brother Frank's time, nicknamed Bi-joshii "The Missing Link"—an acid commentary on the old man's appearance. Small, gnarled, bent with age and probably rheumatism, the medicine man was scarcely handsome. His hair was gray, almost white, and a luxuriant mustache—rare among Navahos—made a formidable brush above a protruding chin.

353

dians have drawn off and left them alone and the old men around here say they will not talk to them any more.

"The Links are expecting trouble any day and are living at a high tension and the least thing may cause trouble to start here at any time. Several Indians have offered to come here and stay, so I do not think there will be [the] least danger in us staying here. . . .

"The more the matter is talked over the madder they get and they have never changed an inch of what they first said, that if you wanted them you would have to come and get them. One of the gang comes down every day and sets around all day to learn if there is any news.

"The Links have told around that if trouble started they would take any good horses they happened to run on to. For that reason some of the other Indians have armed themselves to protect their property. There will likely be something happen to start trouble soon if the Links are not taken care of."

Major McLaughlin was at Sa-nos-tee when Noel wrote this message, but returned to Shiprock to telegraph Secretary Lane on November 20 that Hosteen Nez-bit-chili had surrendered and was being taken to jail at Aztec.

Fed with feverishly inaccurate reports by Superintendent Shelton, newspapers from Albuquerque to Washington published stories to the effect that a large part of the Navaho tribe was in revolt, a horrible massacre was impending, and, if slaughter could be averted, it would be done only through the intrepid action of the United States Cavalry. Anselm Weber, who knew that one small hogan would more than shelter all of the Navahos who defied the government, visualized better than anyone else the real possibilities of bloodshed.

Acting now officially as a mediator at the request of Cato Sells, Fr. Weber went to Gallup with Chee Dodge and Superintendent Paquette on November 23 to talk with General Scott. Arriving there himself only a few hours before, the General received them at his hotel. With all of the eloquence he could command the friar told what he knew of the dispute, beginning with the arrest of the three wives of Hatot'cli-yazzie. He begged the General to use tact and patience. General Scott replied that he had no intention of starting an Indian war, but felt that a show of force was necessary to convince Bi-joshii's band of the seriousness of the situation. He asked Fr. Weber if he would precede him to Sa-nos-tee and there arrange a meeting with the medicine man.

A telegram sent by the missionary the following day from Farmington indicates that Fr. Weber may have gone directly to Shiprock from his meeting with General Scott.[7] In this message, addressed to Charles Lusk, secretary of the Bureau of Catholic Indian Missions, Fr. Weber said he was leaving the same day, with Chee Dodge, Peshlakai, Charley Mitchell, and Fr. Norbert Gottbrath "for the camp of the Indians to induce them to meet General Scott at Noel's Store Wednesday evening [November 26]."

In Gallup, meanwhile, the four troops of cavalry from Fort Robinson arrived on two special trains Sunday night, November 23, going into camp on the west side of town. Considering that their adversaries now numbered twelve men, it was a strong force: 261 men and officers, supplied with 300 rounds of ammunition per man, 256 horses, 40 mules, and 8 wagons.[8]

Again from Shiprock, Major McLaughlin advised Secretary Lane that he was leaving on Tuesday morning for Nelson's trading post, where he expected to meet General Scott. Accompanied by Troop C and its commander, Captain F. T. Arnold, and Deputy Marshall Galusha, General Scott left Gallup in advance of the main body of his squadron and started by automobile the same day for Sa-nos-tee. This was a mistake, as the weather for two weeks had been foul. The General's car mired down in snow and mud and finally had to be abandoned at China Springs, a few miles north of Gallup. From that point on, according to Marshal Galusha, the General proceeded on horseback. Behind him, and a day later, the three remaining cavalry troops followed slowly.

At Tohatchi the General's advance party stopped long enough to clean out the edible supplies of trader Albert Arnold. Pork was roasted that night over campfires around Charles Newcomb's Naschiti store, Newcomb afterward remembering a nervousness among the soldiers.

"As nearly as I remember, there were sixty cavalrymen at Naschiti that night," Newcomb said. "From the questions they asked me I could tell they were uneasy and worried that they might be attacked by Navahos before morning. They built their fires as close to the store as they could safely get."

---

[7] Wilken says that Fr. Weber went from Gallup to Fort Defiance and then, by two-day horseback trip across the mountains, to Frank Noel's store. Galusha told me that the friar came to Sa-nos-tee "from over the mountains." This leaves unexplained Fr. Weber's November 24 telegram, sent from Farmington. Presumably Fr. Weber was not near Farmington at the time and the telegram was sent, over his name, by someone else.

[8] The Gallup *Independent,* November, 27, 1913. In the same story it is reported that General Scott left for Sa-nos-tee on Tuesday, November 25.

Another commanding officer might have made this unease a justification for gathering his full force of cavalry to wipe Bi-joshii and his little band into oblivion. This, however, was Hugh L. Scott, not John Chivington or George A. Custer; there would be no small Sand Creek or Washita ferocity here. Accompanied only by his son and aide-de-camp, Lieutenant D. H. Scott, Deputy Marshal Galusha, and the interpreter Frank Walker, the General went on ahead to Sa-nos-tee. Captain Arnold and C Troop halted at Nelson's Store, twenty miles southeast, where they were met by Inspector McLaughlin and went into camp. Troops A, B, and D, including a jackass battery of Gatling guns, and dragging the escort wagons through mud, joined C Troop there the following day.[9]

Sometime after the General's arrival at Noel's trading post, Fr. Weber came to Sa-nos-tee with Chee Dodge and Fr. Gottbrath. Word was sent to Bi-joshii's camp on Beautiful Mountain, asking him to appear at a council. The medicine man and a number of his people, including several women, came to Noel's store the afternoon of Thursday, November 27—Thanksgiving Day. Before there was any talk, and at Scott's request, the Navahos were taken to the trading post hogan and given a feast of mutton. Afterward, with Chee Dodge as interpreter, the General greeted Bi-joshii in Noel's store. He briefly explained his mission, emphasizing that if the Navahos chose to fight rather than surrender, they would surely die. They had done wrong at Shiprock Agency in taking the law into their own hands, he said, and must now give themselves up and submit to trial.

Frank Noel recalled that when the council was resumed the following day, "some eighteen or twenty Indians were standing around the bull-pen in the store. General Scott, dressed in full uniform, was sitting in a large rocking chair facing them, his back to the high counter . . . Lieutenant Scott stood at one side of him and I on the other. We were all unarmed, but Lieutenant Scott did have a revolver within reach with which to protect his father should the Indians become excited and get unmanageable. Tension was high, and we could see the Indians did not all feel alike about what they should do.[10]

[9] Mounted on wheels and light carriage, a Gatling gun would be broken down and transported by three mules: one mule would carry the gun barrel, another the wheels and carriage, a third the ammunition. Father to the modern machine gun, named for its inventor, R. J. Gatling, the weapon consisted of a cluster of gun barrels which were revolved by a crank, firing up to 600 shots a minute. Gatling guns were common cavalry equipment in the last years of the Indian wars.

[10] Others present and not mentioned by Frank Noel included Anselm Weber

"Over a hundred Navahos of the region—not members of Bi-joshii's band or particularly sympathetic to him—were squatting or standing in groups around the yard outside. Mrs. Noel, with our children and the other white people staying with us at the time, were sitting quietly in the living room of the trading post.[11]

"In opening the council, General Scott let the Indians explain how they felt and tell of their grievances. Then the General spoke, saying that the laws in the land must be kept by whites and Indians alike. He told of the destruction and death and sadness that would result if the Indians made the government use the soldiers against them. He promised that the same soldiers would protect the Navahos if anyone should try to molest them. He explained again why the Indians must come to court for having broken the law, and told them that after their punishment they could return safely and live in peace on the mountain with their wives and children.

"Finally, General Scott asked them to say what they wanted to do. The young men one by one surrendered and asked for peace. Now it was Beshoshie's turn. The old man stepped before the General, and shaking with emotion declared that if it were for himself alone, he would never surrender. He had never been afraid of white sholdiers, and he was not afraid now—but he was not a young man. This wasn't his fight. And if the young men of his band wanted to surrender, then he would go with them.

" 'But I am not afraid of you,' he repeated angrily, and with a sincerity that left no room for doubt in our minds."[12]

General Scott allowed the Navahos to return to their camp on Beautiful Mountain, after receiving their promise to return within two days. From Nelson's trading post, Major McLaughlin telegraphed Secretary Lane: "All the indicted Navajos surrendered this afternoon without bloodshed except two who are hunting in the moun-

and Deputy Marshal Galusha. Although Bi-joshii agreed to come in to talk only if the General's party was unarmed, Galusha told me that he, for one, ignored the agreement. Fearing that there might be trouble, he strapped to his body and concealed under his loose, baggy coveralls, five or six revolvers.

11 There were about twenty persons gathered in the living room. Besides Mrs. Noel and the Noel and Nelson children, they included Miss Louisa Robinson, the children's teacher, who lived at the post; Mr. and Mrs. James Ayres and their son Willard, from the sawmill; Charles Nelson's wife, Emma; and Milton and Jennie Steele, who helped at the store.

12 Deputy Marshal Galusha, recalling the same moment, told me that Bi-joshii waved a gnarled hand almost in General Scott's face as he declared: "I can see blood on this hand. I am afraid there might be blood on this hand again. But I am not afraid of *you*!"

tains [Hatot'cli-yazzie and one other, whom Bi-joshii promised to bring with him on his return]... This ends uneasiness on the reservation as all other Navajos are friendly disposed and much pleased over the happy ending."

True to his agreement, Bi-joshii came down to Sa-nos-tee on Sunday with all of the men in his band, now numbering only seven. Placed in an army ambulance, they were taken to Gallup by Deputy Marshal Galusha and put on a train for Santa Fe. As a condition of their surrender, they were accompanied by Fr. Weber and Chee Dodge, who appeared with them in United States District Court before Judge Pope on December 3. The eighth defendant, Nez-bit-chili, was brought from Aztec jail to stand trial with them.

The day following, Judge Pope dismissed all charges against the Navahos but one: unlawful assembly to seize the three wives of Hatot'cli-yazzie. Bi-joshii and two of his other sons, Atcitty Nez-begay and Bi-joshii-begay, and also Hosh-tah and Ne-do-wille-begay, were sentenced to ten days in jail. Hatot'cli-yazzie and Ne-do-wille-benali were sentenced to thirty days. The charge against Nez-bit-chili, the old medicine man's son-in-law, was dismisssed.[13] Judge Pope directed that the sentences be served in McKinley County jail, at Gallup.

Still smarting because General Scott had ordered him to stay away from the surrender council at Sa-nos-tee, Superintendent Shelton was outraged when he learned of these relatively light sentences. The measure of punishment reflected on the importance he had made of the affair.

"It seems a farce," he fumed in his report to Commissioner Sells, "after the amount of expense and trouble it has taken to get these Indians under arrest... to give them a few days in jail."

Frank Noel had been on friendly terms with Shelton before the uprising. He found now, because of his part as a mediator, that he had won Shelton's enmity. As evidence of his feelings, the superintendent issued a license to Jess Foutz and Sante Bowen for a new trading post at Tocito, only seven miles southeast of Sa-nos-tee and close enough to cut Noel's trading business in half.[14]

13 Criminal Cases, Nos. 152–162, 1913, Federal District Court, Santa Fe.

14 Frank Noel told me that in spite of Shelton's telegram to Commissioner Sells saying "it would arouse suspicion" if Noel left his store to come to the agency, that Shelton in fact had wanted him to come in and, through the trader, Joe Tanner, had ordered him to do so. Noel said he refused to leave Sa-nos-tee, "and that is where Shelton and I drifted apart."

Epilogue

BEAUTIFUL MOUNTAIN was an anachronism. Bi-joshii's defiance was pitiful, absurd, hopelessly brave. Instinctively, the futile uprising recognized, as it tried to deny, this medicine man's old way of life belonged to another era.

Two years later, in 1915, Superintendent Shelton offered a prosaic epitaph when he wrote to C. C. Manning that "our dreams about good roads are beginning to be reality." Indeed they were. In early April, Gallup Mercantile sent out its first truck—the first gasoline vehicle to make the run—to Farmington. In June, Lew H. Miller traveled the ninety-odd miles between Gallup and Shiprock in only ten hours, his automobile sometimes hurtling along at thirty miles an hour.[1]

New dirt roads and lumbering automobiles. As nothing before them could, they demolished the prairie distances. In time they imposed a new order that erased the old Indian trader, opened new dimensions to the pony-Indian economy.

The old-time trader's end was hastened by Commissioner John Collier's stock reduction program, introduced in 1933 and applied indiscriminately and on the same terms to small as well as large owners of sheep and goats. Collier's program was essential, in its basic aim, to halt overgrazing and soil erosion, and certainly it was well intentioned. In the Navaho view, the plan was ruthlessly unfair, dictatorial, and disastrously mismanaged. On his farm at Cudei, on the San Juan side of the Carrizo Mountains, Sam Akeah recalled bit-

[1] The Gallup *Independent*, April 1, April 8, and June 3, 1915.

359

terly that "a fight all the time was going on, people going to jail. Those who talked loud against it were put in jail. They were taken in at night."[2]

Sam Akeah in 1933 was a moderately prosperous Navaho. He then owned 45 goats and 550 sheep. Four years later, because there was nothing else to do, his family had eaten most of the goats and sold all of the sheep at three dollars a head—one-third of their normal value. In 1946, Akeah was elected chairman of the Tribal Council, and served until 1954. On the day he spoke of the Collier regime, in 1958, he was again a farming Navaho, but not prosperous, owning a cornfield, a melon patch, a few goats, and a few horses. No sheep.

John Collier in 1947 understood the consequences of his stock reduction program. "That was twelve years ago," he wrote. "Today, on the Navajo reservation, anguish of spirit is a wolf against the breast, and struggle rages, hardly less than any year before. There are no large lines of the endeavor which the Indian Service would erase if it could go back."[3]

There was no sudden point or day or even year of change, but there was a gradual turning in new directions. Hardships remain, but are diminished. A trader still must be more independently resourceful than his urban cousin, but less so than before. As distances have been overcome by roads, time has been shortened, and the trader's life has become simpler. Once, when the post at Kayenta needed supplies, Ben Wetherill took a string of pack mules one hundred miles to the Hogback on the San Juan. Kayenta traders today lift a boot to the chair rung, tilt back, and wait for the Kimbell truck to unload the week's order on the wareroom floor. Ben Wetherill might have been on the trail two weeks and then lost half his supplies in a gully-washer. The big trucks are rarely delayed more than a few hours, and they lose nothing.

Television sets, radios, and telephones are commonplace in remote regions where the old traders once came to terms with oppressive solitude. Most of the trading posts now are held in absentee ownership—so frowned on in Ben Hyatt's day—and hired managers now may lock up any week night or week end and drive forty to one hundred miles to the nearest town for recreation and companionship.

The exceptional owner-operated posts usually are the most successful: Don Walker's Crownpoint Trading Company is one, Don

2 Interview at Cudei, January 4, 1958.
3 John Collier, *The Indians of the Americas*, 276.

Jensen's Crystal post is another. Camille García's new Chinle store is perhaps singular in that it is the best, or at least the most astonishing, example of what is becoming a trend—the transition of the Indian trader to super market operator. Indians still may, and still do, sell wool and hides and fine blankets at these new stores. Pocketing their gains, they may turn then to gleaming white cabinets of refrigerated meats and frozen foods, fresh farm produce and endless rows of canned goods, to drug and appliance and hardware counters, to racks and counters selling deodorants, hairnets, fingernail polish—and even paperback novels.

Navahos will not find here anyone with time or savvy enough to stitch up an open wound or mend a broken bone or settle a domestic dispute or help to bury a small child. Only at the smaller posts are such traders still found—at Toadlena, for instance, where Bernard Carson found time, not long ago, to lock up at mid-morning and help some Navahos shoot a mountain lion out of a tree.

Until the old days are so far gone as to be forgotten, the virtues of the past may be weighed against the obvious benefits of fresh meat and vegetables and a choice among six shades of lipstick. Progress and change in any case will not be stopped. How much longer the Indian trader can retain his separate identity is problematical, but very likely his time has almost come.

"The new trader," Dorothy Hubbell once said, "is in for a short while. He comes in to make money and get out. But the time is coming when this will change—when the Tribe will open the reservation to other businesses, all sorts of businesses, that will crowd the trader out." To this perhaps Lorenzo might say: "Amen."

BIBLIOGRAPHY

ARCHIVAL COLLECTIONS

New Mexico State Historical Society, Santa Fe.
Bent, Charles. Letters. Benjamin Reed Collection. Microfilm copies in the University of New Mexico Library.

U. S. National Archives, Washington, D. C.
Ledgers of Licensed Indian Traders. (Some twelve to fifteen in number, the ledgers actually are untitled. Entries, in pen and ink, are arranged chronologically rather than alphabetically.)
Navajo File 121.
Office of Indian Affairs, Record Group 75, Classified Files, 71406–11–910; 120395–13–121; 146247–13–123; 150298–13–175, San Juan.
Office of Indian Affairs, Record Group 75, Letters Received, 1882–86, 1892.
Office of Indian Affairs, Record Group 75, Letters Sent, 1881.
Records of New Mexico Superintendency of Indian Affairs, 1849–80, Record Group 75, Letters Received.
War Records Division 1251, Fort Wingate File.
War Records Division, Thomas Varker Keam File.

OTHER MANUSCRIPT MATERIALS

Cason, Ina Wilcox. "The Bent Brothers on the Frontier." Unpublished master's thesis, University of New Mexico, 1939.
Evans, Robert G. Untitled manuscript, n.d.
Noel, Frank. "Eighty Years in America," Typescript memoirs of the Sa-nos-tee trader, 1954.
Tanner, Mrs. Arthur. "History of the Settling of Fruitland and Kirtland." Typescript, n.d.

INTERVIEWS AND LETTERS

Adair, Kenneth (Jeddito Trading Post, Arizona). Interview, August 22, 1958.
Akeah, Sam (Cudei, New Mexico). Interview, January 4, 1958.
Allen, W. R. (Clayton, Missouri). Letter to the author, September 6, 1959.
Arrington, John (Farmington, New Mexico). Interviews and letters, 1957–61.
Ashcroft, K. G. (Tsaya Trading Post, New Mexico). Interview, July 17, 1958.
Ashcroft, Lamar (Bisti Trading Post, New Mexico). Interview, July 17, 1958.
Babbitt, Paul (Flagstaff, Arizona). Interview, August 14, 1959; letter, September 19, 1959 .
Blair, Lodge (Aneth Trading Post, Utah). Interview, September 4, 1959.
Blake, Albert P. (Farmington, New Mexico). Interview, July 21, 1958.
Blake, Mrs. Bessie McFarland (Farmington, New Mexico). Interview, July 21, 1958.
Bloomfield, George (Gallup, New Mexico). Interviews, August 1 and 15, 1958; letters to the author, August, 1958.

Bradshaw, Kenneth (Burnham's Trading Post, New Mexico). Interviews, summer, 1960.

Brink, Paul (Newcomb's Trading Post, New Mexico). Interview, August 1, 1958.

Brown, Elsie (Toadlena, New Mexico). Interview, August 6, 1958.

Bryars, William D. (Clerk, U. S. District Court, Albuquerque, New Mexico). Letter to the author, August 24, 1959.

Burnham, Roy (Farmington, New Mexico). Interview, July 15, 1958.

Carson, Bernard (Toadlena Trading Post, New Mexico). Interview, July 25, 1958.

Coddington, Henry B. (Gallup, New Mexico). Interview, February 5, 1959.

Counselor, Jim (Albuquerque, New Mexico). Interview, January 15, 1958.

Cousins, Mrs. Lucie (Cousins Trading Post, New Mexico). Interviews, February 6 and 7, 1959.

Damon, James (Ft. Defiance, Arizona). Interview, August 18, 1960.

Damon, Nelson (Buffalo Springs, New Mexico). Interview, July 13, 1960.

Davies, Mrs. Ed (Camden, Arkansas). Interview, Farmington, New Mexico, August 4, 1958.

Day, Sam II (Karigan's Trading Post, Arizona). Interviews, September 8, 1958, January 17, 1959, August 24 and 31, 1960.

Des-bah-nez (Crystal, New Mexico). Interview, July 2, 1960.

Dick, Herbert W. (Trinidad, Colorado). Letters to the author, June, 1958, October 9, 1961.

Evans, Robert G. (Albuquerque, New Mexico). Interviews, October 3 and 21, 1957.

Foutz, Alma L. (Kirtland, New Mexico). Interview, July 29, 1958.

Foutz, Ed (Tocito Trading Post, New Mexico). Interview, July 25, 1958.

Foutz, Hugh (Kirtland, New Mexico). Interview, July 28, 1958.

Foutz, Philip (Whitewater Trading Post, New Mexico). Interview, February 6, 1959.

Foutz, R. B. (Tocito Trading Post, New Mexico). Interview, July 25, 1958.

Foutz, Russell (Farmington, New Mexico). Interview, January 14, 1958.

Galusha, J. R. (Albuquerque, New Mexico). Interview, September 19, 1959.

García, Camille (Chinle, Arizona). Interview, August 23, 1958.

García, Ernest C. (Gallup, New Mexico). Interview, January 15, 1959.

Grace, Mrs. Doris (Winslow, Arizona). Conversation, August 13, 1959.

Heap, Merle W. (Clerk, Superior Court, St. Johns, Arizona). Letter to the author, January 29, 1959.

Hegemann, Mrs. Anton (Albuquerque, New Mexico). Interview, October 2, 1957.

Heller, Mrs. Richard F. (Albuquerque, New Mexico). Interview, October 3, 1957.

Herring, Charles (Farmington, New Mexico). Interview, August 3, 1958.

Herring, Mrs. Grace Bloomfield (Farmington, New Mexico). Interview, August 3, 1958.

Hubbell, Mrs. Dorothy (Ganado, Arizona). Interviews, July 13, 1957, August 22 and 23, 1958; letters to the author, July 23, December 8, 1958, February 3, 1959, September 28, 1960.

Ismay, Mrs. John (Ismay Trading Post, Colorado). Interview, September 4, 1959.

Jensen, Don (Crystal Trading Post, New Mexico). Interview, July 2, 1960.

Joeckell, Fr. Emanuel (St. Michaels Mission, Arizona). Interview, August 27, 1960.

Keller, Carl (Albuquerque, New Mexico). Interview, October 3, 1957.

Kelley, Dana R. (Farmington, New Mexico). Conversation, summer, 1959.

Lee, Albert Hugh (Ganado, Arizona). Interview, August 21, 1958.

Leighton, Willard (Farmington, New Mexico). Interviews, August 12 and 15, 1958.

Lucero, Frances L. (Deputy Clerk, U. S. District Court, Santa Fe, New Mexico). Letters to the author, August 25, 1959, January 14, 1960.

McGee, Carr II (Burnham's Trading Post, New Mexico). Interview, July 17, 1958.

McGee, Jewel (Red Rock Trading Post, Arizona). Interview, July 24, 1958.

Manning, Luther (Bruce Bernard Trading Post, Shiprock, New Mexico). Interview, August 14, 1958.

Maxwell, Gilbert S. (Farmington, New Mexico). Interview, July 31, 1958.
Moncus, Herman H. (Tucumcari, New Mexico). Interview, February, 1961.
Nelson, Roswell (Farmington, New Mexico). Interview, October 31, 1957.
Newcomb, Charles G. (Gallup, New Mexico). Interviews, January 16, February 5 and 19, 1959; letters to the author, 1959.
Newcomb, Mrs. Franc (Albuquerque, New Mexico). Interviews, September 3, October 2, 1957.
Noel, Mrs. Eva Foutz (Fruitland, New Mexico). Interview, January 18, 1958.
Noel, Frank (Salt Lake City, Utah). Interview, Fruitland, New Mexico, September 21, 1959.
Noel, H. B. (Fruitland, New Mexico). Interviews, 1958–59.
Owings, Miss Maizee (Hopi Agency, Keams Canyon, Arizona). Interview, August 17, 1959.
Parker, Thomas (Crystal, New Mexico). Interview, July 2, 1960.
Pyle, Frank (Towaoc Colorado). Interview, July 28, 1958.
Reid, Wendell (Cove Trading Post, Arizona). Interview, July 24, 1958.
Richardson, Hubert (Cameron Trading Post, Arizona). Interview, August 17, 1957.
Runke, Mrs. Laura Preston (Flagstaff, Arizona). Interview, August 14, 1959.
Sabin, Lewis L. (Albuquerque, New Mexico). Interviews, January 7 and 14, 1958.
Smith, Mr. and Mrs. Ted L. (Farmington, New Mexico). Interview, January 6, 1959.
Spiegelberg, George A. (New York City, New York). Letter to the author, October 17, 1960.
Stock, Donald (Two Gray Hills, New Mexico). Interview, July 25, 1958.
Stubbs, Stanley (Santa Fe, New Mexico). Interview, September 10, 1958; letter to the author, September 2, 1958.
Tanner, Mrs. Arthur (Kirtland, New Mexico). Interview, July 28, 1958.
Taugel-chee, Daisy (Toadlena, New Mexico). Interview, August 5, 1958.
Tuley, Klee (Toadlena, New Mexico). Interview, August 6, 1958.
Vanderwagen, Mrs. Edward (Zuñi, New Mexico). Interview, February 6, 1959.
Vanderwagen, Ernest (Whitewater Trading Post, New Mexico). Interview, February 6, 1959.
Walker, Donald G. (Crownpoint Trading Co., New Mexico). Interview, July 19, 1958.
Washburn, Del (Hogback Trading Post, New Mexico). Interview, August 14, 1958.
Washburn, Kenneth (Gallegos Canyon, New Mexico). Interview, September 4, 1960.
Washburn, Troy (The Gap Trading Post, Arizona). Interview, August 15, 1959.
Wheeler, Wilfred (Waterflow, New Mexico). Interview, August 14, 1958.
Woodard, M. L. (Gallup, New Mexico). Interview, February 7, 1959.
Woodruff, T. M. (Warden, New Mexico State Penitentiary, Santa Fe, New Mexico). Letter to the author, January 28, 1959.
Wynn, Joe (Farmington, New Mexico). Interview, August 1, 1958.
Wynn, Mrs. Kenneth (Farmington, New Mexico). Interview, September 6, 1958.

NEWSPAPERS

Arizona Daily Sun, Flagstaff, Arizona.
Coconino Sun, Flagstaff, Arizona.
Daily New Mexican, Santa Fe, New Mexico.
Evening Star, Washington, D. C.
Herald, Gallup, New Mexico.
Independent, Gallup, New Mexico.
McKinley County Republican, Gallup, New Mexico.
Times-Hustler, Farmington, New Mexico.
Western Journal of Commerce, Kansas City, Missouri.

REPORTS, LETTERS, DIARIES, ETC.

Calhoun, James S. *The Official Correspondence of James S. Calhoun While Indian Agent at Santa Fe and Superintendent of Indian Affairs in New Mexico,* ed. by Annie Heloise Abel. Washington, Government Printing Office, 1915.

Commissioner of Indian Affairs, *Annual Reports* for 1868–1913. Washington, Government Printing Office.

Frémont, John Charles. *Report of the Exploring Expedition to the Rocky Mountains in the Year 1842, and to Oregon and North California in 1843–44.* 28 Cong., 2 sess., *House Exec. Doc. 166* (1845).

Hafen, LeRoy R., ed. "The W. M. Boggs Manuscript About Bent's Fort, Kit Carson, the Far West and Life Among the Indians," *Colorado Magazine,* March, 1930.

Hammond, George P. and Agapito Rey, eds. and trans. *Don Juan de Oñate, Colonizer of New Mexico, 1595–1628.* 2 vols. Albuquerque, University of New Mexico Press, 1953.

Kappler, Charles Joseph. *Laws, Statutes, Etc.* Washington, Government Printing Office, 1904.

Lee, John D. *A Mormon Chronicle: The Diaries of John D. Lee,* ed. by Robert Glass Cleland and Juanita Brooks. San Marino, The Huntington Library, 1955.

Moore, John B. *The Navajo.* Catalog and notes, privately printed for Moore's Crystal (N. M.) Trading Post, 1911.

Pike, Zebulon M. "The Discovery of Pike's Peak—from the Diary of an Expedition Made Under Orders of the War Department, by Capt. Z. M. Pike, in the Years 1806 and 1807, to Explore the Internal Parts of Louisiana." Boston, *Old South Leaflets,* Vol. XII (1908).

Powell, John Wesley. "Exploration of the Colorado River of the West and its Tributaries Explored in 1869, 1870, 1871, and 1872 Under the Direction of the Secretary of the Smithsonian Institution." 42 Cong., 2 sess., *House Mis. Doc. 173.*

"Report on Employment of U. S. Soldiers in Arresting By-a-lil-le and Other Navajo Indians," 60 Cong., 1 sess., *Sen. Exec. Doc. 517.*

"Report of the Secretary of War Relative to Bill S-3117," 52 Cong., 2 sess., 1892–93. Washington, Government Printing Office.

"Report of the Secretary of War, U. S. War Dept.," 35 Cong., 2 sess., *House Exec. Doc. 2.*

Simpson, Lt. J. H. "The Report of Lieutenant J. H. Simpson of an Expedition into the Navaho Country in 1849 . . . ," 31 Cong., 1 sess., *Sen. Exec. Doc. 64.*

Ward, John. "Indian Affairs in New Mexico Under the Administration of William Carr Lane," from the Journal of John Ward, ed. by Annie Heloise Abel, *New Mexico Historical Review,* Vol. XVI, No. 3 (1941).

BOOKS AND PAMPHLETS

Adair, John. *The Navajo and Pueblo Silversmiths.* Norman, University of Oklahoma Press, 1944.

Amsden, Charles Avery. *Navaho Weaving.* Albuquerque, University of New Mexico Press. 1949.

Bancroft, Hubert Howe. *History of Arizona and New Mexico, 1530–1888.* San Francisco, The History Company, 1890.

Bolton, Herbert E. *Pageant in the Wilderness: The Story of the Escalante Expedition to the Interior Basin, 1776.* Salt Lake City, Utah State Historical Society, 1950.

Bourke, John J. *The Snake-Dance of the Moquis of Arizona.* London, Sampson Low, Marston, Searle & Rivington, 1884.

Brew, John Otis. *The Excavation of Franciscan Awatovi.* Cambridge, Peabody Museum, 1949.

Cohen, Felix S. *Handbook of Federal Indian Law.* Washington, Government Printing Office, 1942.

Collier, John. *The Indians of the Americas.* New York, W. W. Norton & Co., 1947.

Colton, Harold S. *Hopi Kachina Dolls.* Albuquerque, University of New Mexico Press, 1949.

Darrah, William Culp. *Powell of the Colorado.* Princeton, Princeton University Press, 1951.

De Voto, Bernard. *Across the Wide Missouri.* Boston. Houghton Mifflin Co., 1947.

Farish, Thomas Edwin, ed. *History of Arizona.* Phoenix, 1918.

Forbes, Jack D. *Apache, Navaho, and Spaniard.* Norman, University of Oklahoma Press, 1960.

Freeman, Ira S. *A History of Montezuma County, Colorado.* Boulder, 1958.

Garrard, Lewis H. *Wah-to-yah and the Taos Trail.* Norman, University of Oklahoma Press, 1955.

Grinnell, George Bird. *The Fighting Cheyennes.* Norman, University of Oklahoma Press, 1956.

Gregg, Josiah. *Commerce of the Prairies,* ed. by Max L. Moorhead. Norman, University of Oklahoma Press, 1954.

Hodge, Frederick Webb, ed. *Handbook of American Indians North of Mexico.* 2 vols. Bureau of American Ethnology *Bulletin No. 30.* Washington, Government Printing Office, 1912.

———. *Old Dan DuBois.* N.p., n.d.

James, George Wharton. *Indian Blankets and Their Makers.* Chicago, A. C. McClurg & Co., 1934.

Kluckhohn, Clyde, and Dorothea Leighton. *The Navaho.* Cambridge, Harvard University Press, 1946.

Lavender, David. *Bent's Fort.* New York, Doubleday & Co., 1954.

Little, James A., ed. *Jacob Hamblin, A Narrative of His Personal Experience . . . .* Salt Lake City, 1881.

McClintock, James H. *Mormon Settlement in Arizona.* Phoenix, n.p., 1921.

McKenney, T. L. *Memoirs, Official and Personal.* New York, Paine & Burgess, 1846.

McNitt, Frank. *Richard Wetherill: Anasazi.* Albuquerque, University of New Mexico Press, 1957.

Moorhead, Max L. *New Mexico's Royal Road: Trade and Travel on the Chihuahua Trail.* Norman, University of Oklahoma Press, 1958.

Neff, Andrew Love. *History of Utah, 1847 to 1869,* ed. by Leland Hargrave Creer, Salt Lake City, Deseret News Press, 1940.

Parkman, Francis. *The Oregon Trail.* New ed., Philadelphia, John C. Winston Co., 1931.

Pike, Zebulon Montgomery. *An Account of Expeditions to the Sources of the Mississippi and Through the Western Parts of Louisiana.* Philadelphia, C. and A. Conrad and Co., 1810.

Reichard, Gladys A. *Navajo Shepherd and Weaver.* New York, J. J. Augustin, 1936.

Ruxton, George Frederick. *Life in the Far West,* ed. by LeRoy R. Hafen, Norman, University of Oklahoma Press, 1951. First published in 1848.

———. *Adventures in Mexico and the Rockies.* New York, Harper and Brothers, 1848.

Schmeckbier, Lawrence F. *The Office of Indian Affairs: Its History, Activities, and Organization.* Baltimore, The Johns Hopkins Press, 1927.

Smith, Watson. *Kiva Mural Decorations at Awatovi and Kawaika-a.* Cambridge, Peabody Museum, 1952.

Underhill, Ruth. *Here Come the Navaho!* Washington, United States Indian Service, 1953.

Van Valkenburgh, Richard. *Diné Bikéyah*. Paper, mimeographed in limited number of copies. Window Rock, Office of Indian Affairs, 1941.

Welsh, Herbert. *Report of a Visit to the Navajo, Pueblo, and Hualapais Indians.* Philadelphia, The Indian Rights Association, 1885.

Wilken, Robert L. *Anselm Weber, O.E.M., Missionary to the Navaho.* Milwaukee, Bruce Publishing Co., 1955.

Williams, Joseph. *Narrative of a Tour from the State of Indiana to the Oregon Territory in the Years 1841–42.* New York, The Cadmus Book Shop, 1921. First published, 1843.

ARTICLES

Auerbach, Herbert S. "Old Trails, Old Forts, Old Trappers and Traders," *Utah Historical Quarterly*, Vol. IX, No.1 (1941).

———. "Father Escalante's Journal with Related Documents and Maps." *Utah Historical Quarterly*, Vol. XI (1943).

Bloom, Lansing B., ed. "Bourke on the Southwest VIII," *New Mexico Historical Review*, Vol. XI (1936).

Dick, Herbert W. "The Excavation of Bent's Fort, Otero County, Colorado," *Colorado Magazine*, Vol. XXXIII, No. 3 (1956).

Eckel, Mrs. LaCharles Goodman. "History of Ganado, Arizona," *Museum Notes*, Museum of Northern Arizona, Vol. VI, No. 10 (1934).

Flynn, Arthur J. "Furs and Forts in the Rocky Mountain West, Part II," *Colorado Magazine*, March, 1932.

Foster, James Monroe, Jr. "Fort Bascom, New Mexico," *New Mexico Historical Review*, Vol. XXXV, No. 9 (1960).

Grinnell, George Bird. "Bent's Old Fort and Its Builders," *Kansas Historical Society Collections*, XV, 1919–22.

Hafen, LeRoy R. "When was Bent's Fort Built?" *Colorado Magazine*, Vol. XXXI No. 2 (1954).

Hill, Joseph J. "Spanish and Mexican Exploration and Trade Northwest from New Mexico into the Great Basin, 1765–1853," *Utah Historical Quarterly*, Vol. III, No. 1 (1930).

Hubbell, Lorenzo. "Fifty Years an Indian Trader," as told to J. E. Hogg, *Touring Topics*, Vol. XXII, No. 12 (1930).

Jones, Hester. "The Spiegelbergs and Early Trade in New Mexico," *The Southwest Jewish Chronicle.* January, 1936.

McKibben, Davidson B. "Revolt of the Navajo, 1913," *New Mexico Historical Review*, Vol. XXIX, No. 4 (1954).

Matthews, Washington. "A Two-Faced Navaho Blanket," *American Anthropologist*, N.S., Vol. II, No. 4 (October-December, 1900).

Mott, Dorothy Challis. "Don Lorenzo Hubbell of Ganado," *Arizona Historical Review*, Vol. IV, No. 1 (1931).

Parish, William J. "The German Jew and the Commercial Revolution in Territorial New Mexico, 1850–1900,"*New Mexico Historical Review*, Vol. XXXV, No. 2 (1960).

Reeve, Frank D. "A Navaho Struggle for Land," *New Mexico Historical Review*, Vol. XXI, No. 1 (1946).

Rigby, Elizabeth. "Blue Canyon," *Arizona Highways*, August, 1959.

Simms, J. Denton. "Emmet Wirt, Pioneer Extraordinary," *Pioneers of the San Juan County*, Vol. III (1952).

Snow, William J. "Utah Indians and Spanish Slave Trade," *Utah Historical Quarterly*, Vol. II, No. 3 (1929).

Taylor, Mrs. Cresswell. "Charles Bent Has Built a Fort," *Bulletin of the Missouri Historical Society*, Vol. XI, No. 1 (1954).

Telling, Irving. "Coolidge and Thoreau: Forgotten Frontier Towns," *New Mexico Historical Review*, July, 1954.

"Those Green River Knives," *Indian Notes*, Museum of the American Indian, Heye Foundation, Vol. IV, No. 4 (1927).

Utley, Robert M. "The Reservation Trader in Navajo History," *El Palacio*, Vol. LXVIII, No. 1 (1961).

Woodbury, Angus M. "A History of Southern Utah. . . ," *Utah Historical Quarterly*, Vol. XII (1944).

INDEX

Abbott, F. H.: 251
Abert, J. W.: 20, 28–29n., 36
Abiquiu Agency (New Mexico): 47–48, 71, 114–15, 130–31, 293, 305
Abiquiu, New Mexico: 17, 21, 305
Acoma Indians: 4, 117–18ff.
Acoma Pueblo, New Mexico: 54n., 71, 110, 239; destruction of by Spaniards, 4–5; first seen by Alvarado, 116; dispute with Laguna Pueblo, 121–22; Apaches trading at, 128; refugees from, 302–303n.
Acoma Reservation: 117ff.
Acomita, New Mexico: 116n.
Acord, O.: 240
Acowitz (Wiminuche): 310
Adair, John: ix, 85n., 169n., 256n.
Agathla Peak (Arizona): 185n.
Akeah, Sam (Navaho): 359–60
Alamosa, Colorado: 11, 308
Albert, King of Belgium: 236
Albuquerque, New Mexico: viii, 54n., 80, 81n., 110n., 116, 121, 143, 162, 168, 203 & n., 206n., 210, 223–24, 232, 234, 240, 248–49, 259, 296–97, 304n., 314, 319, 331, 334, 354; Heller freights to, 315; Hyde company Navahos at fair, 340
Alcatraz Prison (California): 197, 289–90
Aldrich, Stephen E.: 66, 72, 73n., 223–24, 247, 249, 253, 257n., 279, 282
Alencaster, Governor Joaquín: 8
Algert, C. H.: 196, 259n., 268, 274, 300, 302
Algert, C. H., Company: 300
Allande, Governor Pedro María de: 13
Allantown, Arizona: 327, 330
Allen, Frank: 311
Allen, W. R.: 198
Alosaka (Hopi deity): 190–91
Alvarado, Hernando de: 116; see also Acoma Pueblo

Alvarez, Manuel: 33
Amargo, New Mexico: 307 & n., 311
American Fur Company: 45, 143n.
Ames, A. J.: 309n.
Amsden, Charles Avery: ix, 192n., 201n., 209n., 211, 238, 264, 298n.
Aneth Trading Post (Utah): 47n., 113, 298, 300n.; built by Noland, 309; Byalille incident, 344–45
Aniline dyes: 60n., 209 & n., 255, 257, 260, 268, 344
Animas City, Colorado: 292, 306
Animas River: 291–92, 305
Annuity tickets: 129
Antelope Springs Trading Post: see Babbitt and Roberts Trading Post
Antes, Howard R.: 47n.
Apache Indians: 43, 48, 50, 53, 146, 229, 291n.; Spanish servitude, 5; Mescaleros, 19, 231; Bent post for on Canadian, 32; trade restricted in 1850, 68; trade at Acoma, 128; trade at Zuñi, 241; trade at Flagstaff, 264
Apache Trading Post (Arizona): 266
Arapaho Indians: 27, 36n., 39, 43, 115, 143n.; intertribal peace council of 1840, 33; described by Charles Bent, 34
Arboles, Colorado: 21, 291
Archambeau, Auguste: 23
Arkansas River: 11, 13–16, 25, 35–36, 38; Bent stockade on, 25; Bent's Fort on, 26–27, 42; Indian council on, 33; Cheyennes camped on at Big Timbers, 37; new Bent fort on, 43
Armijo (Navaho): 150n.
Armijo, Governor Manuel: 41
Armstrong, John S.: 131–32, 134
Arnold, Albert: 319, 355
Arnold, F. T.: 355–56
Arny, Cicilia (Mrs. W. F. M.): 159, 161
Arny, W. F. M.: 110, 111n., 113–14, 126–27, 136, 162, 187n., 200, 241; on

employed by Hubbell, 215; part in Dugan murder, 325–27; recalls Cronemeyer, 327–28
Day, William (Willie): 247n., 325
Debus, Wendel: 110n., 112
Defiance Station (New Mexico): 51, 72, 249, 322
Delgadito (Navaho): 150n., 245
Delta, Colorado: 8
Denver, Colorado: x, 134, 298
Des-bah-nes (Navaho): 255n.
De Voto, Bernard: 52
Dewey, New Mexico: see Coolidge, New Mexico
Dick, Herbert W.: 28–30n., 43n.
Dinet-lakai (Navaho): 287, 289–90
Dinét-sosi-begay (Navaho): 348
Dinet-tsosi (Navaho): 182–83, 185
Dinnebito Trading Post (Arizona): 205n.
Dinnehotso Trading Post (Arizona): 295, 300n.
Dirty Devil River: 101
Dittenhoffer (trader): 265–66
Divide Trading Post (New Mexico): 246n.
Dlad (Navaho): 284, 287, 289–90
Dodd, H. W. (Billy?): 46
Dodd, Theodore H.: 46, 109, 172n.
Dodge, Henry Chee (Navaho): 179, 182, 184, 247, 249, 253n., 256n., 257n., 288; partner of Aldrich, 279; with Shipley in Black Horse incident, 279–81; part in Beautiful Mountain Uprising, 349ff.
Dodge, Henry L.: 172n.
Dolores River (Colorado): 21, 310
Domínguez, Fray Francisco Atanasio: 8, 21, 90, 230n., 267, 291n.
Doniphan, Colonel Alexander: 107n., 229n.
Donovan, Michael: 63–64, 66–67, 214n., 253
Doonan, Ed: 332–35
Dove Creek (Colorado): 310
Do-yal-ke (Navaho): 289–90
Doyle, J. B.: 40
Drake, George M.: 306
Drexel, Miss Josephine: 215
Drexel, Rev. Mother Katharine: 250
Drolet, J. M.: 304n.
Drolet's Trading Post (New Mexico): see Newcomb's Trading Post
DuBois, Dan: 69, 136, 156, 205, 242–44, 251; prosecuted by Arny, 162–65; ill-

ness of, 220–21; appearance for Cronemeyer heirs, 330–31
Dudley, L. Edwin: 114, 137, 149–50
Dugan, Frank: 325–27
Dulce, New Mexico: 21, 307–308, 311–12
Dumont, Colorado: 306
Dunn, William H.: 93
Durango, Colorado: 113, 233, 294, 297, 298–99n., 306, 308, 349
Durango, Mexico: 13, 34
Dustin, Al: 294
Dustin, Bert: 300–301, 346n.
Dustin, Sheldon: 300–301

Eastman, Galen: 60–61, 177–80, 244n.; troubles as agent, 166; removed, 167; reinstated, 168; renewed troubles of, 171; links Keam with Miller's death, 172; removal of asked, 173–76; removed, 180–81
Easton, Hank: 151n.
Echo Cliffs (Arizona): 103, 199, 265, 267n.
Echo Trading Post (Arizona): 266
Eckel, Mrs. LaCharles Goodman: 201–202n.
Edie, Volney P.: 249n.
Eighteen Miles Spring Trading Post (Arizona): 274n.
Eldodt, Marcus: 110
Eldodt, Nathan: 110
Eldodt, Samuel: 110
El Morro (New Mexico): 227
El Paso del Norte: 9, 291n.
Enterprise (Farmington, New Mexico): 350
Escalante, Fray Silvestre Vélez de: 1, 8f, 21, 90, 230n., 267, 291, 305
Escrito Canyon (New Mexico): 302–303n.
Espejo, Antonio de: 239
Esteban: 238
Evans, Robert G.: 57, 76 & n., 77
Evans, Will: x, 78–79, 345n., 348n.
Evening Star (Washington, D. C.): 151 & n., 152

Fales, Walter R.: 58–59, 62, 253
Fancher, Charles: 89, 97 & n., 105–106
Farmington, New Mexico: 75n., 81, 84, 295–96, 298n., 303, 304n., 310, 339–40n., 348n.; Navaho uprising at, 173n., 259n., 261n.; founding of, 292–93; Simpson Mercantile Company of, 298; Progressive Mercantile Company

43, 52, 240; traders from, 69; as trade center, 70; range of Utes from, 292, 305

Taos Pueblo, New Mexico: 42 & n.

Taugel-chee, Daisy (Navaho): 261

Taugel-clitso, Mrs. (Navaho): 260

Teec-nos-pos Trading Post (Arizona): 280n., 295, 300n., 301, 343–45, 359n.; built by Noel, 342; sold to Dustin, 346n.

Teec-tso-secad Trading Post: see Burnham's Trading Post, New Mexico

Teller, Henry Moore: 174, 176, 181, 192, 253

Telling, Irving: 232

Tharpe, William: 40–41, 41n.

Thick Lipped Mexican (silversmith): 210

Thomas, Ben M.: 133, 172n.

Thomas, Sterl: 309n.

Thompson, Almon H.: 96

Thompson Park (Colorado): 308

Thoreau, New Mexico: 84, 232–34, 317

Thurland, Ed: 295–96, 341n.

Tice, Dan: 310

Tien-su-se (Navaho): 150n., 151n.

Tierra Amarilla Agency (New Mexico): 131–34; replaces Abiquiu Agency, 305; base for Jicarillas and Capote Utes, 305–306; abandoned, 307

Tierra Amarilla, New Mexico: 21, 130, 135

T'iisnasbas Creek (Arizona): 341

Timpa Creek (Colorado): 27

Timpanogos Lake (Utah): 17

Timpanogos Valley (Utah): 8, 17, 291n.

Timpiache (Capote): 132

Tiz-na-tzin Trading Post (New Mexico): 84, 339 & n.

Toadlena Trading Post (New Mexico): 259–61, 298n., 340, 361

Tobin, Jake: 204

Tocito Trading Post (New Mexico): 300n., 301, 358

Tohatchi Trading Post (New Mexico): 242n., 249n., 251, 319, 335, 337, 340, 355

Tohlakai Trading Post (New Mexico): 249n.

Toiyalone Mesa (New Mexico): 239

Tokens: see trading tokens

Tokesjhay Wash (Arizona): 265

Tolani Lakes (Arizona): 55

Tolchaco Trading Post (Arizona): 250, 266

Tol Zhin (Navaho): 284–86, 289–90

Tombstone, Arizona: 218

Tombstone Prospector, Tombstone, Arizona: 218–19

Tonalea (Arizona): see Red Lake Trading Post

Toner, Samuel T.: 240

Tooly, C. P.: 66

Torreon (New Mexico): 313, 315

Towaoc Agency (Colorado): 308, 310–11

Townsend, Frank: 302, 311

Trade and Intercourse Act, of 1834: 228–29; approved by Congress, 45; appointment of traders, 46 & n.; trading without license, 47 & n.; agency purchases, 47; arms and ammunition, 47–50

Trade customs: pawn, 55–57; credit, 57, 74–86; arrangement of stock, 75, 79; free tobacco, 75–76, 340; rug rooms, 77, 235; guest hogans, 78 & n., 276; use of tokens, 83–86

Trade fairs: 9, 12n.

Trade goods, Plains Indian: 37–38

Trade, Indian: 3, 16–22; at Bent's Fort, 27, 32–33, 35; at Acoma Pueblo, 128; Navaho-Apache, 146; Navaho-Paiute, 147; at Zuñi, 241; Navaho-Ute, 305; see also Comancheros

Trade, Mexican: 16–20, 38, 227–28, 251n.; at Zuñi, 239; among Utes, 305

Trade prices: 51; whisky, 52; lists required, 65; wool, 80–81; freighting, 81; pelts, hides, horses, 81; piñons, 82–83; coffee and Pendleton blankets, 222; Germantown blankets, 235; Crystal blankets, 254; blankets and silverwork, 256, 268; Two Gray Hills blankets, 259, 261

Trade routes: see Chinle Valley, Chuska Valley, Mormon Trail, Río Grande, Río Puerco (of the West), San Juan Valley, Spanish Trail, Wingate Valley

Trade, Spanish: 3, 5, 9–10, 15–17; policy governing American and French traders, 11–14; in slaves, 227–28; at Zuñi, 239; through San Juan Valley, 292

Trade, vagabond: 17–21, 38, 45, 48, 53, 68, 70–71, 227–28; at Zuñi, 239; with Southern Utes and Jicarillas, 305; see also Comancheros

Trade in arms and ammunition: 32,

THE INDIAN TRADERS

has been set on the Linotype in Baskerville, a
recent revival of the mid-eighteenth-century design by John Baskerville, a wealthy manufacturer
whose hobby was printing. He set up his own type
foundry and began experimenting with printing
inks, paper, and the design of type. These experi-
ments led to the design of a typeface which is
enjoying much popularity throughout the Western world on account of its virile, readable form.

UNIVERSITY OF OKLAHOMA PRESS

NORMAN